PHILOSOPHICAL EXPLORATIONS
A Series Edited by George Kimball Plochmann

Juan Luis Vives
and the Emotions

CARLOS G. NOREÑA

Foreword by
GEORGE KIMBALL PLOCHMANN

WITHDRAWN

SOUTHERN ILLINOIS UNIVERSITY PRESS

CARBONDALE AND EDWARDSVILLE

92 91 90 89   4 3 2 1

Library of Congress Cataloging-in-Publication Data

Noreña, Carlos G.
    Juan Luis Vives and the emotions / by Carlos G. Noreña; foreword
by George Kimball Plochmann.
        p.   cm. — (Philosophical explorations)
    Bibliography: p.
    Includes index.
    ISBN 0-8093-1539-4
    1. Vives, Juan Luis, 1492–1540. 2. Emotions (Philosophy) —
History — 16th century. I. Title. II. Series.
B785.V64N674   1989
128′ .3 — dc19   88-36811
                                                           CIP

To my son Carlos

Contents

Foreword by George Kimball Plochmann   ix

Preface   xv

Part 1. Vives' Life and Thought

1.   The Exile from Valencia   3

2.   The Parisian Student   8

3.   The Northern Humanist   17

4.   The Amphibious Man   32

5.   The Mature Thinker   46

Part 2. Vives' Thoughts on Life

6.   Nature   71

7.   Life   81

8.   Sensation   86
The External Senses   87
The Internal Senses   92

9.   Intelligence   95
Simple Intelligence   95
Memory   96
Composite Intelligence   101
Reasoning or Discourse   101
Judgment   105
Contemplation   107

10.   Ingenium   108

11.   Language   113

12.   The Will   119

13.   Sleep and Dreams   124
         Sleep   125
         Dreams   126

14.   Death and Immortality   130
         Old Age and Death   130
         Immortality of the Soul   132

Part 3. Vives on Emotion and Life

15.   The Nature of Emotion   141
         Emotion and Knowledge   146
         Emotion and the Body   151
   Emotion and the Environment   154
         Emotion and Action   156

16.   The Classification of Emotions   159

17.   The Basic Emotions   172
         Love and Desire   174
         Hatred and Anger   180
         Fear and Hope   183
         Joy and Sadness   186

18.   Derivative Emotions   191
Emotions Related to Love and Desire   191
      Emotions Related to Hatred   194
      Emotions Related to Fear   199
      Emotions Related to Hope   201
       Emotions Related to Joy   201
    Emotions Related to Sadness   203

19.   The Dynamics of Emotion   207

20.   The Control and Therapy of Emotion   213

21.   Retrospect   219

Notes   231

Bibliography   255

Index   267

Foreword
George Kimball Plochmann

Aristotle commenced one of the books of his *Metaphysics* by remarking: "The investigation of truth is in one sense difficult, in another easy. A sign of this is the fact that neither can one attain it adequately, nor do all fail, but each says something about the nature of things; and while each of us contributes nothing or little to the truth, a considerable amount of it results from all our contributions" (II.1.993a30–34; Apostle translation). This applies, of course, to Juan Luis Vives, whose labors, regardless of what he actually sought, could not encompass the whole truth, even that regarding a specific subject matter, but which did succeed in advancing human understanding in several parts of that whole. Incidentally, Aristotle might have added that the truths that *have* been found are often forgotten by later arrivals on the field, and this, too, applies to Vives, many of whose sharp and somewhat morose observations and clear-cut descriptions of human emotions were long put aside.

This philosopher-humanist worked in a century that, next to each of the following three, produced few philosophers of the first rank, an epoch, furthermore, when many thinkers were bullied, maimed, and murdered — thinkers to whom the time had given birth and who strove to illuminate it through their varied accomplishments. The sixteenth was a century during which philosophers were so beleaguered that independent thinking belonged only to men of great personal heroism. Michael Servetus, Peter Ramus, Sir Thomas More, and Giordano Bruno were all put to death for their opinions, and Tommaso Campanella spent nearly three decades in prison for his. Vives himself was a little better treated, though his Spanish father was executed at the behest of the Inquisition; the son had already left his native Spain, remaining an exile for the rest of his forty-six years. Troubling portraits of life and death in a troubled time for the European nations. Spain, for one, was stage by stage passing from the zenith of her power and fame, partly because of her overextended economic ties that could not be safeguarded properly, even by a too-costly military and naval establishment.

For nine hundred years, most Jews throughout Western Europe had enjoyed warm hospitality, and often moved into positions of power, their very success eventually causing them to become objects of envy and then hatred. They underwent expulsion from England in the late thirteenth century, from France in the fourteenth, from much of Germany in the next century, and from Spain, Portugal, and Italy in the sixteenth. These nations were seeking scapegoats, as it happened, for the many economic tribulations inherent in the shaky currencies and top-heavy political institutions of the time.

The first victims of the Inquisition were not infidels but allegedly heretical Christians, mostly Albigensians; in Spain, however, there was born a special fear that her large Jewish population, much of it called *Conversos* (but also cursed as *Marranos,* pigs, by the loyal orthodox), were divisive, dangerous, in spite of their having lived in comparative peace heretofore with their native-born Christian neighbors. In this now uneasy religious atmosphere came Vives, so alone: a Jew in a nation of Spanish Christians, a *Marrano* by birth in the smaller society of Jews, a subsequent exile from a life with his family and its foredoomed head. But as a traveler, Vives could become a cosmopolitan in his grasp of the sociopolitical issues on which he later had much to say, as an associate of Erasmus and other intellectuals he could absorb and dispense all the attitudes and lore of the humanists, as a part-time celebrity he could test and expound his convictions regarding human nature, and as a married man, no doubt unhappily, he could strengthen his soul and personal resolves.

It is surely an exaggeration to call the Renaissance a relapse, as did G. K. Chesterton, but it is certain that the gains of wholly fresh information about the world and of new techniques for amassing it, the growing urge to beauty and personal love, the turn to poetry and drama, were not unaccompanied by corresponding losses. The extraordinary rigor of such men as Saint Thomas Aquinas and Duns Scotus at the height of the scholastic period had set a standard not commonly followed again until Descartes, Spinoza, and Leibniz — and not even then. Problems such as whether the soul is immortal, and whether we must believe it to be so, slowly lost their grip on both imagination and intellect. Cultivation of arts of composition and interpretation — grammar, rhetoric, and dialectic or logic — shifted markedly. Subtle examinations of the parts of speech such as that by the Scotist Thomas of Erfurt no longer held currency among the humanists, and the many turns of Aristotle's *Organon,* made even more detailed and perplexing by terminist logicians of the early fourteenth century, were gradually dropped from discussion. Grammar, which had been a theory as well as an instrument, now became a means for teaching beginners. By the time of Peter Ramus, and preeminently through his own labors, logic came to be merged with an art of plain exposition, and the *Organon,* with its harrowing difficulties, was superseded by an openhanded art of thinking and writing on a level near that of a modern high-school textbook. In shifting from *logica docens* to *utens* (Scotus had advocated both), the humanists combined it with rhetoric to achieve clarity of expression in order to persuade readers and hearers. Luther, Ramus, and Erasmus all advanced this movement, and so, in a measure, did Vives. Poets and writers on manners reduced the old catalogue of vices, sins, and virtues offered by Dante, and which he had conjoined with an elaborate cosmic numerology, to a more direct account of human experience, in which the many kinds of loves in the *Comedy* (defective, perverted, moderated, sanctified) were combined into one or two and then directed chiefly to mortal objects.

This is not, however, the whole picture of intellectual Europe in the century of Vives. Though physical theory became simpler in many respects (Aristotle's four causes became one or at most two, his four kinds of motion dropped down to one, and so forth), what served for a science of psychology did not. The soul might be immortal or it might not be, but its everyday complexities, as depicted so long ago in Plato's dialogues (now being read in their full sweep), were restored and rendered in literary and dramatic terms by Marlowe, Plato's great successor, and by lesser men as well.

The Renaissance humanists were all Christians, each in his own way, each with his own sources. If by original upholders of Christian doctrine and faith one means either the primitive Christians (who were by birth, of course, Jews), or the church fathers (who borrowed freely from Greek and Roman texts), or the thirteenth-century scholastic doctors (who learned much of their craft from the Arabs), then the humanist movement must be considered a revolt inspired by still other pagan sources, against ways of thinking similarly pagan in so much of their ancestry. The chief humanists were reviving texts and arts of writing and reading that fell outside the main interests of the three epochs formulating and settling Christian doctrine and practice: Greek writers whose works closely resembled Aristotle's no more than did Plato's; Cicero and Quintilian, whose thoughts were largely shaped in republican and imperial Rome respectively; the later Stoics and Epicureans; and poets, belletrists, and the rest.

Detailed studies of the passions evidently take rise in unhappy times: the waning days of fourth-century B.C. Athenian independence (Aristotle); the incipient nationalism beginning to seethe against the papacy of thirteenth-century A.D. Europe (Saint Thomas); the clash of English commoners and royalists four hundred years later (Hobbes), as well as the factional struggles in France and Holland (Descartes and Spinoza); the eighteenth-century readjustments of economic classes after the Glorious Revolution (Hume); the darkening days of industrialism in the following hundred years (Darwin); and, it goes without saying, the calamities and insanities of every kind in our own time. To this calendar must be added the hectic sixteenth century and the study of emotions by Vives. The questions were almost always standard: How many and what are the basic emotions? What are the derived ones? By what discipline or disciplines are they best studied? Can they be defined, and if so, how? How are they interconnected? What calls them forth? How are they related to sensation, memory, intellect? Can they be controlled? How are they related to the body? But the answers were always different.

Philosophers ever since classical Greece, and up to the present day, have offered lists, either containing a manageable finite number of emotions not reducible to each other (Aristotle), or a somewhat larger number deduced by composition from a far smaller handful of basic emotions (Descartes, Hobbes, Spinoza). The theory propounded by Juan Luis Vives is a sound, worthwhile contribution to the continuing but varied examinations. Vives differs from Aristotle, whose list is for aiding the public orator in finding ways to persuade an audience, and primarily a courtroom audience at that; from the Pseudo-Andronicus, from Saint Thomas, and finally from the post-Vivesian Descartes, though here the differences are less striking. Discovering these means of persuasion hinges, according to Aristotle, upon knowing not only the definitions of emotions but the kinds of persons and sorts of circumstances arousing the emotions. His account, which occupies about eleven pages in the Berlin edition of his *Art of Rhetoric,* is supplemented by a few brief remarks in *On the Soul* and in the *Nicomachean Ethics.* It was not until the later medieval period that Aristotle's emphasis was finally and rather decisively altered to place the detailed classification of these mysterious but ever-present passions clearly in the context of a psychology of human nature *überhaupt,* where it remained until just before the turn of the present century after which it became embedded in physiology (James, Lange, Cannon, Ruckmick), or social interaction (Riesman), the destiny of man (Freud), or even a metaphysic of man's hope (Robert Solomon). There is a swelling literature on the emotions, and the recovery, explication, and criticism of an important sixteenth-century contribution makes the present book an addition of signal worth.

Professor Noreña's exhaustive study depicts an important aspect of one epoch in history and reflects a second: that of Vives and the tireless writers of his time, and that of the twentieth century, with his historians, commentators, and critics at work to unravel the past. We owe a heavy debt to those scholars who have given much of their careers to studying a single thinker, seeking out every relevant detail of his life and thought: Paul Shorey and A. E. Taylor on Plato, Richard Ellmann on Joyce, Sir David Ross and Ingemar Düring on Aristotle, Leon Edel on Henry James, Carl Bode on H. L. Mencken, and others of that dedicated breed. They, too, furnish by their broad diligence invaluable funds of ideas and inspiring models that encapsulate a world in the microcosm of the life and work of a genius to whom these writers have devoted their efforts and their own gifts. None of these books is definitive, if that means closing off further research and interpretation — indeed they all foster it — but they remain nevertheless the stylobates and bases upon which future columns can be erected. With this book and with his other publications, Professor Noreña has, I think, added his name to this list of scholars, and that of Vives to the list of seminal authors who, were they to come alive again, would never dare complain that they had been passed over by all but perfunctory historians picking at bits of their lives and fragments of their authorship.

Until recent decades, by far the largest portion of philosophic research and criticism, at least in English-speaking countries, was directed to what on all sides were termed the major figures in the history of thought: Plato, Aristotle, Saint Augustine, Saint Thomas, Duns Scotus, Descartes — men of that stamp, down to the twentieth century, when different principles of selection have come into play. After World War II, a new spirit arose in those circles making much use of the earlier history of philosophic speculation and analysis. Figures that had formerly received a grudging paragraph as against a chapter began to attract more attention: the individual Presocratics, Cicero, the Skeptics of antiquity, Epictetus, Boethius, Erigena, the later terminists, Pico, Ficino — and now Juan Luis Vives, whose opinions on a multitude of topics as well as the emotions are interpreted by Dr. Noreña. These men were all of great significance for their own times, and should be for ours as well, though the standard histories and anthologies have accorded them less than they deserve. The records are now being rewritten, however, to take this new treasury of materials and criticisms into fuller account. The "tradition" of philosophy will no longer be the same.

Preface

Juan Luis Vives' analysis of the emotions constitutes Book 3 of his treatise *De Anima et Vita*. Published in Bruges in 1538, two years before the author's death, the book belongs to the late and philosophically more interesting and mature stage of Vives' intellectual career, a stage in which he tackled with relentless vigor such complex and disparate issues as the nature of moral wisdom (*Introductio ad Sapientiam,* 1524), social welfare (*De Subventione Pauperum,* 1526), war and peace (*De Concordia et Discordia,* 1529), educational reform (*De Disciplinis,* 1531), and the relation between reason and faith (*De Veritate Fidei Christianae,* posthumously published in 1543). *De Anima et Vita* represents therefore the culmination of Vives' constant effort to understand human nature not as a metaphysician but as a moralist and a pedagogue.

If *De Anima et Vita* encapsulates the best of Vives' thought on human nature, as is generally recognized, its third and final book on the emotions of the soul provides what Vives himself called the "foundation of all moral discipline, private and public." Because I was convinced that this tract on the emotions was essential to the understanding of Vives' thought, my original intent was to open its treasures to the English-speaking world by offering a translation with but a few introductory remarks. Soon, however, those remarks began to expand in scope and eventually became a book-length manuscript. The English translation itself will be soon published in a different book.

A superficial encounter with Book 3 of *De Anima et Vita* could lead the reader to dismiss it as a moralistic and rhetorically bloated rehashing of Platonic, Aristotelian, Stoic, and Patristic commonplaces about the dangers of emotional excess. By natural inclination and by clearly professed choice, Vives was a man of encyclopedic knowledge who combined in an unusual degree the receptivity of the eclectic and the creativity of the pioneer. His thought echoes and emulates not only that of the great thinkers of classical antiquity, but also that of the best European minds in the first half of the sixteenth century. To some extent, Vives' erudition often beclouds the originality of his work. While struggling to translate Vives' book on the emotions, it became clear to me that the translation itself had to be complemented with an analysis of its contents and a study of its relations to some seminal texts on the emotions written before and after Vives. Without such an analysis, only specialized readers might have been able to unravel by themselves all the threads that are woven into this polychromous tapestry or to appreciate Vives' novel contributions to our understanding of emotional responses. Part 3 of this book was designed to help readers to do just that by comparing Vives' thought to that of Aristotle, some ancient Stoic sources, Saint Thomas, Descartes, and Spinoza, and by organizing the entire material under some central headings (nature, classification, interaction, and control of emotions).

The analysis of the text of Book 3 of *De Anima et Vita* also forced me to relate its contents to Books 1 and 2, which precede it, and in which Vives deals with the nutritive, the appetitive, the sensory, and the thinking soul. Vives' philosophy of life, on the other hand, required a careful study of one of his least-known works, a lengthy summary of his metaphysical views published in 1531 under the title *De Prima Philosophia, sive de Intimo Naturae Opificio*. As a good Aristotelian, Vives was convinced that psychology is a part of physics and that physics provides the clue to metaphysics. *De Prima Philosophia* in combination with Books 1 and 2 of *De Anima et Vita* make possible the understanding of Vives' views on the emotions as an integral part of his overall thought on the nature of reality. Part 2 of this book is dedicated to the study of those Vivesian tracts. In Parts 2 and 3 of this book I have often included in the text some of the short but key Latin expressions used by Vives in an attempt to preserve the flavor of the original, although longer quotations have been assigned to the endnotes. I sincerely hope that the readers who know Latin will appreciate this method and that others do not find it too distracting.

More perhaps than any previous discussion of the emotions, Vives' book bears a strong personal character. In spite of its heavy tribute to the philosophical tradition on emotions, the third book of *De Anima et Vita* is highly autobiographical and revealing. One cannot read Vives' musings on friendship, love, compassion, laughter, irritation, cruelty, envy, or pride without thinking of the man who wrote them, the events of his life, the letters he wrote, the joys and sufferings he experienced, the people he loved or disliked. The analysis of the book on the emotions directed me once again to the biography of the man who had experienced them. The purpose of Part I of this book is to relate Vives' thought on the emotions to the author's life and environment. Part I, however, does not pretend to rehash all the biographical detail of my early book on Vives (1970, English edition; 1978, Spanish translation). It merely presents an outline of Vives' life, relates particular events to Vives' analysis of some concrete emotions, and attempts insofar as possible to investigate the connection between Vives' main treatises and the book here under consideration, *De Anima et Vita*. It goes without saying that I have gladly taken this opportunity to respond in a constructive way to my most enlightened critics, to correct some of the inaccuracies of my first book on Vives, and to formulate my thought in what I hope is a much more mature and careful manner while recording in the corresponding endnotes some of the progress in our understanding of Vives' life and thought made since 1978 by Spanish, Belgian, Dutch, French, British, German, Italian, Canadian, and American scholars. Vives' criticism of terminist logic, his relations with Erasmus and Thomas More, the significance of some of his early works (such as *Aedes Legum, De Subventione Pauperum, Somnium Scipionis, Fabula de Homine*), his attitude toward religion, and his position within the history of humanist pedagogy and jurisprudence are among the important topics that have been substantially revised and, I hope, improved in Part I of this book.

The aim of this entire book is therefore to offer the English reader a detailed analysis of Book 3 of *De Anima et Vita* (Part 3) while placing it in the context of the first two books of the same treatise (Part 2) and of Vives' life and intellectual environment (Part 1).

Vives was always grateful to his wife for not having lost one hour of study on her account. I am even more grateful to mine for having lovingly compelled me to trade a few hours of research for the pleasures of her company. Without the emotions I shared with her, this discourse on the emotions could have become embarrassingly long or academic in excess.

I owe my gratitude to Professor John Halverson, Ms. Kate Ellis, and Mr. Howard Robertson for having edited the text with as much patience as expertise. I must also thank the Research Committee of the University of California, Santa Cruz, for their unflinching generosity and their faith in this project. Without the incredible endurance and computer wizardry of Mr. Dan Wenger, Division of Humanities, UCSC, this manuscript could have remained forever undeciphered and undecipherable.

At the 1985 Europalia convention in Bruges I was fortunate enough to meet some of the most distinguished Vives scholars in the world, Professors Angel Losada, Antonio Fontán, Miguel Batllori, José Luis Abellán, Jozef Ijsewijn, Constant Matheeusen, José María de Palacio y Palacio, Angelina García,

Mario Sancipriano, and Juan F. Alcina Rovira. Their enthusiasm, erudition, and personal warmth gave me the last incentive to complete this project. I want also to pay a most affectionate tribute of admiration to the memory of Professor Sebastiá García Martínez of Valencia, a wonderful human being whose sudden and cruel death a few months after we simultaneously became acquainted and close friends at the Bruges meeting left me desolate beyond words.

I sincerely hope that this book will be followed by a wave of scholarly research to be crowned by the festive celebrations of the fifth centennial of Vives' birth in 1992.

Part I
Vives' Life and Thought

I

The Exile from Valencia

JUAN LUIS VIVES WAS born in Valencia, probably in 1493, to prosperous Jewish parents who had converted to Catholicism shortly before or after the 1492 decree of expulsion.[1] From 1507 to 1509 he attended the local "Estudio General" founded in 1501 by a Valencian pope, Alexander Borgia. In the fall of 1509, Vives moved to Paris where he enrolled as a freshman in the University Arts course. He was sixteen years old. So far as we know, he never returned to his home country, in spite of the fact that, as his writings and correspondence abundantly prove, he remained through life deeply attached to it.[2]

The parental decision to send the youngster abroad in pursuit of a university education was normal at that time, particularly in the Kingdom of Valencia. A little more intriguing was Vives' later reluctance to go back home under any circumstances, even when the University of Alcalá bypassed all the formalities and directly offered Vives the chair in rhetoric, one of the most prestigious and progressive academic positions in Spain after Nebrija's death in 1522.[3]

Throughout his life Vives held a surprisingly low opinion of contemporary Spanish culture.[4] In Paris he accused the local Spanish university professors of wasting their considerable wits in stubborn defense of an institution that was nothing but "a fortress of ignorance," a trendy metaphor of an age that relished acerbic criticism. Vives saw intellectual life in Spain threatened by uncertainty and obscurantism, enslaved to hordes of monks who read little, understood less, and were cold and indifferent to the study of the humanities. When his friend Juan de Vergara, the brilliant theologian from Alcalá, tried to persuade him that things were not as bad as he had imagined, Vives replied that he would only change his opinion if he were told that Spain had acquired at least twelve printing presses. Vives' friendship with Erasmus in Louvain did not help matters in any way. The Dutch humanist bluntly confessed he did not like Spain ("Hispania non placet"), even when his ideas were being received there with at least as much enthusiasm as anywhere in Europe. Erasmus was irritated by the emotional exuberance of the Spaniards, contemptuous of Cardinal Cisneros' interest in Scotus, concerned about the threats of Inquisitorial censorship, and predisposed against a nation where "there were more Jews than Christians."[5] The persecution of the Spanish Erasmists in the 1530s—a persecution that did not spare Vergara himself— confirmed Erasmus' and Vives' dislike for Spanish life and institutions.[6]

It is only fair to emphasize here that Vives' judgment on Spanish culture during Charles V's reign was unduly severe. It used to be fashionable— particularly among German and Protestant scholars—to claim that Spain was a "country without a Renaissance" because Spanish humanism failed in the long run to bring about a radical break with medieval Catholic orthodoxy and scholasticism. Today we know better. Anyone who has perused the works of Nebrija, Cisneros, Arias Barbosa, the Valdés brothers, Garcilaso de la Vega, Boscán, Leone Hebreo, Fray Antonio de Guevara, Juan del Encina, López de Rueda, Pérez de Oliva, and Hernando de Acuña—among many others—will have to admit that Spanish literary and intellectual life in the sixteenth century was very much entangled with the main threads of Italian and northern European Renaissance, in spite of the eventual failure of the Reformation in the Iberian peninsula and the blossoming of scholastic philosophy in some Spanish universities. Nor can it be denied that the new intellectual and literary vitality of this period, no matter how different from Burckhardt's one-sided picture of Italian humanism, prepared in some complicated ways the splendor of the Spanish Baroque and the Golden Age. Although as a man who lived most of his life in the peaceful and well-organized municipality of Bruges and as a traveler who became used to commuting between Oxford, Paris, and Louvain, Vives might have had reasons not to welcome the prospect of teaching at the University of Alcalá or returning to the socially restless kingdom of Valencia, his harsh appraisal of Spanish intellectual life can only be seen as a typical case of emotional interference with the mental processes of an otherwise extremely judicious man.[7]

It is beyond any doubt that Vives was not only immune to the growing nationalistic feeling of his Spanish contemporaries, but also was obviously annoyed by some of their temperamental characteristics.[8] Annoyance is described by Vives as a mild form of irritation, the opposite of fondness. If fondness is like a soft breeze, annoyance is the first bite of evil. Vives disliked irritable and temperamental southern people, especially those who had never traveled abroad and simply condemned as barbaric anything different from their own culture, "although what they condemned was frequently better than what they used to see there." It is likely that such a remark was inspired by the behavior of the Spanish students in Paris, the Castilian and Aragonese courtiers who followed Charles V through Europe, and the Spanish soldiers in Flanders. Vives explicitly complained that only Italian mercenaries were more arrogant, rude, and cruel than Spain's professional soldiers. Reserved and self-composed, a harsh critic of excessive laughter and loquacity, self-effacing in the presence of other men and severe with women (as Erasmus accused him in his private correspondence), serious and thoughtful, down-to-earth and realistic, Vives was the very antithesis of the image of the Spaniard perpetuated by the Italian humanists: the disarmingly polished "caballero," the devious politician, the mystic "alumbrado," or the obsequious villain that had tickled the imagination of Castiglione, the admiration of Machiavelli and Guicciardini, the devotion of Vittoria Colonna, and the sarcasm of the Venetian comedians.[9] When compared, however, with other more relevant considerations, these are minor ingredients of Vives' highly emotional reluctance to return to Spain. Vives himself says that the most serious form of irritation is caused, not by overt forms of behavior, but by intellectual habits and preferences that run against an individual's *ingenium* and offend "our reason and will." With the exception of Nebrija—whom he always admired and often praised in his own writings—and a few Spanish Erasmists he had met in Flanders, Vives could not feel much at home in the Spain of Charles V. He probably considered the picaresque novel to be as distasteful as the Italian rhymes of Garcilaso, and the artificial prose of Guevara as offensive as the intense nationalism of the court's chroniclers and at least some of the historians of the American conquest (although sometimes he quoted the latter).[10] The mystic leanings of some of the Spanish Erasmists were certainly alien to his sober soul.

Vives' dislike for the Spain of Charles V was obviously compounded and increased by his fear of the Spanish Inquisition. Fear, Vives taught, causes anxiety, confuses our thinking, provokes the imagination into exaggerated visions, and masterminds our decisions.

Américo Castro and his disciples have claimed that the personal insecurity and resentment of the Spanish and Portuguese "new" Christians, whether they themselves were Jewish converts or the offspring of converts, provides an indispensable key to a full understanding of Iberian cultural life throughout the sixteenth and seventeenth centuries. Although the significance of this consideration can and probably has been occasionally exaggerated, there is little doubt that our understanding of the intellectual, artistic, and socio-economic life in Spain and Portugal during that "conflictive age" (as Castro called it) has been greatly enriched by it.[11]

In Vives' case it seems unavoidable to ask how far his Jewish ancestry helped to shape his emotional make-up, and whether his thoughts on the emotions betray in any way the tensions and conflicts he must have experienced as a Spanish Jew. Such investigation requires, however, a closer look at Vives' individual case. Vives' father was the ideal target of Inquisitorial suspicion and social alienation. He was a successful merchant in a rich agricultural region, a member of a ruling elite that included many other Jews in the professions and in key church and state positions. But he was also the member of a caste held in contempt by the bulk of the Spanish population, the "old" Christians. When Vives was seven years old, old enough to remember, his father was arrested by the Inquisition. For a long time his father remained clear of any charges, but other members of the family were not equally lucky and were sentenced to death. Probably in January 1524, and after a two-year-long trial, Vives' father was also executed by order of the Inquisition. At that time Vives was thirty-two (or thirty-one) years old, married, and teaching at Oxford.

Vives' sadness and bitterness were augmented by concern for his sisters, a concern that was proved more than justified when three years later the Inquisition opened another trial against Vives' mother — who had been dead since 1508 — and found her guilty of having visited the synagogue after her alleged "conversion" to Christianity. As a result, her remains were exhumed and desecrated, and Vives' sisters were deprived of any right to their parental inheritance.[12] We do not know how or if these terrible events affected Vives' attitude toward the Catholic church. But we know from his private correspondence that the news of his father's tragic death and his own concern over his sisters broke his health and seriously affected his entire outlook on life. In *De Anima et Vita,* Vives wrote that sadness causes such a dejection and obfuscation of the spirit that one could become lifeless and misanthropic. Vives' correspondence from 1522 through 1531 presents the heart breaking picture of a man overwhelmed by the "terribly sad news from Spain," deeply concerned about his own economic situation, and exasperated with the religious and political conflicts in Europe. Vives complains about migraines and other headaches, insomnia, nausea, and indigestion. He feels fed up with teaching, listless and callous, withdrawn from society, tormented by imagined dangers, self-destructive, and longing for death.[13]

De Anima et Vita was written a few years later, probably in a more serene frame of mind. But the somber picture of those emotions that "proceed from an apparent evil, make man into a "dreadful and cruel beast," and "destroy the human spirit" is without any doubt heavily colored by the persistent memory of his Spanish ordeal.

Vives' penchant for introspection and self-pity was also reinforced by his choice to carry the sadness of those long years in almost complete loneliness and secrecy. In his book on the emotions Vives seems to profess the odd doctrine that sadness is increased when shared with people we love but decreased when shared with strangers. In life, however, he decided to share his pain with at least one intimate friend, Francis Craneveld, the city attorney of Bruges. But even in this private correspondence, Vives never dared to write the word *Inquisition*. He was so afraid that the letters might fall into the wrong hands—as he himself confessed in one of them—that he decided to write about his father's trial and execution in enigmatic terms and often in Greek, a language he never totally mastered. The first time Vives dared to communicate with Craneveld on this matter, he disguised the truth by touchingly describing his father's problem as a "sickness."[14] It is highly unlikely that being the son of a Jewish "convert" executed by order of the Spanish Inquisition represented a serious threat to Vives' personal safety in Oxford, Bruges, or Louvain.[15] Was he afraid that Erasmus, whose anti-Semitic remarks he had patiently tolerated, would think less of him? Did he fear losing the patronage of Henry VIII, Thomas More, or Cardinal Wolsey? Did he apply to himself the Greek proverb he quoted in *De Anima et Vita:* "Nobody is so excellent and self-confident that he could not be destroyed by a parental disgrace"? That some of these feelings were possible is made clear by Vergara's reaction to the events. In one of his letters to Vives, Vergara—at that time secretary to the archbishop of Toledo—felt obliged to reassure Vives that the tragedy in Valencia ("a circumstance entirely extrinsic to you") had not diminished in the least his love for him.[16]

This well-meant remark and Vives' own cryptic words give us a gloomy intimation of an emotional turbulence we can hardly comprehend. The man who has been described as one of the founders of modern psychology had obviously many personal reasons to be deeply interested in the study of human emotions and motivations. Although Vives' life in his home country was short, the memories of his childhood and of his native town became an important component of his emotional makeup and had a lasting influence on his ways of thinking.

2

The Parisian Student

From 1509 to 1512, Vives attended the University of Paris as a student of Montaigu College and probably obtained a bachelor of arts degree, his first and last academic title. From 1512 to 1514, he probably resided at Paris, where he began his writing career. In 1514, he left Paris and moved to the Low Countries, where he would spend most of his life. His five years in Paris were without any doubt the most formative period of his career. In Paris, Vives became an adult, received for the last time a formal education in an institution of higher learning, and made fundamental decisions that definitively shaped his perception of himself and of the world around him.

It is far from easy to explore the intricate ways in which the emotional and intellectual responses to the new environment contributed to the formation of his personality structure. The analysis of the emotions presented by Vives in *De Anima et Vita* does not help us to simplify this task. On the contrary, as I shall explain in the proper context, Vives recognized with more sophistication than most of his predecessors not only that emotions, cognitive attitudes, and character traits are not clearly differentiated from each other, but also that all three interact in unfathomable ways and are themselves physiologically and socioculturally determined. Vives' overt behavior and written statements (including his private letters) provide us, however, with some significant clues.

We can safely surmise that the emotional reactivity of the Valencian teenager reached a high level in Paris because of the age of the youth and the novelty of his life circumstances. In *De Anima et Vita,* Vives places much emphasis upon the relation between age and emotional response. Young people consider pleasure the highest good, are less burdened by anxiety, tend to be more splendid and generous, experience more joy in life, and need more than others to be tutored into wisdom by the feeling of shame. Vives insists also that novelty intensifies the affective tone of our experiences while custom and habituation tends to dull it. Unexpected good qualities in our beloved ones increase our affection for them, and time diminishes our irritation with their shortcomings and inadequacies. Custom makes evil things more tolerable but leads also to loss of respect and admiration. A novel evil excites our compassion, change delights us and increases our pleasures, and unexpected dangers become the cause of panic.

The young Spaniard shared his Parisian experience with some seven thousand youths of different nationalities who crowded the Left Bank and were immersed not only in the study of dialectic, theology, and canon law, but who indulged also in the pleasures of women and wine, and led a raucous and occasionally violent life on the streets. For the first time in his life, Vives was away from the parental home. He was surrounded by people who spoke a language closely related to his native Valencian dialect, but still incomprehensible to him. Paris in 1509 was the largest metropolis in Christendom, the seat of a powerful monarchy and the capital city of the most populous kingdom in Europe (probably of about sixteen million). The University of Paris was not a new institution like the "Estudio General" of Valencia, but an old and prestigious fortress of Catholic theology surrounded and buffeted by the vigorous winds of Renaissance humanism. Under those circumstances Vives was pressured to make some of the most important choices in his life.[1]

About 1509, Montaigu College had reached a turning point in its two-hundred-year history. The college had been founded in the fourteenth century by the archbishop of Rouen and had exhausted most of its endowments by the end of the fifteenth. In 1493, a Flemish reformer trained by the Brethren of the Common Life, Jan van Standonck (1443–1510), took charge of the college and quickly transformed it into a quasi-monastic institution for the training of the poor. In 1495, Erasmus visited Montaigu and was appalled by the rigor, the filth, and the antihumanistic orientation of the college. Rabelais' observations a few years later were not much more complimentary.[2]

Still, as it had been the case with similar institutions, Montaigu prospered in every sense with the cult of poverty and austerity. When Standonck was replaced by Noel Beda (d. 1536), the college had doubled in size and gifts had accumulated. Beda was a conservative theologian who constantly harassed Erasmus and was much more interested in the scholastic training of the future high clergy than in educating the poor.

It is highly likely that when Vives reached Montaigu both the faculty and the students were divided into two factions: those who attempted to preserve Standonck's reforming zeal and asceticism, and those who were more interested in a promising career and the pleasures of earthly existence. Vives' life and writings clearly show that the young man from Valencia leaned more toward the former than toward the latter group, although he chose a typically eclectic and moderate path between the two.

In one of his later works, the *Exercitatio Linguae Latinae* (1538), Vives presents a few sketches of school life. In the dialogue *Princeps Puer,* he ridicules the laziness, frivolity, and lack of intellectual drive among the sons of the rich and the powerful. In *Ebrietas,* he draws a realistic and repulsive picture of drunkeness. In *Garrientes,* he scorns the quack and the prattler. *Adversus Pseudodialecticos* describes the young students and instructors of Montaigu as "rash and silly," and as having "no understanding, no judgment, and no discernment" (M 3.37, 38, 64; see footnote 8, Chapter 1). *De Anima et Vita* reinforces the impression that Vives never fell into the temptation of frivolity, which he saw as characteristic of the young. As I shall point out later, Vives' attitude toward women and sex was always, if not Manichaean, at least severe and detached. He was instinctively repelled by the abuse of wine and the sight of drunkards (M 4.457; 6.90). He found rich and spoiled young men irritable, proud, and wasteful. But he rejected also the extreme and morose asceticism of Standonck. He praised frugality, but recognized the beneficial results of a healthy diet and the power of a little wine or beer to calm the angry and uplift the sad. He had no taste for shrill merriment but enjoyed banquets, games, and the contemplation of beautiful tapestries and landscapes. What he learned from Standonck and indirectly from the Brethren of the Common Life was a lesson that would guide him through all his career: that any cultivation of the intellect must be aimed at a virtuous life, a life very different from the life he observed and rejected as a student in the University of Paris. But unlike two other Montaigu alumni, Calvin and Ignatius of Loyola, Vives' reforming drive would be aimed at the reform of education rather than at the reform of dogmatic beliefs or ecclesiastical institutions.

Within this context one can begin to understand Vives' preferences for the intellectual alternatives he found within the walls of Montaigu College and in the city of Paris in general. In Montaigu College, Vives studied terminist logic for two full years after having passed the required examinations on Latin and Greek grammar. In *De Causis Corruptarum Artium* (M 3.143), Vives complained about the excessive time dedicated to the study of logic, a mere preparation and tool for further intellectual work. Under the direction of Beda and the Scottish logician John Major (1467–1550), Montaigu had become by 1509 the most prestigious, but also one of the last refuges of strictly medieval logic in Europe. In institutions of higher learning where the humanist influence was felt more strongly, formal logic and semantic theory were being quickly phased out as unsuitable to the legal and ethical instruction of influential laymen.[3] The blossoming of terminist logic at Montaigu went hand in hand with the 1509 statutes that forbade the reading of poetry and discouraged the study of Greek. But Beda's interest in theology conspired with Major's admiration for the medieval tradition to keep alive at Montaigu the interest in terminist logic, an interest that had been preserved at Paris until the end of the fifteenth century by the Scotist Pierre Tartaret (d. 1495) and the nominalist Thomas Bricot (d. 1516). Under the influence of his masters, Bricot and the Spanish logician Jeronimo Pardo (d. 1505), Major began his career with a commentary on Peter of Spain's *Summulae Logicales,* a book he considered "the door to Logic" and the definitive break with the Aristotelian-Boethian tradition that he held responsible for the confusion between metaphysics and logic, and consequently for the wasteful debates on the universals. During his first stay in Paris (1505–1517), Major succeeded in attracting a brilliant group of "dialecticians" that included several Scotsmen, some Frenchmen, and a large number of Spaniards. These people managed to enrich and develop the Parisian and medieval tradition represented by the work of Peter of Spain, and were themselves influenced by the Mertonian school of "calculators" revived in the fifteenth century by the Paduan logicians and natural philosophers Peter of Mantua (d. 1400) and Paul of Venice (d. 1429).[4]

Vives' entire literary and philosophical output amounts to a wholesale repudiation of the instruction he received at Montaigu. Two works in particular spell out his critical response. The first was published under the title *Adversus Pseudodialecticos* in April 1519, six years after his departure from Paris. The second, entitled *De Disciplinis,* was published in 1531, eight years before his death. The documents differ in character but reveal a remarkable continuity in Vives' patterns of thinking. *Adversus Pseudodialecticos* was Vives' first important contribution to the fashionable humanistic diatribes against scholastic *cavillationes* and *garrulitas,* and as such it was also praised with equally fashionable excess by the likes of Thomas More and Erasmus.[5] Erasmus hailed the work and praised the unique philosophical talents of the young Spaniard in his private correspondence, and in the prefatory letter to Vives' *Declamationes Syllanae* (M 2.316). Thomas More read the book in 1520 and shared Erasmus' feelings of admiration and enthusiasm, although with mild irony pointed out the suspicious similarity in phraseology between Vives' and his own pronouncements on the same topic.[6]

The text itself does not make clear when Vives formulated in his own mind the positions he outlined in this wordy tirade. With juvenile lack of modesty — a defect that time would correct — Vives repeatedly claims that he has studied terminist logic with great personal effort and that he is utterly familiar with its most recondite secrets. He also confesses to be very bitter for having spent "so many good hours so badly." (*Tam multas bonas horas me tam male collocare coegit;* M. 3.66). The reader has nevertheless the overwhelming impression that the ideas expressed in this highly rhetorical piece had been brewing in Vives' mind long before 1520. We do know that only two years after he had left Paris, Vives was already echoing some of Erasmus' attacks against the glorification of military heroism, was disparaging the "suicetical" quibbles of his former Parisian masters and recommending the reading of the Latin classics.[7]

Adversus Pseudodialecticos contains few original ideas. It merely repeats in the rhetorical and satirical style of the age a stock of objections against medieval dialectics already raised by Petrarch and Salutati in the fourteenth century; further elaborated by Valla, Ermolao Barbaro, and Politian in the fifteenth; and echoed through northern Europe in the writings of Erasmus and Rudolph Agricola, both of whom were most likely known to Vives during his years in Paris. With only minor variations in emphasis and style, all these masters had taught the descriptive rather than the prescriptive character of all the *artes sermocinales* (grammar, rhetoric, and dialectic), the fundamental similarity and structural relationship of dialectic to both grammar and rhetoric, the interpretation of rigor as idiomatic propriety derived from the *consuetudo* with and imitation of recognized models rather than as formal validity or semantic perspicuity, the conception of dialectic as a tool of persuasion and effective teaching rather than as an end in itself or as a guarantor of apodictic argument. They all had deplored the abuse of dialectic in theology, natural philosophy, and even ethics and the sacrifice of stylish Latin to the technical demands of logical formalism.

Vives' own diatribe did not add much to this fashionable train of thought, but dramatized for us what Erasmus characterized as the "conversion" of the young Parisian "sophister" to the ideals of Renaissance humanism. It also proves that while in Paris or soon thereafter Vives made a radical and lasting choice between the medieval culture represented by Montaigu and those "intelligent, daring, free, and independent men who will rescue individual freedom and bring back to the republic of letters the sweetest of liberties" (M 3.62). Vives' individual case also reinforces the impression that, by the first decade of the sixteenth century, French humanists such as Lefèvre d'Etaples and Budé were not only clearly aware of but had already adopted with peculiar enthusiasm the Petrarchan division of history into a glorious antiquity, a decadent middle age, and a "modern" era of revival, the same division that has remained practically unquestioned as our normative historiographical pattern.[8] The terminist logic he learned at Montaigu was for Vives a medieval monster doomed to extinction in order to make room for a new generation of brilliant and promising minds everywhere in Europe. The University of Paris appeared to Vives as a senile and barbaric institution apparently unaware of the youthful promise of modern men and ideas in other European universities, courts, and centers of learning. To the young and rebellious Spaniard, Paris constituted an antiquated anomaly out of touch with a new world of thought.

The most distinctive qualities of *Adversus Pseudodialecticos* are manners of thinking and expression that seem closely entangled with personality traits and emotional attitudes. The document singles out the Spanish masters at Paris and chastises them with excessive severity. Although Vives attempts to disguise this severity as a patriotic concern for the reputation of his countrymen, the reader also has the impression that Vives was equally inspired by the fear of being unfairly lumped together with them or even by feelings of spite and contempt. Another characteristic of the book is the insistence on the uselessness of terminist logic, an accusation that was certainly familiar to humanist literature but clearly exaggerated by Vives. There is nothing, he laments, more frivolous, wasteful, meaningless, useless, vain, and impractical than terminist logic. These accusations, however, are never backed by reasoned argument or philosophically interesting insight into the aims and method of logical training. The claim that at least logic "sharpens the boys' wits" is simply dismissed by the example of Saint Augustine who, according to Vives, was a good theologian just because he never spoke terminist jargon. The theoretical defects of terminist logic are not reasonably exposed but ridiculed through an accumulation of examples taken out of context (a procedure abused by terminists themselves) and practically unintelligible to all but those thoroughly initiated into the jargon of the sect. In fact, the contemporary reader is tempted to think that, like most of his fellow humanists, Vives never clearly grasped either the shortcomings or the achievements and potential of terminist logic.

The historical origins of terminist logic have to be traced back to the middle years of the thirteenth century when, partially as a reaction against the heavily theological orientation of Thomism, the masters of the so-called arts course, the philosophers, began to write a series of logical treatises on the different ways terms signify things. The best known of those treatises, the *Summulae Logicales* of Peter of Spain (later Pope John XXI), was widely used for the next three hundred years. But it was Ockham in the fourteenth century who gave a radically new philosophical twist to the study of words as the linguistic counterpart to the concepts in our mind. In Ockham's hands, logic becomes severed from metaphysics, a neutral discipline indifferent to any speculative debate, *schola non affectata*. The great Ockhamist masters of the fourteenth century—people such as Johan Buridan (d. 1358) and Albert of Saxony (d. 1390)—partially succeeded in subsuming syllogistics under the basic heading of inferential theory and in binding the logic of terms ("terminist logic") to Ockham's nominalism. Their work was continued in the fifteenth century by a large group of second-rank logicians—such as Pierre d'Ailly (d. 1426), Paul of Venice (d. 1428), and Pierre Tartaret (d. 1495), among many others—who were still very popular in the University of Paris when Vives was a student at Montaigu College.

Like most humanists, Vives was only superficially aware of this important philosophical tradition. His satire was mostly directed against fifteenth-century logicians. The central figures—such as Ockham—played a relatively unimportant role in his criticism. Vives also failed to comprehend the main theoretical shortcomings of terminist logic: the lack of an economical and comprehensive formal system, the inability to subsume the study of inference and implication under a complete logic of relations, the baffling confusion of a semantic theory of supposition and an epistemological theory of signification, the tendency to accumulate examples rather than to choose paradigmatic cases to draw fundamental lessons on the expressive character of language, the failure to construct an adequate and manageable symbolic language. By the same token it also can be said that the humanists failed also to realize the potential of terminist logic. In spite of their fundamental shortcomings, terminist logicians had gone beyond the narrow conception of deductive logic as a study of Aristotle's *Prior Analytics* to the exclusion of other parts of the *Organon*. They had explored at some length and with precision logico-semantical problems such as quantifiers and other operators, the truth-functional treatment of sentential connectives, the problems of naming and definition, the analysis of empty classes and logical paradoxes, and so on. Furthermore, terminist logicians made a great effort to cleanse logical inquiry of any metaphysical entanglement, and most of them were proud of belonging to a school of thought that was—as Ockham had made possible—"a neutral school" (*schola non affectata*). Terminist logic was also promisingly applied to the study of kinetics and to the tentative solution of problems that eventually were made manageable by infinitesimal calculus.[9] Vives' negative attitude toward terminist logic was clearly dictated by a mild form of theoretical skepticism tempered by utilitarian concerns (more about this later), but also by his personal aversion toward the character and life-style of his Parisian teachers. In *Adversus Pseudodialecticos*, Vives describes his teachers as proud and boastful, totally unable to be informed and constructive participants in the conversation of educated partners, ignorant of the arts "that govern life," senile, inept, and sloppy outside of the classroom, lacking common sense and any sense of humanity. Perhaps the most eloquent pages of the tract on emotions are reserved to the description of the narcissistic, contentious, and arrogant intellectuals. Vives' rejection of the medieval *disputatio* as an educational tool was to a large extent an emotional reaction to the obnoxious behavior of the disputants themselves, a behavior condoned by the academic mores of the day and fostered by the very esoteric futility of the topics discussed.[10]

De Disciplinis was written by a more experienced and emotionally balanced man, within the context of an ambitious project of curricular reform that will be examined when we survey Vives' pedagogical ideals in Chapter 5. Vives begins the third book of the first part with a review and commentary on each of the six books of the Aristotelian *Organon*, probably with more objectivity and depth than did any of the contemporary invectives or eulogies. Vives finds the *Categories* too obscure and more metaphysical than logical in content. He believes that *On Interpretation* belongs to grammar rather than to dialectic and criticizes the excessive superfluities of the *Prior Analytics* while reproaching Aristotle for dealing in the *Posterior Analytics* with matters such as opinion, error, and ignorance, which belong to psychology rather than to logic. Finally, Vives finds the *Topics* and the *On Sophistical Refutations* potentially useful, but poorly organized and occasionally repetitious. Vives then proceeds to analyze from his own personal point of view the Greek and Latin followers of Aristotle, including Cicero, Quintilian, and Boethius. The last three chapters repeat basically the same criticism of terminist logic that we found in *Adversus Pseudodialecticos* but in a more sober, less emotional style.

In spite of occasional relapses into his burlesque tone of youthful invective, *De Disciplinis* is not only a less rhetorical and more technical piece, but also less parochial, fairer, and better informed. The criticism of modern dialectic is preceded by some general considerations on the corruption of all human disciplines. Vives, who finished this book seven years before *De Anima et Vita* was published, blames passional disorder for early cultural distortions and misdirections. Ineptitude concealed by conceit and ignorance misled by greed are responsible for the sacrifice of truth to selfish pursuits. In the light of these philosophical reflections, the anti-Spanish feeling of the early document is greatly toned down. Vives seems now more aware that terminist sophists included not only his Spanish teachers at Montaigu but also a medieval Scottish (the "Britannici") tradition and a powerful group of more recent Paduan masters.[11] The book also proves more familiarity with the recent editions and translations of Aristotle, Quintilian's works, and Agricola's *De Inventione Dialectica* (a book that was published in 1515 but had circulated in manuscript for at least ten years before that date).

De Disciplinis makes clear nevertheless that the harsh and by contemporary standards superficial attitude toward terminist logic that Vives adopted in his youth remained basically unchanged throughout his entire life. Some of Vives' more mature works prove, however, that although he never managed to understand the achievements of that logic, he was fully aware of the important philosophical implications of the new humanist attitude toward language.[12] Vives' critical effort in *De Disciplinis* was as repetitious as it was unnecessary. By 1532 terminist logic was quickly fading away, even in the remote classrooms of the universities of Alcalá and Salamanca where some Spanish logicians, including some former Montaigu professors, kept it barely alive until the middle of the century.

3

The Northern Humanist

IN 1512 VIVES VISITED Bruges, where he settled down two years later, becoming a preceptor in residence for the children of a Valencian family of prosperous clothiers who were his distant relatives and members of a large community of Spanish Jewish exiles in the Low Countries.[1] In Bruges, Vives became acquainted with the intellectual elite of the Netherlands, a region that included roughly the present territories of Belgium and Holland, plus the northwestern Rhineland (Münster/Cologne) and the northern sections of what are today the French provinces of Artois and Picardy. In the spring of 1514, before his move from Paris to Bruges, Vives had published in Paris some short devotional books. In 1516 he visited Brussels and Louvain where he probably tutored some students and made a good impression upon some of the faculty members.[2] About this time Vives was personally introduced to Erasmus, who helped to secure his appointment as preceptor to William de Croy, a young clergyman who in 1517 became archbishop-elect of Toledo and cardinal.[3] In March 1517 Vives followed Croy to the Brabantine university city of Louvain, where Erasmus himself lived from 1517 to 1521, helping, among many other activities, to organize the Trilingue College. In 1520 the university allowed Vives to use its premises to give some talks on Cicero, Vergil, Suetonius, and others.

After 1521 Vives' life became much more difficult and full of worries. In January of that year he lost the patronage of Croy, who was accidentally killed while hunting. His professional activity was disturbed by some bickering with Erasmus and by the growing conflict between Erasmus and the more conservative theologians in the university, a conflict that was only exacerbated by the failure of the Diet of Worms to contain the Lutheran rebellion in Germany. There were also signs that this period was a time of indecision and doubt concerning the future of his intellectual and professional life.[4] About this time Vives was shocked by the news of his father's

initial problems with the Valencian tribunal of the Inquisition. In December
1522 Rhodes fell to the Turks. Christendom was assaulted from without and
torn asunder from within. In 1523 Vives rejected the offer to teach at Alcalá,
but sought the patronage of Henry VIII and perhaps too that of Pope Adrian,
with whom he was slightly acquainted. Vives landed in England the spring of
1523.[5]

Vives' decision to take residence in the Low Countries was probably
dictated by practical considerations, but it can also be seen as a clear
indication of a personal intellectual choice. In Paris, Vives became not only a
European Renaissance man but also a man of the northern Renaissance,
decidedly unattached to and partially critical of Italian humanism. Unlike
most of the great humanists of northern Europe—John Colet and Thomas
More, Erasmus of Rotterdam and Rudolph Agricola, Lefèvre d'Etaples and
Guillaume Budé—Vives never made or expressed any desire to make the
customary journey to Italy. His writings make it abundantly clear that he was
thoroughly familiar with the achievements of Italian culture figures from
Petrarch, who "swept off the dust from the works of the classics," to Pico
della Mirandola, whose premature death at the age of thirty-one Vives
lamented in a touching passage of *De Anima et Vita,* Book 3, Chapter 7. That
the work of Italian translators and editors of Greek classic literature was
decisive in the education of this typically self-made man can be inferred from
the frequent references he makes to them in *De Disciplinis,* where, for
instance, he calls Teodoro Gaza "the prince of all translators." Valla's
thought—although partially mediated by Agricola—influenced Vives more
than he was willing to recognize. Marsilio Ficino's Neoplatonic philosophy of
love permeates Chapters 2 through 4 of the third book of *De Anima et Vita.*
Still, Vives' respect for Italian culture was constantly alternated with harsh
criticism. He recommends the reading of Politian but finds him fastidious
and occasionally immoral. He lectures on Filelfo but criticizes him for being
too wordy and tiring. He praises Valla but finds his dialectics full of mistaken
points of view. He likes Boccaccio but hastens to add that he could not be
compared to Petrarch, who was himself "prolix and morose in many
passages." He calls Ficino a "philosophaster" who wrote in "an inelegant
and difficult diction." He thinks that Ermolao Barbaro's style was harsh and
impure, that Patrizi had no critical sense, that Poggio was a "chattering
trifler," and that Pomponio Leto bores the reader with his endless descriptions of ruins. Vives misses no opportunity to praise Erasmus or Budé above
"all the Ermolaos, Picos, Politians, Gazas, Vallas and all of Italy," and finds
the Italians incapable of governing themselves, lighthearted, excessively
nationalistic, too worldly, and formalistic to excess.[6]

The people and the culture of the Low Countries were much more according to his taste. *De Anima et Vita*'s book on the emotions contains a few observations on the temperamental differences between northerners (cold and wet) and southerners (hot and dry). Although Vives bravely attempts to record the positive and negative traits of both groups, in the balance the northerners seem to fare better. Southerners might love with more vehemence, but are "superficial," "unreliable," and "fickle" in their affections. Northern people are more "persevering" and "constantly loyal." Southerners are more prone to anger because of their hot brain humors, while northerners are more "resilient" to this destructive emotion. Southerners are more irritable, become easily jealous about their wives, and are therefore more prone to seek revenge. The only seemingly good traits of the southerners are their ability to experience more joy in life and their natural resistance to deep forms of hatred. But these apparent advantages are outweighed by the stronger social ties among the northern people and by their more developed aesthetic sense. Northern people, Vives says, are less irritable and angry because they indulge more in "friendly parties." Vives seems to have northerners in mind when he praises the ability of some people to enjoy the contemplation of beautiful things because the examples he chooses, green pastures and refined tapestries, evoke Flemish landscapes and crafts. As always, the Spanish Jewish exile proved himself a careful and intelligent observer of his new milieu.

In the Low Countries, Vives found more than congenial people, attractive tapestries, and pastures. He found a culture that was akin to his soul, a culture he probably had sensed in Paris through the lingering influence of Standonck and the writings of Erasmus. While the Italian fourteenth century had been dominated by poets and literary men, the life of the spirit in the Low Countries had been inspired by mystics and reformers. In Italy the centers of learning were mostly secular; in the Low Countries they were monasteries. The only universities in the region were Cologne and (from 1425) Louvain, but both of them remained for a long time bastions of scholastic theology. In the first half of the fifteenth century, Petrarch was read and admired more as an Augustinian moralist than as a secular poet. In the second half of that same century, Italian humanism became better known, but was also increasingly adapted (not without some pockets of resistance toward the end of the century) to the prevailing moral and theological concerns of leading scholars. Probably the most Italianized scholars of the Netherlands were Rudolph Agricola (d. 1485) and Rudolph Langius (d. 1519). Agricola has been compared to Petrarch for his mastery of classic Latin and to Salutati for his influence in the spread of Greek studies.

He and Langius made known in the Netherlands Valla's humanist dialectic, a dialectic that Vives would accept with some important qualifications.

The chairs of poetics and eloquence in Louvain, the profound changes in the teaching of Latin at Deventer, Münster, and Louvain, the spread of a Latin-loving patriciate that provided the social base for a humanist culture, the prodigious activity of the Flemish humanist printer D. Martens in Louvain (the printer of Erasmus, More, and Vives, among many others) and the interest in classic literature in the service of biblical and patristic theology are some of the most salient features of the intellectual environment that Vives found in the Low Countries and that he would help to define with more clarity and vigor.[7]

About 1514, Bruges was still an affluent municipality of about fifty thousand people, although the rising level of silt in the Scheldt River (that linked the city to the North Sea) represented a growing threat to its maritime trade.[8] The municipality was wisely administered by an elective body of senators and councillors that passed legislation, exercised criminal and civil jurisdiction, and left the administration of the laws to a group of lower officials employed by the city. The young Spaniard was greatly impressed by the cleanliness of the town, the smooth social order of the municipality, and perhaps more important, by the polite manners of its well-educated, law-abiding, and socially cohesive population. Vives' admiration and affection for a city he always called "his second home" helped much to form his political and philosophical thought on the social character of the virtuous man, the value of cities as "the seats of human associations," the social teleology of our emotional responses, and on the importance of comradeship in fostering politically and personally rewarding friendships among fellow citizens.[9]

The first friends Vives made in Bruges were typical representatives of culture in the Low Countries: bourgeois, devout, educated, open-minded, well placed in society and great admirers of Erasmus. Mark Laurin (d. 1540) had been a fellow student of Erasmus. John Fevyn (d. 1555) resided in the Princenhof, the old palace of the Burgundian duke, and was related to ambassadors, legates, and Hapsburg officers of the Court. Francis Craneveld (d. 1564) was not only a Hellenist and Bruges' chief municipal magistrate (a "Grand Pensionary") but also a wealthy patron of the humanities. Of the three, Craneveld became and remained throughout life Vives' closest friend, a man Vives loved at first sight, a classic example of that "amazing spiritual sympathy for each other" that binds two people "in a secret and natural harmony," and becomes the model of a good friendship: the lasting friendship between two good persons.

Vives' encounter with Erasmus marked the beginning of the most important intellectual association of his life.[10] By 1516, Erasmus had reached the peak of his fame. From the Brethren of the Common Life in Deventer and Bois-le-Duc he had learned a life of internal devotion centered on the imitation of the evangelical Christ. Under the influence of Colet in Oxford, Gaguin in Paris, and Vitrier in Saint-Omer, he had come to reject the subtle anti-intellectual trends of the *Devotio Moderna* and the monasticism of his years in the Augustinian Abbey of Steyn. In the *Enchiridion Militis Christiani* (1504) he had announced his program of reforming Catholic theology through a return to the study of classical antiquity and described the dangers and weapons of a struggling Christian. The publication by Erasmus of Valla's *Annotationes in Novum Testamentum* (1505) had made known in northern Europe new refined techniques of textual criticism and brought about a promising era of biblical hermeneutics. His fame had reached European proportions in 1508 with the publication of the second edition of his *Adagia* by Venice's most prestigious printer, Aldo Manuzio. The publication in 1511 of *The Praise of Folly* and the feverish activity of editing classic works in the Basel printing house of Froben preceded the "Great Year" of 1516, when Erasmus had truly amazed Europe with the publication of *Institutio Principis Christiani,* the critical edition of the New Testament and the new editions of Saint Jerome and Seneca.

When they met in Flanders, Erasmus was forty-seven years old and Vives was twenty-three. The former was an author of European renown. The latter had written only two short and relatively inconsequential works of devotion. Vives was clearly overwhelmed with respect, a feeling he described in *De Anima et Vita* as "based on the comparison between greatness and smallness" and "mixed always with admiration." Vives' correspondence with Erasmus proves beyond any doubt that his respect for Erasmus survived all the defects he eventually discovered in the master. Erasmus recognized the intellectual promise of the young Spaniard and lavishly praised his initial achievements. There is no doubt that for a time Erasmus was very fond of Vives. In *De Anima et Vita,* Vives says that fondness is "incipient love," but that fondness without love "becomes weaker" and "extremely vulnerable," particularly if we are tempted to think that the other's fondness for us seems dictated by self-interest. Whether Vives' respect for Erasmus and Erasmus' fondness for Vives eventually evolved into a sincere and mutual friendship, is less obvious.

As humanists familiar with the classical ideas on friendship taught by Aristotle, Plutarch, and Cicero (among others), both men had nothing but the most eloquent words of praise for a feeling they considered to be the manifestation of human nature's sociability and the expression in the human domain of the cosmic law of attraction between like objects. Erasmus' thoughts on friendship are scattered throughout his many writings, but two ideas seem to emerge with particular emphasis. The first, of Aristotelian inspiration, is the notion that true friendship is possible only among equals. The second, probably learned from Plutarch, is the claim that one can have only a few friends, that true friendship is always an intimate friendship. By this criterion any friendship that ends badly was never a true friendship: *"Amicitia quae defuit, numquam vera fuit."*

Vives' ideas on friendship are articulated in Chapters 2 to 4 of Part 3 of his tract on the emotions. The love of friendship is never based on self-interest, is always mutual and manifested through actions, particularly in times of "true need" or when the beloved is not loved by others. Gentleness and modesty are the most attractive qualities in a friend. People who "easily criticize us," are inclined "to find fault with our services," or are "easily offended" do not make good friends. People are attracted to each other by common interests, especially by common intellectual pursuits. In some cases, however, the difference in temperament enhances friendship and makes people mutually enriching and complementary. Friendship is threatened by "frequent offenses" and by hypocritical flattery.

The early correspondence between Erasmus and Vives abounds in expressions of mutual affection, particularly in the letters of Erasmus, who was a master in the theory and practice of the epistolary art. But at least some of those expressions strike the modern reader as slightly more affected than affectionate, more inspired by the desire to imitate the classics than by true and honest sentiment. If a friendship that ends badly was never a true friendship, we can sadly conclude that Erasmus had fewer true friends than his large correspondence seems to indicate. His relations with Colet were often overshadowed by dark clouds. He managed to antagonize Aleander and never succeeded in making a real friend in Italy. In France he did not fare much better. His friendship with Budé and his relations with Lefèvre were similarly stormy. He even had some problems with More, "the man for all seasons." For a while the Germans admired and loved him, but in the last ten years of his life the Reformation brought him the betrayal of many "friends" and an unbearable feeling of loneliness.[11] The relations between Vives and Erasmus went through two difficult periods. In 1520, Erasmus asked Vives to write a commentary to *De Civitate Dei* as part of a new edition of Saint Augustine's works. The project turned out to be more difficult and time-consuming than Vives had anticipated. Erasmus, an indefatigable worker but also a man of domineering and impatient character, was irritated by the delay.

Vives' moans and groans finally provoked him. When the book was published, Erasmus wrote the introduction with only a passing reference to Vives. To make things worse, the book was a financial disaster. Erasmus was inclined to blame the failure of their common enterprise on Vives' prolix style. It was rumored that Erasmus had warned Froben not to publish other works by Vives, a charge Erasmus denied. Vives begged for kindness and asked Erasmus to drop the almost insulting formality and aloofness of his rare letters.[12]

The second difficult period was about six years later. In 1528 Erasmus published his *Ciceronianus,* but failed to mention Vives' name among the contemporary masters of Latin prose, not because he had "forgotten it" (as he wrote to Vives) but because he had planned to leave it out unless requested by Vives himself (as he wrote to Conrad Goclenius). From Erasmus' own correspondence we know that he had advised some people to avoid any close contact with Vives. One year later Erasmus published a second edition of Saint Augustine's works but left out all the commentaries written by Vives. In the last six years of his life Vives wrote only three letters to Erasmus, to keep him informed of the fate of some Spanish Erasmists.[13]

From this short account of their personal relations it seems obvious that Vives' unflinching and filial reverence for the Dutch humanist was never an intimate friendship according to a theoretical model presented by either man. What is more important for us is to find out whether their quarrels and progressive alienation represented also a significant disagreement in thought.

No one, I think, will doubt that in some sense Vives was and always remained an "Erasmian." What they had in common was probably more relevant than whatever separated them. Both were Christian humanists. Their main concern as Christians was not to define the dogma with more scholastic stringency nor to reinforce existing ecclesiastical institutions, but to enrich individual and social life with the moral precepts taught by Christ. Christian morality for both of them was not exemplified by monastic withdrawal, not enhanced by sacramental use, nor marked by radical asceticism. Neither of them was attracted to the heroic demands of the "evangelical counsels." Loving enemies or participating in the redeeming sufferings and humiliations of the crucified Christ, had no special meaning to them. Neither of them felt called upon to exemplify in their own lives a heroic or exemplary imitation of Christ. To them Christian morality meant the fulfillment of human nature's individual and social potentialities. Because their Christian devotion was very much bent on improving things on earth, Erasmus and Vives became pedagogues and social reformers. Both men saw the Reformation as a threat to Christian unity, an unwelcome source of new divisive partisanship and another excuse for theological squabbles.

As humanists they admired ancient wisdom and beauty of form but feared the excesses of a blind cult of the past. They considered classical literature as a providential propaedeutic into Christianity, but despised any form of servile imitation and sincerely believed in historical progress. Their notion of progress, however, did not recognize medieval culture, which they judged with a harshness that went far beyond their knowledge of it.

As individuals they had much in common. Both of them were cosmopolitan, pacifistic, self-made, vulnerable to vanity, erudite, and dependent on the patronage of the powerful and the rich. They shared favorite authors and favorite books: Plato, Aristotle, Plutarch, Quintilian, Cicero, Saint Augustine, Origen, Saint Jerome, and Seneca (about most of whom they had similar reservations). They disliked the same types of people: scholastic theologians and dialecticians, paganizing humanists, fanatic reformers and counter-reformers.[14]

In spite of these far-reaching similarities, Vives and Erasmus were strong individuals with distinct ideas and different intellectual and personality traits. By temperament Vives was respectful of others but not a blind follower of anybody. He profoundly disliked any form of partisanship and one-sided sectarianism. He was too critical, eclectic, and skeptic to be the founder or the member of any given school of thought. Although he shared Erasmus' views on Christianity, he was much less eager than the Dutch humanist to antagonize the church authorities or to enter into controversial theological matters. He disliked monks but never wrote against Catholic monasticism or religious vows. In fact, the only time he dared to criticize minor points of Catholic orthodoxy was in his private correspondence and in the commentaries on Saint Augustine that he wrote when he was young and under Erasmus' supervision. For the latter he paid a high price. Erasmus did not appreciate his effort, the Louvain theologians accused him of incompetence in theological matters, and the Jesuits later succeeded in having the book included in the Index of 1584. Devout Christian though he was, he did not emerge as a reformer of Catholic theology, a preacher of evangelical Christianity, or as a champion of biblical hermeneutics and patristic theology, although as a young man he might have contemplated such vocation. Besides his contribution to the edition of Saint Augustine, Vives never wrote a piece of biblical exegesis, nor did he edit the works of a church father. Luther's doctrines on the freedom of the will—which he sincerely rejected— were not enough to draw him deeply into the Reformation debates. A telling sign of his alienation from theological disputes was the fact that while

Erasmus was constantly urged by everybody to take sides at the beginning of the Reformation, Vives was practically ignored by the theologians of either side. In 1525, however, he was apparently asked by Henry VIII to write a reply to a letter by Luther in which the English king was described as a victim of the Roman episcopate. Two years later Vives was also urged by the monarch to give his opinion on the question of the royal divorce. Luther's expected reply was probably never written. Vives never mentions it in his correspondence and the king never used such a document. It is nevertheless certain that Vives complied with the second request and sent his piece to Henry VIII. The document, which has been lost, was never published in any form.[15]

As a humanist, Vives shared Erasmus' admiration for classical culture but was much more severe in his moral judgments of it. Erasmus' enthusiasm for Euripides, Aristophanes, Terence, Lucian, and Ovid did not find lasting favor with Vives. Mastery of Latin and Greek was for Vives a means to learn ancient wisdom rather than a tool to read the Greek New Testament or to improve Saint Jerome's Vulgate Latin translation.

Perhaps the most important difference between Erasmus and Vives lay in the different range of their intellectual concerns. Erasmus' purely literary mind and detachment from strictly scientific and philosophical matters contrasts sharply with Vives' encyclopedic range and with his keen interest in the philosophical and psychological analysis of human nature. Erasmus' chapter on the emotions in the *Enchiridion* was nothing but a stereotypical sermon on the evils of greed, ambition, sensuality, and uncontrolled anger. Erasmus admired Valla as a master of biblical exegesis. Vives thought of Valla as the founder of modern dialectic and a controversial philosopher of language. One can hardly imagine Erasmus writing, as Vives did, a history of philosophy, a summary of metaphysics, a discussion of medieval logic, or a comprehensive psychological treatise such as *De Anima et Vita*.

Vives' early writings reveal Erasmus' influence on him, but also his progressively independent point of view, a widening of his classical education, and new intellectual interests. Most of these publications betray the same unresolved conflict between piety and the love for classic literature that Erasmus had experienced in his youth. As a result, even some of Vives' devotional works, such as *Christi Jesu Triumphus* (1514), *Geneathliacon Jesuchristi* (1514), and *Clypei Christi Descriptio* (1514) are at the same time pious proclamations of Christ as the only true hero worthy of our admiration and love—a typically Erasmian thought—and showy displays of classic erudition (M 7.3–19, 33–41, 110–22). Probably the most sincere religious document of this period is the meditations on the penitential Psalms (1518), one of Vives' favorite religious readings (M 1.162–255). That these intense and beautiful prayers from a contrite heart appealed to Vives so much seems to indicate that his initial contact with the devout men he met in Bruges and Louvain, particularly with William de Croy (to whom the writing is dedicated), brought about a heightening of his religious devotion and a more pessimistic view of man's postlapsarian condition. It even seems that at that time Vives had the intention of dedicating his entire life to the study of *litterae sacrae,* a plan that never materialized.[16]

Vives' devotion of that time was as intense as it proved to be ephemeral. Only in two other periods of his life did he express similar devotion. The first time, in 1529, Vives wrote a lengthy sermon on the bloody sweat of Christ in Gethsemane that he addressed to the people of Bruges victimized by the plague known as *sudor anglicus.* The second time, in 1535, his own misery and suffering led him to write three books of prayers which were nevertheless so neutral in theological content that they became equally acceptable to Catholics, Protestants, Anglicans, Socinians, and Erasmians (M 1.50–165; 7.42–91). Next to these devotional works we find others that are mostly literary in character. Some of them are introductions to the talks he gave in Louvain on Vergil's *Georgica* (1518), on Cicero's *De Legibus* (1514), on Filelfo's *Convivia* (1514), on Suetonius, Hyginius, and on *In Quartum Rhetoricorum ad Herennium* (1514), a rhetorical treatise long attributed to Cicero. Others are rhetorical exercises or *declamationes* that were greatly admired by his contemporaries for their extraordinary inventive power and the mastery of the Valla-Agricola techniques in selecting and organizing material relevant to a subject (M 2.1–13, 83–87, 315–17; 5.494–507; 6.438–39). Erasmus wrote the introduction to the *Declamationes Syllanae* (1520) and recommended them to More, who objected to a few recondite passages (*abstrusiora*) in them.[17] The *Declamationes* are a good example of the *suasoriae* recommended by Juvenal and Quintilian, speeches for and against a given topic, the retention of the dictatorship by Sulla in this particular case. The speeches, however, are more than mere examples of rhetorical exercises. They also provide substantive illustrations of sound political practice and teach by portrayal of concrete examples the sharp contrast between regimes based on fear and those based on the good will of the subjects. For this reason perhaps the declamations were dedicated to Prince Ferdinand, Charles V's younger brother.[18]

The last group of Vives' works in this period defies any generic label, but is the most important in revealing the future direction of his thought. It includes, in chronological order, an allegorical piece on "the dignity of man," an imitation of Cicero's *De Senectute,* a short history of philosophy, the treatise *Adversus Pseudodialecticos,* a commentary on Cicero's *Somnium Scipionis,* two pieces on jurisprudence, and Vives' earliest writings on European politics and on education.

Vives' *Fabula de Homine* (1518) is one of the few of his works that has been translated into English and included in a well-known anthology of Renaissance writings dealing with "the philosophy of man."[19] This short treatise has also been characterized as a mere repetition of Pico's views on the God-like dignity of man, the self-creative microcosmos. Vives obviously shares Pico's enthusiasm for the unique excellence of human nature and places a similar emphasis on the self-defining capacity of free choice. There are, however, significant differences between the two. Vives' mythological allegory is much more compact and less erudite than Pico's lengthy introduction to his almost scholastic treatise. The Neoplatonic conception of the universe as the stage of man's actions is only suggested by Pico but is fully developed by Vives. In spite of its mythological setting, Vives' piece carefully qualifies some of Pico's Pelagian exaggerations. Man, Vives teaches, can imitate Jupiter but never becomes Jupiter. Man can put on the mask of a plant or an animal, but is entirely passive in accepting the costume that makes him look divine. In sharp contrast to Pico, Vives emphasizes that the initiative belongs always to Jupiter. The stage, the roles, the words, and even the rewards have been decided before the performance began. Vives does not accept Pico's suggestion that man's inner essence is identical with his free choices in action, although he accepts that from them we can attain an imperfect knowledge of it. Man's intellectual powers are not unlimited, as Pico insinuates. What makes man special for Vives is his divine origin, the inventiveness of his mind, the mysterious power of his memory, his ability to communicate through language, and his prudence in organizing cities under the rule of law.[20]

Vives' essay on old age, the *De Anima Senis* (1518), an introduction to Cicero's *De Senectute,* presents a much darker and more realistic picture of man's life on earth (M 4.9–22), a picture much closer to the severe description by Aristotle of old age in the second book of his *Rhetoric* than to some of the platitudes found in the works of most Christian moralists or to Vives' own musings in *Fabula de Homine*. In the introduction, Vives confesses that in his youth—he was twenty five at that time—he had always been anxious to imagine himself as an old man, should God allow him to reach an advanced age. (God did not.) Vives' interest in the emotional life of old people was still equally intense at the time he wrote *De Anima et Vita,* twenty years later. The thought of both documents is remarkably similar: the apprehensions of youth became a self-fulfilling prophecy. The soul, Vives says in *De Anima Senis,* is divided into two parts. The lower part is mixed with the body and inhabited by the furies of human passions. The mixture of a cold brain and the bitter experience of life makes old people skeptical, suspicious, greedy, fearful, incredulous, querulous, richer in memories than in hopes, and talkative. The higher part of the soul is the intellect. Old people at their best are prudent because they know how little they know, do not dare to assert anything with certainty, and are ready to place everything under doubt. This awareness of human limitations makes old people the most prudent rulers. At their worst, old people are "twice childish," enslaved to passions that are themselves enslaved to a weak body. The difference in tone between *Fabula de Homine* and *De Anima Senis* echoes not only two different moods but two different conceptions of human existence. The fact that they were written roughly at the same time indicates Vives' hesitations between speculative optimism and sober realism, hesitations that were never totally overcome in spite of all the sufferings life brought to him. Vives' reflections on our emotional life in *De Anima et Vita* display the same ambiguities.

One year before Vives wrote *Adversus Pseudodialecticos,* he wrote a short essay on the history and praise of philosophy under the pretentious title *De Initiis, Sectis et Laudibus Philosophiae* (1518; M 3.3–25). This is certainly a youthful and almost clumsy piece of work, but it manages to open interesting horizons. As a history of philosophy, it is chronologically twisted, crowded, and repetitious. Vives covers not only the history of philosophy but the history of all human learning from Moses to the Buddha, from the Egyptian high priests to the Indian Brahmins, from the Presocratics to the Academic schools. Music, astronomy, mathematics, dialectic, zoology, and botany are all generously included under the name of philosophy. The critical judgments are also overdone. Epicureans are condemned without qualification and Stoics are praised as "true Christians." Aristotle is proclaimed "divine," "lucid and transparent" in every intellectual endeavor. But the lasting guidelines of Vives' own intellectual life are here proclaimed with touching fervor. Philosophy is a divine gift bestowed upon man to help us conduct a virtuous life, to cope with our environment, to control our passions, and to raise us above the life of the beasts. In spite of Vives' enthusiastic praise of Aristotle, the true hero of the young Spaniard was really Socrates, the founder of all Greek schools of thought. Chronological confusions notwithstanding, Vives' erudition and range of knowledge six years after leaving the University of Paris is truly impressive.[21] Sophomoric in style and in content, this intellectual manifesto allows us to observe the growth of an interesting mind and the wanderings of a self-taught man.[22]

This document is nicely complemented by one of the last essays Vives wrote in Louvain before his departure for England, the *In Sapientem Praelectio* (1522), a dialogue obviously inspired by Plato's *Apology* and meant to be "both entertaining and earnest" (*urbanus pariter ac gravis*). A group of Parisian students (including Vives himself) seek wisdom from a grammarian, a poet, a dialectician, a philosopher, a rhetorician, and an astrologer, all of whom fail to satisfy the eager youths' request. The group finally meets a hermit who is also a theologian. Here they finally find the model of the Wise Man, a man whose passions are controlled and whose mind is enlightened by God Himself. That all human learning is corrupted by sinful passions, a clearly Augustinian thought, was already one of the guidelines of Vives as philosopher, moralist, pedagogue, and psychologist (M 4.22–30).

Vives' attempt to write in a satirical vein had previously resulted in one of the most important writings of this period, his introduction and commentary to Cicero's *Somnium Scipionis*. It appeared first in 1520 and, in a more refined form, in 1521 under the title *Praefatio et Vigilia in Somnium Scipionis Ciceroniani* (M 5.62–109).[23] Vives' book represents the first challenge to Macrobius' commentary to the only surviving passage of Cicero's *De Republica*. Cicero's *Somnium,* as interpreted by Macrobius, had been considered through the Middle Ages the compendium of all ancient wisdom regarding the nature of the universe and the meaning of human life, the supreme eclectic synthesis of the Pythagorean, Neoplatonic, and Stoic worldviews. As Dante, Petrarch, and Chaucer before him, Vives too thought that "no volume was ever written within human memory (excepting, of course, "the Sacred Writings of our faith") in which more substance, skill, and eloquence are comprised and condensed" (M 5.106). But Vives rejects Macrobius' Neoplatonic emphasis on contemplative escapism and presents the *Somnium* as a "manual for the education of a perfect prince" in eloquence and virtue, the same purpose of the *Declamationes Syllanae*. Vives' work includes an introductory letter, his own dream, Cicero's text, and the introduction to and the commentary on Cicero's *Somnium*. Vives' own dream is the more satirical part of the book. Vives appreciated Menippean satire as a more effective way of exposing intellectual fraud than the work of those people he called "panegyrici."[24] Erasmus' enthusiasm for Lucian and Seneca might still have had at this time some influence on Vives. But it soon appears obvious to the reader that Vives' satirical sword was dulled by an almost contrived sense of humor. Whenever he tried to be *urbanus* and *gravis,* he managed to be much more the latter than the former. Of much greater significance is Vives' admiration for a worldview that emphasized the benign and orderly character of the universe, the ideal of human perfection as that of an individual and citizen through the imitation of cosmic harmony and concord, the rational belief in Creation and human immortality. In spite of Vives' claim that his own commentary was thoroughly Christian in spirit, the book could have been written for the most part by an enlightened pagan. Vives' comments on the human soul's origins and relations to the body are unquestionably more Neoplatonic than Christian. Vives' *Somnium Scipionis* was the subject of some early talks in Louvain and was also introduced to the Parisian students in 1520. Vives probably chose the *Somnium* because, in spite of its poetical character, the book could be taught at Louvain without the teacher's being suspected of excessive fondness for poetry.[25] To Vives' surprise and to the jealous amazement of Erasmus, the book was well received in Paris, in spite of the fact that it included some harsh criticism of the "Parisian sophists." [26]

Other important works by Vives in this period reveal his youthful interest in legal reform. His introduction to Cicero's *De Legibus*, and particularly his allegorical and philosophical piece *Aedes Legum* (both 1520), are still considered by specialists as influential monuments in the history of humanist jurisprudence, no minor achievement for a young man who probably never had formal training in law. (M 5.494–518; 483–494).[27] Vives' concern with legal reform was not only another manifestation of his interdisciplinary approach—an approach that did not sit well with the more traditionally-minded administrators of Louvain University—but also a clear proof of his growing involvement with all the cultural challenges and dilemmas of an age when orthodoxies were breaking down and it was possible to rethink in a fresh manner the most important issues of human existence. His friendship with the jurist Craneveld and his reading of Erasmus' *Adagia* might have provided the immediate incentive for this tract. In the Low Countries, Vives found a protocapitalistic bourgeoisie that demanded the legal regulation of economic and social structures that could not be encompassed by the literal observation of the *corpus iuris*. In his introduction to Cicero, Vives calls for a legal reform inspired by but not limited to a rehashing of the Roman law of the republican age. Although Vives' project was never completed, the efforts made in such a direction by later jurists contributed a great deal to an extraordinary revival of historical jurisprudence. In the *Aedes Legum,* Vives attacks the greedy contentiousness of judges and lawyers, the archaic jargon of statutory law, and the esoteric and cumbersome medieval tradition of the Italian glossatores (*modus italicus*), the legal counterpart to the abuses of the terminists in the field of logic. Under the influence of Stoicism, Vives describes the entire cosmos as ruled by the eternal and divine law of nature. Human law is only its mute, deaf, and by the very nature of written language, universal and defective expression. What the law literally defines as just needs to be corrected and interpreted by the principle of equity. Otherwise, as Erasmus had written in one of his *Adagia: "Summum ius, summa iniuria."* Servile compliance with the dead letter of the law can be used to sanction the gravest inequality. Vives' explanation of the classic Aristotelian locus on *epiéikeia* (*Ethics,* 5.10. 1137a32) summarizes with extraordinary clarity and vigor a doctrine that had been often misunderstood in medieval jurisprudence and emphasizes, perhaps beyond Aristotle's own intention, not only the corrective but also the interpretative character of judicial equity. Vives' short but precise and vigorous allegory, together with Book 7 of *De Causis Corruptarum Artium,* which deals with the corruption of civil law, has to be seriously taken into consideration in assessing the contribution of humanist jurists (Budé, Cantiunculas, Oldendorp, Alciatus, Zasius, Amerbach, and others) to the history of jurisprudence. Vives' ideas on the limitations of statutory law run parallel to his criticism of scholastic logic and are both founded on a philosophy of language that we shall investigate later. The last writings of Vives in Louvain begin to show his interest in the reform of education and in the political problems of contemporary Europe. All of them, however, belong, in spirit at least, to a new period of his life that began with his residence in England, and will therefore be analyzed in the next chapter.

4

The Amphibious Man

V IVES' FIRST VISIT TO England lasted from the summer of 1523 to the spring of 1524. With Queen Catherine's help (1523) and probably through the direct intervention of Thomas More, Vives was given a readership at Oxford University. At the end of the 1523–24 academic year, Vives returned to Bruges, where in May he married Margaret Valdaura, a distant relative of his in whom he found a loyal companion. By October he was back in England, but had to wait until January 1525 to resume teaching at Oxford because a plague had forced the closing of the university. Vives' tenaciously held optimism about human nature was severely tested by the events of 1525. His health began to deteriorate, his father, as we said earlier, fell victim to Inquisitorial fanaticism, and the religious and political conflicts of what he called "the most chaotic age in the history of the world,"¹ worsened at a rapid pace. Two of his best friends died about this time: Linacre in 1524; Martin Dorp, the Latin professor at Louvain, in 1525.²

When he returned to London in February 1526, he found that his Oxford appointment had been discontinued by Cardinal Wolsey, who had instead offered the position to Erasmus and Goclenius, both of whom declined. In April, he reported to Craneveld that for the first time his life in England had taken a turn for the worse and that he felt he "was sailing against the stream."³ England's alliance with France against Charles V, and Vives' close relations with the Spanish queen began to threaten his standing at Court. Vives could find help nowhere. Erasmus was too far away and not eager to help,⁴ More was completely embroiled in the turbulence of English political life, and Bishop Fisher had many reasons to be concerned about his own future. Between May 1526 and October 1527, Vives crossed the Channel five times, prompting Erasmus to refer to him as an "amphibious man."⁵ In October 1527, and at the insistence of the queen, Vives was appointed preceptor to Princess Mary. Wolsey became increasingly suspicious of

Vives' self-chosen role as counselor to Catherine and of his possible intervention in the Spanish ambassador's communications with the pope and the emperor regarding the queen's predicament. Toward the end of February 1528, Vives was placed under house arrest for thirty-eight days.[6] Catherine advised Vives to leave the kingdom. The Spanish humanist, who never had the timber of even a reluctant hero, was more than happy to comply with Her Majesty's wishes. In November of the same year, however, he returned to England once again, this time as a counselor to the queen's lawyers during the examination of the royal marriage conducted by the papal legate, Cardinal Campeggio. Vives advised the queen not to take part in the trial. Catherine interpreted Vives' advice as a sign of weakness and was "furious" at him.[7] A few days later Vives left England for the last time. He returned to Bruges embittered and impoverished but also better prepared to carry out the most ambitious and profound explorations of his intellectual journey.

The move to England had appeared to Vives as his most reasonable choice and had been carefully planned for several years. Henry VIII was married to a Spanish queen and was at that time a close ally of the emperor against France. England seemed to be distant and isolated from the religious and social upheaval that the Reformation had brought to central Europe. When the Peasants' Rebellion plunged Germany into an orgy of pillaging and slaughter, Vives wrote from Oxford to Craneveld: "The reports from Germany are such that I feel very happy to live in this remote part of the world where the news reaches us rarely and belatedly."[8]

Vives was also convinced that nowhere in Europe could one expect to find more generous patronage from princes and laymen than in Tudor England. The dedications of his books are not only masterpieces of calculated flattery but they also reveal signs of his own hopes and expectations. In 1521 he dedicated to Henry VIII the commentaries on *De Civitate Dei* because he knew "from reliable witnesses" that books were the gift the king "appreciated most."[9] In 1523 he dedicated *De Institutione Feminae Christianae* and *De Ratione Studii Puerilis* to the "Spanish Catherine, Queen of England" (*Ad Serenissimam Catharinam Hispanam Angliae Reginam;* M 4.65–70), the former as "a portrait" of the queen herself, the latter as a guide for the education of Princess Mary. In 1524 the princess herself was presented with *Satellitium Animi* (M 4.33), a collection of two hundred and thirteen aphorisms meant to become the "personal escort" of the future queen. Having taken care of the royal family, Vives proceeded to thank Cardinal Wolsey for the Oxford appointment (which he nevertheless described as a "burden") by dedicating to him in 1523 the Latin translation of two speeches by Isocrates, the orator he had learned from Agricola to admire.

Although Vives' hopes of finding in England a safe refuge from religious and political turmoil were eventually betrayed by the "grave matter" of the royal divorce, his expectations of enlightened and generous patronage were extremely perceptive and, initially at least, greatly fulfilled. Soon after his arrival in England, Vives received a royal pension and was given some grants in the form of commercial privileges.

One of the great achievements of English civilization in the fifteenth century had been the secularization of the charitable impulse and the consequent move away from monastic foundations to the endowment of public schools and the patronage of learning. This trend had been spearheaded by such members of the nobility as the duke of Gloucester, the earl of Worcester, and William Grey, who were just learned enough to admire and support the learning of others.[10]

After the end of the War of the Roses, and at the beginning of the Tudor dynasty, the patronage of learning became particularly intense around the royal court. The increasing prestige of the crown and the growing importance of London as the capital of the kingdom fostered the centralization of English cultural life. Princely education had been maintained at high standards by both the Lancastrians and the Yorkists. The Tudor monarchs only improved it. Henry VII's son Arthur was educated in grammar by men who knew and admired Guarino and Valla, and was himself well read in the classics. Henry VIII was probably more learned than any of his predecessors. More significant perhaps was his firm determination to attract to the court men of high learning and to provide his children with royal tutors of excellent credentials, men like the Greek scholar Sir John Cheke (d. 1557) or Roger Ascham (d. 1568), who inspired in the future Queen Elizabeth her love of the classics and her proficiency in Greek.[11]

Vives' first impressions of English life demonstrated his intuition that the revival of the humanities was centered where scholars like himself could help to reform society and improve the human condition, in London, not far from the king. It was precisely in London, in Colet's Saint Paul's School, where English humanism had come into its own in the first decade of the century. Colet's influence upon Erasmus and Thomas More, and his collaboration with Lily in writing the so-called Eton Latin grammar were destined to bring about an educational reform that would have a lasting impact upon English culture. For Vives the prospect of meeting or becoming better acquainted with people such as Thomas More, Linacre, Tunstall, Latimer, Lord Mountjoy, Grocyn, and Longland compensated by far for the burden of teaching at Oxford, where he disliked the students, the food, the weather, and his private quarters.[12]

Vives' appraisal of Oxford University was obviously clouded by his eager desire to be liked by the royal couple, a desire he confessed to Craneveld in almost childishly candid terms.[13] But Vives' judgment was also partially justified by the state of transition Oxford was going through about 1523. In the 1520s, both Oxford and Cambridge were still centers of learning dedicated to the education of both the clergy and the members of the monastic orders, who, unlike their Italian brethren, had no divinity schools in their own monasteries. Future barristers received training in the common law at the Inns of Court in London. The number of lay students was, however, on the increase. Both universities were enriched about this time with important collegial foundations and although most of those colleges were gifts of important clergymen in the royal service, some of them were more secularly oriented. The teaching of classical Latin as a preparation for an active participation in public affairs, not necessarily ecclesiastical affairs, took a great forward step in Magdalene College at Oxford. The *studia humanitatis* entered both universities, particularly Oxford, through the back door that colleges had opened.[14] Vives' appointment was in Cardinal's College, a college endowed by Wolsey but whose buildings were still in the process of construction when Vives arrived in England. In the meantime, Vives was sent to Corpus Christi College, where Erasmus' influence was clearly felt in the choice of classic authors and patristic theologians.[15] In spite of these promising developments and although the university officials seemed delighted with his services, Vives was unhappy at Oxford. The man who would eventually write one of the most comprehensive and interesting programs of school reform was in 1523 much more interested in counseling kings than in teaching Latin grammar to students he found "lazy and apathetic."[16]

Vives' desire to ingratiate himself with princes and to affect public policy through counsel was greatly fostered by the conditions in England, and probably by his relations with Sir Thomas More. Although these relations remain today partially concealed by the loss of their epistolary exchanges, there is evidence enough in their writings to prove that they knew each other well, that they were well acquainted with their respective families and work, and that for a time at least they were personally bound by mutual admiration and some sincere affection.[17] No matter how sincere or intimate their friendship might have truly been, More's public career as a servant to the king symbolized a partnership of humanistic scholarship and active participation in political life that raised fundamental questions not only about the relations between the theoretical and the practical intellect, but also between the humanistic pursuit of virtue and the implacable demands of political expediency. The potential conflicts between these two aspects of Thomas More's life have been covered up for centuries by a hagiographical tradition that emphasized only the saint's unspoiled integrity rather than the politician's questionable compromises. Recent scholarship has debunked many a myth and offered us a different picture of this extremely complex man.[18]

In 1523 More was forty-six, sixteen years older than Vives. By that time More had already accumulated an impressive record (and equally impressive grants, salary, and other perquisites appropriate to his status) in the service of the king as member of the Royal Council, Royal Secretary, Speaker of the House of Commons, and Under-treasurer of the Exchequer. Two years after Vives' arrival in England, More was appointed Chancellor of the Duchy of Lancaster, a promotion and also a transfer instigated by Wolsey, who was probably restless in the company of a man whose intellectual superiority he had to admit.

Erasmus, who always advised his friends to shun the corruption that public service invariably demands, "felt sorry" for More when he heard that he had been admitted to the Privy Council.[19] There are some indications that More tried to justify himself in the eyes of his fellow humanists by promoting the idea that he had been "forced by the King" into public service. But there is also some evidence that in fact he practically asked for the job.[20] That it was a momentous and difficult decision for him can be clearly seen from the first book of his *Utopia,* written after Book 2, and in which he attempted a justification of princely service and a humanistic exploration of the possibilities of secular life. The dialogue between More and Raphael Hytholday is really a monologue in which More tried to harmonize two incompatible sides of his own personality. More's questionable, frail solution amounted to a rejection of the Platonic ideal of the philosopher-king in favor of an idiosyncratic interpretation of Aristotelian practical wisdom. If humanists cannot be kings, they should at least advise kings by adapting ideal wisdom "to the play at hand" and by attempting to "make as little bad as one can" what "one cannot turn to good." History has abundantly proved that Erasmus' apprehensions were fully justified. The "play at hand" gradually transformed More into a man who has been characterized by some scholars as cruel, hypocritical, and fanatical. Only martyrdom and papal ecclesiastical policies during the Victorian age explain the fact that he was first beatified and later canonized as a saint.[21]

There is some evidence that, like Erasmus in 1517, Vives too had some misgivings about More's political service.[22] In his commentaries to Saint Augustine's *De Civitate Dei,* Vives had expressed his own personal anguish over the corrupting effects of political power. The treatise on the emotions frequently warns the reader against the moral dangers associated with it. Titles of nobility, glory, and riches make us greedy and ambitious. Flattery makes princes violently and doggedly angry. Their power makes them fearful, cruel, and suspicious simply because "those whom many fear have many to fear." Powerful people have no respect for anybody and fall easily into the temptation of pride.

Vives' aversion to the intrigues of political office was deeply rooted in his personality structure. The *Satellitium* he dedicated to Princess Mary offers us a picture of his moral ideals. Virtue meant to him living in peace with others (*sine querela;* M 4.54), seeking the invisible harmony of invisible beauty and nobility of the spirit rather than nobility of blood, shunning honors as burdens of the soul, riches as occasions of injury, and glory as a terrible form of slavery. His ideal was to consider everybody as equal (*homo homini par*). Justice, he urged Mary to think, was its own reward.

Vives' personal aversion to direct political participation was not only a matter of moral ideals. It was also a personal necessity. Unlike More, Vives never had the opportunity to play any significant role in the English court. But the example of More and other English humanists who became involved in politics according to or against their own inclinations was enough to get Vives deeply interested in the political events of his age, although in some occasions he most likely envied the financial security of his powerful friends. But if he ever succumbed to the temptation of envy, his envy was never the diabolical kind—feeling sad over the good of another "just because it is bad for us if others do well"—but the less pernicious envy of "deploring that the good others enjoy does not happen to us in the same manner."

During the period of Vives' visits to England (1523–28), Europe went through the horrors of the Peasants' War (1524), the French invaded Italy and conquered Milan (1524), the king of France, Francis I, was taken prisoner by the Spanish at the battle of Pavia (1525), the Anabaptists set up a communistic theocracy at Mülhausen, the Hungarians were defeated by Suleiman (1526), Rome was sacked by the troops of the emperor (1527), and the Ottoman Empire reached the height of its imperial expansion (1528–29). All these events found their echo not only in Vives' private correspondence, but also in some of his most interesting writings of this period.

In October 1526, Vives published a book that contained a letter to Henry VIII's confessor, two letters to the English king after the battle of Pavia, the English translations of Isocrates, and a dialogue on the Turkish threat.[23] These are interesting writings not because they affected European policy in any visible way, but because they reveal how Vives understood his own role as a royal pensioner and counselor, and because they provide us with Vives' views on the historical events of his own age. His responsibility was not, he felt, to provide rulers with specific solutions or clever courses of action, but rather to remind them of their moral responsibilities. The only partial exception to the moralistic character of these writings is the dialogue *De Europae Dissidiis et Bello Turcico,* which includes a detailed historical background of the Italian wars and explores the causes of the conflict between the claims of the Hapsburgs and the Valois rulers (M 6.252–481). The first letter to Henry VIII about the captivity of the French king contains also the concrete request not to humiliate the people of France by taking abusive advantage of their tragic situation. But even this specific advice is couched in highly moral language. Vives repeats the Augustinian warning that wars and political disasters are divine punishments for the sins of men and in particular for the sins of rulers. Kings should provide their subjects with the example of passional control, a control that is only possible when individuals know the true value of things and adjust their desires accordingly (M 6.449–52). Wars are not conflicts between people but the tragic consequence of the disorderly emotions of princes and rulers.

The Turkish threat was a much more complex issue. It represented, first of all, a real challenge to humanistic irenism.[24] Was it Vives' moral responsibility to urge an alliance of Christian princes to wage war against the infidels? Were there any exceptions to the sanctimoniously proclaimed principle that no war was ever justifiable? The dialogue style of *De Bello Turcico* allowed Vives to offer the reader two antithetical answers to these questions without a firm commitment to either.[25] In fairness to him we must say that three years later, precisely when the Turks began to march up the Danube, Vives had amassed courage enough to proclaim the demands of a radical and uncompromising pacifism.

Suleiman's victory in the battle of Mohacs raised furthermore the specter of what Vives and his contemporaries considered the supreme triumph of evil, the total destruction of Christianity. Such a frightening possibility was for Vives not only a cause of personal anxiety bordering on despair, but also the source of piercing doubts about the meaning of human history and the mysterious relation between evil and Divine Providence. His writings oscillated between a philosophy of doom and one of hope. Resigned as we are now to the threat of a nuclear catastrophe, it is difficult for us to comprehend that in his more pessimistic moments Vives saw Suleiman the Magnificent as the man who could destroy everything that Christian humanists considered civilized and divinely ordained. The temptation to despair—an emotion that Vives mysteriously avoids in his *De Anima et Vita*—was nevertheless the catalyst to profound philosophical reflections on the cosmic and moral order of reality and on the problem of evil and providence, reflections which would find their final expression three years later in one of Vives' most ambitious and significant works, *De Concordia et Discordia in Humano Genere* (1529). Furthermore, Vives' writings on European problems show a heightened European consciousness that is of extreme interest to our own times. More research is needed to decide whether Vives merely reflected or at least partially contributed to the perception of Europe as both a well-defined geographical whole and, more important, as a political entity.[26]

The social awareness of English humanism, best exemplified by More, and Vives' own experience with urban poverty in the Low Countries provided the inspiration for one of Vives' most celebrated writings, *De Subventione Pauperum,* published in Bruges in March of 1526.[27] Records from the middle of the fifteenth century show the English monarchy's concern over the problems of poverty and unemployment. The Poor Laws of the late fifteenth and early sixteenth century had begun to cope with the social upheaval caused by growing capitalism and mercantilism. Philosophers such as John Major had developed the idea that public welfare was the duty of the state rather than the charitable obligation of the church. Begging had to be outlawed. In one of his dialogues, *Ptojologia,* Erasmus had sarcastically described the advantages of professional mendicancy. Thomas More in *Utopia* had severely criticized the enclosure of lands for pasture and the resulting impoverishment of farmers who were forced to flee to the urban centers where they became poor vagabonds. English humanists, following Erasmus' example, had opposed on several occasions Wolsey's severe new taxations. The meager harvests of the mid 1520s had aggravated the problem in the British Isles, while the Peasants' War in Germany and the French wars in Italy had brought to the Continent much misery and poverty.

It is very likely that while in More's home at Chelsea, Vives met two administrative officials of the Low Countries: the president of the Great Parliament at Mechlin and the former burgomaster of the Senate of Bruges. In the *De Subventione Pauperum's* dedication to the councilors of Bruges, Vives confesses he had written it at the request of their former burgomaster, Louis de Praet. It is also probable that Vives and the two Flemish officers discussed the program of public welfare just enacted by the commune of Ieper, in the southern part of western Flanders. It is, however, difficult to ascertain who influenced whom in drafting this plan of assistance to the poor. In his correspondence with Craneveld, Vives made some references to the work he had at hand but was oddly secretive and reluctant to reveal the details of his plan.[28] He also seemed worried about the reaction of the ecclesiastical authorities to a plan that completely secularized what had been considered so far an obligation of Christian charity. Vives was so aware of the dangers involved in presenting his ideas on the subject that he admitted to Craneveld that he had "gone mad" in writing such a book.[29] His worries were fully confirmed. The Ieper plan was condemned four years later by the theologians of the Sorbonne. In 1527 Nicolas de Bureau (d. 1551 in Bruges), bishop of Sarepta and suffragan of the diocese of Tournai, accused Vives of being a Lutheran heretic, probably because he thought that Vives and some of his fellow humanists in the Low Countries were guilty of an excessive admiration for the handling of the mendicancy issue by two nearby Protestant towns, Strasbourg and Nürnberg.[30]

Vives' proposals represent one of the most detailed and comprehensive programs of social welfare written in a century rich in suggestions and legislative innovations regarding the problems of poverty.[31] Vives calls for action by the state at the municipal level to provide relief for the poor, the unemployed, the handicapped, the old, the mentally ill, victims of natural disasters, war refugees, and orphans. Vives demands not only *ad hoc* measures to relieve those needs, but a fully organized system of public welfare, a system that begins with a census of the population and is handled by public officers or overseers paid with public money.[32] Vives' tract shows in similar proportions a Christian concern for the needy and a bourgeois contempt for the lazy vagabond. To Vives, unattended poverty represented a possible cause of civil disorder, a disastrous waste of human resources, and the rousing cause of destructive emotions. But the same man who unveiled the temptation of covering up social injustice with showy displays of Christian charity saw also the dangers of the welfare state, the possible abuse of public assistance without work and the risks of creating a parasitic bureaucracy (ecclesiastical or secular) that would make a living out of the business of helping others.[33]

Thomas More's direct or indirect influence on Vives during this time was focused on other sources of possible human disorder that are more directly linked to man's emotional life such as the turmoil of sexuality, the conflicting relations between men and women in and out of the state of matrimony. We do not know whether Vives was cognizant of More's complex attitudes toward women and sex, or whether during their long periods of close personal contact they discussed these topics as married men tend to do. We know indeed that Thomas More used to expatiate on these matters in Latin with some of his male friends and in the presence of his second wife, who was ignorant of Latin. In any case, it is both fascinating and enlightening to compare what these two men, who had so much in common, thought about sexuality and what their sexual behavior actually was.

Modern scholars have not only investigated More's controversial public career but also the more intimate and personal traits of his private life.[34] Here, too, the contrast between the hagiographical tradition and modern research is a sharp one. More's eulogists have described him as a prodigy of unruffled affability, gentle piety, and relentless but harmless humor. His early writings, however, demonstrate an almost morbid capacity for severe melancholy, a tragic sense of the absurdity of life, a strong inclination toward vindictiveness and chauvinistic patriotism, a penchant toward antifeminist cynicism and even pornographic voyeurism.

In *Utopia,* More had tried to harmonize and synthesize the paradoxical and antithetical aspects of his personality and thought. But in the end the book offered the reader a self-destructive idealism, a penetrating critique of the irrational consequences of even an ideally rational world. It seems tragically ironical that the man who died for opposing the royal divorce (and all its implications) made divorce extremely easy to obtain in the utopian island of his dreams. No wonder that later in his life More came to wish the book had been burnt.[35]

More married twice, the first time in 1504 when he began legal practice at the Bar and abandoned the Carthusian monastery where for four years he had lived as a monk "without vow." Erasmus says that More married because he preferred to be a chaste husband rather than a licentious priest.[36] He married not the woman he lusted for but her older sister, as he thought propriety demanded.[37] Marriage to him was almost exclusively a remedy to lust, the only possible way to reconcile piety and sensuality. One month after his first wife died in 1511, More married again, this time a woman whose lack of beauty he used to mock in the presence of his close friends. Erasmus says that More married this second time only because he needed a woman to take care of his children. As a father he was kind and enlightened but extremely authoritarian. He provided his daughters with an education that was denied to most women at that time, but required from them an austere discipline. That the sexual life of the new couple was far from satisfying can be inferred from the fact that More secretly wore a hairshirt under his formal robes to mortify his body and control his lust. The least admirable side of his sexuality was revealed by an unexpected event. Luther's marriage provoked a storm of indignation in More. The man who had envisioned married priests on the island of Utopia could not accept Luther's bold attempt to fulfill that very ideal, to be at the same time a priest and a married man. More's obscene attacks on Luther seemed to be inspired not only by his loyalty to ecclesiastical orthodoxy but also by poorly concealed feelings of spite, vindictiveness, and even envy.

There is no trace in Vives' life or writings of similar turbulence and conflicts. Because Vives' personality lacked the sharper edges of More's internal contradictions, his attitudes toward sex, women, and marriage were, although undeniably harsh, less bitter than those of his friend. Nor did Vives need a Lucianesque persona to cover up his own inner conflicts. Still, Vives' ideas on sexuality are similar to those of More and typical of the northern humanistic attempt to reconcile a devout life with the claims of the body.

At the age of thirty-one, Vives decided to get married. He confessed to Craneveld that in his younger years he had thought of becoming a priest to secure some ecclesiastical benefice. But the choice between priesthood and married life was for Vives a choice between two different careers rather than a truly religious choice between heroic celibacy and a more mundane existence. Vives' ideas on marriage are contained in two moral treatises written or planned during this period of his life. The first was *De Institutione Feminae Christianae* (1523; M 4.70–297), a title he objected to for mysterious reasons.[38] The second was its logical counterpart, *De Officio Mariti* (1529; M 4.305–421). Vives began his discussion of marriage with an explicit rejection of Manichaean views (M 4.172) and with a straight refusal to enter into the hotly debated issue of whether philosophers ought to marry or not (a topic proposed by Rudolph Agricola as ideally suited for dialectical treatment). Perhaps his most complete definition of marriage is found at the end of the introduction to *De Officio Mariti* (M 4.315). Before Adam's fall, marriage was meant by God as the condiment of life to provide companionship in the loving union of male and female. In our postlapsarian condition, however, the spice that was meant to add flavor to life has to be taken as a medicinal herb. In this condition, marriage is "permitted" as remedy to our concupiscence (*Permissae sunt nuptiae in remedium libidinis;* M 4.178).

Vives' decision to take the medicine of marriage had to be a difficult one. The marriage to Margaret was probably arranged by her parents, a custom Vives recommends. Engagement was certainly not preceded by any romantic rapture, a practice Vives condemned in the most severe tone and often ridiculed with uncharacteristic sarcasm.[39] Although he often confessed that a good wife could be a man's priceless companion, his ideas concerning women in general and on the qualities of a good wife were of a kind that would make marriage an extremely risky proposition for all males. Throughout the treatise on the emotions, women are constantly grouped together with children, the sick, or the old. Their emotional responses are in most cases the responses of weakness. Women—like the old and the sick—excite chiefly our compassion because "they are no match for the suffering of extreme hardship." Children, women, and simple-minded people are prone to excessive laughter, easily irritable, and given to tears. In the first chapter of *De Officio Mariti* (M 4.315–46), where Vives advises men to be extremely cautious in choosing a wife, his language becomes obnoxiously explicit. Gender, he says, makes some human passions stronger in women than in men. Woman lacks the heat of the man. She is therefore "a weak animal" (*animal imbecillum*) both in physical strength and in passional control. Women are fastidious, greedy, distracted by trivial details (*occupata in cura rerum minutissimarum*), suspicious, envious, querulous, fretful, irritable (*continuo inflammatur ira*), vindictive (*ultionis cupidinis*), superstitious, and talkative. These defects are stronger in women than in men, but they can also be found among effeminate men, children, and senile people. Any man about to enter into matrimony must remember that women can be improved but not changed by the education they have received from their fathers and by their submission to the "virile" authority of their husbands (M 4.320-21). Training a woman, Vives wrote to Craneveld, can sometimes require more than persuasion.[40]

The first book of *De Institutione Feminae Christianae* (M 4.70–172) gives a somber picture of the way young women should be prepared for marriage. A woman's exclusive care should be to preserve her purity, as it becomes a future wife and mother. Girls should be allowed to play only with other girls, since they are more "pleasure seeking" than are boys. Their toys should be little kitchen utensils rather than pretty dolls. From a very early age they should learn knitting and cooking. Their intellectual education should be exclusively in moral philosophy. They should read the Bible, the church fathers, Plato, Cicero, Seneca, and some Christian poets. But since the exclusive purpose of their education is to protect their chastity ("I have never known a learned woman who was impure"), they should totally avoid obscene poems or books, such as Ovid's *Ars Amatoria,* Boccaccio's *Decameron,* or even worse, the pestilence of chivalric romances. Science, grammar, dialectic, history, and mathematics are completely unwarranted in the education of women whose vocation is only to attend to domestic duties. A young woman's worst disgrace is the loss of her virginity outside of marriage. To prevent such disaster Vives recommends that young girls never leave home, except for reasonable causes, that they sleep few hours, avoid boredom, and absolutely shun any cosmetics or fancy attire that might make them more attractive sexual objects. If young women must leave the house (to go to church mostly), they must cover their entire bodies (particularly the neck and breasts) and remain silent in the presence of males. A woman destined to be man's companion and servant must at all costs avoid becoming a seductress (M 4.70–155).[41]

It is highly likely that Margaret Valdaura was as close to Vives' ideals as one could expect to find anywhere on earth. When Vives announced to Craneveld his intention of getting married, he emphasized that he had not been impressed by her wealth or her looks, but rather by the "simple and honest education" Margaret had received from her parents, whom Vives had known for twelve years as a preceptor of the Valdaura children. A few months later he reported his wedding to Erasmus, and cheerfully commented that things were going well and that the marriage had met with general approbation of relatives and friends.[42] That the wedding itself was an austere ceremony can easily be assumed, since Vives had constantly forbidden any feasting or dancing on such a serious occasion.

Vives' married life with Margaret was probably peaceful but not exciting by normal standards. The first years of their marriage were constantly interrupted by his long visits to England, visits he always undertook alone. Margaret seems to have been the totally submissive, home-bound, and self-effacing wife that Vives considered ideal. Three years after his wedding, Vives considered his married life a success because his wife had not made him waste "one hour of study."[43] They never had any children, but that was no great disappointment, to him at least, since on repeated occasions he confessed he could not understand why people should desire to have them. In what can only be described as a bitter and almost cynical chapter of *De Institutione Feminae Christianae* (Book 2, Chapter 11), Vives attempts to persuade Christian women to give up any desire to have and raise children, a task full of "incredibly tedious annoyance" (*incredibilis molestiae ac taedii*), "pain, anxiety, inconvenience, and eternal fear" (*dolores, fastidia, sollicitudo, aeternus metus*). What joy is there in having children? Vives asks. They are nothing but a burden in infancy, a cause of fear in adolescence, a source of terrible pain if they deviate from virtue and of apprehension if they are good. Women deprived of children, Vives says, should first of all blame themselves rather than their husbands, because, "as most great philosophers agree," sterility is more often the woman's than the man's fault. Furthermore, women should think that sterility is a divine gift because it is better not to have children at all or even to give birth to a snake or a wolf than to deliver to the world an evil child. These dark, somber pages of the *De Institutione Feminae Christianae* acquire a particularly tragic character if, as it is suspected by some scholars, Margaret Valdaura was a syphilitic and permanently sterile woman.[44] It is a reasonable guess that Vives' sexual life with

Margaret was far from what we today would call normal and healthy. *De Institutione Feminae Christianae* and *De Officio Mariti* present a rather bleak concept of sexual pleasure, in spite of Vives' anti-Manichaean proclamations. The body is described as "dirty," and "the most vile slave" of the soul. The sex act "blinds our intelligence" and lowers us to the level of the beasts. Sexual pleasure is "unworthy of the soul" and should be avoided as soon as the wife becomes pregnant. Women are forbidden to initiate sexual intercourse.

In 1524, Vives published one of his most read books, *Introductio ad Sapientiam* (M 1.1–48), a book that was translated into German, English, Spanish, and French in the first half of the sixteenth century. This book, which is essential to the understanding of Vives' growing interest in the study of emotional responses, describes human nature as including a divine part, the soul, and an animal part, the body. Wisdom consists in knowing the true value of whatever appears good to us, including the pleasure of sex. The soul itself is divided into two parts: one is the seat of our intellectual powers; the other is the seat of our passions. Order demands that the lower part of the soul obeys the higher part, that the body be subjected to the soul, and that both soul and body be obedient to the Creator. Sin is disorder, the lack of harmony and concord, the rebellion of the lower against the higher, uncontrolled passion. It is within this more philosophical and larger picture that we can begin to understand Vives' ideas regarding sex and his concern with the dynamics of intellect and emotion, knowledge and passion, body and soul.

In *De Anima et Vita,* Vives deals with sexual love and pleasure in Book 3, Chapters 2, 3, 4, and 9. Although the style of the text is less moralistic than the tracts he had written in England (or shortly thereafter), the content is basically the same. Chapter 2 presents an entirely Platonic picture of Love and its relations to Beauty including the severe warning that bodily beauty is by far the lowest of all. The greatest good of an adult, Vives claims, is not pleasure but "respectability." Vives describes the body as a prison, recognizes that bodily love seeks bodily union, and that separation between lovers is always painful. Soon, however, we are told that sexual love is the origin of most human troubles and that it was probably invented in a "torturing chamber." Sex is the pleasure of vulgar people. It tends to make lovers ridiculous and mindless beings and is the lowest and least enduring form of pleasure. Sexual pleasure brutalizes us and is totally incompatible with the pleasures of the spirit.

When Vives left England for the last time, he was a man whose only hope in life was to cultivate "the pleasures of the spirit" in intense intellectual activity. The return to Bruges in 1528 marked also the beginning of his most productive and mature stage as a thinker.

5
The Mature Thinker

I N THE LAST TWELVE years of his life (1528–40), Vives the individual seems to disappear behind the reflective and mature author of lengthy and momentous writings. The private correspondence of this period, partially lost, includes only two or three letters to each one of his old friends Craneveld, Erasmus, and Juan de Vergara. Except for a few personal letters to new friends and former disciples, the rest are limited to formal and polite exchanges with prospective patrons or to fashionably obsequious dedications of books. After his return to Bruges, Vives' heart seems to have experienced a rekindling of affection for Spanish (or Hapsburg) friends and patrons.[1]

After his hasty return from England, Vives was emotionally spent and had to fight constantly the demon of poverty. The royal pension he had been receiving from Henry VIII was discontinued in 1528 (M 7.143). His life was outwardly as uneventful as it was intellectually productive. Most of the time he resided in Bruges with his wife, but occasionally he traveled to Paris, the imperial court in Brussels, and the University of Louvain, seeking the help of powerful patrons or the financial rewards of temporary lectureships. There is some evidence that around 1530 Vives met in Bruges the future founder of the Jesuits, Ignatius of Loyola, but neither man has left us a personal recollection of such an encounter.[2] In 1532 his financial situation was alleviated by a modest imperial pension. In 1537 he became preceptor to Doña Mencía de Mendoza, the wife of the duke of Nassau in Breda, North Brabant. At her request and as "a break from more strenuous endeavors," Vives wrote the most uncharacteristic piece of this period, an allegorical interpretation of Vergil's *Bucolics* (1537; M 2.1–71).

After 1530, Vives' concern for his health became almost obsessive. The Christian humanist who aspired to live up to the challenge of a dignified old age and kept writing about the blessings of the afterlife was severely tested by a long struggle with gouty arthritis, real or imagined stomach ulcers, and an almost hypochondriacal fear of certain foods. On May 6, 1540, Vives died in Bruges, probably of a kidney stone. He was one of the few men of that sectarian and intolerant age who died without enemies and without followers. His wife outlived him by twelve years.

Most of the books to which Vives owes his fame were written in these years of poverty, solitude, and crumbling health. That he was able to accomplish so much precisely when his personal circumstances and Europe's religious and political situation were invitations to cynicism and despair was probably his greatest achievement as a human being and as a thinker. Through the hardearned and sober optimism of these writings, through their calm and sustained reflection, northern humanism reached a wider scope and a new philosophical depth.

The first masterpiece of this period and one of Vives' pivotal books was *De Concordia et Discordia in Humano Genere,* published in Bruges in 1529 (M 5.193–404).[3] *De Concordia,* as the book is generally known, seeks to understand in metaphysical terms not only the events of current history discussed in the writings of the English period, but also the critical moral questions raised by the *Introductio ad Sapientiam. De Concordia* exemplifies the humanist attempt to harmonize Stoic metaphysical and ethical conceptions with Augustinian religious views.[4] We know from Vives' letters to Erasmus that after his return from England, Vives immersed himself in the study of Seneca and in the revision of his commentaries to Saint Augustine's *De Civitate Dei.*[5] *De Concordia* was published in the same year as Erasmus' second and greatly improved critical edition of Seneca's works, an edition that brought to a climax the humanistic rediscovery of the true Roman Stoic. The almost mythical Seneca of the Middle Ages, venerated as a "friend" of Saint Paul and superficially known as the sage-author of a few quotations taken out of context, began to be studied with sustained admiration but also with a new critical perspective.[6]

Most sixteenth-century humanists, including Vives, were well aware of the incompatibility between the Stoic emphasis on the immanence of the divine and the mortality of the soul on one hand, and the Christian revelation of God's transcendence, the creation in time, and personal immortality on the other.[7] Most of them rejected as a Stoic fallacy the teaching of the inseparability of all virtues. At least some of them understood also that the naturalistic character of Stoic ethics was incompatible with the Christian sense of man's fall into sin and the need for repentance and divine forgiveness.[8] That most of the humanists followed Petrarch in rejecting as impossible and undesirable the Stoic teaching on *apátheia* proves that their understanding of the role played by emotion in the dynamics of human personality

was also significantly different from that of the great Roman Stoics, a topic
we shall discuss in Chapter 15.9 Here we shall restrict ourselves to exploring
what appears to be an unresolved conflict between the Stoic and the
Augustinian elements of Vives' moral philosophy.

Vives had nothing but admiration for the eclectic, syncretistic, and severe
moralistic character of Roman Stoicism. The Stoic conception of virtue as
the reflection in the human domain of the order and harmony that Divine
Reason imposes upon the cosmos appealed to Vives as an expression of
Hellenistic wisdom clearly compatible with the Christian faith in the Divine
Providence and human free will. Vives, however, discarded the tendency of
some Stoic philosophers to restrict to an enlightened elite the rational
perception of order and hence the possibility of perfect wisdom and virtue,
and translated into Christian terms the equally Stoic doctrine of human
brotherhood. Discord, the opposite of love and peace, "prevents us from
being humans" (*homines nos esse non desinit*) because God created us as
social beings endowed with every faculty required to fulfill all the potential
of our nature. He gave us memory to preserve the achievements of past
generations and make possible a progression toward an ever-growing cultural
stock. He gave us language to make possible social intercourse, and a face
capable of expressing and sharing with others our deepest emotions. He gave
us a natural dislike for solitude, a natural need to seek the help of others, and
an equally natural inclination to be with and love others. Finally, God gave us
a natural capacity to understand and to live by these truths. Even the
Christian precept of loving our enemies is for Vives a precept of "natural
law" (*hoc naturae lex postulat*). A Christian is nothing but "a human being
reinstated in his nature" (M 5.196–201).

If Vives' emphasis on the reasonable and natural character of what is
morally good brings him close to pagan Stoicism, his explanation of disorder
and evil is profoundly Augustinian. Unlike the Stoics and very much like
Saint Augustine, Vives had a keen sense of the historical cycles of order,
corruption of order, and recurrent movements of reform. Furthermore, like
Saint Augustine himself, Vives was convinced that the present condition of
humanity could not be God's original plan but the result of man's fall from
innocence. Unlike most Catholic theologians today, Vives was convinced
that Adam's original sin was not only a revealed dogma but also a truth
that could be reached, and historically had been, by the unassisted powers
of natural knowledge. The overwhelming conviction of man's sinfulness and
of the ensuing corruption of humanity that one tends to associate with
Lutheran reformers rather than with Erasmian humanists was central to
Vives' thought.

Vives' interpretation of man's fall and of the conditions of personal redemption is, however, plagued by fundamental ambiguities. Man, he says, lost his true humanity by the proud desire to be like God Himself. Uncontrolled pride and excessive love of one's self brought about all kinds of passional disorders: flattery, stubbornness in defending one's opinion, the surrender to pleasure, greed, ambition, envy, and the desire for revenge. War among nations is nothing but the result of emotional conflicts within individuals (M 5.204–15, 229–34). The only way to recover our nature is self-knowledge, the knowledge that we are not capable of knowing anything with certainty, the knowledge that our will is weak and blind, the knowledge that our body is nothing but misery, the knowledge that earthly goods are contemptible and transient. Only this form of self-knowledge is capable of making us bear the adversities of life with calm and serenity (*aequo animo*), of raising the wise to the heights of peace, of making rulers powerful instruments of harmony and human concord. Without such knowledge, the individual is in disharmony with himself and with others. Hence all the wars and disasters among nations (M 5.338–61).

Vives' prescription for self-redemption represents, in my view, a partial relapse into Stoic naturalism and rationalism. *De Concordia* is naturalistic in the sense that it lacks the truly Augustinian insistence on the powerlessness of man, on the total reliance of man on God's grace and assistance. There are, of course, occasional appeals to Christ's redemptive work and example, but they have none of the religious intensity that characterizes the writings of Saint Augustine or Luther. Vives' appeal to a secular prince, Charles V, in favor of an ecumenical council to resolve the theological differences within Christianity—an attitude very displeasing to Pope Clement VII—seems also to bypass or at least to undermine the *magisterium* of the Church. The book is also rationalistic, for Vives seems to relinquish the Augustinian conception of order as an "order of love" (*ordo amoris*) in favor of an almost Socratic insistence on the primacy of enlightenment and right judgment. On the other hand, his belief in the positive role of controlled passion in the dynamics of human action and his respect for the mystery and energy of the human will separate him from the Stoics and bring him closer to the author of *De Civitate Dei*. The tension between the two attitudes is never satisfactorily resolved.

De Concordia was immediately followed in the same year by a similar but much shorter treatise entitled *De Pacificatione* (M 5.404–47). The book repeats many of the central ideas of *De Concordia* but adapts them to the person to whom the book was dedicated, Alfonso Manrique, the archbishop of Seville and Grand Inquisitor of Spain. In unusually passionate tones, Vives exhorts the archbishop and all the people endowed with authority to use it in the service of peace. The frequent references to Christ, the peacemaker between Man and God, give this document a particularly religious tone. As the bitter son of an Inquisition's victim, Vives daringly questions the excessive authority of the Holy Tribunal and stresses the frightening responsibility of priests and popes (M 5.405). In a touching passage, Vives reminds the archbishop of the plight of those who were forced to leave their country in the pursuit of a peaceful coexistence with their neighbors, and rejects any concept of noble ancestry based on blood rather than on the nobility of the spirit and the true imitation of Christ (M 5.409, 428).

It is very likely that the intriguing and small essay *De Conditione Vitae Christianorum sub Turca* (M 5.447–60) was also published in 1529, the year the Ottoman Empire reached the height of its expansion in the Balkans.[10] In this vigorous document Vives repudiates those who in a selfish or naïve way confused the love of peace with a total surrender to the Turk. Freedom does not consist in escaping the obligations of a Christian citizen, but in compliance with the law. Religion and culture would perish under Ottoman rule. Realistic and eloquent as it is, *De Conditione* manages to avoid the basic dilemma of all radically pacifist postures. Is there ever a justification for violent self-defense? Is peace the supreme value in human society?

These books represent principal steps in Vives' intellectual journey not only because they provided an extremely clairvoyant and pessimistic diagnosis of European disintegration and discussed it at the deep level of sweeping metaphysical considerations, but also because they seminally contained the only possible means of healing the disease: an educational reform inspired by a new vision of culture and based upon a sound knowledge of the human psyche and behavior.[11] We have reasons to believe that the two monumental works in which Vives carried out both phases of this ambitious project, *De Disciplinis* and *De Anima et Vita*, were written about the same time (between 1529 and 1531), although the former appeared in 1531 and the latter in 1538.[12] *De Disciplinis* was published in Antwerp (1531) in a massive volume that included seven books on *De Causis Corruptarum Artium* (this treatise is also known as *De Causis*), five books on *De Tradendis Disciplinis*,[13] and eight books on the arts, *De Artibus*. These books on the arts include three books entitled *De Prima Philosophia*, a metaphysical treatise, two books on *De Censura Veri* that correspond roughly to the first three books of the Aristotelian *Organon*, a book on *De Instrumento Probabilitatis* and another on *De Disputatione Veri*, both of which represent an attempt to develop some of the ideas of Valla and Agricola on probable arguments. The last eight books were probably written at the same time or even before *De Disciplinis*.[14]

The 1531 Antwerp edition is a telling proof of Vives' almost incredible intellectual productivity during the two years that followed the publication of *De Concordia*.[15] *De Disciplinis* is obviously Vives' most comprehensive and mature work on education. But his lasting reputation as one of the most interesting pedagogues of the sixteenth century is solidly based on this and other writings that preceded or followed the Antwerp volume. *De Disciplinis* had been preceded by *Adversus Pseudodialecticos* (1519), *De Institutione Feminae Christianae, De Ratione Studii Puerilis* (both in 1523), and *De Officio Mariti* (1529), all of which have been discussed in their historical contexts. *De Disciplinis* was followed in 1532 by *De Ratione Dicendi*, in 1534 by *De Conscribendis Epistolis,* in 1538 by a short review of Aristotle's main works, *Censura de Aristotelis Operibus,* and finally, also in 1538, by *Exercitatio Linguae Latinae,* a most successful collection of dialogues aimed at teaching the proper vocabulary and idiomatic expressions in Latin, once again in the spirit of the recommendations contained in *De Tradendis Disciplinis*.[16] To these we must add Vives' writings on legal reform, *Aedes Legum, In Leges Ciceronis Praefatio,* and on the education of the poor and unemployed in *De Subventione Pauperum*.

Vives' pedagogical ideas need to be carefully discussed because to a large extent his small treatise on the emotions represents their psychological basis. It is also interesting to observe how the theme of emotional disorder and its impact upon the activities of the mind becomes a recurrent topic through all of Vives' works on education. These works surpass the effort of any previous humanist in scope, detail, and erudition. Petrarch had a vision of a new culture that entailed radical innovations in the educational system but never wrote a pedagogical treatise. Vittorino's personal example at Mantua was itself a lesson in pedagogy, but the man wrote practically nothing on the theory of education. Vergerius' *De Ingenuis Moribus* is a short letter dedicated to an Italian *condottiere,* hence limited in scope and content. Bruni d'Arezzo's *De Studiis et Literis* deals almost exclusively with women's education. Pius II's *De Liberorum Educatione* is only a short letter addressed to the king of Bohemia and Hungary. Guarino's *De Ordine Docendi et Studendi* is mostly relevant to the history of the school of Ferrara and the teaching of Greek in the early Italian Renaissance. Palmieri's *La Vita Civile* provides a more detailed blueprint for education, but its psychological views are still relatively crude and its aims strongly nationalistic. Trend-setters and historically significant as these early classics of humanist pedagogy might be, they cannot compare in scope and maturity to Vives' works.

Vives and his sixteenth-century contemporaries belonged to a self-confi-dent generation that had largely achieved the aims defined by Petrarch.

Classical texts had been resurrected and correctly printed. Latin (and to certain extent, Greek) was written in a masterly way by such men as Erasmus and Alberti. The problems of textual criticism and the standards of imitation had been thoroughly discussed and no longer belonged to the burning issues of the day.[17] The challenges of educational theoreticians in the first half of the sixteenth century were: a) to define the aims of education; b) to clarify the role of classical models and languages in the liberal arts; c) to specify the character of dialectic and its relation to the other *artes sermocinales* of the *trivium;* d) to elucidate the role of poetry, history, and philosophy (metaphysics, theory of knowledge, and ethics) in the *studia humanitatis;* e) to improve and expand the teaching of the *quadrivium* into a thorough exploration of nature; f) to explain the relation between liberal and professional education; g) to adapt professional education to contemporary needs; h) to refine the environmental and physical aspects of education; and, finally, i) to provide a program for the training of teachers and a justification for a secular and public system of education.

In meeting these challenges, Vives remained naturally bound by some of the values and opinions of his contemporaries, but succeeded in articulating them with deeper philosophical insight and in venturing, however tentatively, into more modern grounds.[18] Although some of Vives' philosophical reflection was touched off by the writings of two of his predecessors, Valla and Agricola, it can justifiably be claimed that Vives forged ahead of the leading educators of his day—Colet, More, Erasmus, Budé, and Sadolet, among others—and together with Melanchthon made possible the significant pedagogical innovations in the second half of the century in harmony with Sturm, Thomas Elyot, Ramus, Cordier, Ascham, Gilbert, Rabelais, Montaigne, and the Jesuits' *Ratio Studiorum.*

This does not mean that Vives' ideas on the aims of education share little with those of the humanist tradition, for both are inspired to a large extent by the writings of Plutarch and Quintilian. Vives enthusiastically accepts the fundamental humanist premise that to educate means "to bring out" (*e-ducere*) by "instruction and exercise" (Erasmus) or by "attention and practice" (Vives) the different *ingenium* of each individual.[19] Without education, natural talents are "blind" (*natura sine disciplina caeca*). The main aim of education is self-fulfillment, the actualization of all human potentialities (Aristotle). But these potentialities are different in each person within some specific boundaries. Education therefore needs to be carefully tailored to individual needs and characters. Growth is an important part of the process of self-definition that human nature makes possible and imperative (Pico).

Vives readily agreed with the Erasmian principle that "Man is not born but made." While many humanists, following Plutarch, emphasized the flexibility of the infant's mind, in *De Disciplinis* Vives was particularly interested in secondary, higher, and professional education. He placed special emphasis on the training of memory, the need to study the differences in personality, the nature of our emotional responses, and the relation among imagination, judgment, and passion. *De Anima*'s sections on memory and *ingenium* (Book 2, Chapters 2 and 6) and the entire third book on the emotions were written by one of the pioneers on educational psychology.

Self-fulfillment, for Vives, meant becoming a virtuous and useful member of the human community at different levels (family, village, state, church) rather than a clever and elegant scholar, as some of the early Italian humanists seem to have had in mind (as with Guarino Veronese). Well within the tradition of northern humanism, Vives' moral concern was of paramount importance. The central message of *De Causis Corruptarum Artium* is the idea that the immorality of the learned leads always to the corruption of culture and also to the enslavement of reason to uncontrolled passion. In the *Somnium Scipionis,* Vergil and Cicero are presented not only as masters of golden latinity but even more strongly as moral guides. Equally characteristic of Vives is the emphasis on the practical aims of education. In the *Fabula de Homine*, human beings are presented as godlike precisely because they are endowed with an *ingenium* sharp enough to meet human needs and to utilize the word in a reasonable manner.[20] In the *Somnium Scipionis,* Vives did not hesitate to reject the down-playing of active life that Macrobius had learned from his Neoplatonist masters. According to Vives, only those who, like Scipio Africanus, have served the community well deserve an eternal reward.[21] Action and intelligent production are not only reconciled with contemplation but made into the highest purposes of education and culture. This emphasis on social usefulness is in sharp contrast with the early importance attached by Italian humanists to "dignity of mien," to polite manners or witty conversation. Furthermore, Vives was much less interested than was Pius II in preparing young men to be "future crusaders" of the church and would have never characterized "training in the Arts of War" as an alternative to "Letters," as Vergerius had done. The refined *cortegiano* and the cunning *condottiere* were never Vives' ideals of an educated man. The practical and the ethical aspects of education were more important to him than the purely aesthetic, contemplative, or recreational. Eloquence without virtue was to him more dangerous than desirable.

Vives' respect for the models of classic antiquity and for the important role of Latin and Greek in liberal education is unquestionably rooted in the humanist tradition and shares some of its historical limitations. But Vives'

critical attitude toward the ancients, his ideas on the importance of the
vernaculars, and his emphasis on the educational value of sense-observa-
tion[22] correct to a certain extent the naïve and uncritical admiration for
classic letters of some early humanists, and partially overcome the backward
and bookish character of some humanist educators. In that sense, Vives
represents a more advanced stage in the long history of "la querelle des
'anciens' et de 'modernes.' "[23] Vives never questioned that education is
imposssible without books (*cognoscenda sunt ex libris omnia*). He also
practically assumed that early humanists had satisfactorily justified the
reading of pagan letters. The pedagogical problem in the age of the printed
book was rather to select from the large amount of available material.[24]

Still, Vives' attitude toward the classics was significantly different from
that of other scholars and writers, because, for one thing, it lacked the
nationalistic overtones of some early Italian humanists. Reading Latin
classics was to him not a means to "recover a national treasure," but rather a
means to master a language that was "the shrine of erudition" and to open the
gates to our knowledge of ancient wisdom. The Erasmian idea that a
thorough knowledge of Latin and Greek was necessary to the project of
retrieving the purity of primitive Christian ethics, impressed the young
Vives for a while, but it never became of paramount importance in his more
mature and original works. In *De Disciplinis,* Vives' reference to Christianity is limited to a short recommendation that the teacher ought to imitate
Christ's humility and gentleness.[25]

Probably the outstanding difference between Vives and all his predecessors was his unremittingly critical attitude toward any kind of authority.
Early humanists had often warned against the moral dangers of reading some
ancient authors like Ovid and Horace. Others had discussed the incompatibility between Christianity and certain schools of Hellenistic philosophy,
such as Epicureanism or Academic Skepticism. Erasmus had freely criticized the credulity of Livy, the obscurity of Aristophanes, the severity of
Seneca, the excessive speculation of the Neoplatonists. But Vives' critical
attitude toward classic models went far beyond these ethical, religious, or
aesthetic objections because it was based on an intelligently articulated
theory of learning and a profound philosophy of history that was applicable
not only to medieval interpreters and translators, but to the classic masters
themselves and to recent and even contemporary humanists.

De Causis Corruptarum Artium describes man as initially poor in material
things but endowed with a mind "spontaneously active" (*sponte actuosum;*
M 6.8) and inventive. Necessity first and then convenience sets this mind into
motion. The result is what Vives calls "the arts," the human stock of cultural

knowledge. But these arts were not even initially "pure." There was never a "Golden Age" of cultural achievement. On the contrary, from the very start, all human intellectual accomplishments were spoiled by uncontrolled passions and by the ignorance of our own limitations.[26] It is precisely those limitations that make possible and even necessary individual and historical growth. Truth was not given to a single author or to a single generation. Truth is subject to historical growth (*veritas, temporis filia*). Vives not only remarks that Aristotle himself knew more in his old age than in his youth, but even ventures the then-novel idea that he experienced also a process of intellectual change and maturation.[27] We know more than Aristotle did, although he was in Vives' opinion "by far the wisest of all philosophers" (M 3.18). Vives' criticism usually intensifies toward the people he admired most, Plato, Aristotle, Cicero, Seneca, Quintilian, and Valla, among others. There are, however, some interesting exceptions. Vergil, Lucan, Plutarch, Saint Augustine, Saint Jerome, and, among the more recent humanists, Agricola, Erasmus, Melanchthon, Nebrija, and Budé received nothing but generous praise. Because Aristotelian philosophy (not, of course, its medieval distortion) is in Vives' opinion the highest form of ancient wisdom, he submits it to the most probing, detailed, and unforgiving critical analysis ever carried out by any of his fellow humanists. Vives not only rejects the *Ethics* as clearly incompatible with Revelation and with a religious conception of human existence,[28] but frequently ridicules the hasty character of some inductions and criticizes both the style and the content of most Aristotelian writings, particularly the *Organon* and the *Metaphysics*.[29] Vives is not only opposed to a servile imitation of Ciceronian style—which he nevertheless admired enormously—but proceeds beyond the concept of "creative imitation" to that of challenging competition (*imitatio paullatim eo debet progredi ubi jam incipiat esse certamen*).[30] Vives' ideas on the relative importance of classic languages and the vernaculars are a baffling mixture of humanist commonplaces and potentially innovative insights. There is no denying that Vives considers Latin the "shrine of ancient wisdom" and the lingua franca of Europe's intellectual elite. Consequently, like many of his contemporary humanists, Vives never used the vernacular in his writings and clearly overestimated the importance of Latin. He was also partially blind to the fact that some of the most creative talents of his own day (particularly in Aragón, Cataluña, and Valencia) were already turning to the vernacular and that Neo-Latin literature was doomed to be an interesting but short-lived chapter of European letters.[31]

But the exile who had to learn French, Flemish, and English besides his own native languages (Castilian and Valencian), also expressed significant insights on the necessity of mastering the vernacular and formulated a philosophy of language (to be analyzed in Chapter II) that was logically incompatible with the privileged status of any given language. In his treatise *De Institutione Feminae Christianae,* Vives reminds mothers that they have the privilege and responsibility to teach children to speak their native language well. Mothers must be very careful in choosing well-spoken nursemaids, must see to it that children understand prayers in the vernacular, and must supervise the correction of early speech.[32] In *De Disciplinis,* Vives extends those recommendations to the fathers and the teachers of elementary education. From the latter in particular Vives expects more than a mastery of correct speech and writing. He wants them to know the history of their native language from its origin to the present.[33] The maternal tongue is important simply because it provides the foundational and first verbal expression of the child's apprehension of reality. Language is a conventional tool for communicating with others and opening the doors to the knowledge of the arts. In this respect all languages are alike: it is not more valuable to know Latin and Greek than to know French or Spanish (*nec plus esse Latine et Graece scire, quam Gallice et Hispane*). A correct sentence in Spanish or French is preferable to an incorrect sentence in Latin (M 6.345).

Vives' ideas on the vernacular represent some progress beyond those of his master Erasmus, but seem less emphatic and forceful than those of Thomas More, an accomplished writer in both English and Latin, who warmly recommended Linacre's Latin grammar with English explanations, urged the English translation of recent books in Latin, and shared the enthusiasm of his closest friends (Grocyn, Colet, Lily and others) for the learning of classical Latin through English (*discere ex verbis non tua tuis*) as practised in Magdalen College.[34] To Vives, the plurality of languages was only "a consequence of sin" (*peccati enim poena est tot esse linguas;* M 6.299). Latin is the ideal ecumenical language only because it is pleasant to the ear (*suavis*), learned (*docta*), and rich (*facunda*). It is also widespread, useful to the propagation of the faith, and to the expression of sacred truths.

Vives' opinions on vernacular languages are closely tied to his guidelines for the study of the three *artes sermocinales*. These guidelines are mostly trite repetitions of popular, up-to-date commonplaces and are similarly inspired by the humanists' firm belief in the value of correct, articulated, and persuasive speech. The only difference seems to be that Vives had assimilated in a more thorough and explicit fashion the revolutionary ideas of Valla and Agricola on the character and the central role of dialectic. Vives consistently applies to all the *artes sermocinales* the purely descriptive character of all linguistic rules. More emphatically perhaps than most of his immediate predecessors, Vives insists on the descriptive character of grammar. He was so persuaded that popular use dictates the rules of language and that grammarians merely describe and systematically organize them, that, in spite of his admiration for Nebrija, he did not hesitate to question the necessity of grammars for the study of living languages and made the obviously exaggerated claim that languages are almost entirely changed by use roughly every hundred years.[35] Because languages that are not used anymore by any living group, such as Latin and Greek, ought not to be "dead" but alive, Vives opposed Valla's literal imitation of Cicero and Quintilian. He therefore claimed for himself the right to introduce neologisms into the Latin vocabulary, a right he generously used in his *Exercitatio Linguae Latinae*.

By far Vives' most interesting and influential contribution to the study of the *trivium* centers on the character of dialectical training and its relation to rhetoric. His thinking in this matter is consistently dictated by the changed aims of dialectical and rhetorical training. The purpose of dialectic is not to sharpen the mind for scholastic speculation, but to provide it with abundant avenues to the investigation of any subject matter and to prepare the young for a useful life in society. The central aim of rhetoric is not to adorn discourse but to make it clear, efficient, and persuasive. Mental inventiveness and articulated speech go hand in hand. Dialectic and rhetoric are neither reduced to one another nor confused in their tasks, but they are obviously brought close together by making them serve two mutually complementary ends.

This change in purpose presupposes and is based on philosophical views that Vives explicitly states. In their daily existence, in their intercourse with others and the world around, human beings are guided more by probable beliefs than by absolute and certain truths. Even rigorous deduction starts from premises that are not themselves demonstrable but held only in belief.[36] Dialectic and rhetoric are the internal and the external, or the mental and the language-related sides of the art of the probable, an art in which feeling and emotions play no insignificant part. This new art entails the rejection of a culture dominated by medieval logic—as we saw in *Adversus Pseudodialecticos*—and ushers in a mild form of pragmatic skepticism of great significance in the history of modern philosophy. The practical character of dialectical training excludes also the technical jargon of scholastic logic. There is not, nor should there be any gap between the language of ordinary life and that of discourse and philosophical reflection.

The Antwerp volume of 1531, *De Disciplinis,* includes three small treatises that are meant to give an idea of what this new dialectic ought to offer. In

De Instrumento Probabilitatis, Vives sketches a theory of knowledge (more about this in Chapter 9) and offers a "confused and disorganized jungle" (*confusam et permixtam quandam instrumentorum silvam*) of topics or *loci* of invention (M 3.86–87). The treatise is a typical example of what has been called "the commonplace tradition," a tradition which in spite of its "zany confusion"—as Father Ong has called it—cannot be dismissed as trivial or as limited to the art of imparting knowledge but which extends to a technique of acquiring knowledge.[37] In *De Censura Veri,* Vives deals with the problems of synonymy, analogy, metaphor, and the distinction between categorematic and syncategorematic terms. The small book proves a familiarity with philosophical technicalities that was unusual among most humanists, and reveals the more traditionally Aristotelian aspect of Vives' thought. *De Disputatione* is closer to the Aristotelian rhetoric but gives it a typically Vivesian twist. The author seems much more interested in the internal confrontation between the two sides of an argument and the role emotions play in it than in the struggle of the orator to persuade a less sympathetic audience. Persuading oneself can be and is often more challenging and strenuous than persuading others.

On the basis of all these reflections, I think it is unfair to say that Vives placed little value on the learning of rhetoric.[38] It is true that he placed less value on *ornamentum* and *copia verborum* than some of his contemporaries and predecessors. Against the former, Vives insists that, as any form of beauty, the beauty of style can be both edifying or poisonous. Against the latter, Vives is eager to warn that ornate prose can easily degenerate into "silly verbosity." "I prefer," Vives wrote, "the mumbling of the wise to the verbiage of the fool" (*indisertam malim sapientiam quam stultam loqua-citatem*).[39] The purpose of discourse is not to delight the audience with the flourish of words, but to get and retain its attention. Vives' admiration for Quintilian did not blind him to the shortcomings and exaggerations of the Roman orator. Quintilian's almost Machiavellian teaching that the public speaker must at least make the outward impression of being an honorable man in order to manipulate his audience was not enough for the Spanish humanist. But to claim, as Quintilian did, that the art of speaking well involved the art of living well was to Vives an unforgivable confusion of two different orders, the aesthetic and the ethical.[40]

One of the glaring defects of the medieval *trivium* was the curious neglect of literature, history, and philosophy. Literary models were mostly used to teach grammatical correction and rhetorical embellishment; they were seldom read for their own sake or for pure aesthetic enjoyment. One of the great achievements of Italian humanism had precisely been the rediscovery of literary beauty in all its forms. Vives himself was extraordinarily familiar with Greek and Latin poets, and often expressed in vivid terms his delight in the charm of poetical creations. On the other hand, he never wrote a poem worthy of that name and made every possible effort, particularly during his early years at Louvain, not to antagonize the theologians by introducing himself as a philosopher rather than as a poet and by making clear that his interest in literature was "healthy" and morally safe. His writings on Vergil's *Georgics* (1518) and *Bucolics* (1537) are inspired by a warm admiration for Vergil, Homer, and Theocritus. In the work on the *Bucolics,* published three years before his death, Vives violates his own guidelines and relapses into a medieval and patristic interpretation of Vergil as a prophet of the Messiah. But as a severe moralist and philosopher deeply indebted to some fundamental Platonic views, Vives feared the power of poetry to affect the imagination and stir up uncontrollable emotions. The ambivalence between his aesthetic delight in the poetical, and his self-righteous and moral condemnation of it, was never resolved. The tone of his remarks depends mostly on historical circumstance or on the different character and aim of the work at hand, whether it was a piece of literary criticism or a moral admonition. In *Veritas Fucata I* (1520) the young Vives had condemned poetry as devilish poison and counterfeit, smeared Truth.[41] About this same time Vives wrote *Sapientis Inquisitio,* a dialogue that is partially inspired by Socrates' *Apology* and in which poets are characterized as liars and fools. *De Institutione Feminae Christianae,* written in a highly moralistic vein and addressed to a woman, included a violent attack on "pestiferous books" (*de pestiferis libris*) including the medieval romances, the *Celestina,* the works of Poggio and Boccaccio. In *De Causis Corruptarum Artium* Vives praised the pleasing harmonies of verse but bemoaned the corruption of most poetical themes (M 6.93–101).

Vives' more judicious pronouncements on poetry can be found in an early dialogue also entitled *Veritas Fucata* (and known as *Veritas Fucata II*), in his later pedagogical work *De Tradendis Disciplinis* (1531), and in a treatise on style, *De Ratione Dicendi* (1532). In *Veritas Fucata II* (M 2.517–31) Vives probably tried to minimize the negative, antihumanistic impact of the early dialogue of the same name, but as the subtitle indicates ("How far poets are allowed to part from truth"), deals with a slightly different issue, the reconciliation of fiction and truth. In this surprising document, Vives goes as far as he could in the attempt to rehabilitate poetry. Poets can use fiction sanctioned by popular use (*fama publica*) or concerning obscure facts of ancient or, as he calls it, "pre-Olympic" history. Events of recent history can be embellished by rhetorical devices, provided such embellishments tend to promote moral values and the events themselves remain credible, decent, and consistent with other facts. Poets are also allowed to invent fables, comedies, and dialogues if their intention is a moral one.[42]

The third book of *De Tradendis Disciplinis* presents a lengthy critical review of ancient and modern literature, a survey in which both the merits and faults of classical and contemporary authors are pondered with some equanimity. But in Chapter 5 of the same book, Vives reprimands Plutarch for having only "diluted the poison" of poetry, and does not hesitate to recommend a severe censorship. *De Ratione Dicendi* condemns once again the *fabulae licentiosae* or novels that under very liberal conditions had been approved in *Veritas Fucata II,* but offers also a small treatise on poetics that is almost free from any moralistic posturing.

Italian humanists had also rediscovered the great historians of the classical age. In Caesar, Livy, Sallust, and Tacitus, among others, they had learned not only to appreciate the beauty of Latin prose but had also become acquainted with and fascinated by their own historical past. Like most northern humanists, Vives left aside the nationalistic interest of his Italian counterparts and approached the study of history from a literary and a moral perspective.

In Book 2, Chapter 4 of *De Causis Corruptarum Artium* (M 6.93), Vives suggests that the knowledge of history (and that of poetry) is closely related to grammar. If popular use changes language every hundred years or so, then the study of any given language becomes a historical task. Linguistic changes are historical changes not only in the sense that they have a history of their own, but also in the sense that they echo the institutional and social changes of the people who imposed them. Vives' sharp criticism of medieval commentators and translators is based on the allegation that they ignored the historical background of classical texts.

The detailed review of historical books presented in Book 5, Chapter 2 of *De Tradendis Disciplinis* and in fact in all Vives' works—including one of his devotional writings (*De Tempore quo, id est, de Pace in qua Natus est Christus*) and two rhetorical exercises (*Declamationes Syllanae, Isocratis Oratio Areopagitica*)—betrays an extraordinary familiarity not only with classical but even with recent historians who had written in the vernacular and for whom he felt great admiration.[43] Vives also wrote a short account of Rome's fall, *Quinam Fuerint Gothi, et Quomodo Romam Ceperint* (M 6.440–49), and a few additions to Suetonius, *In Vita C. Julii Caesaris, De Gente Julia, Caesarum Familia,* and *Ortus Caesaris et Educatio* (M 6.438–40).

Vives' use (and abuse) of edifying historical anecdotes demonstrates his interest in history as the *magistra vitae,* a commonplace of all humanist literature. But even in this respect Vives' critical insights sound strikingly original and modern. Students must have in their minds a clear outline of universal history (M 6.327–28). The chronological sequence of the historical process has to be learned accurately in order for the student to perceive its organic interconnections (M 6.392). Nor can historical events be confused with mythical ones, as Greek poets and historians were prone to do (M 6.101–5). The writing of history needs to be undisturbed by evil emotions. Anger and hatred can lead to the glorification of war and war heroes, and nationalistic pride can result in ridiculous exaggerations (as in the case of Plutarch). Only under these conditions can the study of history become the basis of practical wisdom and foster the higher moral life of citizens, rulers, and scholars. History is a moral teacher, laying bare what remains constant through ever-changing social contexts, the interplay of human passions and their impact on the process of choosing and acting. Vives was more interested in the covert side of human actions than in the mere sequence of external events (M 6.389).

Vives was also more helpful than most of his fellow humanists in reforming and widening the scope of philosophical education. The corruption of dialectic and the abuse of disputatio (once again, the evil effect of an emotional disorder) had led to the debasement of the entire philosophical enterprise and to proud and divisive sectarianism (M 6.27–35, 49–57). With some honorable exceptions, the philosophical curriculum of most universities had degenerated into a painfully long study of terminist logic and an equally painfully short acquaintance with ethics and physics. Metaphysical speculation had practically become a theological footnote. To remedy these abuses, Vives placed special emphasis on the reform of moral philosophy, metaphysics, and the philosophy of nature. Vives' moral books, however, were much richer in exhortations and aphorisms than in ethical theory, probably because he never questioned in his mind the basic premises of Christian morality. He nevertheless considered the third book of *De Anima et Vita* "the foundation of all moral philosophy" because it probed the psychological dynamics of the moral act (M 3.299).

In spite of his moderate skepticism and antispeculative frame of mind, Vives included in the 1531 Antwerp volume, *De Disciplinis*, the lengthy treatise *De Prima Philosophia, sive de Intimo Naturae Opificio* as an example of what a clear and worthwhile textbook on metaphysics should be, an investigation guided not by the "dim and malignant light" (*obscurae lucis malignaeque*) of pagan authors but by "the solar beam Christ brought to the world" (M 6.351).[44] Vives rejects the hair-splitting of Aristotelian philosophy but recommends all eight books of the *Physics* and the first six books of the *Metaphysics. De Prima Philosophia,* however, lacks the clear and orderly exposition that was promised in *De Tradendis Disciplinis,* and only partially succeeds in providing a synthesis of Aristotelian views (teleology, theory of sensation, hylomorphism, the metaphysics of substance and accident, analogy of being), Stoic doctrines (common notions), and Christian truths (natural knowledge of God's existence, original sin, immortality, creation in time, existence of the angels). But that synthesis is tightly circumscribed in scope by some typically Vivesian caveats on the adequacy and limitation of our intellectual powers, on the value of ordinary language in philosophical speculation, on the relativity of all human knowledge, and on the possibility of cultural progress. Probably the most interesting part of the book is suggested by its subtitle, "About the innermost operation of nature." What Vives tries to do with only moderate success is to enrich our observation of the natural domain (physics) with some reasonable conjectures about the essential and therefore partially hidden chains of causal relationships that link the world to God and underlie all natural processes. Metaphysics thus conceived becomes the inner side of physics, the ever-unfinished human project of reaching an understanding of the world that points toward God and both satisfies and stimulates a humble but open-ended desire to know. I must add that, although *De Prima Philosophia* was in Vives' intention one of his most ambitious speculative projects, it actually turned out to be one of his least influential works. As a unique example of Renaissance peripatetic philosophy, *De Prima Philosophia* nevertheless deserves more attention than it has received so far, and will therefore be discussed in detail in Part 2 of this book.

Vives' understanding and appreciation of contemporary work on physics, what he called *Suisethi cavillationes* (a reference to the medieval logician Richard Suiseth) was undermined by his inclination to dismiss any form of knowledge that was not clearly practical and was still dressed up in "scholastic" jargon. On the other hand, his pedagogical recommendations and guidelines with regard to the scope and method of the *scientiae reales* of the *quadrivium* were, if not revolutionary (as they have been occasionally characterized), certainly illuminating and novel among his fellow humanists. Our knowledge of nature, Vives claims, is not a mere contemplation inspired by curiosity nor a rigorous science seeking indubitable truth, but a probable conjecture (*verisimilia consectamur*) aimed at meeting the necessities of life and at fostering our pious recognition of God's majesty. Speculative overindulgence leads only to superfluous quibbling, a serious shortcoming of Aristotelian physics that was only exaggerated by medieval commentators, particularly by Averroës (M 6.185–98).

Vives, however, had a great admiration for certain books written by or attributed to Aristotle, such as *Meteorology, History of Animals,* and *On the Universe.* Vives' short appraisal of these books can be read in *Censura de Aristotelis Operibus,* published two years before his death.[45] This practical and conjectural knowledge of nature is mostly acquired through sense experience and observation. Those who generalize from experience need to proceed with some caution. Vives frequently criticizes Aristotle's penchant for hasty inductive conclusions. At least in Belgium (*in hac Belgica*), he writes on two occasions, it is false to conclude that animals that have thin legs also have thin arms (M 6.43, 183). Books summarize and preserve for posterity the observations that others have accumulated of the world. As such, they are limited but useful tools to the scientist. Vives recommends some Aristotelian short treatises, also some by Pliny, Pomponius Mela, Aratus, Hyginius, Manilius (with some qualifications), Ptolemy, Strabo, Theophrastus, Dioscorides, and others. One of the great benefits of these readings is to provide the student with a general picture of the universe, an outline within which all particular observations regarding plants, fishes, heavenly bodies, oceans, and gems find their natural context. Bookish learning must be enriched by our own experiences and also by the experience of those who are more closely related to the natural environment, such as gardeners, husbandmen, hunters, and shepherds (M 6.347–51).[46] It is clear from this that Vives' encyclopedic interest in the study of the natural world went far beyond the four *artes liberales* of the classical *quadrivium* (arithmetic, geometry, astronomy, and music).

Vives' philosophy of mathematics represents a difficult compromise among Platonic, Aristotelian, and Stoic views. As other humanists before him—particularly Vittorino da Feltre and Pius II—Vives too accepted Plato's insistence on the disciplinary value of mathematical training in the journey toward true knowledge. Vives' division of the mathematical disciplines echoes the curriculum and the conception of the *Republic*. Arithmetic deals with the quantity of number, geometry with the quantity of volume. Astronomy is geometry applied to the heavenly bodies and music is arithmetic applied to harmony (M 6.203, 639). The emphasis on mathematical abstraction from matter is clearly Aristotelian, but the explanation of axioms and definitions as based upon the innate "anticipations" impressed in our minds reflects a Stoic theory of knowledge.

Vives' interest in astronomy—which he always separated from astrology— dates from his youth. Vives' first publication was an edition of Hyginus' *Poeticon Astronomicon* (1514), a work on astronomy probably of the second century A.D. and attributed to the Palatine librarian under Augustus, whom

Vives calls in one of his early books *"conterraneus meus."* This "mediocre textbook" (as Ijsewijn has called it) had often been printed since 1475 and had been edited twice by Jan Dullaert. It is also probable that Vives lectured on Hyginus at Paris in 1514.[47] Astronomy led Vives to the consideration of music—the sound of the heavenly spheres. He appreciated the power of music to soothe violent emotions but seemed convinced that European culture had lost the appreciation of "subtle sounds" since the collapse of the Roman Empire due to the ignorance of rhythm and the lack of refined musical instruments among the German tribes (M 6.207).

Vives' strong emphasis on the practical aims of the liberal arts helped to bridge the gap between liberal and professional education. The self-fulfillment that liberal education seeks entails the fulfillment of oneself as a useful member of the human community. The *artes sermocinales* of the *trivium* are not tools for a theoretical speculation unrelated to daily existence, but tools to enhance the art of communication among ordinary people in their private or professional tasks. The *artes reales* of the *quadrivium* are even more relevant to professional education. Mathematics is the foundation of all the arts of measurement, perspective, optics, and acoustics. Perspective is closely associated with architecture and the visual arts. Optics is essential to the study of mirrors and lenses. Acoustics—a quantitative theory of sound that Vives believed to be possible and desirable though it did not yet exist—would be extremely useful to musicians. Astronomy is a necessary complement to agriculture and the art of navigation (M 6.371). Students should be encouraged to enter shops and factories, and to ask questions from craftsmen in order to learn from them the details of their crafts (M 6.374). The study of mathematics, both theoretical and applied, must be followed by the study of technological progress in the arts that pertain to eating, clothing, dwelling, husbandry, herbs, and means of transportation (M 6.373–74). Vives' insight into the unlimited possibilities of applied mathematics went far beyond the Aristotelian tradition and echoed some of the more promising and revolutionary trends of his age. But here, too, his fear of speculative excess prevented him from mastering a body of theory that could degenerate (as in the study of infinite quantity) into "an anxious inquiry" (*sollicita horum inquisitio*) that "leads people away from the business of life" (*a rebus vitae abducit*).[48]

Vives was seriously concerned with the reform of professional education, except in the field of theology on which he was very careful not to trespass. His writings on jurisprudence—which we have discussed in their historical context—are an eloquent testimony to his zeal for legal reform. Here I shall analyze his contribution to the reform of medicine.

In the first appendix to Book 5 of *De Causis Corruptarum Artium*, Vives offers an interesting account of the origin and corruption of the medical art (M 6.198–203). The decadence of medicine was due not only to emotional disorders (greed increased by the physician's power over life and death, the seeking of glory and novelty) and to the adulteration of classical sources, but, more important, to methodological failures. Although Vives often warns the reader that he is not an expert on medical matters—a lack of expertise that is obvious in any event—his writings prove that he had at least perused some of the numerous editions and translations of classical authors dealing in particular with the proper method in medicine.[49] In tracing the origin of dietetics and the medicinal art (the preventive and therapeutic aspects of medicine proper), Vives presents the Hippocratic method as the paradigm of all forms of *téjnē,* the model of all applied sciences sketched by Plato in the *Philebus* and adapted to a radically empiricist epistemology in the Stoic definition of art: "A complex of percepts exercised together for some useful end in life." Although the term *percepts* had been misread as *precepts* by some Latin translations of Galen, Vives interpreted Galen's definition in his usual eclectic manner and devised an analysis of scientific methodology that in my judgment avoids some of the hesitations of the first book of the Aristotelian *Metaphysics*.

Vives emphasizes that art differs from useless speculation since it is aimed at a practical end. It differs from unlearned skill, combining experiments (observations or "percepts") with judicium to yield what Vives calls "general rules" (*canones generales*). What makes medicine a special art is the fact that the initial experiments were prompted by desperate needs (and possibly helped by divine intervention) and that the results of such experiments had to be valued in light of such variables as the time and location of the disease at hand, and the individual conditions of the patient. Results had to be carefully judged as to the nature of the remedy, the time and the location of the disease, and the individual conditions of the patient. "Precepts" that are not supported by enough "percepts" are as dangerous as the latter are useless without the former (M 6.198).

The proper training of physicians therefore involves the right balance of theory and practice. Theoretical training begins with the study of the four elements, their combinations in metals, plants, and animals, the anatomy of the human body, and the study of symptomatology and pharmacology. The study of medicine is for Vives an endless, lifelong, and all-absorbing task. Physicians must leave aside any distraction, even the study of the literary arts, even the reading of Cicero and Vergil. A practicing physician must always keep abreast of the latest theoretical discoveries, although not every physician is called upon to become an "investigator" or, as Vives says, "a master of his craft" (*velut antistites quidam artis*). Practical training involves dissection of human bodies, experiments with animals, and consultation with more experienced physicians. Physicians should dress neatly, try to remain healthy themselves, and never prolong any disease for reasons of greed or vainglory (M 6.378–85).

Vives' attention to the demands of the body is also reflected in his remarks on the impact of the environment on the educational process and the proper care of the students' health. Few educators have been as concerned as Vives was with the right location of schools.[50] The site chosen for a school should be healthy but not lush (unless the school is dedicated to the study of poetry, music, or history), distant from noisy factories and shops, but not isolated. Schools should be far removed from the court, from maritime and commercial cities, and from public highways and international borders (M 6.272–73). In the third book of *De Anima et Vita,* Vives provides the psychological justification for this concern about the environment. External circumstances (as we shall see in Chapter 15) play an important part in the emotional and therefore intellectual life of children and the young.

Proper bodily care is also highly relevant to emotional susceptibility. Vives often insists on the importance of a well-balanced diet, a diet adapted to individual "temperaments" (M 6.273, 275, 319). Like all humanist pedagogues, Vives also recommends physical exercises, sports, and recreation (even card games), but forbids excessive corporal punishment and any martial arts.

De Disciplinis strongly reinforced the tendency toward the secularization of public education and toward the professional training of teachers. The treatise does not include a single reference to the educational responsibilities of the church. Public education is clearly preferred to household and private education, although Vives was not totally unaware of the dangers of schools too distant from home and discouraged parents from sending children to boarding schools. Vives boldly asserts that each municipality should have its own school and that each territorial jurisdiction (*provincia*) should have its own academy, that only men who were academically and morally qualified and well-trained teachers should be paid with public moneys (M 6.272–85).

Three years after Vives' death, and at the request of his widow, Francis Craneveld published and dedicated to Paul III the unfinished treatise *De Veritate Fidei Christianae* (1543). From Craneveld's letter to the pope, we know that Vives had been working for several years on this book, second only to *De Disciplinis* in size and scope. This testimony and a vague reference to the treatise in *De Anima et Vita* proves that both were written at roughly the same time. *De Veritate* makes explicit the religious beliefs that underpin the philosophical assumptions and psychological analysis of *De Anima et Vita*. Hence its great relevance to our project.

Although Craneveld reports that Vives' intention in writing this book was to contribute as much as possible to "the important religious debates of the times" (*tantae de rebus ad religionem pertinentibus quaestiones*), the treatise scrupulously avoids every single theological issue raised by the Reformation. One has the overwhelming impression that Vives' religious beliefs, though profoundly theocentric and unquestionably Christian, were never dogmatically specific enough to enter into an adversarial course with Protestant or Reformed theology. The first four and endless chapters of Book I represent a repetitive and occasionally passionate justification of the attempt to facilitate or reinforce the act of faith by human reasoning. Chapters 5 to 7 of the same book introduce us to perhaps the most brilliant and mature account of human nature ever written by Vives, and draw the conclusion that the final purpose of human existence necessarily points to a life after death. After two chapters (8 and 9) on the true nature of God, Vives presents the Catholic dogma on the creation of the world in time (10 and 11), the angels (12), the sin of the angels, and the original sin of man (14 to 17).

The second book deals with the Trinity (2), the Incarnation (3–6), the Old Testament (7), the Gospels (8, 9, and 10), the doctrine of Christ (11), the miracles and divinity of Christ (12–14), the death of Christ (15–16), the Eucharist (17), the Resurrection (18), the primitive church (19–20), and eschatology (21–24). This quick outline proves that Vives' Christian beliefs went beyond a purely humanistic admiration for Christian ethics, as Erasmus' *philosophia Christi* has sometimes been characterized. Still, whenever he approached themes that could lead into a theological debate with Protestant reformers, Vives was extremely cautious. The chapter on the consequences of original sin, a touchy topic, is strongly permeated by Augustinian pessimism, but manages to avoid any language that could have been offensive to the church's *magisterium*. Papal authority is not even mentioned. Sacramental theology is limited to a short discussion of the Eucharist where Vives cleverly avoids any theological strictures by simply declaring that Christ's presence in the sacrament is "incomprehensible to us" (*modo quodam nobis incomprehensibili*). The central theological concept of grace is almost entirely omitted from discussion. That the chapter on predestination was never finished could be another sign of theological timidity. It goes without saying that, in spite of all these precautions, Vives submitted the entire writing to the approval of the church and willingly declared himself prepared to change any opinion that could be in the least offensive to "the judgment of the Holy See" (*Santissimae Sedis arbitrio;* M 8.iii).

Vives' interest in Catholic dogma did not seem aimed at refuting Protestant views but rather at rejecting Jewish Rabbinic theology and proving the superiority of Christianity over Islam, the explicit purpose of Books 3 and 4. The third book is a dialogue between a Christian and a Jew, a "troublesome and complex" task. With obviously sincere conviction and impressive Biblical expertness (in spite of his self-confessed ignorance of Hebrew), Vives, the Jewish son of an Inquisition's victim, addresses himself to his ethnic brethren, "people of shameless obstinacy" (*genus hominum impudentissimae pervicaciae*) and tries to persuade his partner in the dialogue that Judaism has become a narrow-minded ethnic sect more than a religion of all humanity. Vives accuses Judaism of being bound to a literal and materialistic interpretation of the Scripture, embroiled in silly ritualistic precepts, deprived of any desire to proselytize, a religion of fear rather than of love.

The fourth book is also a dialogue, this time between a Christian and a Moslem theologian. In this part of the treatise, clearly prompted by the Turkish threat in eastern Europe and by his own social intercourse with the large Morisco population in Valencia, Vives demonstrates nothing but spite and contempt for a self-destructive religious belief he believed to befit people of poor intelligence. Vives was convinced that Mohammed was only "a thief, a violent robber, a murderer, and a repulsive adulterer" (M 8.375). Vives felt the utmost contempt for a religion that approved polygamy and divorce, and debased eternal blessing into an orgy of sensual delights.

The last book emphasizes once again the superiority of Christianity, the religion of love ("the most powerful passion"), the only religion that provides consolation in the face of death, and the only religion that heals all our emotional disorders and makes therefore possible the attainment of our true vocation in life, to live with others in peace and harmony. If *De Veritate Fidei Christianae* reveals to us Vives' mature thought on religion, *De Anima et Vita,* written about the same time, lays bare before our eyes Vives' reflection on human existence and the demands of moral life. The rest of this book represents an attempt to understand this reflection in as much detail as possible.

Part 2
Vives' Thoughts on Life

6

Nature

Vives' *De Anima et Vita* bears only a general resemblance to the Aristotelian treatise on the same subject. The first book of the Aristotelian treatise, in most of which Aristotle expounds and criticizes many of his predecessors, has no counterpart in Vives, who had nothing but contempt for the "absurdities" written by the ancients on the nature of the human soul. Aristotle's discussion of the proper definition of the soul (Book 2, Chapters 1 and 2) was also bypassed by the Spanish humanist, who, in a much quoted and partially misunderstood passage, defiantly confessed to his not being interested at all in getting to know "what the soul is" (*anima quid sit, nihil interest nostra scire;* M 3.332).[1] The most insightful chapters of Vives' book—the chapters on ingenium, language, the learning process, common notions, the will, dreams, old age, death, and immortality—are either completely original or far more elaborate and richer than Aristotle's hesitant pronouncements on the same topics. "Aristotle," Vives says, "was, as usual, inscrutable and evasive" (*Aristoteles, more suo, tectus est, et vafer;* M 3.299). Vives' long third book on the passions of the soul has no counterpart in Aristotle's *On the Soul*, although his positions are stated with some care in Book 2 of the *Rhetoric*.

These differences in the structure of the two treatises and Vives' apparent lack of interest in speculative questions should not, however, be exaggerated to the point where they could conceal from us the metaphysical direction of Vives' enterprise and the fundamental similarity between his and Aristotle's conceptual framework. An account of Vives' conception of human nature needs therefore to be preceded by an introduction to his metaphysical views on the character of nature in general as they are expounded in the books of *De Prima Philosophia*, which, as I have pointed out, contain his more mature philosophical outlook.

In spite of explicit protestations to the contrary, Vives' philosophical task

in *De Prima Philosophia* and, to a certain extent, in *De Anima et Vita,*
remains basically Aristotelian: to know the hidden and permanent *ousía* of
everything through the observation of its sensible actions and passions.
"Internal features are revealed through external actions and passions"
(*Interiora illa per externas actiones et passiones proferunt se ac ostendunt;*
M 3.226). To know the definition of the soul might not be important to Vives,
but to know what kind of reality the soul is by knowing what its operations
are, is indispensable to his conception of metaphysics as a form of inquiry
that goes beyond the mere satisfaction of our speculative curiosity. "We are
not interested at all in knowing what the soul is, but *we are very much
interested* [my emphasis] in knowing what kind of reality the soul is and what
its operations are. God, who commanded us to know ourselves, did not
intend for us to know the essence of our soul but the operations of the soul
that relate to our moral conduct."[2] The very titles of Vives' books, *De Anima
et Vita* (On the life of the soul) and *De Prima Philosophia sive de Intimo
Naturae Opificio* (On first philosophy, or the internal workings of nature)
reveal the character of this project.

This operationalist approach to the knowledge of the essential is as
Aristotelian as the basic metaphysical principles and concepts by which we
seek to infer the covert essence of natural agents from the overt operations we
perceive through the senses. Still, the differences between the two philosophers are almost as significant as their linguistic and conceptual approxima-
tions. These differences are dictated by Vives' pervasive theocentrism,
moderate skepticism, and strong pragmatism. All three conspire to shape a
theory of knowledge never explicitly stated that radically weakens the
cognitive rigor of metaphysics as a "science." God, Vives often claims, has
made possible for us that degree of knowledge that is adequate to the pursuit
of our final end. "The edge of our mind is not so dull that it cannot perceive
the truth in as much as it is conducive to humanity. To have such a power is an
inmense gift of God to man" (M 3.185). "The same God who in His infinite
Wisdom ordered us to seek our end, wished in His Goodness that we be
endowed with the required powers and tools, and was All-powerful to confer
them on us" (M 3.189).

God's purpose in granting us knowledge is also the measure of the
knowledge we can rightly expect. Whatever God has not revealed to us
through the law-sanctioned regularities of Nature is and should remain
beyond our cognitive domain and aspirations. It is, for instance, wasteful and
potentially immoral to pry into the reasons that God had for creating as many
heavenly bodies as He did, to ask whether the matter of the heavens and the
sublunar matter are the same or not, to speculate why there are so many

species of animals and plants. Such immoderate curiosity leads us to "enter forbidden territory and to interject ourselves shamefully into the secrets of the Divinity."3

This God-given capacity to know whatever we need to know in order to reach our eternal destiny was weakened but not erased by Adam's original sin. Although we are not totally "blind and orphans," we certainly have lost forever the "quickness in knowing," and constantly suffer the rebellion of the body and the passions (M 2.190). Christ's example and doctrine are a powerful help, but have not restored us to a paradisiac condition. Human knowledge in our postlapsarian status remains a difficult and arduous task, mostly because of passional excess and rebellion. Our knowledge of the natural world is particularly difficult, Vives claims, because Nature is not ours but God's work: "We see how the artificial work is done because the art is ours. But we do not see how the work of nature is done because it is the work of God."4

Furthermore, the human artificer works "from the outside" by adding, taking away, or mixing what is already there. Nature's operations, on the other hand, are "silent and hidden," a "recondite and intimate process."5 Our attempt to infer the nature of invisible causes from perceived effects is also frequently frustrated by our inclination to assume that whatever has preceded the effect in our limited experience must be reckoned as the cause of that effect, by the possible but often unnoticed concurrence of several causes, by the dissimilarity between causes and effects, by the possible coexistence or succession of causes and effects, and once again, by the disturbing impact of prejudice and passion.

As a result, our knowledge of the natural world remains limited, conjectural, subject to revision and growth, necessarily incomplete, dependent on the observations of others, often leaning on universal consensus or even on the opinion of a select majority. The unfinished character of all human effort to reach a full understanding of Nature was to Vives another proof of the immortality of the soul, a proof that the pagan Aristotle miserably failed to ponder (M 3.191).

Our knowledge of Nature's hidden operations might be more reliable than our knowledge of moral principles, but it still lacks the certainty of mathematics and the evidence of sense perceptions (*De Veritate Fidei Christianae*, Book 1, Chapter 4; M 8.23). Consequently, Vives' metaphysics of nature is nothing but a complex of beliefs made reasonably persuasive by a constant appeal to observations derived from our routine interaction with the world and by their direct or indirect utility to us as moral agents or practical producers. Vives' intent is clearly not to evince agreement by the use of apodictic deductive inferences but rather to persuade the reader through the cumulative convergence of loosely tied dialectical arguments. This rhetorical treatment of even the most challenging and puzzling metaphysical questions gives *De Prima Philosophia* and *De Anima et Vita* their unique Renaissance flavor.

The existence of God as the intelligent and provident Creator of everything is quickly confirmed by the order of the natural world, by an appeal to humanity's consensus, and by the universality of religious feeling in times of particular sadness or joy. Vives proves that the world was not necessarily created by God by the argument that there could be no logical reason why the number of herbs on earth or the number of hairs on our heads is precisely what it is. The world's creation in time is made believable by the constant emergence of novelty in the universe and by the daily reminders in our experience that everything is subject to a process of birth, progress, and decay. The tormenting problem of evil is cleverly bypassed by a charming thought on the "stunning ornament and unspeakable beauty of the discordant."[6] Metaphysical questions about the origin of multiplicity from the essential simplicity of God are quickly resolved by comparing God to a prolific scholar who shows the wealth of his knowledge by writing a book on grammar, another on dialectic, and another on the philosophy of nature (as Vives himself did).

What makes *De Prima Philosophia* and *De Anima et Vita* both strikingly original and occasionally baffling is the fact that these dialectical (and controversial) arguments are nevertheless loosely structured within the theoretical framework of Aristotelian metaphysics and sometimes expressed in Aristotelian jargon. The notions of matter and form, substance and accident, act and potency, the doctrine of the four causes, the four elements and the ten categories, the theories of inductive generalization, action and passion (to mention only the more important) are as central to Vives' thought as they were to Aristotle's. To them Vives adds other more scholastic notions such as that of intellectual abstraction and the analogy of the concept of being. To a certain extent, the structure of *De Prima Philosophia* is loosely organized—more like an intelligent discourse than a rigid textbook—around the Aristotelian four causes, the categories, and other metaphysical distinctions of Aristotelian or medieval origin: substance and its constituents (form and matter) and subdivisions (infinite and finite substance), accidents in general, action and passion, quantity and quality, place and time. The last part of Book 3 is only a summary of the Aristotelian theories of quantity, the continuum, the rejection of vacuum, the definition of time, and so on. But even in this respect, there are remarkable differences between Vives and

Aristotle. Vives makes an explicit effort to avoid speculative subtleties, to illustrate the abstract with a profusion of simple but enlightening observations, and to translate most of his philosophical reflection into plain, everyday language. For instance, Vives rejects the Aristotelian theory of privation, shows some uneasiness with the Aristotelian jargon on potential being, and virtually bypasses the categories of relation, position, and state (M 3.202). Furthermore, basic Aristotelian concepts are occasionally enriched with post-Aristotelian speculation, such as Stoic epistemology, Christian theocentrism, and Renaissance physics.

Our knowledge of Nature begins with the perception of sensible objects, what Vives calls *sensata*. A *sensatum* has two different layers: first, an external mass (*moles exterior*) "covered and clothed" (*tectum et quasi convestitum*) with sensible accidents; and second, something imperceptible, (*nec ulli sensui est pervium*) internal and hidden (*intus latens*). Actions and operations proceed from the latter. The study of sensible accidents and operations belongs to what Vives calls *secunda philosophia* or *physics*. The task of first philosophy is to investigate the imperceptible grounding of perceived accidents which is also the covert source of overt operations.

In developing these basically Aristotelian notions, Vives succeeds in giving them an original, idiosyncratic flavor. The moderate skeptic never ceases to emphasize the mysterious and hidden character of the essence of things, an essence that constantly eludes our efforts to comprehend it. "Confined in the body, our mind fails to picture itself a substance deprived of its external accidents" (M 3.201). Precisely because actions and operations are the only link between the sensible and the hidden, Vives constantly seeks to enlarge the very concept of action and operation. Action and operation are understood by Vives as any manifestation of the "interior force" (*interna vis*) that transforms the inert and sluggish mass of everything into a thing with its proper specific differentiation. Leaves, flowers, and fruits are the operations of a tree as much as thinking is an operation of man or barking and chasing rabbits are the operations of a dog (M 3.197).

In spite of this obvious exaggeration and his tendency to make a sharp contrast between the inert or sluggish (*abjecta et torpida*) character of matter and the energetic or active (*generosa et actuosa*) character of form, Vives criticized Aristotle for calling matter and form causes, a term he reserved for the efficient and the final cause. To Vives, matter and form were constitutive elements of natural objects rather than manifestations of finite causality.[7] Matter was created by God all at once (*semel cuncta est producta*) to be worked out and shaped by the forces of Nature. Matter can be split, joined, combined, and moved. But it never increases, decreases, or ceases to exist.

Matter lacks any force (*nullam omnino habet vim*), is close to nothingness, and does not have any specific nature of its own. The transformation of matter by form requires, however, some immediate preparation, as the dough mixture requires careful kneading before the yeast begins to act and to transform it into bread with the instrumental help of heat (M 3.216–18).

Form is "an internal force and faculty of acting" (*interius vis et facultas agendi*), an invisible artificer (*opifex*), a "making" (*effectio*), as Cicero calls it, or an "act and energy" (*actus,* or *energeia*) in Aristotelian terms. This "internal force" (Vives' favorite terminology) is the principle of specific differentiation and the source of all natural operations. These operations, however, depend sometimes on proper instruments. The human soul, for instance, uses the eye as an instrument to see and the ear as an instrument to hear. This force does not "inhere" in matter as accidents inhere in substance, but rather subsists (*inest*) in it with various degrees of dependence on matter. Form shapes matter, and lends support to all the accidents that give each thing its proper "face" (*facies*) and "looks" (*species*).

Nature as a whole is "a force spread through the entire universe" (*vis sparsa per orbem totum*), the sum total of "the laws originally sanctioned by God." These laws bind everything together, guarantee the concord and harmony of everything, and subordinate the welfare of the part to the welfare of the whole. Vives emphasizes this ecological interrelation of all the parts of the universe by comparing the natural to the civil domain and by proclaiming as a law of Nature the general principle that "nothing private will survive if the public interest is threatened" (*nihil privatum salvum fore, si male sit reipublicae*). In this sense, the universe is like a clock, except that the Divine Craftsman never abandons the machine to its own forces but is always present and active in its operations like a puppeteer with his creations (M 3.212).

Vives understood Aristotelian teleology as the reflection on the natural domain of God's infinite wisdom. The immense variety of created agencies, the subordination of means to ends and the hierarchy of ends, the relation between parts and the whole not only within living organisms but also within the universe as a totality, the proportion between faculties and their instruments, the exact proportion between the necessary and the convenient, the mutual balancing of contrary activities and qualities are nothing but traces of a benevolent and wise creator.

The harmony of Nature, however, does not exclude the constant tension and conflict between contraries. There is nothing finite and created that does not have something contrary to itself (*quum nihil sit quod contrarium non habeat*). The generation of a new form always entails the corruption of another: finite beings thrive at the expense of each other. The life process of all living organisms is like the trajectory of a projectile: after an ascending line of maturation and growth, the organism reaches a moment of repose followed by a descending line of old age and decay. Vives borrows from contemporary works on kinetics the guiding lines of his metaphysics of old age, a recurring theme in many of his works and private correspondence (M 3.276, 282). Furthermore, finite beings were created from nothing and gravitate into nothing, particularly those that have incurred the curse brought about by the sin of man, their master (M 3.279).

This view of the universe as wounded by sin is not only a Christian revision of Aristotelian cosmology, but the metaphysical foundation of Vives' philosophy of history and of his austere conception of man. Only constant effort, exercise, and toil preserve things in their allotted degree of perfection. Stagnant waters become polluted and murky, culture is corrupted by indolence, neglected soil becomes barren land, and sloth transforms men into beasts by enslaving their languid minds to the tyranny of passion (M 3.279–80). Vives' metaphysical vision of the conflictive character of the material universe adds to Aristotelian philosophy of motion a note of dramatic intensity that is more Christian and baroque than Greek and classic. The form is conceived by Vives as a force that "compels and retains" (*contineat et coerceat*) within the substance all those "conflictive accidents" (*dissidentia inter se*) that "tend to separate from each other and are reluctant to inhere together in the same subject" (*conatu suo unumquodque ab alio separaretur et dissiliret, praesertim quum invita videantur cohaerere;* M 3.204). The action of finite agents is not only mediated by time, but involves the overcoming of some resistance on the part of the subject of change. This is obvious not only in the case of changes that go against the nature of the "patient" but also in natural changes. Contemplation is natural to the human soul, but because the soul is "burdened by the mass of the body" (*deprimitur enim mole corporis*), contemplation often becomes arduous. Furthermore, no matter how natural an action might be, all action represents an attempt by the agent to penetrate and divide the medium in which the action takes place. The medium resists this attempt (*medium vero quantumcumque molle penetrationi renititur*) because division is always a harbinger of corruption. The more dense the medium is, the stronger the resistance becomes. That is why it is easier to fly through the air than to swim through water and why a "sharp" mind can understand "matters" that are "too hard" for others. The variety of human ingenia, as we shall see in Chapter 10, is the result of the different densities of the brain (M 3.268–69).

Vives' universe is not only more torn by conflict than is Aristotle's cosmos, but it also appears to our limited knowledge as being less tidy and more resilient to our taxonomic aspirations. Vives constantly teaches that it is neither always necessary nor even possible for us to provide a neat definition of everything and that it is difficult to place every specific entity in its exact niche within the hierarchy of a universe that reflects in myriads of ways the unfathomable perfection of the Creator. There is, Vives claims, still ample room for an unthinkable number of possible degrees of perfection between two apparently consecutive links in the chain of created beings. The gap, for instance, between the human soul and God seems to Vives so disproportionately large that human reason, he thinks, is naturally led to guess the existence of spirits unattached to matter, an existence we only know for certain through Christian revelation.

Our knowledge of essential nature is further complicated, according to Vives, by the fact that almost everything in the universe reaches its essence through a gradual process (*paulatim veniunt ad essentiam*). This large group includes all living things, all things that have some mass (*mole*) and are subject to quantitative changes, such as stones and metals, the accidents of those material substances, and even the achievements of our mind, such as culture, virtue, and vice. The only things that "achieve their essence all at once" (*statim total simul essentiam nanciscuntur*) are angels, our souls (in their specific perfection), and those accidents that have no parts and are therefore not subject to increase or decrease (*et quae inhaerentia partes non habent, nec crescere dicuntur nec minui*). But even some of these are still subject to the flow of motion and time. The human soul changes in location because of its attachment to the body and is therefore bound to time. In some cases, nature itself establishes the "point" and "boundary" (*certi termini ac tamquam puncta*) at which time, and not before nor after, a given thing finally reaches the fullness of its specific perfection. Before birth, a human being is a fetus, and after death it becomes a corpse. (The example is literally taken from Vives, who was apparently unaware of all its possible moral complications.)

In most cases, however, the measuring rod is not provided by nature, but by our minds. To call something large or small, rich or poor, depends as much on human subjectivity as to decide how many grains it takes to have a heap, how many people make a crowd, how many soldiers constitute an army, or even how much flowing water it takes to form a river. Even those entities that share the same specific perfection can be said to be more or less what they are depending on some accidental perfections or relations of similarity. Thus, Vives says, it is possible to say that the Greeks were more human than the Scythians, that native citizens are more citizens than naturalized citizens, that the crocodile is more a snake than a fish. In all these matters, nature does not provide us with an "indivisible boundary" (*meta insectilis*), but rather with a "broad border ground" (*latus est limes*) that has to be assessed by an "unexacting and crass judgment" (*crasso judicio crassa sunt objicienda*). Hence the variety of opinions among human beings and the differences in values and emotional responses (M 3.209–12).

The unstable balance and baffling complexity of the universe does not make our rational inquiry totally impossible. God has given us the knowledge we need to master nature and make it serve our human projects. But such knowledge remains arduous and difficult. Intense observation reveals constant interaction between the four elements (fire, earth, air, and water) and the four qualities (cold, heat, dryness, and wetness). Vives' thought on this matter betrays not only an Aristotelian but also a Hippocratic influence, the latter through the mediation of Galen, and represents the foundation of his physiology of life, sensation, and emotion.

The very sight of fire makes us understand its quick vigor and active nature. The motionless density and cold listlessness that our tactile sensations discover in earth betray its role as the firm foundation of the material universe. Air, akin to fire, and water, close to earth, make up the connecting links (*vincula*) that secure the harmony of contraries. Water—cold, dense, and wet—keeps earth sticky and prevents it from crumbling apart while parrying the destructive power of fire. Air—volatile, light, and sleek—feeds but also weakens fire with its own commotions; it penetrates the body and fosters the process of growth.

The four elements are therefore bound together and tempered (*connexa et temperata*) by the combined action of the four qualities. Humidity prevents pulverization and dryness stops dissolution. A wet heat is less sharp than a dry heat. Heat and fire seek the heights close to the heavenly bodies where they can spread without impediment. Heat absorbs humidity and dries up the bodies. Air is not cold as the Stoics thought, but assimilates the temperature of its own environment. The wetness of water and the dryness of air mediate between the heat of fire above and the coldness of earth below. Cold is lazy and slow; wetness is the agglutinant of bodies. Dry bodies shrink; wet bodies expand. The hardness of a body is in inverse proportion to its wetness. What is dry and cold is less malleable than what is wet and warm. Whatever is impressed in the former lasts longer than what is impressed in the latter (M 3.218–22), a principle that helps us to understand the different ways memory apprehends and retains its objects (M 3.346).

Vives refuses to speculate whether all four elements enter into the composition of every specific entity. But observation tells us that some things seem to be mostly earth (rocks, metals), others mostly water (snow, hail, oysters, and starfish); that wherever fire is present all the other three elements seem to be there, albeit in minimal quantities; that life is impossible without some small amount of fire and water (heat and humidity); that living organisms capable of sensing must be endowed with forms that exceed the nature of the four elements and should be properly called "heavenly souls" (*animae coelestes*); that human beings capable of understanding differ from other earthly creatures by a "divine gift" (M 3.225).

Natural objects—be they simple or composite—need to be carefully distinguished from human artifacts. Whatever has been produced through the mediation of a human choice and design is "artificial," although the capacity to produce such things is and must be called "natural." Art imitates nature: matter is transformed into iron when it receives the corresponding form, and iron is transformed into a sword when it is fittingly shaped by the human craftsman. Art, however, never reaches the perfection of the natural because it always works from the outside; the natural never reaches the perfection of the divine because the imitation is never equal to the model. That is why the contemplation of natural beauty provides more lasting therapy for emotional disorders than does the contemplation of human artifacts.

The power to act, known to us through its actions, can be necessarily linked to a single effect (as is the case of fire that cannot but burn) or can be mediated by choice (as in the case of human agents). What man can naturally do can also be subject to choice. Man can naturally walk, but walking at a given moment in time is (or can be) the result of a free human choice. Habit imitates nature and results in a "second nature": it is perfectly natural for an irritable man to be easily irritated. Some actions are "beyond" nature: to raise a millstone is "beyond" the nature of a child. Other actions are "against" nature: it is "against" the nature of a rock to ascend by itself while it is in its nature to fall by itself (M 3.232).

Vives' effort to draw a clear line between the natural and the artificial (not an easy task!) and also between the necessary and the voluntary, sprang from his humanistic concern with the domain of human actions and choices. His picture of the natural world in *De Prima Philosophia* was only an introduction to his intense and reflective study of human life in *De Anima et Vita*. Nature to Vives was not only the stage where man lives and decides his eternal destiny, but also the mysterious, active, complex, and only partially understood reflection of the Divine Goodness whose possession constitutes the final end of all human desire.

7

Life

IN THE DEDICATION OF *De Anima et Vita* to the duke of Béjar, Vives announces that the treatise is to be divided into three books: the first, on the soul of the brutes, the second, on the rational soul, and the third, on the "affections" (*De affectionibus*) of the soul. Vives, however, did not exactly follow the original plan. The first part is especially disorganized. A general introduction on nutrition is followed by two chapters on growth and reproduction (Chapters 1 and 2), eight (Chapters 3 to 10) on sensation, one (Chapter 11) on "the rational soul" (*De anima rationabili*), and one on the soul in general (Chapter 12). For the sake of clarity I shall begin this discussion with a chapter on life in general, after that taking up the subject of sensation in a subsequent chapter. The last two chapters of his Book 1 will be discussed later.

Vives begins his study of life by reminding the reader that the distinction between lifeless and living things is exclusively based, as with all our knowledge of essence, on their different operations (*Ex solis operationibus*). Spontaneous locomotion, nutrition, and growth are the visible operations of life. Vives fails to make clear whether all three are cumulatively required in all living things, but he explicitly claims that, according to our observations, life is obviously inseparable from the last two, which are themselves inseparable from each other. Whatever is endowed with the "nutritive faculty" (*facultas autrix*) is also capable of growth. Whatever is alive, feeds itself and grows. It remains, however, questionable in what sense plants and sessile animals are said to move besides the motion that accompanies growth. The notion of growth as a sign of life is also complicated by some of Vives' statements in the first chapter, where he characterizes as "not absurd at all" (*haud prorsus est absurda;* M 3.306) the opinion of those who maintain that metals are alive and "grow" from within.[1] On the other hand, the idea that fire is "alive" is quickly dismissed by Vives as a peculiarity of

Roman religion with no other foundation than the close linkage between heat and the process of lively growth.

After failing to make altogether clear the general distinction between lifeless and living things, Vives proceeds in a similarly careless manner to divide the domain of life into four different "levels" (*quattuor gradus;* M 3.300). The first and lowest category of living things includes those organisms capable of feeding themselves and of growing, as all the plants are. The second group (such as sponges and shellfish) enjoys also the capacity to sense. The third group, which includes all birds and quadrupeds, has also a "cognitive life" (*vitam cogitativam;* M 3.300) capable of "memory and thought" (*sunt praedita ad memoriam et cogitationem;* ibid.). The last and highest form of life is "the life of reason or human life" (*vita rationalis seu humana;* M 3.301).

Vives' blurry taxonomies and incomplete characterizations betray a certain reluctance to spend his own intellectual energies in a patient and time-consuming study of the physical and animal domain. They also reveal a strong but inaccurate dependence on ancient learning, particularly the Aristotelian writings. Leaving aside the fact that Vives failed to provide a thorough description of vegetal life, his rash introduction to the study of life proves that he was not as sensitive as Aristotle to the finer distinctions between the highest forms of plant life and the lowest forms of animal life.[2] Nor can it be denied that Vives failed also to make a clear distinction between the different degrees of animal sensibility, and that in the process of characterizing its higher forms he used a language that tended to obscure the all-important distinction between nonhuman and human cognition.[3]

In several of his treatises, Aristotle observed that some animals seem to be capable of learning and are more intelligent than others because they show signs of being endowed with memory and imagination.[4] Vives' reference to the memory and *cogitatio* of the third group of living things—which Aristotle does not extend to all birds and quadrupeds—is probably a casual rendition of this Aristotelian teaching. By assigning *cogitatio* to the higher animals, Vives seems to be weakening the humanistic emphasis on the radical superiority and uncompromising uniqueness of man's "rational life," a term he nevertheless reserved to human ways of knowing. In any case, it seems obvious that Vives' humanism was not incompatible with the Aristotelian emphasis on the continuity of the scale of living forms. The force that directs the feeding of a plant, the sensation of a dog, and the rational processes of a human contemplative mind is the force of life that permeates all of nature and that manifests itself in different degrees of perfection. Reason, nevertheless, remains a unique gift of God to human beings.

The second and longer part of the general introduction deals with the nutritive soul (*anima alens*). Vives' account of the process of digestion is closer to the Hippocratic than to the Aristotelian tradition. It also avoids the highly abstract level of Aristotle's corresponding chapter in *On the Soul* (Book 2, Chapter 4) and constantly prefers the term *vis* to the traditional Latin term *potentia*. Although primitive in linguistic expression, its basic content is not incompatible with the nineteenth-century discovery that digestion can be explained in terms of chemical processes. Digestion, Vives teaches, is the transformation of food into an animated body by the power of the nutritive soul. This soul has two physical instruments: the primary instrument of heat and the secondary instrument of humidity (*calor et humor;* M 3.301). The latter tempers the heat of the body and prolongs life. When heat needs to be tempered by humidity, the body becomes thirsty; when both heat and humidity need to be reinforced, the body becomes hungry. Solid food is required to preserve the solidity of living organisms. The staple of all human beings includes bread or a bread substitute (*nationes omnes pane uti vel re aliqua quae panis vicem impleat;* M 3.303). Pure water lacks any nutritive value. The process of digestion includes the combustion of the food and the dissolution of food into its basic components. Animals are fed by "the like" and cured by "the contrary" (*perspicuum fit nos et similibus nutriri, contrariis curari;* M 3.302).[5]

The functions of the nutritive soul include therefore the power to attract, to retain, to burn, and to expurgate foods. It includes also the power to eliminate waste and to distribute the digested substances through the body and to assimilate them into one body. All these functions are mutually related, being constantly at work and distributed throughout the body, although not in the same proportion. Following Galen once again, Vives teaches that the combustion of food is performed by the stomach, the combustion of blood by the liver. Thirst and hunger are two forms of appetite. All living things were endowed with appetite for their own preservation. Appetite seeks what is useful and avoids what is harmful to life. These general principles, as we shall see later, apply equally to human emotional responses.

After this poorly organized introduction, Vives deals in the first chapter of *De Anima et Vita,* Book 1, with the power and process of growth that is found in all living things, but not found at all times. The nutritional process is constant. The power to reproduce is given to most living things only when they reach maturity. The power to grow is given until that point in time when the living organism stops growing and begins to shrink before death. Natural growth does not consist in the external juxtaposition of parts (*non est additio*

extrinsecus; M 3.305), but in the increase of observable magnitude by the
transformation and distribution of food through the inner recesses of the
body. All living organisms are therefore porous in nature. Size increases
through growth are limited by the Creator of nature. Man will never reach the
size of an oak, nor can the powers of the human soul be contained within the
body of an ant. Environmental circumstances affect size: sea animals are
bigger than terrestrial animals and terrestrial animals are bigger than birds.
Among humans the people from the North are generally more corpulent than
the people from the South.

The growing process of all living things is like a "second creation" (*velut
secunda creatio;* M 3.307). Although Nature cannot create from nothing, it
can "create" from such feeble beginnings that our judgment can hardly
distinguish those beginnings from nothing (*tam tenui principio, ut iudicio
nostro non valde videatur abesse a nihilo;* M 3.307).

The second chapter of Book I deals with the power of reproduction that
nature gave to "most" living things (*generatrix in plerisque;* M 3.305). Vives
departs from the Aristotelian opinion that "nutrition and reproduction are
due to one and the same psychic power,"[6] and proceeds to give an account of
the reproductive process (Chapter 2) that is a baffling mixture of sharp
observations and blind acceptance of such traditional ideas as spontaneous
generation and the incompleteness of the female with respect to the male. It is
also plagued by such naïve beliefs as the generation of monsters by human
mothers. The power of reproduction, Vives teaches, resides more in the seed
than in the matter where it is received. But if matter is not congruous with the
seed (*congruentem materiam;* M 3.309), nature produces monsters, as it
happens in Italy, Flanders, and Belgium, where women who eat too much
cabbage and drink too much beer give birth to animals or to children who are
half animals. The seed too can be responsible for these deformations. In the
case of sexual reproduction, the more important features of the offspring
proceed from the paternal seed; the more base ones from the maternal matter
(*ex materia matris*) in the same way as the nature of the soil affects the
growing process of a plant. Females are nothing but "incomplete males"
(*mas imperfectus*), males that have been deprived of the "right proportion"
of heat (*cui iusta defuit caloris mensura;* M 3.310).[7] The wisdom of the
creator ordained that in some cases life be born from the combined effort of
the strong and the weak. The offspring that bears resemblance to the father is
stronger and brighter than the offspring that takes after the mother. Plant
seedlings are more similar to their begetter than are animal offspring to their
parents. Brute animals, on the other hand, are more similar to their progeni-
tors than humans are, because their imagination is less agile than ours. Vives

never bothers to explain what the role of imagination might be in the reproductive process.

Some living things are born by spontaneous generation, such as flies, mosquitoes, ants, and bees, who are sexless. Others are born by sexual reproduction, as man, the dog, the horse, and the lion. Rats can be spontaneously born from waste or sexually from intercourse. All plants are spontaneously born from the seeds that the Creator delivered to "the power of the soil" (*vi terrae*), although human industry and care can make some of them "more suitable to our use" (*usui nostro aptiora*). There are trees, such as the tamarind, that yield no fruit and only reproduce when nature or man cuts off a stem from them and the stem grows roots in the soil.[8]

The reproductive faculty includes the male's power of ejecting the seed, the capacity in the female to receive and keep it, the power to mix the paternal seed and the maternal matter, the power to form and to push out the formed fetus at the proper time. An admirable variety of bodily parts and members corresponds to this variety of the soul's powers.

8

Sensation

V IVES' DISCUSSION OF SENSATION in *De Anima et Vita*, Book I, follows very closely the order of its Aristotelian model in *De Anima*. A short general introduction on sensation (Chapter 3) is followed by an analysis of the five external senses (Chapters 4–9). The section ends with a chapter on imagination and common sense (Chapter 10). While this structural similarity tends to accentuate Vives' dependence on Aristotle, it can also mislead the reader into underrating the significant differences between the two thinkers.

It is obvious that Vives shared with Aristotle some fundamental assumptions. Both considered sensation a form of cognition that placed animals above the vegetative life of plants and just below the rational life of human beings. But Vives was more eloquent than his master in bringing out the radically new perfections and complexities that even the lowest form of cognition adds to the mere process of nutrition and growth. Cognition opens up a living organism to the outside world. A plant is "enclosed in itself" (*quum tota plantae vita introrsum spectet*), totally unaware and deprived of any conscious interaction with the rest of the universe (M 3.311). Through its senses, an animal becomes cognizant of and reacts to the life-enhancing and life-threatening circumstances of its environment. In a rational universe, sensation is the necessary and sufficient condition of appetite. The same Creator who endowed animals with the capacity to become aware of the dangers and gains presented by the environment gave them also the tendency to avoid the former and seek the latter.

This teleology of the senses provides Vives with a principle with which to emphasize the difference between external and internal sensation, to justify a reasonable conjecture about the number of external senses that would belong to a "perfect animal," and to establish a hierarchy among the five external senses themselves. External sensation makes the animal cognizant of bodies present (although distant in some cases) and primarily serves bodily needs. Vives does not hesitate to call this type of sensation "bodily sensation" (*corporalis sensio*). Internal sensation is called "internal cognition" and through it the animal is capable of knowing corporeal things that are absent and of reaching higher forms of cognition, although such capacity is actualized in different degrees in brutes and human beings. In humans internal cognition represents the bridge between sensation and intelligence.

The External Senses

Vives reasons that, since animals have bodies and live among bodies, we can surmise that a perfectly endowed animal should have no less nor more than five external senses: the sense of touch to come into contact with the earthy, the sense of taste to know the watery and the moist, the sense of smell to feel thick air, the sense of hearing to detect air in motion, and the sense of sight to perceive "fiery" light (M 3.322).[1]

But Vives also stresses that not all senses are equally necessary to the preservation of life, nor are all of them given to all animals. In Book 3 of *De Anima et Vita* (Chapter 9), he compares the senses and the pleasure they afford in their relation to desire. In his discussion of the external senses, Vives limits himself to rank the senses according to the service they provide to animal life. In this respect, the most essential and complex sensory equipment is that of the sense of touch because it provides the animal with a wealth of information about the four elementary qualities (hot and cold, dry and moist) that, in their different combinations, determine the harmful and the beneficial character of all parts of the universe. For that reason the sense of touch, which is also the sense of pain, was not only given to all animals without exception, but is extended, with different degrees of sensitivity, through the entire body of the animal (*tactus est universis animantibus tributus et per universum corpus;* M 3.318). Man in particular was given an extraordinary tactile sensitivity on his fingers so that he could test, without much harm, the possible threats around him. Furthermore, nature made touch receptors "more sluggish" than visual or auditory ones to prevent the damage and fatigue that would follow from a sense that operates through contact. For the same reason, the sensations of touch and taste (that also require contact) are both more tiring and generally shorter than other sensations.

Touch and taste are therefore essential to animal life; vision and hearing are not. Fish do not hear but sense the motion of the water.[2] Vives considers the sense of smell a useful but not an indispensable aid to the sense of taste. Nature gave a good taste to the beneficial and a bad taste to the harmful, although not everything that is tasteful is beneficial nor everything that is distasteful is harmful. The sense of smell is the weakest among humans and "can easily be blunted or perverted" (*quin et facile in nobis tum obtupescit hic sensus . . . tum etiam corrumpitur;* M 3.324), not only by an inbalance of our bodily humors but also by vice and custom. There is no great harm—the moralist complains in a bitter and contrived tour de force—in losing the sense of smell when "our private and public morals are as corrupted as they are" (*haud parva molestia . . . praesertim ut nunc sunt mores privati et publici;* M 3.324). Education and custom have deformed nature to the point that what is pleasurable to smell is often harmful to the body and vice versa. We must conclude, therefore, that not only our emotional responses (as we shall see in the third part of this book), but even our animal appetitive reactions have to some extent lost their primitive innocence and reliability.

Vives calls sight the "most simple and best known" of all the senses, the paradigm of all cognition, the "private guide and master" that reveals to animals the face of the earth. Humans consider it the "most noble" (*praestantissimus habetur*) and the "most dear" (*carissimus*), the "author and inventor of all the arts and disciplines." Hearing is the sense of learning. Deaf animals, such as worms, "cannot be taught anything." In spite of all this, Vives seems to feel that seeing and hearing are not essential to animal life, and that they were given by the Creator only to those animals that "have to seek in the distance the food they need" and to those that use them in the service of "interior cognition" (*cognitioni serviunt interiori*) rather than in the exclusive service of bodily needs (M 3.324–25).[3]

These interesting but questionable generalizations on the proportions between animal needs and the operation of the five external senses are followed by some remarks on their interactions and the fallibility of their reports. The customary observation about the ways nature "compensates" the blind and the deaf with increased responsiveness in other senses, such as touch, is broadened with the more original and controversial claim that blind and deaf persons are also "compensated" with a more powerful memory and a clearer intelligence.

In dealing with the old controversy about the fallibility of sense reports, Vives carefully avoids any relapse into scholastic hairsplitting. He strongly emphasizes the "friendship and communion" (*communionem quasique amicitiam*) of sight and touch. The latter, for instance, corrects the illusion of three-dimensionality that a picture might convey. Vives reiterates also the traditional teaching that the senses cannot be deceived because they make no judgment and are merely passive, like a mirror. But he sounds a little more skeptical when he admits that the senses can nevertheless deceive the mind if the sense organ is defective, if the object is beyond or appears suddenly in the sensory field, or if the medium is not adequate to the sense. When all the proper conditions obtain, any false judgment of the mind about sense reports must be attributed to insufficient attention. This insistence on mental attention, one of Vives' recurring themes, is his way of translating into an educational language what he saw as the cosmic demand for strenuous effort in the achievement of perfection.

Vives' analysis of each external sense roughly follows the equally rough outline of the Aristotelian model. It deals, more or less in order, with the object, organ, and medium of the five senses. Still, the metaphysical implements so dear to Aristotle (the potential and the actual, the contrary and the like, action and passion, the mover and the moved) are more sparingly used. On the other hand, Vives' physiological descriptions of sense organs and his physics of sense stimulation reflect the modest advances of Renaissance science up to the first half of the sixteenth century. Vives' discussion is also enriched with frequent observations, some of them borrowed from either Aristotle or Galen.

Like Aristotle, Vives makes a distinction between a proper (*germana et vera sensilia*) and an improper or incidental (Vives does not use any one term) sense object. Substances, for instance, are never the proper object of any sense, since they are always "inferred by conjectures and reasonings" from their accidents.4 In Aristotle's *De Anima,* the clear definition of the proper object of each sense is the central task because of the general taxonomic principle that "objects specify faculties." Although Vives assumes the same principle, he enlarges the scope of the discussion by describing the sense organs with more detail and by explaining more carefully the impact of the medium upon the senses' operations.

The distinction between proper and incidental sense object is particularly important to Vives in relation to the sense of sight. The primary and proper object of sight is light, the secondary (but still proper) object is color, the third and incidental object is whatever is lighted and colored. Color is the light "that can be seen on the outer surface" (*lux quod in extima facie conspicitur*) of bodies that have a dense matter (*densiorem nacta est materiam*). A transparent body is a body of less density that has absorbed all the light into itself. White bodies are those that retain most of the light, black bodies those that retain a minimal amount of light. All colors are combinations of white and black. The sense of sight is so relevant to higher forms of cognition that the language of sight is applied to objects that are incidental to sight but are the proper objects of other senses ("Don't you see how sweet this apple is?") and even to rational knowledge itself ("Don't you see how sharp this argument is?"). To say "I see a king or a musician" is—Vives warns the reader—an improper manner of speaking (I only see an object that I know or believe to be the king) that has nevertheless been sanctioned by ordinary linguistic usage.

To decide whether the proper object of hearing is either the clash between two solids or the air set in motion by that clash is not only difficult but "absolutely unnecessary" (*difficilis ad explicandum questio et minime necessaria*). We know, however, that the clash between two soft bodies— such as wool and linen—does not produce any sound.[5]

The proper objects of touch are the four primitive qualities: the hot, the cold, the dry, and the moist; and their combinations: the hard, the soft, the rough, the smooth, the heavy, and the light. The names of the objects of taste and smell coincide with the names of their corresponding sensations.

The external organ or "instrument" of sight is the eye; the internal, the nerve that links it to the brain. Light reaches the eye through the pupil in "the shape of a pyramid" (*in formam pyramidis*). The base of the pyramid is the object seen; its top is the portion of the pyramid that penetrates through the pupil. When the object is large, the pupil tries to catch all the lines of the cone through its center by "turning around with extreme quickness" (*se circumvolvit mira celeritate*). Some people need magnifying glasses to see the contours of distant objects. Others must contract the pupil to see the detail of small ones. The eye, Vives says, works like a mirror. When the lens of the eye becomes concave, the image is magnified; when the lens becomes convex (*tumentia vero specula, et oculi exstantes*), the image is reduced in size (M 3.314). Primitive as this description of the focusing activity of the lens and the refractive power of the eyeball might appear to us, it certainly adds something to the information provided by Aristotle, while revealing some of the significant progress made in optics during the sixteenth century.

The external organ of hearing is the ear; the internal is the nerve that links it to the brain. Some people claim that the buzzing we hear when we plug our ears proves that they contain some air. Vives, however, thinks that the ears contain rather "a light and spongy humor" (*tenuem humorem ac spongiosum*) that is motionless and silent. The buzzing we hear when we plug our ears is caused by the external air that is pressed into the flaps of the outer ear (M 3.316).[6] In the same passage, Vives confesses his amazement at the sound produced inside a golden globe "without cracks" (*absque ulla rima*) that belonged to his last patroness and pupil, Doña Mencía de Mendoza. He was equally perplexed by the report that some fish seemed to have ears and often surfaced on the water to "hear" with apparent admiration or horror the sounds above the sea waves. These, he wrote, are "mysteries of nature that are incomprehensible to us" (M 3.316).

The organ of the sense of touch consists of the flesh and the nerves that link it to the brain. The organ of taste is "the nerve spread through the tongue." This nerve is most sensitive on the tip of the tongue (as human fingers are) and is capable therefore of processing its information with extraordinary quickness to the part of the tongue that touches the palate, where the sensation of taste properly takes place. The organs of smelling consist of the mucous membrane (*sensorium est in carunculis narium*) inside the nasal cavity and the nerves that link it to the brain (M 3.318).

Vives' observations on the impact of the medium on the operations of each sense are perhaps the most original part of this small treatise on sensation. He considered the influence of the medium on the sensation itself in terms of causality (*habet quoque medium causam aliquam*) and proportion. Light is not only the original object of sight but also its proper medium. As a medium, light must be proportionate to the organ; we do not see at night nor when we are blinded by excessive light. This proportion differs from animal to animal. The eagle can stare unharmed at the sunset that hurts our eyes. Because light is also the object of sight, it is impossible to see an object that is not lighted even if there is light between it and the eye. On the other hand, a lighted object can be seen through the intervening darkness. People who carry torches at night can be seen by others, but they do not see them (M 3.314). This is also the reason why things that absorb more light are more visible at night, such as cinders, diamonds, snow, mirrors, copper, and fireflies. Light as a medium also requires a certain distance between the object and the organ. Objects that touch the eye are as invisible as those that are too distant. Sight is also disturbed by the motion of the object, the intervening air, or another medium of higher density (such as water and glass).

Vives' explanation of sound phenomena such as the cracking of a whip and the echo effect follows Aristotle very closely. But he valiantly tries to explain why the last part of an echo is heard more clearly than the beginning, an explanation that Aristotle did not provide. He emphasizes more strongly than Aristotle that every noise is constantly echoed through the universe, even when it becomes imperceptible to us. The motion of air itself weakens other sounds. That is why we hear better on a calm night than on a windy day. Sound waves propagate in circles, but the circles become disrupted when the medium itself is in a state of flux, as we see when we throw a stone into water in motion (M 3.317). Saliva is the medium of the sense of taste and is therefore insipid (the medium is always neutral with respect to the sense-object). A dry tongue is not capable of tasting anything. The saliva of sick people spoils the good taste of pleasant food (M 3.319–20).

The Internal Senses

Under the general title of "internal cognition," Vives undertakes the study of imagination, fantasy, memory, common sense, and the estimative. Vives thinks that the existence of these internal faculties is implied by the obvious fact that both the brutes and man are capable of perceiving corporeal things that are absent, an argument that unfortunately does not always apply to the estimative faculty and only in a peculiar way to common sense.

Imagining for Vives is an internal seeing of what is not present, and he conceives of the imagination as "the eye of the soul" (*imaginativae actio est in animo quae oculi in corpore;* M 3.327). Although he sees no great harm in calling imagination and fantasy by the same name in ordinary language, he asserts that it is more correct to make a clear distinction between the two. Imagination and fantasy are two different faculties because their operations are different. The former is merely passive, while the latter is "marvelously free and active" (*mirifice expedita et libera;* M 3.327) in combining and separating whatever the imagination has merely received. Imagination is also more tied to bodily changes, as one can see in the imagination of sexual matters and in the case of pregnant women whose imagined objects of desire become erratic and unpredictable. Although both imagination and fantasy are found in humans and in animals, Vives' attention seems to focus almost exclusively upon the moral consequences of human imaginings and fantasizing. Human imagination, assailed by the spiritual promptings of good and evil spirits, can be the source of uplifting thoughts but also the origin of disturbing passions that need to be controlled by reason (M 3.327).

Vives defines common sense as the sense "by which absent sensibles are judged and those that belong to different senses are discerned" (*quo iudicantur sensibilia absentia, et discernuntur ea quae variorum sunt sensuum;* M 3.327). Through common sense, taste is capable of discerning between the present sensation of sweetness and the absent sensation of bitterness.7 Through common sense, we are also able to distinguish between the color and the taste of a fruit and to attribute both to the same object, an example that I take literally from Vives (M 3.322). In this passage, Vives mentions also the *sensilia communia* — such as motion, size, number, figure, shape, and location — which are usually assigned to common sense and which Vives apparently overlooked in the introductory definition. Here, as on other occasions, the reader has the overwhelming impression that Vives was much more interested in those operations of the soul that are directly or indirectly related to the study of man's emotional and moral life than in those operations that are more relevant to a speculative theory of knowledge.

The estimative (*extimativa* or *extimatrix*) is, Vives writes, "the faculty that causes the impetus of judgment from the sensible species" (*facultas quae ex sensibilibus speciebus impetum judicii parit*), a judgment about the beneficial or the harmful aspects of what is perceived. It involves a double action: first, a judgment about the nature of the perceived object, then, a second judgment about "how convenient or harmful it might be to us." The first judgment follows our sensation of sight or hearing. In the second, the mind is "forcefully seized and moved by a secret stimulus of nature" (*in posteriore animus occulto naturae stimulo agitur et rapitur impete*). The sheep flees from a wolf it has never seen before and humans run away from monsters. The judgment of the estimative faculty is followed by a desire for the beneficial or an aversion to the harmful. Desire and aversion are followed respectively by motion toward or motion away from the object. These instinctive reactions and physical movements explain animal behavior and also play an important part in the understanding of human emotions and actions (M 3.328).8 Vives postpones his study of memory until Book 2, where he deals exclusively with human memory. The instruments of the internal senses are localized in different parts of the brain: the imagination in the front, the fantasy and the estimative in the center, the memory in the back. Although the internal senses have their "different workshops" (*ceu diversas officinas*) localized in different parts of the brain, Vives suggests that at least some of them are less body-dependent and more active than the external senses. These, he repeats, are merely passive, as a mirror in which something is reflected or as the wax in which something is impressed. Furthermore, external sensations are not projected outwards but "received inside." The fact that most external sense organs are shaped as receptacles (ear, nose, eyes) betrays their passive character. What is received inside are the "sensible species," a term that Vives simply interprets as an impact made by the external object on the sensorium or organ through the motion of air or light and through direct contact. Such is not the case with at least some internal senses. When we imagine something, the impression is merely received. But when the fantasy separates or combines the parts of what has been impressed in the lucid spirit (*in lucido spiritu*), it becomes an activity of that spirit.

All the ambiguities and difficulties that are inseparable from the doctrine of animal spirits are also an obstacle to our understanding of Vives' thought on the relations between the body and the soul and on the active role of the imagination in the process of rational cognition. In the next chapter, we turn our attention to this task.

9
Intelligence

In Book 2 of *De Anima et Vita* Vives discusses the operations of the rational soul. In the introduction, he lists three "faculties," "powers," or "functions" of the rational soul: intelligence, memory, and will. He recognizes that to investigate the beginning, progress, decay, and breakdown of these powers is a most difficult and arduous task because humans are not endowed with a faculty higher than the intellect to observe their own rational operations. The intellect can observe the operations of the senses much better than its own. Still, the study of our rational life is the most beautiful and useful of all endeavors.

In attempting to carry out this imposing and promising research, Vives gradually extricates himself from the self-imposed limitations of Aristotle's *On the Soul,* Book 3. The first five chapters of Vives' Book 2 seem to follow the Aristotelian speculation about the intellectual process that leads from simple understanding to rational inference, judgment, and contemplation. But even they include significant departures from pure Peripatetic doctrine. Chapter 9 represents a clarification of the central notions of opinion, science, and wisdom. This is the part of Vives' treatise that I intend to discuss in this chapter. The rest of Vives' study leaves Aristotle behind and shows at his best the Christian humanist in his lifelong effort to comprehend the human resources that play an essential role in moral choices and in education, a topic to be analyzed in later chapters.

Simple Intelligence

Intellectual knowledge begins with a "first and simple apprehension" of those things that are offered to the mind by the external senses if the object is present, or by the imagination if it is absent. This cognition is called "simple" not because it is limited to the knowledge of what has no parts, but rather because it is a form of knowledge involving neither any comparison nor inference. The simple intelligence (*simplex intelligentia*) of suprasensible things is only possible when reason offers to the understanding the conclusions of its own inferences. In this case, therefore, simple intelligence grasps the conclusions but is not involved in the inferential process that led to them. As in the case of corporeal things with which we have never been acquainted, the fantasy attaches to this concept of suprasensible things an image constructed from those material things that have been given to us by experience. Vives emphasizes that images are never universal, no matter how "blurred and tenuous" (*confussisima ac tenuissima;* M 3.344) they might be. Only a concept that is reached by a rational discourse is universal. Vives thus disposes of the lengthy and sophisticated scholastic debate on the intellectual knowledge of the singular in a single paragraph.

Soon his attention turns to more mundane and practical matters. What are the images and concepts of the blind? What are the internal and external impediments to this first and simple apprehension by the intellect? How can we prevent the mind from being blocked by obsessive thoughts or from wandering when it encounters the distraction of superficial and unconnected thoughts? How does the body interfere with this first step of the cognitive process? What is the impact of bodily fatigue upon intellectual sharpness? How can we control the negative impact of strong and irresistible sensations or emotions? What is the relevance of mental attention, novelty, recreation, proper diet and pleasant feelings to intellectual life? (M 3.344–45)?

Memory

Vives proceeds to claim that the second step in the cognitive process is required by the limited nature of our mind and by the temporal character of human existence. Since we are not capable of thinking all the time nor capable of thinking of everything at the same time, we need to store our thoughts in the "receptacle" of our memory, where, as William James would put it, they remain "liable" to be "recollected" when we need them. As one could expect from the writings of a humanist seeking to understand the psychology of the learning process and the interaction between memory and emotion, Vives' chapter on memory is strikingly original and characteristic. One can certainly hear in it the voices of the classics, but they are all conveniently modulated to serve Vives' own philosophical tune.

Still, Vives' basic teaching on memory does not represent an important departure from Aristotle's *On Memory and Reminiscence*. Both writers teach that memory is the necessary condition of learning, that remembering is different from recollecting, and that retentiveness in remembering differs from excellence in recollecting. They also think that remembering is a function that human beings share with those animals capable of perceiving time and that recollecting, on the other hand, represents a "mode of inference" and "a sort of investigation" that belongs exclusively to persons.[1]

Vives, however, enriches Aristotelian thought by making a distinction between the *recordatio* that is caused by a simple intuition (*simplici intuitu animi*) and that which is gradually achieved through discourse (*per gradus quosdam et discursum*). We share the former with some animals; the latter, which is more properly called *reminiscentia* or *recultus*, is an exclusively human function and is preceded by what Vives calls *consideratio* (M 3.345–46).

Both Aristotle and Vives emphasize the relevance of age and of the emotional strength of the original impression to retentiveness of memory. Aristotle, however, seeks with characteristic tenacity a clearly articulated understanding of some theoretical but fundamental questions about memory and recollection that Vives, with his typical detachment from subtle speculation, almost entirely ignores. Aristotle's first concern is to define the proper object of memory and to specify whether memory is perception or conception, a function of the senses or a function of the intellect. Aristotle teaches that memory always involves a presentation that relates to a past presentation as its likeness. Memory, however, is not the presentation as such, but rather that "state or affection" of the presentation by which it is related to a past one, an affection that implies the perception of the time elapsed. He therefore defines remembering (or memory) as "the state of a presentation related as a likeness to that of which it is a presentation." As such, memory is "a function of the primary faculty of sense perception, i.e., of that faculty whereby we perceive time."[2] Sensible objects are therefore the proper objects of memory; intellectual objects are only incidental to it.

Vives defines memory as "the faculty of the soul by which it retains in the mind what it had known through some sense, external or internal." The seat or "workshop" of memory is found in the occiput of the brain. Memory has two powers, as do the hands: the power to grasp and the power to retain. These powers depend on the humidity of the brain. Moist brains learn and forget quickly while dry brains are slow in grasping but also in forgetting. The best memory is found in the proper balance of both qualities (moist and dry), as in children. Bodily health, a proper diet, and good sleep are "a great help to memory" (M 3.435–46).

Vives' thoughts in Book 2, Chapter 2 of *De Anima et Vita,* and his inclusion of memory among the internal senses as the "faculty" that retains the images received through the senses and impressed on the imagination

(M 3.326) seem to coincide more or less with the Aristotelian doctrine of memory. But Vives tends to obscure matters by dealing with memory under the general heading of "rational life," and as one of the three faculties (together with the intellect and the will) that God gave exclusively to human beings as the proper equipment to seek and reach their eternal destiny.[3] He also fails furthermore, to provide a clear explanation of the way in which past thoughts can be remembered or how our discursive reason can make use of them in the process of thinking.

Aristotle was also more careful than Vives in defining the process of recollecting and in distinguishing it from relearning and rediscovering. His magnificent effort to explain the assumed fact that we are able not only to sense a present image as the likeness of a past presentation, but also to distinguish between a greater and a smaller time or between a determinate or an indeterminate time-notion, finds no intellectual sympathy in Vives.[4] Instead of conceptual accuracy, Vives strives after psychological descriptions based on introspection. Vives' descriptions of the different types of forgetfulness—a theme Aristotle forgot to analyze—and of the processes of recollection are not only much richer in psychological detail than anything Aristotle wrote on the topic, but also bear a charming personal touch that one would never hope to find in the works of the Greek master.

Vives compares the four types of forgetting to the way an image appears on a canvas. The image might have been completely erased, partially damaged, hidden from the viewer, or "concealed by a veil" (*quasi velo quodam contecta*). The "most evident and certain truths" that were given to us by nature itself can also be forgotten "as if" we had learnt them from nature (M 3.348).

The first type of forgetting demands a whole new learning. The fourth type requires the rehabilitation of bodily or mental health. Only the second and the third types are subject to that process of "investigation" or "restoration" that James compared to the "rummaging of a house in the search of an object lost." Vives' description of this process is doubtless one of the most original sections of his entire treatise.

The description begins with a concrete example. A golden ring reminds us of its craftsman, the memory of the craftsman evokes that of the queen's necklace, the queen's necklace leads us to remember the war that the queen's husband waged, the war brings back the memory of the army's captains, the captains direct our thought to their ancestors or to their children, from there we come to think about the disciplines they studied, and so on without end. This chain of associations can sometimes be more structured. The cause evokes the effect or vice versa, the effect is associated with the instrument, the part with the whole, a location with a person, the similar with the similar or with its opposite. This journey can proceed gradually or by leaps. Scipio makes me think of the Turks (a very personal association), the name of Cicero brings back the name of Lactantius (who imitated Cicero), and Lactantius brings back the memory of copper engraving.[5] This entire process of tracing back our memories can happen spontaneously or be directed by a command of the will. The spontaneous association of a present with a past experience can itself be the result of a past association of that experience with sensations of either pleasure or pain. If a sound is remembered as associated with a happy feeling, we tend to feel happy whenever we hear the same sound. Even animals welcome the sound of a voice they associate with a pleasurable taste and run away at the sound of a whip. Vives confessed that he could not eat cherries without feeling sick because as a child they had given him painful indigestion. He observes also that in the case of spontaneous recall the less important tends to evoke the more important rather than vice versa. The house of a friend made him always think of the friend, while the sight of the friend did not always bring back the memory of the house (M 3.349–50).

These and similar passages reveal the vivid contrast between Aristotle's speculative inquisitiveness and Vives' penchant toward introspective analysis. Their different talents correspond neatly to their respective intellectual vocations. Thus, in the particular case of memory, probably the best way to obtain a more accurate profile of Vives as a thinker is to compare him not to a contemplative philosopher such as Aristotle but to other moralists and educators such as Plutarch and Quintilian.

Plutarch's influence on humanist educators, including Erasmus, was also strongly felt by Vives. To Plutarch, memory was "the storehouse of learning" and "the Mother of the Muses." But it was also the only human resource that reached its peak in childhood and therefore made imperative what Erasmus called the "early and liberal education of the child."[6] While Plutarch insisted on memory training for children, Quintilian emphasized its importance in the education of a prospective orator. To Quintilian, memory was "the treasure-house of eloquence," the indispensable condition of the speaker's power.[7] As a moralist and educator, Vives too recognized the retentive power of children's memory and the urgent necessity of early memory cultivation. But in *De Disciplinis* and *De Anima et Vita,* Vives was more concerned with the role of memory in higher education and with the analysis of mnemonic processes in the adult.[8] Nor was he exclusively interested in the "art of memory" that facilitates the instant recall that Quintilian required from the perfect orator. Vives' analysis and observations on the ways memory is either reinforced or weakened surpassed in both scope and detail those of his classic models.

The original impression in memory, Vives teaches, is deepened by attention and emotion. By "attention'" Vives means not only the absence of distraction, but also the presence of care and concern (*attente accepta et cum cura;* M 3.348).[9] Whatever is strongly "apprehended" by our minds is also better retained in them. That is why children with a short attention span, sick people, and drunkards soon forget what they have superficially grasped. Emotion, too, deepens the original impression. "Whatever entered the mind with great joy or pain is remembered for a very long time" (*quae cum maxima laetitia vel dolore sunt in animum ingressa, horum longissima est memoria;* M 3.3438). Although Vives is convinced that no other faculty of the soul could thrive more with exercise or weaken more with inactivity, he still criticizes the excessive medieval emphasis on memorizing and the fashionable abuse of mnemonics. Following the example of Erasmus, Vives often recommends the use of notebooks, a significant departure from the medieval stress on oral learning. Vives joins Quintilian in rejecting Plato's claim that the use of written characters is a hindrance to memory, and he is convinced that the very effort to put into orderly writing the material to be remembered is a powerful way of engraving it more deeply on our memory.[10]

As a psychologist and educator, Vives makes other interesting observations on the different types of memory. Some people remember words better than facts. Others remember the trivial better than the important, the distant better than the recent past, public events better than private gossip, what affects others better than their own interests, verse rather than prose. Recall is often misled by similarity or by some secret association. We use the word *problema* instead of *enthymema*, we call Gregory George, we take Xenocrates for Aristotle, and we confuse Cicero with Demosthenes. To recall what we forgot is much more difficult than to recognize it when it is presented to us. Speaking a foreign language is harder than reading it, and recalling the name of Socrates' father is more difficult than answering the question, "Was Democritus Socrates' father?" Memory is reinforced during sleep. What we learn at night before going to bed becomes more deeply engraved in our memory than what we learn during the day. Children have better memory because they are not distracted by worries and concerns. What we sometimes fail to recall often comes back to our minds when we are thinking about other matters or even during sleep.

Composite Intelligence

In the shortest chapter of *De Anima et Vita,* Book 2, Vives tries to explain the difference between simple and composite intelligence and between composite intelligence and judgment. Composite intelligence differs from simple intelligence in that fantasy adds to the simple imagination "its own figments and other forms that are derived from those qualities and actions apprehended through the senses" (*addit ei phantasia simulacra et formas alias ex iis qualitatibus, quae hauriuntur sensibus*). The fantasy, however, "does not affirm or deny anything by means of the copula" (*nihil coniungit aut separat per copulam*). It simply gathers together the elements of a possible judgment: "this such or not such, this acting this way or another" (*hoc tale vel non tale, hoc modo aut alio*). This explains why children and ignorant people tend to accumulate nouns without connectives in their speech. Composite intelligence is nevertheless more than just a complex perception. Composite intelligence adds to perception an act by which it compares the parts that make up the perception itself and adds to them the understanding—not yet formulated in an explicit judgment—of the logical relations between those parts. Composite intelligence is therefore richer than complex perception but stops short of the final act of judgment. Vives' full explanation of the difference between composite intelligence and judgment—an obviously difficult enterprise—does not emerge until his introductory remarks in the chapter on memory (Chapter 5).

Reasoning or Discourse

Reasoning, Vives teaches, follows understanding, consideration, and comparison. It consists essentially in "the inferential progress from one or several things into another or others" (*est collationis progressio ab uno ad aliud vel alia;* M 3.353). This progress can be gradual and continuous (*per suos gradus continua series discurrens*) or intermittent and by leaps (*transiliens et medios aliquos intermittens;* M 3.354).

Having defined the process of reasoning, Vives proceeds with great care to specify the role the imagination plays in it. Although basically in agreement with Aristotle, Vives' analysis is also tinted with Platonic influences. Furthermore, the vivid metaphors and the moralistic tone of this section seem more inspired by ethical than by purely epistemological preoccupations.

Expedite discourse needs the assistance of fantasy (*opus nihilominus est ad expeditum discursum ministerio phantasiae*), but should not be carried away by it. Discourse uses the figments of the imagination, but must not "get mixed with them." The imagination provides only pictures of "individual accidents" while reason "glides over them and looks at them from the distance" (*aspicit procul;* M 3.354). When discourse gets entangled with the visions of our fantasy, it "slides down" into a slippery path and risks getting carried away by "a gushing stream." The art of reasoning well about the proper subject matter requires "great mental health" and a proper division of mental labor. The senses serve the imagination, the imagination helps the fantasy, the fantasy assists consideration and recollection, recollection facilitates comparative scrutiny, and scrutiny ministers to discourse. The senses see shadows, the fantasy images, the intelligence bodies, and reason powers and forms (M 3.354).

As in the case of most rational processes, rational discourse can be either spontaneous or commanded by the will. In the first case, the principles of operation are less clearly known than in the second. In general, the human mind proceeds from the singular to the universal, from the material to the spiritual, from the effects to the causes, from the better known to the more hidden and recondite. There are many types of argument (*loci*): from negation to affirmation (not this, therefore that), from negation to negation (neither this nor that), from affirmation to negation (this, therefore not that), and from affirmation to affirmation (this, therefore that).

The relation between our speculative and practical discourse is better understood by comparing the way in which brutes and human beings encounter and are attracted by the good. What is good for irrational animals is clear (*apertum*) and bodily. Brute animals "do not live in darkness" (*tenebras non habent*). Their estimative faculty is an "inclination" (*pronitates*) that makes them move toward any individual good that is presented to their senses. Animals are simply "drawn to the first good that is presented to them" (*ad primum oblatum bonum rapiuntur*). But the good that the human will seeks to embrace is "hidden in the mind" (*occultum in mente*), a good that can only be found by "an investigation of a truth shrouded in darkness" (*opus fuit investigatione veri in tenebris*). The rational discourse that searches for the true and rejects the false is called "speculative reason." The rational discourse that tries to find the good and avert evil is called "practical reason." Practical reason offers its findings to the will (*transit ad voluntatem;* M 3.355). Speculative reason stays within itself (*sistit sibi*). Practical reason about the good is called prudence; practical reason about the useful is called art. Practical reason thrives with experience and speculative reason is sharpened by education.

Vives seems to be telling us that human beings were endowed with reason for the main purpose of finding what is truly good for them, a good that is incorporeal (God), and the knowledge of which requires a faculty superior to sense and imagination. The attraction toward the good that man, "the most excellent being under the sky" (*quo nihil est sub coelo praestantius*) possesses in a higher degree than animals presupposes a capacity for rational investigation that enables man to transcend the domain of the sensible. In asserting, however, that such is the primary task of reason, Vives abandoned the traditional interpretation of Aristotle, according to which the knowledge of what is good as good was merely the task of right deliberation and not the supreme end of reason at its best, speculative reason. This blending of truth and goodness that probably lay at the root of Vives' moral pragmatism signifies, in my opinion, a decisive departure from Aristotelian authority. This opinion is further confirmed by Vives' chapter on contemplation, his last chapter on man's cognitive life.[11] Nature, Vives contends, has provided human beings not only with an attraction toward the good, but also with some rules about good and evil. These rules have been partially obscured by original sin, but not totally erased. The theologians call them *synteresis, conscientia* (Saint Jerome), *iudicatorium* (Saint Basil) or *lux mentis nostrae* (Saint John of Damascus). The philosophers have called them *anticipationes* or *naturales informationes*. Vives calls them *mentis nostrae sive lux sive censura* (M 3.356), and thinks that they cause us to praise virtue and condemn vice. Not everybody is equally aware of those rules. They become more clearly defined through experience, education, and reflection (M 3.356).

The identification of truth and goodness leads Vives to extend the theological notion of moral conscience to the theoretical and speculative level. While rejecting Plato's contention in the *Meno* that "to know is to remember what the soul had known before birth," Vives freely subscribes to the more Stoic teaching that man was born with a "propensity toward the truth," a propensity he characterizes as the "seed of all knowledge," "the beginnings and origins of the arts, practical prudence and all the sciences."[12] This seminal knowledge is nevertheless limited to the domain of those things "that are naturally constant " (*de cognitione rerum natura constantium*) and does not include skills acquired by experience or the knowledge of human contrivances, such as languages.

The purpose of human discourse is to extend our knowledge beyond the domain of sensible things, to infer the unknown from the known. As such, rational discourse is an exclusively human power. Vives criticizes Plutarch for having failed to provide philosophical reasons to back this claim and characterizes Valla as "blind" for having upheld the "absurd" opinion that animals can also reason. Animals can reason, Vives writes, in the sense that they can proceed from A to B, but not in the sense that they can infer B from A by comparing the classes to which A and B belong. This conclusion is confirmed by the fact that animals have no religion: their minds are unable to rise above the sensible and to infer the existence of their Creator. It is further confirmed by their lack of speech and by their external appearance, always bent down to the earth. The hierarchy of the universe also demands that animals occupy an intermediate rank between plants, which cannot sense, and humans, who can reason (M 3.358).

In *De Anima et Vita,* Vives merely claims that the human mind is able to "rise above sense and fantasy," to understand that "we are surrounded by darkness" as a person who is in a room "understands" but does not "see" what lies beyond its walls (M 3.361). A more careful description of the intellectual process that makes metaphysics possible by leading us from the knowledge of the material to the knowledge of the immaterial can nevertheless be found in *De Prima Philosphia* (M 3.194–96).

The senses see, hear, touch, taste, and smell their proper objects. Common sense apprehends size, number, rest, motion, figure, state, and the absence of sensible qualities (darkness, silence). Fantasy assisted by memory and without any inferential discourse knows the subject (man, lion, goat) of the sensible qualities. From actions fantasy knows the agent, as from the perception of heat it knows the presence of fire. All these forms of knowledge are common to man and brute.

By a simple judgment and by simple reasoning, man proceeds from the cause to the effect, from the effect to the cause, from the action to the end, from the instrument to the action, and through similar inferences, to realities not immediately given in experience but that nevertheless "consist of things of this external nature" (*quae omnino exterioris hujus naturae constant;* M 3.195). Vives calls such entities *deprehensa.* There are, however other entities that are incorporeal — such as God, the angels, the devils, the mind, immortality, vice, virtue, science, prudence — and which the human mind reaches only through a "difficult ascent above the senses" (*ardua quadam assurrectione supra sensus*), following not a straight but "a winding and treacherous" path. Vives calls these incorporeal entities *indagata sive inquisita.*[13] The mind can also know what Vives calls *excogitata,* contrived by our minds for the sake of an end, such as the human disciplines (the arts, mathematics, geometry, public administration, music). There are also the objects of fiction or *conficta* — such as honor, insult, offense — that would be nothing if we were not persuaded of their existence, and things that are never real, such as centaurs and chimeras. Finally, there are objects that we envisage in the future (*prospecta*) or remember from the past (*respecta*). Everything that is, shares being: "that which God gives first of all to everything that He creates." The Latin language, Vives says, made extensive use of the word *res,* but the word *ens* is a better translation of the Greek *tò ōn,* an expression, that, as Quintilian noted, cannot be translated into a single Latin term (M 3.194–97).

In this rather hasty and simple manner Vives tackles and disposes of some of the most abstruse metaphysical questions that had been thoroughly debated by medieval scholastics and, *mutatis mutandis,* would be later discussed by Kant and his followers and critics. In *De Anima et Vita,* these important epistemological claims are stated simply, in vivid metaphorical language, but are not carefully analyzed nor convincingly proven by argument. Vives was much more interested in describing the different types of intellectual temperament and the practical obstacles to a sound reasoning than in analyzing the process of reasoning itself. In this, as in many other instances, the psychologist clearly overpowered the philosopher.

Judgment

Vives' relatively short chapter on judgment (Chapter 5) is of capital importance to an understanding of his theory of knowledge, his conception of dialectic, his views on the complex relation betwen cognitive performances and emotional responses, and his typology of personality structure. The chapter also represents a moderate form of Academic skepticism probably derived from Cicero's *Academica,* but alien in many respects to the Peripatetic tradition (although not incompatible with some of the suggestions we find in the *Posterior Analytics*).[14] Vives' psychological rather than logical description of the act of judging is clearly couched in forensic terms. Judgment for Vives is more than the simple act by which subject is linked to the predicate by the copula. During the process of reasoning the judgment rests, listening to and pondering the evidence at hand. When the discourse has been completed, the intellect renders its judgment on the validity of the procedures and on the conclusion reached by them. In assessing correct procedure, the judgment relies on the rules of logic (procedural law). If the judgment finds out that the discourse was not properly conducted, it restrains itself and refuses to pronounce any sentence, unless the conclusion reached is so congenial to our prejudices and emotions that we are willing to overlook formal violations. If the conclusion appears to be validly inferred but in conflict with a previously held opinion, the judgment is upheld (*haeret judicium*) until we are forced to change our opinion by the force of the argument itself, the only force capable of moving our intellect. Well-educated and prudent people are more reluctant to rush into a judgment, as they are more aware of all the possible objections against it. Temperament also plays an important part: people who have little confidence in themselves can more easily be influenced by the opinions of others. A strong emotion, on the other hand, such as fear, can cloud our judgment and prevent it from pronouncing its final sentence. If we fear enough the truth of the conclusion, all possible objections to it—even the invalid ones—become aggrandized and overwhelming.

A healthy and proper judgment is more important to our intellectual and moral life than experience, erudition, and sharpness of intellect. The difference between intellectual mediocrity and intellectual excellence is based exclusively on the capacity to judge well. Assent is the judgment that the conclusions of an argument are true and therefore congenial to our mind. Dissent is the opposite of assent. Belief (*fides*) is a strong assent; suspicion, a weak one. Doubt or ambiguity is the suspension of judgment between assent and dissent. Credulity and incredulity are names of mental habits. Credulity is strengthened by hope and fear and is often found among kind, simple, and humble people. Incredulity is fostered by ignorance, by conflicting expectations, by excessive hope, by accumulated experience, or by an arrogant inclination not to believe anything one has not found by oneself. People who are envious, greedy, ambitious, perverse, or old people who have been hardened by many bad experiences, or people who have spent their life in risky dealings tend often to suspect the worst or to exaggerate the reasons that make them incredulous. A feeling of security makes us more gullible than a feeling of being threatened. We are more inclined to believe tales than to yield in a scholastic debate. Rhetoric is more powerful than dialectic in persuading simple folk.

In Chapter 9 (*De cognitionibus seu notitiis*), Vives clarifies his concept of opinion. Wisdom is the supernatural knowledge of God, the "changeless and eternal nature."[15] Opinion is the knowledge of what is generally the case but admits of some exceptions, such as "Mothers love their children," "This type of medicine heals this type of disease," and so forth. The arts are based on such opinions. Science is the knowledge of that which remains constant through change (*quod est in natura mutabili perpetuum et constans*), a knowledge that is based on "the light we received from nature" (*lucem habemus a natura inditam*). This light shines with great power over the initial steps of our reasoning process, but is darkened in the long run, not by the nature of things themselves but by our manner of cognition.[16] Hence the perplexing variety of human opinions about the true and the good. Age, bodily constitution, health or sickness, habits, actions, emotions, all of these affect the intellectual and moral temper of individuals.

Contemplation

Contemplation is the repose that follows reasoning and judgment, the "quiet and safe inspection" of what has been attained by the process of reasoning and the approbation of judgment. This inspection is not used as a means to reach an end but causes by itself a pleasure that is based on the congruity between our intellectual faculty and its object, between our natural desire to know and the truth we have attained. The quality and amount of this pleasure depends on the individual's *ingenium* and on the nature of the truth he has reached. Nature has provided human beings with a strong desire to know the causes of everything. This desire is so compelling that even pagans were willing to give up everything to enjoy the pleasure of contemplation (M 3.381).

The most blissful and secure contemplation will be the vision of God in the eternal life. Vives emphasizes the restful and secure character of human contemplation so much that he seems to think that, at least in its full measure, contemplation is reserved for those who, either temporarily in this life or eternally in the next, are free from the responsibility of making urgent moral choices or from securing their own material survival.

10

Ingenium

BETWEEN THE CHAPTERS ON judgment and contemplation (*De Anima et Vita,* Book 2), Vives interjects four original chapters dealing with *ingenium* (Chapter 6), language (Chapter 7), the process of learning (Chapter 8), and opinion (Chapter 9). Having discussed the last of these in connection with judgment, we proceed to analyze here the complex concept of *ingenium* and its relation to learning. Vives' doctrines regarding language deserve separate treatment.

The humanists' rejection of what they considered formal and useless abstractions led naturally to a keen recognition of human individuality. Humanist educators recommended an intelligent respect for and a careful observation of the pupils' individual traits and aptitudes. Renaissance writers, painters, and sculptors explored in many different ways the riches of individual uniqueness. The philosophers, on the other hand, limited themselves to repeating some of the observations made by Quintilian or to expanding Galen's classification of temperaments.[1] Vives was also cognizant of this classical tradition, but more than most of his contemporaries, he was able to enrich it with his exceptional gift for psychological observation and introspection.

All that Vives has to say about human individuality is encompassed under the term *ingenium,* a word that he took from the classics but which he uses in a complex though not always well-defined manner.[2] In classical Latin, *ingenium* (from *ingigno*) was applied both to human beings and to inanimate objects to mean either natural disposition, temperament, mood, the character of a place (*ingenium loci*), or the natural inclination, natural desire, literary talent, cleverness, skill, ingenuity, or the person or thing endowed with such qualities. In Vives' writings, the prevalent sense of the word is laid out at the beginning of Chapter 6 (Book 2) of *De Anima et Vita:* "We call *ingenium* the whole power of our mind as exercised and revealed with the aid of our (bodily) organs" (*universam mentis nostrae vim ingenium nominari placuit, quod se instrumentorum ministerio exerit et patefacit;* M 3.364). In this strict sense then, *ingenium* means human intelligence conditioned by bodily temperament. In other contexts, however, and even in this very chapter, the meaning of what is conditioned and the meaning of what does the conditioning is greatly expanded.

By "the power of our mind" Vives can mean the following: ability to control the imagination, judgment, creativity, mental laziness or alertness, intuitiveness, mental perseverance or instability, patience or impatience, attention to detail or the span of attention, talent for specialization or generalization, speed in grasping, retentiveness of memory, power of recall, excellence in analyzing or in synthesizing, ability to speak or write, learning habits, motivation, problem-solving capacity, manual or speculative ability, power to imitate, professional vocation and aptitude, and mental control of emotion and passion. Much of what modern psychology investigates under the headings of growth and development, motivated and emotional behavior, individuality and personality, type and trait theories of personality, and ability testing and measurement of intelligence was discussed by Vives under the heading of *ingenium* in a sketchy manner, no doubt, but also with the striking originality of an authentic pioneer. It goes without saying that, as a good Aristotelian, Vives was much more interested in describing the qualitative difference among individual intelligences than in providing quantitative measurements of intellectual performances. Nor is there much need to remind the reader that Vives' conclusions were exclusively based on a combination of accepted theories and personal observations rather than on controlled laboratory experiments.

If Vives understands what is conditioned in a variety of ways, he also stretches that which does the conditioning to include many different factors, both inborn individual traits and environmental situations. Clearly Vives avoids any simple solution to the nature-nurture dichotomy and vaguely suggests the unanalyzable complexity of the interaction between natural talent and environmental factors. He makes evident, however, that all factors affecting mental performance are not only bodily or body-related characteristics or events (perceptions, acts of the imagination, memory patterns, passional disturbances, habits and dispositions), but also external circumstances perceived by the body and that bear upon it.

Vives' discussion of *ingenium* therefore represents an original attempt to understand the relation between mind and body in psycho-physiological rather than in metaphysical terms. Behind this attempt we find once again the practical concerns of the moralist and the pedagogue rather than the speculative curiosity of a contemplative philosopher.[3] The human mind, Vives says, is immaterial in the sense that it is capable of transcending the domain of the material, but not in the sense that it can dispense with its material instruments (*non quod sine instrumento materiali aliquid hic possit*; M 3.365). The body is the room that the soul inhabits. Whatever the soul sees depends on the clarity of the windows through which it looks out onto the world outside. The soul moderates its dependence on bodily instruments because it is aware of such dependence and because it is capable of compensating for its effects. The soul is led by the senses but can also correct their information (*tametsi ducitur a sensibus, eos tamen corrigit*) and compensate for their weakness (*homo fulcit sensuum imbecillitatem;* M3.364).

One of the fundamental differences between animals and human beings is that only the latter are capable of understanding the fallibility of their senses and of making up for their weakness. Animals are at the mercy of their sense perceptions. It is true, however, that sometimes even the human senses, like rebellious horses, can resist the leadership of the mind and slow down its operations. Sense perceptions can distract us from the contemplation of the sublime and make us fall into the trifles of sensual games.

The operations of the senses and all mental activities are dependent on the physiology of the body. In explaining this impact, Vives follows very closely Aristotle's theory of the four qualities and Galen's primitive endocrinology. The instruments of our rational activity (*organa functionis rationalis*) are some "very thin and bright spirits" (*spiritus tenuissimi et lucidissimi*) that are "exhaled" from the pericardial blood and reach the brain (M 3.365). The heart is the origin of the spirits; the brain is their workshop. If the spirits do not reach the brain, the mind is not affected by them. Such is the case in courageous and self-controlled people: they remain undisturbed by danger because the heat of their pericardial blood (*effervescit in praecordiis*) never reaches their brain (M 3.365).

If those spirits are cold, mental activity (both intellectual and emotional) is languid and slow (*segnes et languidae*). If they are not, mental actions are quick and prompt (*celeres et concitatae*). This simple metaphorical translation of the vigor of fire and the languor of cold into the qualities of our mental life is the fundamental taxonomic principle of human ingenia in Vives' work and, as I will point out later, a decisive perspective in the analysis of emotional responses.

The vital spirits proceed mostly from the blood but are also affected by the quality of all the body's humors: the pituitary gland (whose division into two lobes was not known to Vives) secretes phlegm, the liver secretes yellow bile (*flava bilis*), and the spleen secretes black bile (*atra bilis, bilis fusca, furva bilis*). Blood is hot, phlegm is cold, yellow bile is dry, and black bile is wet. The coldness of phlegm slows down mental operations (*pituita humores gignit crassos, functionesque intelligentiae lentas*). Yellow bile produces "sudden and extremely quick" mental reactions that are restrained by the resistance of black bile (*cogitationes ex flava bili concitatas temere sistit atra bilis*). Black bile leads to melancholy, depression, outbreaks of anger, and weakening of the entire body (M 3.366).

The balance or temperance of all four humors results not only in physical but also in mental health. Excessive heat leads to insanity and excessive cold to obtuseness. When the wetness of black bile is combined with the heat of the blood, the vehemence of yellow bile is restrained and the power to concentrate and understand is greatly increased. Genius is always mixed with madness (*nullum excellens ingenium sine mania*).[4] The melancholic and phlegmatic are diligent and persevering. The sanguine and choleric are weak and inconstant. The choleric tend to improve when they calm down and the phlegmatic tend to deteriorate when they grow cold. The prevalence of one of the four humors and their different combinations account for the incredible variety and incompatibility of human *ingenia,* a variety that is reflected in the diversity of facial features and is known only to the Creator of Nature.[5]

Bodily temperament itself is conditioned by time, place, and environmental circumstances. Age plays an important role in intellectual development and emotional control.[6] In infancy, the intellect cannot rely on its bodily instruments because they are not yet ready, in old age, because they have already deteriorated with prolonged use (*magno usu detrita et corrupta*). Young prodigies tend to deteriorate with age. If their early heat is drowned in obesity or gluttony, they become stupid. If the same heat increases, they fall into madness. Other children improve with age if their early hot temper is dampened or their harmful or excessive humors are progressively cleansed. Well-balanced children experience fewer changes.[7] Climate is also relevant: high summer temperatures or the weather of southern regions tend to heat up the body's temperament. Diet, occupation, bodily health, the subject matter of study, emotional makeup, habits, and personal customs also have much to do with the *ingenium* of each individual. The habit of laziness, or the sybaritic life, represent strong impediments to attention and to sustained mental effort. Pride makes some people incapable of carrying out any compulsory task. The minds of people can be manly or childish, humble or pretentious, sober or insane, straight or crooked, shy or showy, obedient or rebellious. Inconstant people start fast and tire quickly. Shy, fearful, and angry people cannot work without frequent interruptions. Strong characters are always mentally alert.

Vives' description of different *ingenia* is characteristically rich in psychological detail but poor in systematic guidelines. No effort is made to assimilate each type into a clearly defined category. On the contrary, the reader is implicitly led to believe that the baffling and extraordinary diversity of human *ingenia* can only be roughly explained as the complex result of some or of all the factors that enter into their constitution. The direct pedagogical application of Vives' effort to describe the variety of *ingenia* can be found in the second book of *De Tradendis Disciplinis*. One of the most important responsibilities of educators is to diagnose the *ingenium* of each pupil. To this end, Vives prescribes a careful scrutiny before the child enters school and regular meetings of the teaching staff to determine the *ingenium* of their pupils. The purpose of these examinations is to determine what the child is "specially fitted for" and to adapt instruction to the individual's talent and vocation.

Following Aristotle, Vives teaches that pleasure enhances performance, while "unwilling minds that are driven to uncogenial work" will end by being "wrong and distorted." Sharpness in observing, capacity for comprehending, and power in comparing and judging are natural powers that cannot be "taught" but must be taken into consideration by the teacher. Manual ability and speculative subtlety are seldom found together in the same individual. The ability to write poetry does not entail the ability to write prose. Some people are witty in matters of jest but stupid in dealing with serious research. Some have the sharpness of a needle and others the cutting edge of a sword. Demosthenes belonged to the latter type. Cicero was admirable in both respects (M 6.289). Some students are naturally inclined to respect their teachers' authority, others to question it. Some make good use of what is found out by others, but are themselves deprived of any creativity and originality. Again, some students thrive when they are guided with kindness, others prefer to be led with a strong hand.

Classical authorities had offered different means to find out the intellectual prowess of each child. Pythagoras thought that nothing displays the sharpness of the mind so much as the process of reckoning that arithmetic requires. Quintilian considered memory a better indication of mental ability than a talent for arithmetic. Competitive games were recommended by others. Vives thinks that the testing of natural intelligence is always a complicated process that must itself be adapted to the *ingenium* of each individual.

II

Language

D*E ANIMA ET VITA* (Book 2, Chapter 7) deals also with language, a subject previously discussed by Vives in several works. His theory is centered around the notion that language is first of all the necessary implement of man's social nature. Human beings do not need words to speak to themselves or to God "who lives in the secret recesses of their heart." "Language was given to human beings on account of other human beings" (*hominibus hominum cause tributus est sermo*).[1] Consequently, Vives frequently characterizes language as "the instrument of that society and communion to which nature disposes people toward one another" and the "agglutinant of our social life" (*linguae et voces glutinum sunt communis vitae*).[2] On at least two occasions, Vives did not hesitate to claim that as "a bond of human association" language is even stronger than justice.[3] The power of justice is "silent and slow" (*tacitas habet vires et lentas*) because it "appeals to reason and deliberation" (*rationis et consilii vim admonet*). The power of language is "more conspicuous and faster" (*sermo vero habet vires praesentiores et magis celeres*) because it "excites the passions of the soul" (*animi motus excitat*).[4] Furthermore, justice is a "mild and soft" virtue (*mitis et blanda*) that rules only among "minds that are properly educated" (*in solis mentibus recte ac probe institutis*) while language "entices the minds and provokes the passions, whose reign over the entire human being is all-powerful and heavy."[5]

God gave animals endowed with no other cognitive powers but sensation and feeling the capacity to express the latter by means of "backward and crude sounds." These sounds can be compared to the interjections in human language. But God gave human beings endowed with reason and destined to live in society the gift of speech. This is also why those animals that "join in fellowships which somehow imitate human society" (*quae ad imaginem quandam societatis congregantur*), such as the apes and the bees, are also capable of using signs that are "closer to human speech" (*signa edunt propinquiora humano sermoni*).[6] Human nature can only fulfill its social vocation if people can communicate with each other, if the soul that is "hidden by so many dense layers of the body" (*animus tot involucris et tanta densitate corporis occultus*) manages to "reveal itself" to others.[7] For this reason God has endowed human beings with two exclusive gifts: the gift of language and the gift of a face capable of expressing our deepest emotions and feelings.[8] To emphasize the close connection between the invisible mind and the spoken (*voces*) or written (*litterae*) language, Vives constantly follows Democritus in comparing language to a stream that proceeds from the mind: *"tamquam ex fonte rivus."*[9]

In *De Tradendis Disciplinis,* Vives nevertheless makes it clear that what naturally flows from the human mind are neither the different tongues spoken by mankind (*linguae*) nor the different scripts (*litterae*), but rather the very "capacity to speak" (*peritia loquendi*). This capacity is as natural to us as the possession of a rational mind, but to speak this or that particular language is a matter of "art." "As far as language proceeds from human reason, it is as natural to man as reason itself" (*quandoquidem sermo ex ratione utitur, tam naturalis est homini sermo quam ratio;* M 3.371). This *peritia loquendi,* which is necessarily conditioned by the nature of the human mind and its relations to the body, is the foundation of those general characteristics of all human languages that are not yet mediated by circumstantial contrivance or "art." Since those general characteristics are dictated by man's nature, they form the main subject of Vives' discussion in *De Anima et Vita.*

Language is basically a "sign" of the soul. But while animals can only signify their affections, man is capable of signifying both his thoughts and his emotions. In *De Ratione Dicendi,* Vives makes an interesting claim about the relation between these two roles of human language. Both before and after Adam's fall, man has always felt the need to share his thoughts and his emotions with others, but the need to combine the two in what rhetoric calls persuasive speech is only a consequence of the original sin. Before the fall, when man's nature was "unspoiled" (*integra*) and the affections did not interfere with the process of thinking, speakers did not have the burden of persuading others by accumulating probable arguments or by enlisting the powerful help of their passions and emotions. It was enough for everybody "just to bring out through language whatever was in their minds" (*ut quisque per eum sermonem foras ad alios proferat, quae mente apud semetipsum concepit;* M 2.156). Whenever that happened, the listener immediately understood with great clarity whatever the speaker meant (M 2.156). Adam's language was such that it "revealed the nature of things" (*quorum verba rerum naturas explanarent;* M 6.299). Such ideal conditions, however, disappeared in our fallen condition: the essential natures of things remained the same, but our minds were darkened with an inability to understand those natures and therefore to express them by means of words: "things are not covered with darkness, but our minds are" (*neque enim tenebris sunt res coopertae, sed mentes nostrae*).[10] The challenge of language itself is therefore to make oneself understood to others, to articulate, expound, and communicate to others one's own thought: "truly the only purpose of language is to explain thought." In our present condition, however, we impose upon language three "other roles of our own," roles that depend not on the nature of language but on the corruption of human nature by sin: "to persuade, to move, and to retain the attention of the listener" (*tres autem nostri fines, probare, movere et animum oratione pascere quod detinere nominemus;* M 3.157).

These fundamental ideas regarding the roles of language provide the philosophical background of Vives' thought on the characters, purposes, and relations between the three *artes sermocinales*. Since language is the means by which people communicate their thoughts, language not only makes human culture possible but determines its range and limitations. The corruption of language entails the corruption of culture and the renewal of language amounts to a renewal of culture. In this fundamental sense, Vives remains a faithful disciple of the great linguistic rebirth initiated by the generation of Petrarch, embodied in a new pedagogy by Guarino and his followers, and transformed into a fundamental critique of traditional logic by Valla and Agricola.[11] In *Adversus Pseudodialecticos,* Vives attacked the language of medieval logicians as an artificial and contrived instrument totally unrelated to the ordinary language through which people communicate and through which they mold their reality, the world of their perceptions and thoughts. Any unbridgeable gap between the language of culture — be it the language of law, theology, science, or philosophy — and the language of ordinary life leads to a corruption of culture itself and to a decline in the quality of human life.

For the same reason, Vives enthusiastically supported Valla and Agricola on their insistence on the eminently practical character of the three *artes sermocinales* and on the intimate connnection between them and those sciences that deal with reality itself (*scientiae reales*). Descriptive grammar guarantees that the young learn to speak according to the rules created by the practice of speaking itself. The critical and inventive roles of dialectic correspond to the two basic roles of language, to explain one's thought and to persuade others with a convincing accumulation of probability. Vives was also sympathetic to Agricola's inclusion of rhetoric under the general heading of teaching: "the first and primary role of speech is to teach the listener something" (*primum et proprium habere videtur officium ut doceat aliquid eum qui audit*).[12] Vives' more qualified characterization of rhetoric represents, however, a slight departure from Valla and particularly from Agricola, who, in the opinion of the Valencian humanist, placed too much emphasis on the importance of ornament.[13] The aim of rhetoric, Vives insists, is not to "please" the audience, but rather to "retain" its attention. Vives frequently insists that in our fallen state the attention of the listener is the indispensable condition for speech to be effective. Rhetoric in a way represents the finishing touch of liberal education. It presupposes a thorough training in grammar and dialectic, requires mature familiarity with the psychology of feeling and emotion, and is impossible without knowledge of the real world, accumulated personal experience, good judgment, and a sense of "propriety" (*decorum*) that defies any strict regulation.[14]

Vives explains the primary role of language—to signify thought—by discussing in detail the relation between language and thinking, and the relation between language and reality. Unlike some of his humanist predecessors, particularly Valla, Vives' account of those relations remained unequivocally Aristotelian and traditional.[15] As the simile of the source and the stream clearly indicates, Vives believed in an intimate linkage between mind and language. Simple words emanate from simple ideas, compounded terms from fantasy, words that are joined and connected from our linking and discerning reason (*ex ratione coniungente et separante*) and speech from the combined effort of our discursive reason and the judgment that frames propositions (*ex judicio aptante clausulas*).[16] Because of this intimate connection, Vives claims that the development of language parallels the development of the mind. The language of children and of the uneducated tends to consist exclusively of "disjointed words" because their reason is "weak." In the first book of *De Censura Veri,* Vives claims that the use of syncategorematic terms (terms that do not have a definite signification by themselves and must be used in connection with other terms, such as *every, none, some,* or *only*) presupposes a language "polished and refined by usage" (*linguae excultae jam usu atque expolitae;* M 3.144).

In spite of their close interdependence, language and thought—so Vives teaches—are not identical. Some simple thoughts need to be articulated in composite words while simple words are complicated in our understanding by the work of the imagination. We also have thoughts for which we find no words (*multis desunt verba;* M 3.370). Furthermore, the expression of thought in language is conditioned by circumstantial factors that are neither linguistic nor exclusively mental in character. In *De Anima et Vita,* Vives deals mostly with psychological and educational factors. Individual *ingenium* affects linguistic habits. People with poor imagination and weak memory "express laboriously what they mean." People who are quick but inaccurate are often loquacious, but never eloquent. Some people excel in storytelling but are almost speechless when they need to articulate arguments. Reflective and thoughtful individuals are usually less talkative than those who are effusive, superficial, or even insane. Talking, listening, and reading are also linguistic functions subject to many variations. Most people are more capable of understanding a foreign language than of speaking it, but some, especially those who have learned a language through books, cannot understand, when they hear them, expressions that they can themselves use properly. There are even those who cannot understand what they can speak, but understand it when they hear it from others. Gifted speakers are sometimes poor writers. Bodily fatigue, sickness, and emotional disturbance impair our faculty to speak. Those who try to imitate too closely the language of others usually betray ordinary language for the sake of contrived expression (M 3.370–72).

In Book 1, Chapter 6 of *De Causis Corruptarum Artium,* Vives explains the decline of medieval culture as a result of linguistic ignorance. The correct understanding of a language that was once a living language depends not only on the accuracy of manuscript copies and translations of the original text, but also on thorough familiarity with the historical and cultural milieu (social customs, political and legal institutions, religion, art, literature, etc.) which that language helped to shape and by which it was shaped. For Vives, the meaning of a word is so relative to the culture in which it is used that he did not hesitate to deny that the Latin term *homo* and the Greek term *anthropos* could be considered as synonyms.[17]

Vives' closer analysis of what *significatio* means is also conservative and traditional. To signify means "to make a sign, to indicate something to somebody" (*signum facere, indicare aliquid alicui*).[18] Spoken and written words are signs. Through them the mind signifies "whatever the alert mind understands in one way or another." Although Vives carefully avoids any scholastic controversy, he seems to accept the traditional interpretation, according to which words are direct symbols of concepts and indirect symbols of the objects themselves (Boethius, Saint Thomas), and to reject Scotus' and Ockham's teaching that words are direct symbols of objects and secondary symbols of concepts.[19] To signify cannot be taken absolutely, however, but always in relation to the user of the sign and to his social context. The Spanish blind, Vives says, use among themselves a language not understood by the rest of the population. Thieves and diplomats communicate through a code that signifies nothing to others. Cicero and Atticus shared an intimate idiom that makes understanding their private correspondence extremely difficult. All this proves that the relation of signification is a purely conventional one among the speakers of a given language, the result of "a pact, a contrivance, and agreement among those who speak the same language" (*ex compacto, ex conventione, et quadam loquentium conspiratione ac consensu*). A significant word (with the possible exception of some interjections) can therefore be defined as " a common sign by which people explain to others the notions they conceive in their minds." Usage is therefore "the master of signification" (*magister significatuum;* M 3.143).

Besides these basic thoughts on language, *De Censura Veri* presents a summary of the fashionable theory of signification, the division of terms into *significativa* or *categorematica* and *cosignificativa* or *syncategorematica,* the problems of synonymy, the difference between terms of first and secondary intention, the distinction between univocity, equivocity, and analogy, and even a perfunctory section on supposition. What is striking about this mini-treatise of logical theory — whose exaggerations and distortions Vives criticized severely both in *Adversus Pseudodialecticos* and *De Disciplinis* — is that Vives manages to remain scrupulously neutral and noncommittal in ontological matters. On the other hand, his treatise *De Explanatione Cujusque Essentiae* presents a theory of universal concepts that is strictly Aristotelian and traditional (M 3.121–25).

12

The Will

$D_{E\ ANIMA}$'s CHAPTER ON the will (Book 2, Chapter 11) is particularly important to our purpose, introducing as it does Vives' general theory of appetite and its relation to knowledge. Such a study of the will is a necessary prelude to an understanding of emotional responses and particularly to an understanding of their teleological and intentional character. The psychological considerations of *De Anima et Vita* need, however, to be considered with Vives' more metaphysical speculations on the character of the will and its relation to the rest of the created universe.

In Book 1, Chapter 1 of *De Veritate Fidei,* for instance, Vives presents the human will as a manifestation on the human level of that *appetitus naturalis* by which the Creator intelligently provided each species with the proper inclination toward its assigned end. This inclination serves within the general plan of the cosmos and lovingly binds everything to God as the first and final cause of the universe.[1] According to this Christian synthesis of Aristotelian teleology and Augustinian emphasis on the will, which Vives probably learned from the leaders of the Florentine Academy, inanimate objects and plants tend toward their end by virtue of their own essence, brutes by virtue of their instincts, and human beings by virtue of their will.[2] This is why, in the very first sentence of Chapter 11 (Book 2) of *De Anima et Vita*, Vives proclaims the metaphysical principle that "all knowledge was given [by God] to make possible the pursuit of the good" (*cognitio omnis propter bonum expetendum est tributa*) in desire and in action. The sensual appetite of brutes is guided by sensation. Human will is guided by reason.

Having thus quickly provided the metaphysical framework of an analysis of the will, Vives proceeds in *De Anima et Vita* to the psychological study of its relation to knowledge. The main purpose of such a study is to explain how, in spite of their intentional character, human volitions remain free and self-determined. Vives says that the will is "guided" (*ut dirigat*) but not "mastered" (*non ut regat aut torqueat*) by reason. In doing so, Vives makes a novel and significant departure from other Renaissance writers on the subject. Early Renaissance literature on the will had been clearly inspired by a new confidence in the power of man to master his own destiny and to conquer the goddess Fortune with the daring of youth (Petrarch, Machiavelli, Alberti). Florentine Platonism had expressed similar notions in highly speculative terms, by contrasting the self-creative and self-defining character of human nature with the pre-determined and unwilled nature of everything else in the cosmos (Pico, Manetti, and—to a certain extent— Bouvelles). During the Reformation, literature on the will became highly theological and polemical. In the great debates of the age (Erasmus vs. Luther, More vs. Tyndale, Eck vs. Karlstadt, Luther vs. Zwingli, etc.), biblical texts were endlessly analyzed in an attempt either to reconcile human freedom with divine foreknowledge and providence or to sacrifice the former to the latter. Valla and Pomponazzi, on the other hand, had discussed free will in a more rationalistic vein. The fascination for astrology, which Salutati and Ficino felt and finally overcame, was another source of Renaissance thought on the freedom of the human will.[3]

Although *De Anima et Vita* adopts a clear anti-Reformation stance in proclaiming human freedom, and is obviously congenial to Neoplatonist speculation (without any of its exaggerations) and to the Renaissance affirmation of human self-determination, it quickly disposes of the theological docrine (the will is not necessitated by grace) and astrological issues (the will is not directed by the heavenly bodies) in order to engage in a careful, sober, and strictly philosophical and psychological analysis of the relations between cognition and volition, an analysis which I think is unmatched in the humanist literature of the age.

Vives' analysis of this relation is centered around the simile of the relations between a powerful but blind ruler and his personal counselor. The simile itself is topical and traditional; but its careful and sustained unfolding is unquestionably original. Vives begins by distinguishing two acts of the will: the propensity toward the good (*propensio seu amplexus boni*) and the aversion from evil (*aversatio mali*). But Vives adds to these traditional reflections on the motions of the will a more original one. The will is not only attracted by the good and repelled by evil, but can also remain unmoved when it "does not lean toward either." This he calls "avoidance" or "deprivation" (*orbatio*). In all three cases, reason judges and persuades, but the will remains the master (*voluntas quidem ipsa domina est omnium et imperatrix*).

An act of the will is "conceived" (*gignitur*) by reason but "delivered" (*paritur*) by the will itself. The Creator of human nature decided that the human will could not want but what appears to be good and could not reject but what appears to be bad. Whenever reason offers something good to the will, the latter can abstain from willing it, but cannot reject it or hate it. Whenever reason presents the will with something bad, the will can abstain from hating it, but cannot embrace and love it. By giving the will the extra power not to move in either direction when confronted with good or evil, Vives makes a bold (and controversial) statement about the will's mastery over its own actions, and firmly denies the quasi mechanical attraction of the good and the repulsiveness of evil.[4]

What Vives calls "the liberty of the will" is further analyzed in the internal domain of choice and in the external sphere of action. Internally, the will is free before, during, and after the process of deliberation or consultation. *Before* deliberation, the will is free to bring or not to bring the matter to deliberation. *During* deliberation, the will is free to delay further deliberation, to silence any deliberation (*in universum silentium indicere*), or to distract the mind with other matters, just as a ruler can refuse to listen to his counselor, force him into silence, or order him to talk about something else. *After* the deliberation, the will remains free to reject the advice of reason or to command a new and more comprehensive inquiry. This is always possible, even when reason makes a strong case, because the mere suspicion that another choice might be also acceptable is enough to give the will the power to accept the former and to reject the latter. The complexity of human affairs and opinions reinforces the will's tendency not to accept blindly the initial guidance of reason. Furthermore, just to prove to itself its own authority and mastery over the situation, the will is sometimes inclined to reject even the most persuasive advice of its counselor, human reason. Human rulers also sometimes think that is better for them to reject even the best advice than to convey the impression that they themselves are blindly ruled by their counselors. Rebellious adolescents behave in the same manner and for the same reason.

It is worthwhile emphasizing that in this context Vives is discussing the possibility and not the morality of a free choice under the circumstances described. His words cannot be construed as a sanction of probabilism nor as a condemnation of rigorist probabiliorism, although it is possible that this text (or at least this conception of the will's freedom) might have had some influence on the seventeenth-century debates between Jesuits and Jansenists. The pejorative reference to despotic rulers and to rebellious adolescents seems nevertheless to condemn any form of behavior that might be free but also whimsical. Still, Vives' explanation of freedom threatens to reduce the will to an unpredictable and irrational power that decides not to act according to the best advice given to it by man's cognitive faculties for a paradoxical reason, in order to establish its final independence from the rule of reason.

The freedom of the will is also manifested in observable behavior. The will might accept the advice of reason but refuse to translate it into action, interrupt its execution, or carry it out irresolutely and reluctantly. Brute animals are always driven by their instincts to act as strongly and quickly as they are able to. If they sometimes seem to behave with more power and swiftness, such change in pace is due not to their voluntary decision but rather to new external stimuli or to their physical condition, as fire flames up with oil or with a strong wind. Those human beings, however, who are driven by their appetites more than by their reason are in this respect very similar to beasts. Brutes never deliberate, even when they appear to. Human beings always deliberate, even when their emotions are vehemently agitated and seem overpowering. Sinners deliberate also; their passions deceive their reason into believing that the present pleasure they expect is more important than the uncertain reward or punishment in a distant future. The freedom of the will, Vives concludes, is a great gift of God by which and "with the help of His grace and help" (*opitulante illius favore et gratia*) we are made capable of deciding what we would like to be and of transcending the "necessary and fateful" destiny of the brutes (M 3.385).

Having clearly proclaimed the freedom of the will, Vives proceeds to analyze all the influences to which it is subject. The will is, first of all, indirectly and remotely moved by whatever moves our intellect. It is also moved by the "higher spirits" (*a mentibus superioribus*), such as angels and demons. The will is mostly moved by God, by Whom alone it can be "coerced" (*a quo solo potest cogi*), since God is the author of both our will and our being. Although Vives fails to explain the meaning of such "coercion," he seems to profess a Thomistic compatibilism between the freedom of the will and the determination imposed upon it by God's irresistible power. What follows is probably the shortest of all theological discussions of how to reconcile the divine attributes with our free will. Divine foreknowledge (*praevidentia*), Vives says, in imitation of Valla, does not any more take away my own freedom than "your looking at me acting" prevents me from acting freely. Divine providence (*providentia*), which Vives defines in an Augustinian vein as "the will governing everything with infinite Wisdom" (*voluntas consilio immenso universa gubernans*), not only does not prevent but in fact wills human (and angelical) freedom. No event in the past, present, or future can in any way escape the intelligence and order of a God who, as eternal, is always present in every instant of our time (M 3.386).

Vives' rejection of astrology is strong and unequivocal. His main objection, clearly inspired by Pico della Mirandola, is that inanimate objects cannot be the causes of contrary effects because they "necessarily produce one determinate effect" and are therefore incompatible with the freedom of the human will. The popularity of astrology is mostly due, Vives claims, to the arrogance of selfish and power-seeking mathematicians (M 3.386).

Human will is sometimes moved or neutralized by its conflicting inclinations, by an attraction to the forbidden and novel, or by morbid curiosity. The will's power over the body is also limited by nature. It is up to us to listen or not listen, to speak or not speak. But it is not within our choice to interrupt, delay, or accelerate some of our bodily motions, such as the beat of our heart or the motion of the animal spirits.

In *De Anima et Vita* (Book 2, Chapter 15) Vives deals also with a subtle force affecting the acts of the will and other human faculties: the force of habit (M 3.398–99). Some faculties act naturally as soon as they have reached their maturity. Their activity is not preceded by exercise or deliberation: children can see as soon as they are born, dog puppies have to wait about nine days. Other faculties, however, require some practice and repeated use to acquire a certain "propensity to and easiness in acting" (*facilitas ad agendum et pronitas*). This inclination is called *héxis* in Greek and *habitus* in Latin and covers both actions and passions. A habit reinforced by long use "acquires almost the force of nature." It increases the attraction of what is pleasantly familiar and makes more tolerable the pains we are used to. Habits were given to us to enhance our nature by making duties more attractive and suffering less painful. Habits grow with time but are weakened by lack of activity (M 3.398–99).

In the introduction to Book 3 on the emotions, Vives reminds the reader that the Latin term *affectus* means not only the act of an appetitive faculty, but also the faculty itself and the habit that arises from the repetition of an act (M 3.424; Introduction, 33–35). And, in fact, throughout the tract on the emotions the ambivalence between emotions as acts and emotions as habits or personality traits is never fully resolved.

13
Sleep and Dreams

As a young humanist, Vives was greatly interested in the dream vision as a literary form. The *Somnium et Vigilia in Somnium Scipionis,* the subject of his first informal lectures at Louvain, reveals his great admiration for Cicero's *Praefatio et Virgilia in Somnium Scipionis Ciceroniani,* which he considered at that time "the most distinguished and divine writing in the entire corpus of philosophy" (*Nullumque est in tota philosophia prae-stabilius opus ac divinius;* M 5.63). Vives' youthful composition also demonstrates extensive familiarity with Macrobius' commentary to Cicero's vision, with Lucian's *Dialogues of the Dead,* with Seneca's *Ludus de Morte Claudii,* and with the eleventh book of Ovid's *Metamorphoses.*[1]

Vives' allegorical and symbolic portrayal of the precincts the god Sleep inhabits is therefore a part of a long literary tradition that has been described as "the poetic exploitation of the dream-experience."[2] In his own *Somnium,* Vives is "peacefully and enticingly" taken to the swamps of Maeotis where he finds the palace of the god Sleep, who is the son of Night. Night itself is the daughter of Earth. The doorkeeper of the palace is Repose, and Silence is its prefect. The only sound to be heard is the sleep-inducing murmur of the River Lethe. Physical noises, the disturbing nuisance of human litigation and passional conflict, are kept away from the mansion where the "placid" Sleep and his wife Security live with their daughters: Cowardice, Inertia, Torpidity, Forgetfulness, and Laziness. Some of the god's servants do not have any time off. Newborn babies and infants, she-bears, and sea-calves form Sleep's intimate circle. At dinner, the god sits between his sister Death and his paternal cousin Life, but closer to the former than to the latter. The watchmen of Sleep are called *Somnia.* One of them, *Insomnium,* makes human spirits think in their sleep that the hopes or the fears they had while awake have been fulfilled. *Insomnium* rules over lovers and over the greedy, the fearful, and the gluttonous. Another henchman is called *Phantasma* or

Visus and presents himself to our senses when we are half-asleep, between the two powerful kingdoms of Slumber and Wakefulness. Vision's daughter Epialtes is the mother of nightmares. Morpheus, Icelos, and Fantasy crowd our dreams with extraordinary figments without substance.[3]

In his dream Vives witnesses a debate in the Senate about the interpretation of dreams. The Pythagoreans, Socrates, Plato, and the Stoics seem convinced that Sleep will bring tranquil and true "visions of peacefulness" to those who live well. Aristotle, on the other hand, rises in the Senate to declare that dreams might occasionally foretell the truth—as a man who throws javelins all day will sometimes hit the target—but are not reliable means of forecasting. Finally, Carneades sweeps away all confidence in dream-oracles by introducing to the audience a wretched man who had found coals instead of the treasure promised to him in dreams (M 5.65–76). Vives himself does not take part in the debate and seems to leave the question open to further discussion.

In *De Anima et Vita*, written eighteen years after the *Praefatio et Vigilia in Somnium Scipionis Ciceroniani*, Vives tackles once again the perennially interesting subject of sleep and dreams, but in a totally different vein. The allegories and symbols of the youthful classicist are almost completely sacrificed to a pervasive naturalism that makes only a few concessions to religious beliefs. Nevertheless, the topical conception of sleep as an "image of death" (*somnus autem, imago quaedam mortis;* M 3.390) or as the "borderline between life and death" (*interliminium vitae mortisque;* Ibid.) and the Platonic and Christian picture of death as an awakening from a fleeting dream into an eternal life are still referred to in *De Anima et Vita*. They also continue to appear in Vives' private correspondence.[4] But the main concern of *De Anima et Vita*, Book 2, Chapters 13 and 14, is to provide a physiological explanation of sleep and of dreaming. Even the psychological approach of Aristotle is abandoned in favor of Galen's anatomy and physiology. The allegorical language of *Praelectio in Somnium Scipionis* is replaced by the language of qualities, humors, and animal spirits.

Sleep

In Book 2, Chapter 13, Vives characterizes sleep as a requirement of animal life. Sleep is the cessation of sense operations, but not the cessation of all the mind's activities. Nature, which is always "benign in providing what is necessary" (*benigna est in necessariis natura;* M 3.390) gave animal life the therapeutic rest it needs, since all sense operations lead to fatigue.[5] Vives tries therefore to provide a physiological explanation of how fatigue leads to

sleep and how sleep tends to restore the energies of the body. This physiological explanation is obviously rudimentary and it is heavily dependent on
Galen's terminology.

The process of digestion causes a vapor that condenses like a cloud (*nubis
in morem*) in the humid and cold mass of the brain and spreads from there to
the entire body. If the nerves are tired and cold through the loss of heat in
exercise, they surrender easily to the invading humor. As a result, the body
loses control of itself and collapses (*impos sui consternitur*). The eyes,
because of their proximity to the frontal and most humid part of the brain,
close (except in the case of the fearful rabbit and some human beings).
Common sense, similarly located in the forehead, is rendered inoperative.
The sense organs take "a placid rest" (*quiescunt placide*). Sleep is not a
disease; it lacks the numbness of a sudden blackout, fainting spell, stupor, or
coma (M 3.391).

The relation between emotions and sleep is also gauged in purely physical
terms. Sadness and fear make us sleepy because they are cold and dry. Love,
anger, and greed disrupt our sleep because they are hot passions.[6] Bodies that
are hot and humid, such as the bodies of little children, fall easily into sleep.
The old cannot sleep well because their bodies are cold and dry. The sick
cannot sleep well because they are hot as well as dry.[7] Hot-tempered people
are great sleepers. We sleep better after a good meal and in rainy days or
places. Our will can to some extent prevent us from falling asleep. The body
is restored by sleep as a plant is restored by irrigation. In sleep, the heat of the
body concentrates inward. This move cools off the extremities of the body
but fosters the unimpeded activity of our nutritive soul.

Waking up from sleep can be caused by internal or external factors. We
wake up when the vapor that ascends from the stomach to the brain is finally
dissipated, when we are disturbed by some bodily pain or by some violent
passion, particularly by those passions that are hot, such as anger, love, or
desire. Fear is a cold passion that both causes and interrupts the tranquillity
of sleep. Noises, motions, blows, and the like are some of the external causes
of awakening.

Dreams

During sleep, the senses' operations are in abeyance but the mind remains
active (*dormiente corpore non consopitur animus;* M 3.393). The activity of
the mind during sleep is called dreaming, the subject of Book 2, Chapter 14
of *De Anima et Vita*. Dreams in fact prove beyond any doubt the existence of
an internal reality different from the body and from the vegetative and the

sensitive soul. Vives, however, is not very interested in the psychological study of dreams or in the epistemological problems raised by them. He certainly agrees with Aristotle in saying that to dream is to be mentally active while asleep, but clearly misunderstands him by dismissing as an irrelevant verbal question the Aristotelian claim that in dreaming "we think something else over and above the dream presentation."[8] The problem for Aristotle was obviously not whether dreams should or should not be called *phantasmata*, but rather whether they involve both a mental presentation and an assertion or judgment.[9] That Vives did not hesitate to accept the Aristotelian affirmative answer to that question can be inferred from his own words. In dreaming, Vives says, "people probe, investigate, reason, and find solutions to problems they could not resolve while awake." The only difference between dreaming and being awake is that, in the former condition, the fantasy, "free from the censorship of reason" (*a rationis censura soluta*), draws its material from memory "without any order and control" (*sine modo ac ordine;* M 3.393). Vives also supports the Aristotelian conception of dreams as residuary movements of our conscious life. "Often," he says, "we dream of what we did or said the same day" because our fantasy is still occupied with the same images or because such images were deeply impressed in the fantasy through a "vehement disturbance of the soul" (*perturbatio animi aliqua vehemens*), such as fear, love, greed, anger, or envy (M 3.394).

These are the only psychological observations on dreams included in this chapter of *De Anima et Vita*. The rest is mostly dedicated to the etiology and interpretation of dreaming. All dreams are at least influenced by the humors that reach the brain from the heart. Dreams reveal the quality of those humors. If they are affected by the humidity of the pituitary gland, we dream of water. If affected by blood, we dream of blood. If affected by black bile, we dream of sad things, and if affected by yellow bile, we dream of struggles and conflicts. The succession of different humors is responsible for the erratic character of our dreams.

The motions of the body we imagine in dreams mimic the motions of the heart. If the heart is raised by some vaporous spirit, we dream of climbing a dangerous and steep hill. When that vapor is conquered by the heat of the heart, we dream of going down. If such humor suddenly disappears, we dream of falling over a terrible precipice. If our heart is oppressed by a humor for a long time, our dreams become anxious, restless, and nightmarish. The attempt to get rid of such humors causes dreams of an impossible and lengthy struggle against invincible odds. When our blood is cleansed from "sordid humors" our dreams are "pure and authentic" (*pura et sincera*), as it often happens at dawn when we are through with the process of digestion. Such dreams, however, do not become more "truthful." Like tales, they can be more elegant but still totally fictitious. If the animal spirits are "thin and cool" (*tenuior et temperatior*), the dreams filter down like a placid brook. Red-hot spirits make the fantasy gush forth in a most disorderly and disturbing fashion. Rome and Paris become interchangeable, Caesar and Pompey are brought to the present, and the same character appears as king and slave. If the dream is about extremely happy or sad events, it is possible to dream that we are dreaming or to dream that we are not dreaming. Dreams tend to echo the images of our conscious life and vice versa: children are often terrified while awake by the fantasies of their own dreams.

Dreams can also be caused by sensory impressions that manage to have an impact on our sensitive soul even when we are asleep. But such impressions are magnified out of any proportion because the judgment of common sense is "depraved" during sleep. A small noise is dreamed as a "horrible uproar" (*ingentes fragores*). If we get warm, we dream of being burnt alive, and if some humor is left in our arteries, we dream of drowning in a huge stream. This is why physicians use the dreams of the sick to diagnose their diseases (M 3.393–94).

Vives was particularly interested in the study of that condition of drowsiness and somnolence that mediates between sleep and being awake (*medium quiddam inter somnum et vigiliam*; M 3.395), a condition he calls *dormitatio*. In that state we often imagine that we are dreaming what we are really sensing, no matter how feebly. By the same token, when we are suddenly awakened and our common sense is not yet entirely alert, we perceive some sensations but interpret them in the most extravagant manner. There are occasions when we talk to ourselves in sleep and imagine that we are listening to somebody else or that we are reading a book we can hardly understand.[10]

Not all dreams are remembered the same way; some are remembered in detail, some confusedly, others are completely forgotten. It is also possible for the animal spirits to be so "crammed and turbid" (*spirituum incrassatio et perturbatio*) that dreaming becomes utterly impossible, as with the drunk, the newly born, and the embryo. World travelers report that some people never dream. There are people who claim to have never had a dream and refuse to believe that others do (M 3.395).

Vives' naturalism shows both its depth and its limitations in short but unequivocal reflections on the interpretation of dreams. Dreams are never the "cause" of future events. Dreams are only "signals" of the condition of our animal spirits. Some of our nocturnal visions might fortuitously prove to be true. Some do because of their connection with a preceding passion or an obsessive thought. God and the devil can sometimes put dreams into our minds, as the Bible reports in the case of the Pharaoh, Nebuchadnezzar, and Saint Joseph. In most cases, however, dreams are natural events to which we, misled "by passion or by a bold belief," assign a supernatural origin. Except in a few cases, therefore, the misinterpretation of dreams as more than mere natural events is, generally speaking, one more unwarranted result of emotional excess.

14

Death and Immortality

Old Age and Death

VIVES' VISION OF LIFE and death was more in tune with the austere piety of the *Devotio Moderna* than with the joyful "rediscovery of earthly existence" we tend to identify as one of the attributes of Renaissance culture. To him, life was a short and painful pilgrimage toward eternity, a dream of the soul in the "dark and dreadful" (*carcer obscurissimum ac teterrimum*) prison of the body, an exile full of "misery and torment" (*vita aerumnae ac miseriae*), the "dark and constricted " (*angustia et tenebris*) embryonic preparation for life after death. In a similar vein, Vives considered death the awakening to an eternal life, the beginning rather than the end, the moment of birth after the "laborious service" (*absoluti ab hac laboriosa statione*) of earthly existence.[1]

Few if any Renaissance men were as detached from life and as obsessed with the thought of death as Vives was. In his daily prayers, he liked to compare his bed to the grave from which he expected to awaken to the vision of God[2] and constantly asked for the gift of being inspired by a "desire for the other life."[3] At the age of thirty-six he found life most unattractive (*non nimis jucunda*) and rejoiced at the thought that he had already lived most of it.[4] Three years later he considered old age "an incurable disease" and complained about his poor health with such asperity that death seemed to him not only less terrible than most people think, but even highly desirable.[5]

In his youth Vives had drawn a psychological portrait of the "Soul of an Old Man" (*De Anima Senis*) in which he contrasted the advantages and disadvantages of old age, following the lead of Cicero's *De Senectute*. As I pointed out in Chapter 3, Vives teaches that old people can be led by the "inferior" part of their souls to be skeptical, cautious, irritable, qualmish, and wistful, but that they can also be lifted by their "higher" part to become prudent, dignified, and self-controlled ideal counselors in public affairs. This modest sketch of developmental psychology is complemented in Book 3 of *De Anima et Vita* with interesting observations on the emotional life of the old.

In Book 2, Chapter 16 of *De Anima et Vita*, Vives' study of old age retains the physiological approach of the chapters on sleep and on dreams. Aging is, for Vives, an inexorable consequence of the union of body and soul. The same nature that transforms matter into bodily instruments to be used by the soul dictates that such instruments be gradually worn out by use (*deteruntur usu ipso*) and finally totally corrupted and destroyed (*corrumpuntur penitus ac intereunt;* M 3.400). The life of an animal, following the shaping of the bodily instrument in the maternal uterus, is divided into four seasons regulated by the balance or imbalance of heat and humidity. The spring of infancy is dominated by an excess of warm humidity (hence the almost constant sleep); youth, the summer of life, is characterized by a proper balance (*contemperatio*) of both qualities. Old age is cold and dry. The most evident sign of advanced age is wrinkling, caused by the dryness of the skin, particularly noticeable in those who have an excess of black bile. Baldness is also due to dryness. For that reason, those who have curly hair (and Vives assumes that curly hair is particularly dry) become bald sooner than others. Baldness begins in the frontal part of the head, which is also the "less solid and dense" (*minus est solida atque spissa*). The secretions of the pituitary gland are responsible for white hair (M 3.400–401).

The balance of heat and humidity decides the length of life and is itself affected by such external circumstances as diet, the quality of the air we breathe, weather, and physical exercise. Against the opinion of Aristotle and in agreement with Hippocrates and Pliny, Vives maintains that life expectancy is shorter in warm regions than in cold ones. But he follows the Peripatetic school in teaching that life in the tropics is shorter and more vulnerable to disease than life in other parts of the world. Vives rejects the common view that women live longer than men and attributes the premature death of most males to sexual excesses.[6] Small animals have shorter lives because they contain less heat. Trees live longer than animals because they have a "more dense mass" (*densiores sunt mole*). The palm tree lives the longest because it is "the warmest of all trees" (M 3.401–3).[7] As the carpenter stops working when he loses his tools, the soul abandons the body when the bodily organs are finally corrupt and inadequate. Death does not result from any incompatibility between body and soul but rather from the corruption of the body itself. The immediate cause of natural death is the extinction of bodily heat. The flame of an oil lamp disappears when it has used all the oil. Blood is mostly responsible for the proper balance of heat and humidity that is the precondition of life. For that reason, the heart is the most important organ of the body, the first to come into life and the last to die. Next in importance are the organs in the proximity of the heart, such as the liver and the lungs. The brain is only passingly mentioned by Vives as one of the other "vital organs." The hands, arms, feet, legs, and eyes are classified as "less significant" (*viliora*). In sharp contrast with the heart, the eyes are the "last to begin living and the first to die" (*oculi incipiunt postremi vivere, et primi moriuntur;* M 3.404).

Immortality of the Soul

Chapter 19, the last chapter of *De Anima et Vita,* Book 2, and the longest in the entire treatise, deals with one of the favorite themes of Renaissance philosophy, the immortality of the soul. More perhaps than any other of his writings, this fascinating chapter reveals what is distinctive about Vives' manner of thinking and his conception of human nature. That Vives considered this the most mature expression of his thought can be surmised from the fact that the chapter was included, with insignificant variations, in his last work, *De Veritate Fidei.*

The chapter on immortality reveals, first of all, the secondary role of physiology in elucidating those central questions that concern the final destiny and the moral worth of human existence. Vives' interest in Galen's humors and qualities is left behind as a worthwhile but relatively unimportant manifestation of intellectual curiosity, as a legitimate but unessential part of the human mind's never completed project of understanding reality at different levels. More significantly, perhaps, the chapter presents an outstanding example of Vives' conception of dialectical reasoning. Vives goes about proving the immortality of the soul as a lawyer tries to convince a jury, by accumulation of evidence. The purpose, however, is not, as has been misleadingly stated about sixteenth-century humanists in general, to amplify a subject for the purpose of entertaining or manipulating an audience or for the purpose of embellishing that subject with rhetorical ornament. Accumulation and convergence of proofs is here a heuristic device to find true conclusions, to persuade oneself rather than to elicit the assent of a sympathetic audience. Formal rigor is replaced by convincing persuasiveness. Proofs reinforce each other not by virtue of any formal rule of logic, but rather by the psychological impact of the convergence itself upon those persons who ponder their persuasiveness. The mind is compelled to yield assent by a process that is closer to that enhancement of evidence characteristic of a forensic orator than to the quasi-mathematical rigor of deductive inference. The moral rather than the apodictic certainty attained by this method provides the necessary and sufficient foundation for a moral conception of human existence.[8]

More as a teacher and counselor than as a rigorous philosopher, Vives begins his chapter on the immortality of the soul with some important reminders. First, he reminds the reader that this topic has traditionally been more clouded by moral turpitude than by intellectual ignorance. Second, he makes a robust and direct affirmation of the possibility of metaphysical knowledge. Only brutes, Vives says, live circumscribed by "this mass of matter" (*hanc molem*). Human beings know realities that they cannot sense in the same way as they can know the existence of fire from the sight of smoke or the proximity of a corpse from the smell they perceive. Vives' metaphysical approach is nevertheless carefully limited by a firm resolve not to get entangled in the traditional disputes about the individuality of the active intellect (Saint Thomas vs. Averroës) or the independence of intellectual operations from the body (Cardinal Cajetan vs. Pomponazzi).

The immortality of the soul, like the hidden essence of things, is known to us through many signs: signs taken from the nature of causes, from the proportion of causes, from the dignity of man, from the goodness of the Creator, and from our own utility. But before he proceeds to ponder those signs, Vives completes his preliminary moves by attempting to steal the thunder from the specious but potentially disturbing objection that no one has returned from the other life to ascertain its existence. Leaving aside the fact that Revelation teaches us that some spirits have in fact done so, Vives replies that to deny the existence of an afterlife for that reason would be as foolish as to have denied the existence of the Indies before the discovery of America. The journey and communication (*commercium*) between the corporeal and the incorporeal is obviously much more difficult than the navigation between Europe and the American continent. Furthermore, the inhabitants of the afterlife have too much to enjoy or too much to suffer to be distracted by the trifles (*nugis*) of this earthly exile. Those who would like to return *are not* allowed to, and those who *are* allowed to have no desire to return (M 3.405–6).

The first series of arguments for the immortality of the soul is based upon the soul's essential attributes, known to us from the soul's operations. The analysis of man's cognitive operations provides Vives with an initial proof basically Platonic in spirit. Knowledge is the reflection of images in the mirror of the mind. There is therefore some "proportion" between the object known and the faculty of knowledge. Our knowledge of things that are either absent or "deprived of quantity" (*quantitatis immunia*) requires that the mirror of our own mind be itself immaterial and spiritual. Vives does not even bother to explain how material things can be reflected in the mirror of an immaterial mind. On the contrary, he expands the proof by claiming that a soul capable of understanding what immortality means must itself be immortal. This parallelism between the objects of our cognition and the nature of our cognitive faculties is further insinuated, Vives claims, by the alleged fact that human reason "easily" understands immortality but not eternity, which is God's unique and mysterious manner of being (M 3.407).

The argument based upon the reach of our cognition gives Vives one more opportunity to pursue with renewed vigor the typically humanistic emphasis on the radical difference between human beings and brutes. The souls of brutes are a product of nature. Human souls are created by God in a unique manner "beyond the powers of matter and nature" (*supra vires materiae ac naturae hujus*). Although the creation of a human soul is not a miracle in the strict sense of the term, it reveals the fact that at least its most noble part (unlike our body or our senses that are bound to the material) "belongs exclusively to God " (*mens vero solius est Dei*).[9] What God has created in a unique manner and belongs exclusively to Him cannot share the corruptibility of the material and the natural. The human soul is immortal (M 3.408–9).

Vives' second, far more interesting and eloquent set of arguments for the immortality of the soul is derived from the study of man's appetitive operations. The appetites of brutes are limited to the here and now (*feruntur pecudes solum ad nunc*). Man, on the other hand, can know and therefore desire "endless being" (*interminabile esse*; M 3.409).[10] Craving for fame, which even those who deny the hereafter experience in themselves, is only a clear sign of a misguided desire for immortality. God would be extremely cruel if He gave man a desire that cannot be fulfilled. The idea that death could be the definitive end of any existence terrifies a thoughtful person, even under circumstances that make life on earth extremely painful. The prospect of bodily death, on the other hand, shocks the sensual part of ourselves but leaves the mind serene and undisturbed. Obviously the immortal mind is only concerned about immortality while the bodily senses are exclusively interested in this earthly existence. It is true that in times of desperation, sickness, mental confusion, emotional upheaval, and moral perversion the mind can be more scared by the possibility of bodily death than by the denial of the soul's immortality. On the other hand, Vives asks, whose judgment deserves more our attention, that of a confused, sick, corrupted, or ignorant mind, or the judgment of a "sober, healthy, serene, quiet, learned, innocent, and pious" soul (M 3.410–11)?

Of all human desires Vives emphasizes most the desire to possess the truth. How could God have given man a desire doomed to be forever futile and vain? How could God have given animals eyes to see if there was nothing to see?

Vives shows little sympathy for the topical pagan complaint about the brevity of life.[11] The brevity of life on earth should have made clear to those pagans that human fulfillment was not of this life. Life on earth is long enough for us to understand that God has destined us for a life without end. More interesting perhaps is the unusually harsh attack that Vives mounts against Aristotle in this context. The heavy Aristotelian flavor of *De Prima Philosophia,* written only five years before *De Anima et Vita,* does not prepare the reader to accept Vives' characterization of Aristotle as "a usually obscure, slippery and cunning" thinker (*obscurus est, lubricus, vafer*) whose positions on the soul's immortality were rash and even inconsistent (*non satis est pro acumine ingenii illius animadversum*).[12] Although Aristotle seemed to have suggested that the mind could exist apart from the body and the senses "as the immortal [can exist apart] from the perishable" (*ut immortale a caduco*), he conditioned such possibility on the ability of the intellect to operate without the help of the fantasy. Vives, who knew but refused to become involved in the scholastic debates between Ficino and Pomponazzi regarding this matter, criticized the Aristotelian hypothetical argument because he was convinced that, as long as the soul is united to the body, "it must understand everything in corporeal terms" (*non potest nisi corporaliter omnia intelligere*). Vives also was emphatically convinced that the proof of the soul's immortality should not be based on any questionable epistemological theory about the role that images play in the process of understanding (M 3.416).

Man's pleasures also reveal the true nature of our soul. The most noble minds (*praestantissimas ac generosissimas mentes*) find more delight in the operation of the internal senses than in that of the external, more pleasure in the activity of the intellect than in the vagaries of the fantasy, more self-fulfillment in contemplation than in the use of practical intelligence, more enjoyment in the contemplation of the immaterial and the eternal than in the contemplation of this physical universe. This hierarchy of pleasure lays open the spiritual nature of our souls (M 3.411–12).

Our bodily makeup also manifests our eternal destiny. Unlike the brutes, we walk erect, facing the skies, looking up toward our eternal home. The maternal womb is an image of life on earth. Both are only preparations for a higher form of existence. In the womb we get ready for the life of the body; in the body we get ready for the eternal life of the spirit. The trauma of birth and the trauma of death are only rites of passage to higher levels of life (M 3.413).

In the last section of Book 2, Chapter 19, Vives turns his attention to the relationship between immortality and morality. If man's end were to eat, drink, sleep, and indulge in sexual pleasure, man would be more miserable than the beasts while religion and Divine Providence would be totally meaningless. If evil and goodness were indifferently treated, if morality were not guaranteed to coincide with happiness, God should not be worshiped as the Infinite Wisdom who cares about the actions of human beings. If God is not watching and passing judgment, why are human beings naturally inclined to praise such unworldly virtues as modesty, moderation, gratitude, piety, kindness, patience, and fairness (M 3.413–14)?

The moral consent of all of humanity, not only that of philosophers and civilized nations, but even that of the most primitive and barbaric people, is enough argument for the immortality of the soul. How could it be that in this important matter the most respected philosophers—Pythagoras, Socrates, Plato, Zeno, and many others—are wrong, while "the most ignoble of all the masters of philosophy," those who overestimated the pleasures of the body, are right? The wise and the good disagree with the ignorant and the perverse. Whose judgment should we prefer? How is it possible that some people ridicule Epicurus' or Pliny's opinions on nature but accept their false teachings on providence and immortality? Only those who have a vested interest in denying God's eternal Justice can fall into such absurdities. If the good are not going to be rewarded in the afterlife, what is the meaning of their sufferings on this earth? Only immortality explains why evil people shun the thought of immortality and the just rejoice in it. How could death be the end of the wise man's contemplation? How could we long for a rest if there is nothing after our journey? "How could that which is non-existent enjoy rest?" (*Quomodo enim quod non est quiescit?*) Does God need a lie to restrain our passions (M 3.417)?

Vives ends the chapter by confessing that one could bring, and in fact other philosophers have brought, many more arguments on behalf of the immortality of the soul. After all, truth is "extremely spacious" (*veritas latisssime patet*) and is not monopolized by an individual and finite mind. Still, these arguments—Vives teaches—are enough to persuade "the tribunal of reason" (*tribunal rationis;* M 3.419). Only a jury hampered by stubborn passion (*tribunal affectionis pravae ac pertinacis*) could resist this massive evidence. Do we need to see the soul leave the body as the smoke leaves the flame behind? The immortality of the soul has never been defined as an article of faith because—as Vives reminds the reader—it can be proved sufficiently by reason alone. If all these arguments are not enough, how can we expect any scientific truth? Do we have stronger arguments to support the knowledge of those natural causes that we consider "most certain and clear"? What is more insane than to proclaim that the soul is immortal according to our faith and mortal according to our reason? Truth does not have two faces, but only one. How can we debate for hours speculative details about the nature of the soul and place in doubt that attribute of the soul that is the foundation of all morality and religion? (M 4.419–20). Only a mind befuddled by uncontrolled passion can resist the compelling force of so many converging proofs of the soul's immortality.

It is in this context that the study of emotions becomes to Vives the key to the knowledge of our own humanity and the indispensable propaedeutic to the moral life.

Part 3
Vives on Emotion and Life

15
The Nature of Emotion

THE LAST AND LONGEST book of *De Anima et Vita* deals with the "affections" of the soul, the study of which is understood by Vives as the supreme task of philosophical inquiry, "the foundation of all moral training, both private and public" (*fundamentum universae moralis disciplinae, sive privatae, sive publicae;* M 3.299; *Praefatio*). In Vives' mind, the first two books of the treatise are only an introduction to the third, as the third is itself an introduction to ethics. Morality is embodied in action, action depends on choice, choice is affected by emotion, and emotion is guided by knowledge. Readers might nevertheless be disappointed if they expect to find in Vives' book a full-fledged theory of the nature of emotional response. Still, the two first chapters of the third book contain enough clues to reveal the general outline of Vives' philosophy of emotion.

As has become customary among writers dealing with most subjects but particularly with this one, Vives begins by characterizing the study of emotions as "complex," "important," and "neglected by former writers" (M 3.421).[1] More concretely, Vives proclaims his independence from the Stoics, who had "corrupted the entire subject with their fallacies" (*omnia argutiis suis perverterunt;* M 3.421; Introduction, 1–4) and from Aristotle, who "dealt with it from a purely political perspective" (*tantum de materia hac exposuit quantum viro politico arbitratus est sufficere;* ibid.). But one should not be excessively impressed by these words. Vives' relations to the Peripatos and to the Stoa were much more complex than he himself was willing (or able) to recognize. It is unquestionably true that Vives was temperamentally antagonistic to Stoic dogmatism and excessive subtlety and a little weary of the predominantly forensic character of the Aristotelian analysis of emotions in the *Rhetoric*. But a careful study of Vives' sketchy theory of emotions will help us to understand that Vives' relatively original thought on emotions was nevertheless deeply indebted to a long and complex philosophical tradition.

Aristotle considered emotions to be a part of human nature. As a Christian, Vives considers them the actual exercise of some God-given powers, an integral part of life. To share His existence with us—Vives teaches—God gave us (and all animals) the instinct of self-preservation. To share His beatitude with us, God gave us the power to seek the good and avoid evil. Emotions, therefore, are part of the divine plan of creation, the sources of human dynamism. The divine origin of our emotions guarantees their purposiveness (M 3.421; Introduction, 6–17). Aristotelian teleology and Christian theology are the foundations of Vives' thought on the emotions.

One is almost tempted to see this positive, optimistic attitude toward the emotions as a radical departure from the disparagement of emotional life that was generally associated with Platonism and Stoicism. The truth is, however, that Vives also pays some tribute to both traditions. As we shall see in the next chapter, Vives divides emotions into two large groups: those inspired by the good and those representing our reactions to evil. In a highly rhetorical manner, Vives characterizes the latter as those emotions that transform human beings into "most ferocious beasts" (*affectus qui ex opinione veniunt mali mirum in modum exasperant atque efferant humanum animum;* M 3.471), a phrase that could have been used by Seneca or Epictetus. This, however, cannot mean that the emotions inspired by the good are always uplifting and that emotions inspired by evil are always degrading. As Vives himself teaches, the love of wealth and honor can be as morally objectionable as jealousy or envy. Vehement desire or unrequited love can be as torturing as fear or hatred. Excessive reverence can lead to shyness and submissiveness. Compassion can be painful. Furthermore, as Vives emphatically states in most of the chapters dedicated to their analysis, even the emotions provoked by evil were intended by God as means to desirable ends. God gave us the capacity to be irritated to warn us of the presence of evil. God gave us the emotion of anger to foster in us a desire for exemplary behavior. God made us capable of indignation to reinforce the demands of distributive justice. Fear is a divine gift because it protects us from the bite of evil and shame, and because without it, life in society would be impossible. Even pride was originally natural and good because enlightened self-love could have led man to the desire and love of things heavenly and eternal. Tears and laughter are gifts of God because they attest to our feelings for others and awaken the feelings of others toward us.

If such is the case, why are we "brutalized" by our emotional reactions to evil in the world? Why does Vives say that the study of emotions is necessary to provide medication "for very severe diseases" (*ut tantis malis adferamus remedium morbisque tam saevissimis medicinam;* M 3.421)? Can love, desire, and pleasure become morbid and degrading? What Vives obviously means is that emotions are such that they can be either used or abused, that they can enhance our life and maximize our powers or render us sick and morally objectionable. Some emotions can become diseases of the soul while others are powerful means toward self-realization.

In the introduction to the third book of *De Anima et Vita,* Vives makes a further distinction among the emotions by dividing them according to their intensity, and by suggesting that only the violent and powerful emotions can be considered as "disturbances" of the soul (*perturbationes*). In describing these "disturbances," Vives uses the classic metaphors that Stoic philosophers applied to all passions: the soul becomes the victim of an external blow, blinded, paralyzed, and irrational. But the threat to rationality proceeds not from the emotion itself, but from the excess of emotion, a distinction Stoic philosophers were unable to make.

Vives' considered an eclectic attitude toward emotion avoids the excessive rigor, pessimism, and intellectualism of both Platonism and ancient Stoicism. There is no doubt that for most of his philosophical career Plato had been deeply suspicious of emotion: he considered emotional appeals as unworthy of reasonable speakers and associated all forms of poetry with irrational feelings. Philosopher-kings had to be denied family and property to be shielded from disturbing passions. Zeno and Cleanthes restated and reinforced the radical positions of the young Plato. Emotions, they taught, were irrational and morbid not only because they originated in a irrational part of the soul but also because they were uncontrolled, exaggerated transports of the entire soul. The Aristotelian notion of *metriopátheia,* moderate passion, was to Zeno of Citium and Cleanthes a contradiction in terms. Chrysippus reached the same conclusion, in spite of his monistic psychology and strong intellectualism. Emotions cannot be controlled by reason because they are, by definition, irrational judgments of the soul. The only possible cure is to wipe them out.

Vives' views on emotions were not only closer to the Aristotelian emphasis on moderation but were also partially influenced by the more realistic and eclectic masters of the Middle Stoa and the Imperial Age. Panaetius and Posidonius tried to remain faithful to the founders of the school by reinstating the opposition between the Logos and appetite (as *dúnameis* of the soul, not as parts of it), but followed the Peripatetic line by condemning only those emotions that were not duly controlled by our higher and dominant power, the *hegemonikōn.* Panaetius recognized the existence of human drives that are not only natural but morally worthy: the social drive, the desire for knowledge, competitive striving, the will to order. Posidonius considered appetite the driving and creative force of all cultural life, and demanded only that it be constantly guided by reason. Both of them made Stoicism more palatable to Roman ears by praising *"le joie de vivre"* or *euthumía* as life-enhancing and perfectly compatible with wisdom. Even Seneca admitted that some initial feelings (*prospátheiae*) are morally neutral and irrelevant to wisdom. The sober eclecticism of Panaetius and Posidonius was reflected in some of the most important catalogues of emotions written by rhetoricians and philosophers during the Imperia Age. The Pseudo-Andronicus' *Perí Pathōn*, which I shall describe more in detail in Chapter 16, makes an unexplained but fundamental distinction between "the irrational movements of the soul" (sadness, fear, desire, pleasure) and "the good passions" or *eupathéiae* (rational acts and inclinations of the will, joy).

Although Vives might have learned something from these Stoic thinkers, he still objected strongly to their occasional relapse into rigid forms of dogmatism and to their scholastic subtleties, particularly to their attempt to uphold their misconceived and dehumanizing ideal of *apátheia*. In his passionate apology for tenderness, sympathy, and compassion, Vives urges the reader "to forget the Stoics, who through pedantic cavils tried without success to convert into stones what nature had shaped as human beings" (M 3.461). Vives' harsh words for the Stoics might have been partially inspired by Plutarch's criticism of Stoic ethics and provoked by the occasionally exasperating word-games Vives found in Seneca's writings, two authors with whom he was very familiar.[2]

Vives defines the "affects" of the soul as "the acts of those faculties which nature gave the soul in order to seek the good and avoid evil" (*a natura sunt ad sequendum bonum vel vitandum malum actus;* M 3.422). He also reminds the reader that, depending on the context, the term *affect* can mean the orectic faculties, their acts, and the habits that arise from the repetition of those acts. It should be noted that the Latin term *affectus,* meaning a passive condition ("that which is affected by"), seems to contradict the definition of *affect* as the act of a faculty. Vives does not bother to resolve this tension perhaps because he was aware that in this case, as in the case of "sense impressions," accepted philosophical language had emphasized more the receptivity of the soul to external stimuli than the soul's active response to them. In any case, by *affect* Vives certainly does not mean that emotions are pure inert passivity, but rather activities provoked in the soul by an agent different from itself, an important point that the English word *emotion* unfortunately conceals.

Vives' apparent inconsistencies are not unique to him. Saint Thomas' *Summa Theologiae* reveals exactly the same tension.3 It is more difficult, however, to explain the difference between Vives and the scholastic tradition regarding the "faculties" whose acts are supposed to be affects or emotions. To Saint Thomas and most scholastics, the *passiones animae* reside in the sensory appetite of the soul rather than in the intellect, the will, or the physical organism. According to Saint Thomas, to "feel hot or stiff" is not a passion of the soul. By the same token, to "feel reluctant" or to "feel suspicious of an argument" might be a disposition of the will, or an intellectual attitude, but not a passion. Under "passions of the soul" (*Summa Theologiae,* IaIIae. 22–48) Saint Thomas understands those acts of the sensory appetite which are common to man and other animals, acts that always involve a physiological modification and are caused by our imagining sense-good or sense-evil. Only insofar as emotions are subject to the control of reason and will are they distinctively human and subject to moral judgment (IaIIae. 24). Saint Thomas' explicit definition of emotion as a psychosomatic event involving the sensory appetite was dictated by methodological and philosophical considerations. Although most of Part 2 of the *Summa Theologiae* was concerned with man's journey to God (goal of life and human activity regarding that goal), the section on the "Passions of the Soul" explains not those acts that are exclusively human, but those acts that are common to man and other animals. As a Christian moralist and Aristotelian philosopher, Saint Thomas was eager to explore those acts of human nature that are inextricably rooted in the animal and material part of ourselves, the acts of our composite substance while on earth.

On several occasions, nevertheless, Saint Thomas was compelled to forgo (or, at least, to qualify) these self-imposed limitations on the study of emotion as the movement of just the sensory appetite. Charity, he says, does not belong to the sensory orexis, but to the will (IIaIIae. 24, 1 ad 1). Love has to be understood not as an emotion seated in the sensory appetite, but as including intellectual, rational, animal, and natural love (IaIIae. 28, 6 ad 1). Longing for spiritual goods is sometimes called desire either because it resembles desire or because the longing is so intense that it spills over into the sensory appetite (IaIIae. 30, 2 ad 1). Although hope involves an awareness of the future, animals can be said to hope and to despair because their sensory appetite is guided by the intellect of nature's Creator (IaIIae. 40, 4). Anger in some sense involves reason, but animals are capable of being angry because they are endowed "with a natural instinct for internal and external reactions" that is analogous to reason's operations (IaIIae. 46, 5). Hope and human anger are, therefore, not only the result of intellectual knowledge, but are also instinctive and animal. Joy is the pleasure derived from the possession of objects intellectually desired and is therefore a distinctively human pleasure (IaIIae. 31, 3). Sorrow is the pain resulting not from exterior sense-perception, but from interior perception by the intellect, and is therefore a distinctively human pain (IaIIae. 35, 2). The pleasure of contemplation, which is seated not in the sensory but in the intellectual part of the soul, can nevertheless assuage the pain felt in the senses because it often spills over into the lower parts of our nature (IaIIae. 38, 5).

Subtle distinctions and qualifications of this kind are totally missing in *De Anima et Vita*. To Vives, emotions are movements of either the sensory or the intellectual appetite, movements which are in different degree related to physiological changes and bodily expression. No attempt is ever made to formulate a unified theory, except in a most sketchy manner. Vives does not even try to explain the difference between emotions on one side and feelings or acts of volition on the other. By far the largest portion of *De Anima et Vita,* Book 3, is dedicated to the description of each emotion. Whatever general theory is presupposed is either formulated in the two short introductory chapters or scattered through the treatise by way of perfunctory remarks. Such general theory includes the following points: emotions are movements of the appetite guided by knowledge, inextricably connected with preceding and resulting physiological changes, modified by internal and external circumstances, naturally seeking a bodily expression and their manifestation in observable behavior.

Emotion and Knowledge

No philosopher has ever denied that emotions are in one way or another mediated by and dependent on cognition of some sort, although different explanations have been given for that mediation and dependence. Even empiricist philosophers, who like Hume emphasize that emotions are feelings, recognize that such feelings are "derived from" or "produced" by cognitive experiences such as original impressions or derivative ideas of pain and pleasure. Whether this simple mechanism is enough to explain the complex intentional structure of emotions, to identify each emotional state, and to justify our attempts at emotional control and rehabilitation, is certainly a much more controversial matter. In general, those philosophers who, like the Stoics and Spinoza, were persuaded that such control and rehabilitation were well within our power and a necessary condition of human happiness and moral worth were inclined to emphasize the cognitive determinant of emotions. To them unhappiness and vice were, as Socrates had said, forms of ignorance and error.

In spite of his harsh words about the Stoics, Vives belongs to this rationalist tradition while avoiding some of its most radical and intellectualist exaggerations. Zeno's and Cleanthes' doctrine that emotion can be eradicated by insight led to Chrysippus' exaggerated teaching that emotions are judgments, not theoretical judgments about the truth or the falsity of a proposition but practical assessments about the goodness or badness of a thing, assessments that incite an excessive agitation of the soul.[4]

Chrysippus' exaggeration was rejected by Posidonius and Panaetius for obvious reasons. The theory confuses the partial cause or the necessary cause of an emotion with the emotion itself, presupposes that the rational principle acts against its own standards, and fails to explain why it is possible to have the judgment without the corresponding emotion or why emotions abate while the judgment about their object remains the same. In spite of these serious objections—which I intend to discuss more in detail in a different context—Chrysippus' excessive intellectualism reappeared in Seneca, in the work of Spinoza, and within a different philosophical horizon, in the opinions of Sartre and those contemporary philosophers who see emotions as judgments, as ways of interpreting ourselves and our modes of being in the world.[5]

It is difficult to say whether Vives was fully aware of Chrysippus' doctrine, although his reading of Galen and Plutarch should have been enough to impart to him some knowledge of it. In any case, Vives does not make any explicit reference to it nor does he indulge in any direct refutation. But the entire treatise *De Anima et Vita* presupposes that while judgment is essential to emotion, the two are different. Our intent here is to explore how Vives explains the essential relations of thought to emotion (and vice versa), and to see how far his opinions on this matter are compatible with some of the interesting insights raised by those philosophers who identify emotions with judgment.

Vives begins by teaching that God gave man the power to desire the good because he was created to enjoy the Eternal Good. Man was given intelligence because appetite without cognition would be entirely blind. The will, Vives says, "has not light of itself, but is enlightened by a rational judgment." The will cannot wish or avoid anything but that which has been put forth by reason" (*voluntas non expetet nisi intelligat;* M 3.341). The act of the will "is conceived by reason and delivered by the will itself." In fact, "all cognition was given for the sake of seeking the good, sense cognition for the sake of seeking the sensory good, intellectual cognition for the sake of seeking the intellectual good" (*cognitio omnis propter bonum expetendum est tributa, sensualis propter sensuale, mentalis propter mentale;* M 3.382).

This typically Aristotelian and scholastic teaching is conveyed through the traditional metaphors: cognition is seen as static, as light; appetite is seen as dynamic, as motion. The metaphor of motion that Vives constantly uses incorporates both the Stoic sense of movements within the soul (effusion, lifting, expansion, shrinking) and the Aristotelian sense of the soul's moving toward or away from the object. And it is in the latter sense that cognition plays a more evident role. A being capable of moving toward or away from an object cannot move unless the object becomes known as either desirable or repulsive. In spite of its traditional jargon about "faculties" of the soul, Vives' teaching lacks any metaphysical pretense. Knowledge and appetite are not ontologically different parts of the soul but two aspects or powers of our being that are essentially intermingled. As desire is blind without thought, thought is paralyzed without desire. If "all cognition is for the sake of seeking the good," even speculative knowledge is permeated by the desire to know the truth, a conclusion that Vives suggests, even though he fails to present it in explicit terms.[6]

The intimate relationship between thought and emotion explains why, as thought guides emotion, so too emotion affects thought in many different ways. Authentic love perfects knowledge while selfish love misrepresents the value of the loved object. We tend to neglect the study of those disciplines that irritate us because they do not go well with our own intellectual talents. Jealousy fosters false illusions and imaginations. Envy distorts judgment; it exaggerates the trivial and misrepresents beauty. Fear "drives away any wisdom from the soul." Pride makes people intellectually stubborn and impervious to intelligent advice. Memory retention is reinforced by the strong emotion associated with events and objects. Irritable and hasty people can rush to unwarranted conclusions. Fear, anger, and shyness can slow down and even halt our entire reasoning process. Intellectual incredulity is a creature of suspicion, and suspicion can be fostered by lack of self-esteem, diffidence, and fear. The unfathomable and complex interactions between thought, emotion, bodily temperament, and environmental circumstance explain the extraordinary variety of personality traits, a variety that Vives attempts to study in his pioneer reflections on *ingenium*.[7]

Judgment is essential to emotion in the sense that no emotion is possible without some form of preceding cognition. Vives, however, admits that there are some "natural impulses" of the soul that precede any judgment. The problem is that such natural impulses include not only bodily sensations (thirst, hunger, pain) but also the desires accompanying them (desire to eat or drink), the sadness or joy associated with feeling sick or healthy, and the irritation caused by pain. These "natural impulses" of the soul that "arise from the affected body" alone are neither preceded nor controlled by judgment. Vives discards their consideration not only because they are uncontrolled by thought, but because as such they are independent of choice and morally neutral, although as we shall see later they are, together with judgment, important codeterminants of our emotional and moral existence.

Vives also admits that some emotions are so abrupt and violent that they "seem sometimes to precede judgment" (*praevertere nonnunquam animi judicio putantur;* M 3.422; Introduction, 62–63). The reason is that by "judgment" Vives does not understand a formal proposition stating the conclusion of a reasoning process, but any form of cognition, including "a mere commotion of the fantasy bearing any resemblance to the belief or judgment that something is good or bad," a commotion which is enough to disturb our soul with all kinds of emotions (M 3.423). Vives' notion of "the visions of the imagination" (*imaginationis moventur visis;* M 3.423) as the minimal cognitive determinant of emotion stands halfway between the Stoic concept of "judgment" (*krísis*) and the rich contemporary explorations into the intentional components of emotions.[8]

Vives' thought-provoking appeal to the role of the imagination and consequently to that of memory in explaining the etiology of emotion is closely linked to his insistence that the object of any emotion is never what is really good or bad but only "what the individual judges to be good or bad" (*quod quisque sibi esse judicat bonum vel malum;* M 3.422). Anger is caused not by the harm done to us by another, but by the *belief* that somebody has done something that we *believe* to be harmful to us. Unfortunately, that belief is itself reinforced by the pride and the suspicion of the person who holds such a belief (M 3.476). Indignation is caused not by the undeserved good fortune of another, but by the *belief* that another is enjoying what we *believe* to be good fortune and by the *belief* that the other does not deserve it. In fact, indignation presupposes an individual perception of "just deserts" that is deeply rooted in what today we call the value system of the individual. Reflective people fear more often because they think more about what they believe to be dangerous.

Emotions, therefore, do not inform us about reality itself, but only about the way reality is perceived by each individual. Democritus, Vives says, was always laughing because he was amused by the follies of man. Heracleitus was always crying because he sympathized with all human miseries (M 3.423). But since our opinions are themselves affected by emotion, the world view of each person shapes and is shaped by his emotional life, a life that includes emotions, motivations, character traits, beliefs, memories, and moods. This explains not only the immense variety of opinions, but also the possibility of both error and enlightenment. The baffling variety of human opinions and beliefs is matched by the equally baffling variety of human feelings, emotions, moods, and motivations. In this restricted sense it is true that emotions define us and our relation to the world, that we are partially responsible for them, and that affective interpretation and personal identity mutually help to constitute each other. Emotions are not judgments but entail them; emotions are not pieces of behavior but dispose people to some forms of behavior. To have an emotion is no doubt to hold a normative judgment about one's situation, but the emotion does not coincide with the judgment itself. Emotions have a dynamism of their own, hence one may have a judgment about the goodness or evil of something without experiencing the corresponding emotion, to see the emotion fade with fatigue while the judgment remains vigorous and unchanged.

It is certainly possible for some people to work themselves up into some emotion for the purpose of manipulating other persons. But most emotions, particularly the strong ones, are more "suffered" than planned. They are responses to perceived situations rather than strategies with a purpose. To be overcome by grief denotes an emotion we are subjected to rather than a self-engineered form of manipulative behavior, although the way grief overcomes the individual, and, even more so, the way grief is expressed in observable behavior are themselves a function of the individual's *ingenium* and of different environmental variables, social, cultural, historical, ethnic, and so forth. The sadness we experience at the sudden death of a person dear to us fits much better into the classic paradigm of "passion" than into the existentialist model of "purposive self-definition." Vives was wise to uphold here a model itself sanctioned by the wisdom of ordinary language.

Thought—even as "a vision of the fantasy"—is not only a necessary condition for the possibility of having emotions, but also the final ground for discriminating between them. Vives' definition of each emotion depends on whether we *think* that the object is good or evil, present or future, past or possible, possessed or not possessed, easy or difficult to obtain, magnificent or abject, harmful or favorable to us, deserved or not deserved by others, novel or familiar. The fact that emotions are to a large extent caused and determined by thought makes possible a therapy of emotion based upon intellectual enlightenment, reflective reassessment, the education of our fantasy, the cultivation of proper memory associations, and so forth. On the other hand, the fact that thought is only one of the determinants of emotions—albeit an indispensable one—explains why Vives envisions such therapy as a complex strategy that, as we shall see later, involves not only cognitive but also environmental and physiological factors.

Emotion and the Body

Although Vives makes a distinction between bodily appetites that "ignore and bypass judgment" (*transilit judicium neque illi auscultat;* M 3.437) and emotions, the distinction remains blurred. According to him, emotions are appetites preceded by judgment. But since the term *judgment* is extended to include any form of cognition, emotions themselves constitute a complete series that begins with such "earthly" desires as the desire to eat, prompted by the sensation of hunger, to the desire of God caused by our alleged knowledge of the First Cause. In the chapter on pleasure (Chapter 9), Vives presents such a hierarchy of emotions: emotions of pleasure that "stretch out" all the way from the pleasures derived from the sense of touch, "the earthly sense," to the pleasures made possible by intellectual contemplation. The same could obviously be said about pain, a topic that our philosopher discusses only under the topics of "irritation" and "sadness."

This hierarchy of emotional reactions exemplifies once again Vives' deep commitment to the principle of substantial unity between body and soul. As we saw in the chapter on *ingenium,* the soul cannot dispense with the instrumentality of the body. All human cognition begins with sensory cognition. All human emotions are psychosomatic events, not only the passions triggered by "the visions of the fantasy" but, in one way or another, even the highest forms of pure love and desire.

As earlier suggested, Vives, more perhaps than any other philosopher before him, was eager to explore in detail the physiological aspect of our emotional life. This emphasis on the inextricable union of body and soul as reflected in emotional activity, an echo perhaps of the Renaissance interest in the body and of the rediscovery of Galen's endocrinology, may well have had a significant influence on Descartes' *Traité des passions de l'âme,* a work that obviously betrays similar concerns, though from a different philosophical perspective.

Since all human cognition is rooted in sensory knowledge, and that knowledge is made possible by bodily organs, our emotional reactions to cognitive experiences are also deeply ingrained in our body. This is why, Vives claims, emotions are called warm, cold, dry, or wet (M 3.423), the same qualities that determine bodily temperament. Love, joy, and pride are hot passions. Irritation, hatred, and sadness are cold and dry. The quality of our bodily temperament depends itself on the quality of the "animal spirits" that exhale from the pericardial blood and from the balance of the four basic humors (hot blood, cold phlegm, dry yellow bile, and wet black bile).

To Vives, the most obvious manifestation of the body's impact upon our emotional life is the fact that bodily temperament predisposes individuals toward a particular set of emotions, an aspect of Vives' thought we have previously discussed in the chapter on *ingenium*. "Some emotions," he says, "were given to us by nature according to our bodily constitution" (*sunt quidam affectus a natura inditi ex constitutione corporis;* M 3.425).[9] The desires of hot temperaments are—like fire itself—vehement and fickle. The desires of cold temperaments are sluggish and stubborn (M 3.437). Resemblance in bodily constitution accounts in some cases for the initial attraction between lovers (M 3.429).

Whatever affects bodily temperament affects our emotional habits. The temperament of the body is affected by internal and external circumstances. Among the internal circumstances are the emotions themselves. Vives, always alert to the complex and sometimes mysterious interactions between causes, hastens to make clear that emotions "not only reflect but contribute also to the temperament of the body" (*affectus enim rationem corporis non recipiunt modo, sed praestant;* M 3.423), a topic we shall discuss later. Here we are more concerned with those material circumstances, such as food, drink, age, and diseases, that are or become internal to the body and produce physiological changes that alter the temperament of the body. The Valencian exile who hated the sausages of Oxford and the rotten fish of Louvain was more than willing to accept the Hippocratic teaching about the importance of diet. People who drink water are irascible and passionate. People who drink wine or beer are less excitable (M 3.479). A diet of warm and moist food mixed with some wine helps to heat up the black bile and weaken the emotion of sadness (M 3.499–500) Wine is particularly effective in reinforcing confidence and dispelling fears (M 3.506). Cholerics become less excitable with a wholesome diet of fat foods and cold drinks (M 3.481).

Age and state of health are also determinants of emotional reaction. Desire, for instance, depends on them for its object. The young desire pleasure, adults seek respectability, the sick long for health, old people worry about maintenance, and rulers lust after glory (M 3.437). An abundance of warm pericardial blood in the young and the drunk inspires confidence and assuredness. Compassion is common among the old and ambition among the young. Even a small health problem is enough to destroy great and intense pleasures (M 3.468). Old age and sickness make people irritable, angry, and highly sensitive (M 3.479). Hunger and sickness make people melancholic and hateful (M 3.484). Bodily fatigue invites irritability (M 3.473).

As one could expect from a man who was practically forced to leave the balmy weather of Valencia for the rougher, cloudy skies of northern Europe, Vives placed great importance on the way climate and seasonal changes affect emotional disposition. The Hippocratic parallel between bodily temperaments and weather conditions—hot or cold, dry or wet and their different combinations—pushed him in the same direction. People, Vives teaches, tend to have the same passionate make-ups as the climates in which they live: they are either hot and dry or hot and wet, cold and dry or cold and wet. Because of personal experience all the way from Mediterranean Valencia to the northern Atlantic regions (Flanders, Brabant, and southern England), Vives was especially bent on contrasting the hot and dry temperaments with the cold and wet. Sadness, a cold passion, finds more victims in northern Europe than in Spain or in Italy, more on winter nights than summer days (M 3.499).

The somatic aspect of emotion goes far beyond the physiological conditioning of our emotional habits and dispositions. Emotions are not only fostered by our bodily temperament, but are also accompanied by distinctive physiological changes. Although these changes are as inseparable from the emotions themselves as the soul is inseparable from the body in its terrestrial journey, Vives clearly makes a distinction between them by considering emotions as causes and physiological changes as effects. This analysis is specially striking in the study of paradigmatic, strong, and clearly defined emotions. In the case of intense love, Vives writes, heat is diverted from the heart to the brain. Hence the pallor of face and body, the hard breathing, the tears and moans, the fluctuations in blushing or turning pale according to the concentration or the recession of the blood (M 3.447). Joy expands the heart so much that some people can die of it (M 3.463). The description of "the terrible effects" that anger causes in the body is clearly inspired by classical sources, such as Seneca's *De Ira*. The blood heats up, the heart swells and beats hard, the facial expression changes, the voice quivers, speaking becomes blurred, and the whole appearance of man becomes "more bestial than human." The brave become pale when angry because their blood seeks refuge in the heart. Cowards blush when angry because their blood goes up to their head (M 3.477). Envy causes a livid face, deep eye wrinkles, loss of weight, and a devious glance (M 3.487). Sadness contracts the heart to such an extent that the heart of persons who have died of sadness "is not much thicker than a membrane" (*non latius membrana;* M 3.499). This cold and dry emotion emaciates the face, ruins our health, and causes weeping and wailing (M 3.499). Fear weakens the heart, shakes the body, increases the heartbeat, makes the voice deeper and shaky, and makes one's hair stand on end (M 3.503).

Physiological changes brought about by an emotion are called expressions of that emotion when they are easily observable and identifiable. Beside all the changes we have just summarized, Vives describes in more detail the laughter generally associated with joy and pleasure (Chapter 10) and the tears generally associated with sadness (Chapter 20). Laughter, however, is not always an expression of emotion, for it can be a "bodily reaction" (*corporalis prorsus;* M 3.469) caused by the expansion of the diaphragm. Gladiators wounded under the armpit "laughed" that way. Vives himself laughed for the same reason while eating after a long fast (M 3.469).[10]

Nor is all laughter caused by joy and pleasure. There is also a "false" laughter caused by sadness, indignation, and anger. Descartes follows Vives in this point by emphasizing that such laughter is "feigned and contrived." Laughter, Vives continues, is a unique human privilege. Animals cannot laugh, not because they do not experience joys and pleasures, but because their face is "stiff and motionless" (M 3.470). Vives also tries to explain, without much success, the laughter associated with humor and our sense of the ridiculous. All laughter thrives on novelty. That is why ignorant people, children, and women (once again!) are more vulnerable to distasteful outbursts of laughter.

Vives gives a simple and quick explanation of tears. Tears are only "a humor trickling down through the eyes from a brain moistened and softened by heat" (M 3.500). The heat of excessive grief or long-lasting sadness is enough to dry up the tears, an observation that Descartes repeats almost word for word. All the warm emotions are capable of provoking us to tears: grief, love, desire, anger, envy, shame, joy, admiration for a noble deed. Nevertheless Vives suggests that all tears are "tears of compassion" for ourselves or others, a sense of compassion that can easily be triggered by the mere imagination of impending or possible evils.

Emotion and the Environment

Beside the physical conditions either internal to the body or directly affecting the body, Vives mentions other external circumstances of the environment that shape our emotional habits and dispositions. In his pedagogical writings, Vives insists that the location of a school is of primary importance in fostering the love of learning among youngsters.[11] The contemplation of a serene and beautiful landscape plays an important part in the therapy of emotion (as I shall point out in Chapter 20). Good architecture and pleasant music can instill confidence and joy (M 3.506).

Emotional disposition and expression are mostly affected by the situation of the individual within a given ethnic, social, and cultural environment. Emotions both reflect and reinforce the social bonds that tie individuals to a group, a cohort, a class, a nation, or a culture. For social life to be possible, human beings must not only be endowed with the capacity to feel certain emotions but also with the capacity to express them in a way that other humans can easily recognize. For instance, Vives teaches that a man incapable of feeling and expressing compassion for others is "completely inhuman," a "stone," or a "statue" (M 3.460, 461).

The emotions that humans experience and the way they express them are not for Vives the direct and unadulterated manifestations of natural inclinations and needs. Unlike animal emotions, human emotions are to some extent relative to their ethnic, historical, social, and cultural milieu. Ethiopians are not ashamed of being black, pygmies are not ashamed of being short (M 3.512). Southern people are much more disposed to jealousy than northerners (M 3.491). The feeling of compassion dwindles among soldiers in the midst of war or among obtuse peasants in times of peace (M 3.461). Social gatherings with friends discourage sad or even serious thoughts about personal obligations and duties (M 3.464), while public festivities can sometimes, by contrast, exacerbate feelings of self-pity and sadness (M 3.499). Community of interest and the sharing of risks enhance love and mutual attraction (M 3.439). Merchants are disposed to greed, rulers to cruelty, and scholars to pride. Spoiled children are more irritable than those children who have been properly trained (M 3.473). The feeling of envy thrives most among peers, people whose standards of performance and achievement have been clearly defined by society: "potters envy potters, beggars envy beggars, and poets envy poets" (M 3.488). The emotions felt in times of novel or long-lasting prosperity are different from the emotions that follow an unexpected misfortune, a sudden loss of property or reputation, the onset of a serious disease, the death of a friend or relative (M 3.459).

The social environment not only determines the range of possible emotions, it strongly influences the manner of their expression. Although Vives seems to assume that there are some unvarying forms of emotional expression, such as the laughter of joy and the tears of sadness and compassion, he is eager to emphasize that, in some cases at least, different people express the same emotion in different manners. Thus, he says, the Romans took off their hats as an expression of submissive respect, while western Europeans in the sixteenth century genuflect for the same purpose (M 3.455). Children, women, and ignorant peasants show their joy with outbursts of laughter, but mature and intelligent men display their joy with a smile (M 3.470).

The impact of the nonphysical environment upon human emotions can be gauged by the baffling complexity of human emotional life. False opinions about value that are perpetuated by education and custom have added to the number of true human needs a cumbersome load of artificial and culturally conditioned wants and desires, "an enormous and superfluous weight" (*immane pondus adjecimus superfluitatum;* M 3.424). This complexity of emotional life separates human beings from the simple and straightforward emotions of an animal. Animal emotions are mostly rooted in the present, directed by instinctive sensory reactions to the challenges of the environment, free from the whimsical constructions of fantasy, unaffected by moral or religious values. Animals are not saddened by the haunting memory of past evils nor excited by the prospect of future good. Animals are neither greedy nor proud, cruel nor indignant. Noble ancestry, political power, riches, reputation, and glory are never within the range of animal desire (M 3.437). Man, Vives says, is "a difficult animal" (M 3.474). To the irritations that any animal can feel, he has added an impressive number of exclusively human irritations. Animals are irritated by pain, hunger, thirst, heat. We, too, are irritated by all of those but also by the lies of others, by our own shortcomings, delays, false opinions, rumors, the strange and unusual behavior of others (M 3.472–74). Unlike animals, humans become "intolerable to others and find others intolerable" (*nec ipse tolerabilis est cuiquam nec potest alia tolerare;* M 3.474).[12] Remorse, shame, boredom, anxiety, objectless sensations of fear, embarrassment, nostalgia, contempt, and shyness are emotions that originate in the complex web of human society, and only in a derivative sense can they be ascribed to animals.

Emotion and Action

To Vives, human action is the visible, external manifestation of the will. Emotions are not forms of behavior but are externalized in behavior. Anger is not "to anger-behave," as modern behaviorists would have it, but rather the motive to behave in an angry manner. External behavior and action manifest an emotion at the same time as the motive to behave according to that emotion. The inextricable link between emotion and behavior is part of the teleology of emotion that God the Creator has wisely implanted in our nature. God, Vives teaches, "provided all animals with emotions as incentives to move souls destined to inhabit bodies," incentives that work as "spurs to move the soul this or that way, or as reins to restrain it from running into the harmful" (M 3.423). In contrast with the Stoic tradition, Vives sees emotions not necessarily as irrational excesses to be denied and canceled, but as potentially positive sources of energy and as divinely ordained parts of human nature. Evil would certainly find more victims if humans were not endowed by God with the capacity to be irritated immediately by its presence. Life in society would be impossible if its members were incapable of feeling ashamed of improper forms of behavior. Without compassion life would be "fierce and cruel" (M 3.460). To Seneca's claim that one can help the needy without being handicapped by the painful feeling of compassion, Vives answers that without compassion no one would be motivated internally to help others in the long run and would be unable totally to provide them with the most profound consolation: the awareness that others share their pain and their suffering (M 3.460–61).

De Anima et Vita presents some exquisite, detailed, colorful descriptions of emotional behavior. Vives' profound dislike of intellectual arrogance speaks eloquently through the pages of the last chapter, which is about pride. The proud man, he says, thinks that he is always entitled to the best, despises everybody as unimportant and beneath his dignity, envies the good qualities or fortunes of others, constantly seeks to make an impression, and to be honored by others. The proud man is showy and ostentatious, afraid to reveal his shortcomings, talkative, and loud. The proud man dresses, plays, and walks in a characteristic fashion, seeks novelty for the sake of novelty, refuses to follow orders or advice. The proud man feigns wealth and power, is insolent and threatening to others, always irritating and irritable. The proud man refuses to learn from others or to change his opinion, is sectarian and intellectually stubborn. The proud man is angry, vengeful, suspicious, contentious, sometimes even proud of condemning his own pride. Pride is to Vives the main culprit for the "corruption of the arts" and the greatest obstacle to their progress.

Similarly revealing of Vives' personal attitudes is his spicy description of the ways lovers behave (Chapter 4). Lovers ignore the deformities and defects of those they love, constantly think of them with great intensity, seek to be in the same place, and to see and talk to them. Lovers flatter each other with reciprocal praise, are eager to prove their love with challenging deeds, are always anxious and apprehensive, ingenious, and active. Lovers are particularly vulnerable to jealousy and to envy. Lovers engineer melodramatic quarrels for the sake of enjoying pleasurable reconciliations. Heavy breathing, frequent moanings, pallor of the face, and generous tears are telling signs of passionate love. Lovers often burst into song, stare at each other, by turns grow cold or hot, are restless and impatient, awkward in their praise of the beloved, and suddenly irritated by trivial details. Lovers enjoy silly conversations, trivial gossip, worn-out jokes. Lovers are incapable of extended and serious dialogue and indulge frequently in expressions of endearment that others find ridiculous and contrived. Lovers think acutely, become eloquent and poetic, obsessive, resourceful, inventive, and witty.

Vives also provides rich descriptions of the behavior inspired by hate, envy, jealousy, fear, and embarrassment. People full of hatred are given to slander, cruelty, violence, and chicanery (M 3.485). Envious people also enjoy slander, tend to distort everything they hear or see, exaggerate petty details, lose their power of fair and realistic judgment (M 3.488). Jealousy causes insomnia, leads to hatred, titillates the imagination, and fosters desires for disproportionate revenge (M 3.491). Fear is often accompanied by depression, self-incrimination, suspicion, submissiveness to others, anxiety, agitation, laziness, and desperation (M 3.505). Embarrassment and shame cause confusion, dispel sober thinking, increase self-diffidence and shyness (M 3.512–13).

We could summarize Vives' views on this general topic by saying that emotions are affections of the orectic powers of the soul, either the will or the sensory appetite that, according to God's Providence, help us to avoid evil and seek what is good for us; that they are responses to cognitive encounters with the world through sense, memory, imagination, or judgment; that as such they entail and reflect the individual's perception of reality and are commensurate with bodily temperament and disposition and therefore partially determined by those physiological and environmental circumstances which directly or indirectly affect the body; that they involve physiological changes that are partially manifested in external gestures and behavior; that they presuppose and reinforce social ties and bonds, and that consequently they are also partially determined by the ethnic, historical, social, and cultural environment of the individual; and that, finally, emotions are inextricably tied to external behavior as motives and incentives to act in a certain manner.

16
The Classification of Emotions

IN THE FIRST CHAPTER of *De Anima et Vita*, Book 3, Vives provides a sketchy classification of emotional responses. Each one of the ensuing chapters begins with or includes a short definition of each emotion. This emphasis on taxonomy and definition, no matter how light and unsystematic it might be, is characteristic of a Western philosophical tradition that stretches from Plato to at least Hume, and sets Vives apart from contemporary ways of thinking. Most philosophers today distrust abstract theories that disregard "the muddles that come from staying too close to the descriptive ground," recognize the fact that "our vocabulary (regarding emotional responses) is in disarray," are suspicious of natural kinds, have abandoned the hope of making a clear distinction between emotions on one side and moods, motives, attitudes, and character traits on the other, and emphasize the complex and sometimes overlapping intentional structure of interacting emotions.[1] Contemporary philosophers are therefore more keen to provide us with rich and detailed descriptions of emotions than with simple and elegant dichotomies and schematic diagrams, more inclined to borrow from the language of neurophysiology, psychology, biology, and anthropology than from a metaphysical language about "soul partitions" or the "formal object" of our "faculties." In this chapter, I shall present Vives' taxonomy of the emotions, assess his position within the philosophical tradition, and draw some conclusions about the originality of his thought.

To make such assessment possible, I have chosen five concrete points of reference which I find particularly relevant: Aristotle's *Rhetoric*, the medieval Latin translation of Pseudo-Andronicus' *Perí Pathōn*, the *Summa Theologiae* of Saint Thomas, Descartes' *Traité des passions*, and finally Spinoza's *Ethica*.

Aristotle's classic treatment of the emotions can be found in Book 2 of the *Rhetoric*, rather than in *On the Soul* where it seems to belong. At the beginning of the latter treatise, Aristotle limits himself to proclaim that everything that affects the soul affects also the body (403a16), and that for this reason alone the study of the soul belongs to the physicist. A complete definition of an emotion involves therefore a reference to the bodily movement—the concern of the physicist—and a reference to its efficient and final cause—the concern of the dialectician. While the physicist would define anger as a boiling of the blood, the dialectician would say that anger is the appetite for returning pain for pain (403b29–31). Unfortunately for us, the Aristotelian corpus has not preserved any analysis of emotional life combining the material and the formal, the physiological and the phenomenological. The physiology of emotion is never offered anywhere, except for some scattered observations on the role of emotion in recollection and dreams. The "dialectical' study of emotional responses is presented in Book 2 of the *Rhetoric,* as part of Aristotle's analysis of what he calls "modes of persuasion." Rhetoric for Aristotle was the counterpart of dialectic, the study of argumentative modes of persuasion in the courts of law (forensic rhetoric), in political debate (political or deliberative rhetoric), and in praising virtue or censuring vice (epideictic rhetoric). These modes of persuasion include the power of evincing a personal character that makes a speech credible, the power of stirring the emotions of the hearers, and the power of proving a truth. The study of emotions in Book 2 is aimed at enhancing the power of stirring emotions. Such a goal dictates the scope and the limitations of the inquiry. Aristotle selects the following emotions: anger, friendship, fear, shame, pity, indignation, and emulation. In each case he studies the disposition and conditions that give rise to that particular emotion, the objects to which it is directed, and the typical grounds on which it is felt. Aristotle's limited catalogue of basic emotions makes no attempt at classification. But the Aristotelian description of those emotions—partially complemented by the study of the affective reactions of an audience to tragedy in the *Poetics*— remained a classic point of departure to any philosophical study of emotional life. Vives, too, while complaining about the merely political character of Aristotle's analysis, freely borrowed from the master.

The Pseudo-Andronicus' catalogue of definitions of emotions is generally accepted as a highly eclectic compilation of Platonic, Peripatetic, and mostly Stoic sources written in Rome during the Imperial Age, translated into Latin by Robert Grosseteste in the thirteenth century, and well known to Saint Albert and Saint Thomas. I am not suggesting that the Latin translation of Pseudo-Andronicus' classic was known to Vives. What is important is that the *Perí Pathōn* (Concerning the passions), summarizes in a most reliable and thorough manner the same Stoic ancient sources that had inspired the compendia Vives had no doubt easy access to, such as those written by Diogenes Laertius, Cicero, Plutarch, Galen, and Saint Clement of Alexandria.[2]

Saint Thomas' thorough study *De Passionibus Animae in Generali* in *Summa Theologiae* (IaIIae. 22–48) is considered here in spite of Vives' apparent detachment from this classic medieval text; the contrast between it and Vives' tract highlights the striking difference between the systemic rigidity of scholastic philosophy and the looser descriptive approach of Vives. In many ways the difference between Saint Thomas and Vives epitomizes the change from medieval to Renaissance patterns of thinking.

Descartes' and Spinoza's great works are particularly relevant to us not only because of the latter's relation to the former and Descartes' acknowledged familiarity with Vives, but also because the authors' ambitious efforts to classify all the emotions represent the last rationalist attempt to formulate a grand theory of emotion. This confident attempt provides a sharp antithetical background to contemporary thought and helps us to assess Vives' modernity.

Vives' classification of emotions (which he significantly calls "a catalogue of emotions": *enumeratio affectuum;* M 3.426; title of Chapter 1) proceeds according to some traditional parameters, emotions toward the good, away or against evil, emotions about present, past, future or possible and imagined objects, intense and weak emotions, stable and fleeting emotions, incipient and deep-set emotions. The incipient movement of the soul toward the good is called attraction (*allubescentia*). A deep-seated attraction toward the good is love (*amor*). The love of a good actually possessed produces joy (*laetitia*) and pleasure (*delectatio*). Under love we find the (less generic?) emotions of fondness (*favor*), reverence or respect (*reverentia*), and compassion (*misericordia*). The love of a good not yet possessed produces desire (*cupiditas*) and hope (*spes*). The incipient movement of the soul away from evil is called annoyance (*offensio*). A deep-seated and well-established annoyance turns into hatred (*odium*). The hatred of a present evil produces sorrow and sadness (*moeror*). Under sadness we find the (less generic?) emotion of bereavement (*desiderium*). The hatred of a future evil is fear (*metus*). The motion of the soul against a present evil is anger (*ira*) or envy (*invidia*) and indignation (*indignatio*). The movement of the soul against a future evil is either confidence (*fiducia*) or daring (*audacia*).

That this classification of emotions was not very important to Vives is obvious from the fact that in writing his own treatise on the emotions he did not hesitate to deviate from it or even to ignore it without further explanation. The order of the treatise subverts the initially promised order of classification. Fondness (Chapter 5) is discussed after love and pleasure, the analysis of hatred is followed by a chapter (Chapter 12) on contempt, anger precedes sadness (Chapter 19). Confidence and daring are treated as afterthoughts within the chapter on fear (Chapter 21). Attraction and bereavement are summarily dismissed (M 3.428, 498) while annoyance deserves a full chapter (Chapter 11), a detail that might have some significance for understanding Vives' character and attitudes. Contempt, jealousy, desire for revenge, cruelty, and shame are not even mentioned in Chapter 1, but are discussed at length in the rest of the treatise (Chapters 12, 16, 18, and 23). Pride is described by Vives himself as "a monster composed of many emotions" (M 3.426).

The parameters of intensity and stability are virtually ignored, except in the case of attraction-love and annoyance-hatred, even though Vives explicitly remarks that some emotions, such as love and hatred, are "naturally powerful" (*natura sunt validi;* M 3.427) while others, such as fondness and reverence, are less intense and more stable. The fundamental distinction between emotions that have the good as their object and those that deal with evil and "brutalize the human soul" becomes a nuisance to Vives when he is dealing with several emotions. It is a nuisance in dealing with compassion, a noble emotion that evil makes possible; when dealing with envy, an ignoble emotion caused by the good of others; and when dealing with hope, an emotion about a good, but about a good that we, as finite and contingent beings, do not yet possess. In fact, in the second half of the book, Vives discusses hope, putting it in the somber company of such emotions as sadness, fear, shame, revenge, hatred, and anger. Nor does it seem totally correct to say that all the human emotions that react to evil in the world are themselves evil and that they brutalize our spirit. Vives himself proclaims that irritation is good in the sense that it makes us recoil from evil at the first encounter with it (M 3.474) and that anger makes us strive after what is best and beyond any possible reproach by others (M 3.483). How can the contempt for the vile be vile itself? Who could say that the hatred of evil brutalizes man? Indignation is praised by the Scriptures, as Vives explicitly admits; and compassion, caused by the undeserved evil of another, is an important Christian virtue. Without being capable of fear, man would constantly hurt himself. Social life would become impossible if we were deprived of the feeling of shame, as Vives himself emphasizes (M 3.514). Even pride, Vives says, is not bad in itself. Pride helps us to recognize the excellence of our origin and our spiritual destination (M 3.520). In fact, the only emotion that Vives characterizes as essentially evil is "authentic envy," the sorrow we feel when we think of the good of another without any consideration of our own interest, beyond the fact that we think it bad for us that others do well. This is the way the Devil envies, Vives says. Other forms of envy were given to us by God as "stimuli to desiring and preserving important goods" (M 3.490).

Vives' frequent emphasis on the distinction between those emotions that shun evil (*a malo*) and those emotions that challenge and defy evil (*in malum*) seems to fade away in his attempt to contrast the emotions of hatred and sorrow on one hand and anger, envy, and indignation on the other. The same applies to the contraposition of fear and confidence-daring. More significantly, perhaps, the temporal parameter (present-past-future) plays a negligible role in the definitions of most emotions, except for the definition of desire, fear, confidence, daring, and revenge. It is particularly striking that Vives, the former editor of Saint Augustine's *De Civitate Dei,* had almost nothing to say in his lengthy chapter on shame (Chapter 23) about such Christian emotions directed toward past actions as remorse and guilt. Renaissance-like considerations of worldly propriety, fame, and honor seem to prevail over more eschatological and religious concerns.

Vives' lackadaisical attitude toward the taxonomy of emotions represents an interesting departure from tradition. The *Perí Pathōn* organizes all emotions as species of four generic passions: sadness and fear, desire and pleasure (in this order). The distinction between these generic emotions is derived from two related sources: the presence or absence of evil and good, and the psychological reaction of the soul to that presence or absence. The terms that the Pseudo-Andronicus — or rather Chrysippus, from whom the definitions were obviously taken — uses to describe such psychological impact, can still be found in Vives. Sadness and fear are described by Vives as "contractions" of the soul (*animi contractio;* M 3.498 and 502), a term very similar to the term *constrictio* used by Grosseteste in his medieval translation of the Pseudo-Andronicus. On the other hand, the Stoic characterization of desire as an irrational "lifting of the soul" (*elevatio*) and of pleasure as an irrational "expansion" (*diffusio*) of the soul, are abandoned by Vives in favor of more Aristotelian terms. The Pseudo-Andronicus lists twenty-four species of sadness, thirteen of fear, twenty-five of desire, and five of pleasure. Only in the case of desire do we find a modest attempt to make a distinction between species and subspecies: under anger we find the subspecies of *furor* (incipient anger), *chólos* (inflated anger), *mēnis* (lasting anger), and *kótos* (anger patiently waiting for revenge).[3]

The Pseudo-Andronicus' catalogue, like many others of Stoic extraction, betrays only a modest amount of philosophical concern, and sounds more like a rhetorician's lexicon than a philosopher's analysis of emotion. Still, the very enterprise of classifying emotions under generic headings seems to be inspired by an Aristotelian commitment to the principle that human language is neatly grouped into a structure of classes and subclasses and that such a grouping corresponds and reflects the natural kinds that make up the essential texture of reality. In this way the Aristotelian drive toward biological taxonomy was extended by the ancient Stoics to all the varieties of emotional responses. But if the principle behind the attempt to classify emotions was profoundly philosophical, the execution of the project was not. The endless variations under the four generic emotions are simply listed without any visible organizing principle, as a lexicon rather than as a system.

Vives' classification of emotions differs from the catalogue compiled by the Pseudo-Andronicus in some interesting respects. Unlike the author of the Stoic compilation, Vives makes no attempt to subsume all emotions under a small number of generic ones, although some of them (love, hatred, desire, fear, joy, and sadness) emerge as the main emotions and others are clearly derivative (attraction, favor, reverence, compassion, anger, envy, etc.).[4] Nor does Vives try to list all possible variants of each emotion, as only the Greeks could do. In fact, Vives' passing remark that the Greek vocabulary on emotions was much richer than its Latin counterpart (M 3.438) suggests the remote possibility that he was acquainted with the Latin translation of *Perí Pathōn* although a reading of Cicero's *Tusculanae Disputationes* could have had a similar effect on him. Of the sixty-seven Greek terms listed by the Pseudo-Andronicus to name the varieties of sadness, fear, desire, and pleasure, Grosseteste found only twelve that could be translated into ordinary Latin (*misericordia, invidia, zelus, calamitas, paenitudo, confusio, nemesis, luctus, cura, agonia, ira, furor*). The other fifty-two were just transliterated into Latin and remained unacceptable jargon (words such as *deima, thórybos, deilía, katáplēxis, dysnoia*, and so on).

The initial drive toward the sytematization of emotions that we find in ancient Stoic catalogues reached its full expression in the *Summa Theologiae*. The most striking difference between the Stoic and the Christian classification of emotions is the central role that love plays in the latter. To the Stoics, *eros amicitiae* or love of friendship was only a species of desire, like anger. To Saint Thomas, love is the "first of all passions" (*prima passionum;* IaIIae. 25, 3), the cause of all emotions, even the cause of hatred, since "it is precisely because one wants some good that one rejects the opposing evil" (IaIIae. 25, 2). Saint Thomas nevertheless emphasizes that in some sense the four principal emotions are joy and sorrow, fear and hope, for "in them all the others have their end and fulfillment" (IaIIae. 25, 4). It is worth noticing that this short list coincides with the Stoic generic emotions except for the substitution of hope for desire, a variation that Saint Augustine preferred but that Saint Thomas sacrificed to the authority of Boethius and to the argument that hope rather than desire represents the last stage of the soul's movement toward the good.[5]

Saint Thomas' own classification of emotions was completely dictated by systematic principles derived from the metaphorical concept of emotion as a movement of the soul. The division of emotions into species is organized by the different directions (approach or withdrawal) and the different stages (initial reaction-movement-repose) of motion. The direction of motion is dictated by the formal object of the emotion. Goodness provokes a movement of pursuit and evil a movement of avoidance. But in our fallen condition, good can be perceived as good as such or as arduous. The arduous good attracts as good but repels as arduous. In a similar fashion, evil can be perceived as simply evil or as an evil that can be challenged and managed by us. A manageable evil repels as evil but can be challenged as manageable. Emotions that deal with good and evil as such are called *concupiscible* emotions. Emotions that deal with good and evil as arduous or manageable are called *irascible* emotions. Love is the first pursuit of the good, desire the full motion of the soul toward the good loved, pleasure the repose in the possession of the good. Hatred is the first movement away from evil, aversion (an emotion Saint Thomas neglects to analyze in more detail) is the first motion of the soul away from the hated evil, pain the result of an evil possessed. Hope is the movement toward an arduous good as good, while despair is the movement toward an arduous good as arduous. Again, fear is the movement of the soul away from an evil perceived as unmanageable. Courage is a movement of the soul that challenges a manageable evil perceived as such. Anger is a movement of the soul against a present or past evil that cannot be avoided. In this neat manner all the emotions—except anger—are organized in pairs of contraries: love-hate, desire-aversion, pleasure-pain, hope-despair, fear-courage.

Saint Thomas' elegant systematization is complemented by a whole array of clarifications. The relations of contrariety, specificity, and causality are carefully analyzed. Love and hatred, for instance, are contraries only when they bear upon the same object. Sorrow is opposed to joy as pain is opposed to pleasure. Sorrow and pleasure, however, are not only not contrary, but are akin with regard to different objects: rejoicing in goodness is akin to sorrowing over evil (IaIIae. 35, 5). Hope is the contrary of despair, though not in the same way that love is the contrary of hate because in the concupiscible emotions the soul approaches or withdraws from different objects, while in the irascible emotions the soul approaches or withdraws from the same object (IaIIae. 40, 4). The fact that anger has no contrary emotion is fully explained (IaIIae. 23, 4). In the case of anger there can be neither a contrariety based on a different object, nor any based on a different attitude to the same object, since an evil that is happening or has already happened cannot provoke the impulse to take flight from it. Calm, or the cessation of anger, is not the contrary but the negation of anger (IaIIae. 40, 4).

The relation between generic and specific emotions is also clearly differentiated. Pity, envy, anxiety, and torpor are not genuine species of sorrow because what is added to the genus-concept of sorrow to arrive at their definitions is not virtually but only extrinsically contained in the genus-concept (IaIIae. 35, 8). Unlike sorrow, which "happens in many different ways," pleasure is not subdivided into different species (ad 1). Anger involves a number of emotions, not as genus does species, but rather as an effect embodies its cause (IaIIae. 46, 2).

In a brilliant page of the *Summa Theologiae* (IaIIae. 25, 1), Saint Thomas establishes the relations of temporal priority, causality, and intensity between the concupiscible and the irascible emotions. These relations are ruled by two dynamic principles. Rest is first in intention and last in occurrence; irascible emotions display no element of repose. Irascible emotions precede therefore those concupiscible emotions which involve coming to rest in some good state of affairs: hope precedes joy, since every irascible emotion has as its term one of the concupiscible emotions that involves coming to rest, joy, or sadness. Concupiscible emotions that involve movement precede the relevant irascible emotions: desire precedes hope and aversion precedes fear because both hope and fear add something to desire and aversion. Furthermore, the relation between cause and effect explains a priori why emotions that are caused by other emotions are always weaker. Appearances notwithstanding, love, the cause of all emotions, is also the strongest emotion, certainly stronger than hatred (IaIIae. 29, 3). For the same reason, joy is stronger than hope and fear is stronger than sadness.

Vives' classification of emotions no doubt preserves some of the internal structure of Saint Thomas' study. Like him, Vives understands emotions in terms of movements of the soul. But unlike him, Vives does not use the metaphor as a paradigmatic matrix. Saint Thomas' efforts to explain how in one respect pleasure consists in being at rest and in another respect pleasure is a kind of movement (IaIIae. 31, 1 ad 1) makes little sense to Vives. As in the *Summa Theologiae*, love, hatred, desire, joy, sadness, hope, and fear occupy a central place in Vives' initial taxonomy. But the systemic rigidity of the great medieval scholastic plays no part in Vives' analysis of emotions. The central distinction between concupiscible and irascible emotions is abandoned by Vives, who objects explicitly to the tendency of Aristotelians to "attribute the performance of great deeds to the irascible part of the soul." To call "irascible" what is nothing but "a warming up of the blood" is only an abuse of the word, Vives writes (M 3.476). By abandoning this distinction, Vives escapes some of the pitfalls of the Thomistic classification, a classification which would force us to call hatred and grief "emotions of desire" and would place hope and fear among the "angry emotions."[6]

Saint Thomas' distinction between emotions that deal with either good or evil as such and emotions that deal with an arduous good or an avoidable (or unavoidable) evil is nevertheless echoed by the Vivesian distinction between emotions that shy away from evil (*a malo*) and those that challenge evil (*in malum*). But the distinction, which Vives explicitly makes in the first chapter of the treatise, fades away in the treatise itself, except to explain the contrast between fear and courage. The fact, however, that both courage and despair are almost ignored by Vives points to one of the shortcomings of his approach. He sacrifices the neatness and elegance of Saint Thomas to descriptive detail and to psychological and therapeutic concerns. Vives' tract falls at a midpoint between the disorganized lexicon of the Stoics and the rigid systematization of medieval scholasticism. There is no emphasis on contrariety or generic-specific relations. Causation is certainly analyzed by Vives, but never in the highly systematic manner of Saint Thomas. Vives is interested in describing the subtle and complex interaction between different emotions in as far as such description is conducive to self-knowledge and emotional rehabilitation, and thus useful to teachers, lawyers, priests, and diplomats. As a humanist deeply influenced by Rudolph Agricola, Vives' descriptions of each emotion follow in most cases the rhetorical model of a discourse *per locos,* a procedure that explains the redundant copiousness of some of the chapters of *De Anima et Vita.*[7]

Descartes approaches the classification of emotions with reservations more akin to Vives' lack of interest in theoretical schemes than to Saint Thomas' elegant systematization. The number of emotions, Descartes warns in the *Traité,* is "indefinite." The task of the philosopher is only to "enumerate" (*dénombrement,* a literal translation of the Latin term used by Vives, *enumeratio*), the "principal" emotions, a task that had not been fully accomplished, he claims, by previous writers. Like Vives, Descartes, too, rejects the Thomistic distinction between concupiscible and irascible emotions, a distinction that he wrongly thought presupposes a real division of the soul into parts (II, 68). His *enumeratio* includes six principal emotions. The rest, he says, are either "composed of some of these six or are species of them" (II, 69), a claim that sounds more scholastic than Vives' own designs. The first emotion, wonder (*l'admiration*), is unique in not being originated by the consideration of good and evil, but only by the consideration of the object's novelty (II, 70). There are two species of wonder, esteem (admiration of the novel and great) and disdain (admiration of the novel and small; III, 159). Impudence is disdain of fame and glory (III, 207). Cartesian wonder and Vivesian *allubescentia* show in common an attempt to give a name to the very first reaction of our appetite, although, as I will point out in the next chapter, there are significant differences between the two. Still, it is not impossible that Vives' original terminology might have had some influence upon Descartes. The other five principal emotions consist of two pairs of opposites (love-hatred, joy-sadness) and an emotion that has no opposite, desire.[8]

Descartes teaches also that love has different degrees (simple affection, friendship, devotion) and two different kinds (love of the good, and love of the beautiful or attraction [*agrément*]). Hatred, on the other hand, knows of no degrees "because we do not to the same extent notice the difference that exists between evils" (II, 84), a teaching that signifies an interesting departure from the scholastic and Vivesian doctrine that evil happens in many ways and provokes therefore a larger variety of emotions than the good. Descartes' outlook on life was obviously more positive and optimistic than that of Vives.[9] Echoing the division of love into two kinds, Descartes recognizes two kinds of hatred, the hatred of evil things and the hatred of ugly things, which he calls "horror" or "aversion" (III, 85).[10] Indignation, an emotion to which Vives dedicates an entire chapter, is dealt with by Descartes in the last part of the *Traité* as one species of hatred (III, 195). The different species of joy and sadness are not as neatly contrasted as the kinds of love and hatred. Descartes strikes a most original note in describing the feeling of joy we have when we see that worthy people other than ourselves enjoy good things, a feeling that is opposed to envy and pity in different ways and is derived from the recognition "that things happen as they should" (II, 72). Neither Saint Thomas nor Vives seem to have found in themselves a noble feeling of this kind.

Descartes departs even more from tradition by opposing the feeling of self-satisfaction to that of repentance (II, 73). The good done by others without relation to us provokes in us the feeling of favor.[11] If the same good has relation to us, it provokes gratitude (II, 64). Indignation and anger are directly opposed to favor and gratitude. The analysis of anger in articles 199–203 proceeds along traditional lines and repeats some of Vives' thoughts in Chapter 13 of *De Anima et Vita*. More interesting, perhaps, are Descartes' observations on three emotions he thought had been neglected by previous writers: tedium or sadness provoked by the duration of what is good (II, 67 and III, 208), gaiety, a joy excited by the passing away of some evil (II, 67 and III, 210), and regret, a bitter sadness caused by the memory of lost pleasures (II, 67 and III, 209).[12] Descartes' analysis of desire is probably the most controversial part of his work. Hope and fear are presented as two kinds of desire, the desire of things that we can probably obtain and the desire of things that are difficult to obtain (II,68). Jealousy is a species of fear, confidence is excessive hope and extreme fear becomes despair. Irresolution, courage, bravery, cowardice and emulation are all related to the selection of means in the pursuit of what is difficult to obtain (II, 68). Irresolution, courage, bravery, cowardice and emulation are all related to the selection of means in the pursuit of the arduous and are thus related to fear (II, 69). Like Vives himself, Descartes paid the price of some intellectual obscurity for his abandoning the Thomistic distinction between emotions that relate to the good or evil as such and the emotions that relate to the arduous good or the manageable evil. Nor was Descartes unquestionably correct in assuming that such a distinction was necessarily linked to a metaphysical theory about the division of the soul.

As a whole, Descartes' taxonomy of emotions is both theoretically tighter than that of Vives and richer in content. The *Traité* manages to combine in a novel manner the conceptual clarity of scholastic thought with the descriptive detail of Vives' style. The fact that Descartes' reference to *De Anima et Vita* deals with an autobiographical remark on Vives' inclination to laugh after breaking a long fast reveals, I think, the aspect of Vives' work on the emotions that Descartes appreciated and could not forget.[13] The Cartesian taxonomy was enriched by naming and finding the proper location in the map of the emotions for some subtle forms of feeling such as wonder, self-esteem, irresolution, emulation, self-satisfaction, contentment, cheerfulness, tedium, regret, and remorse that had remained nameless or misplaced in the philosophical tradition and had only been referred to by Vives in passing remarks. In the *Traité,* Descartes gave philosophical expression to the rich portrayals of human emotions that helped make possible the plays of Racine, Molière, and especially Corneille.

Spinoza's rigid classification of the emotions was dictated by clearly formulated definitions and postulates. As I have already pointed out, emotions for Spinoza were affections of the body that either increase or decrease the body's power of action together with the idea of such affections (III, 3rd definition). The mind acts when it has adequate ideas, and is passive insofar as it has inadequate ideas (III, prop. 1). The essence of anything is the *conatus* by which it endeavors to persevere in its being (III, prop. 6). The idea of what increases or decreases the acting power of the body also increases or decreases the thinking power of our mind (III, prop. 11). All emotional life is therefore determined by desire, which is "the very essence of man," and by either joy, an increase in human perfection, or sadness, a decrease of human perfection. All human emotions are nothing but variations of desire and of two basic emotions: the positive, joy, and the negative, sadness. Since desire has no opposite—as Descartes emphasized—opposite emotions can only be found among the variations of joy and sadness. Thus, for instance, love is opposed to hatred, attraction (*propensio*) to aversion (*aversio*), hope to despair, favor to indignation, humility to self-contentment (*acquiescentia in seipso*). The variations of desire, on the other hand, are not organized into pairs of opposites. Emulation, gratitude, benevolence, and desire for revenge (among others) have no opposite emotions. This theoretical inflexibility compels Spinoza to describe aversion as a form of sadness rather than as the opposite of desire, to describe *desiderium* as a form both of desire and of sadness opposed to the joy we experience with the absence of things we hate, to deny that clemency is a passion (III, 38, explanation), to characterize pusillanimity as a form of fear (which is itself a form of sadness) opposed to audacity (which is itself a form of desire, III, 41, explanation). Gluttony (*luxuria*), ebriosity, avarice, and lust are all described by Spinoza as kinds of desire and of love, which is itself a kind of joy. More basically, perhaps, Spinoza's extremely comprehensive use of the terms *laetitia* and *tristitia* has encouraged some of his followers and interpreters (especially those with a Freudian perspective) to see love, devotion, esteem of others, and self-confidence as forms of pleasure. By the same token, Spinoza has been interpreted as characterizing fear, compassion, contempt, and humility as forms of pain.[14] Subsuming love under joy (or pleasure) runs against a solid scholastic tradition. Saint Thomas, for instance, makes a clear distinction between love and pleasure, and between pleasure and joy (IaIIae. 31, 3). *Laetitia* for Saint Thomas means one of the effects of pleasure, the swelling of the heart.[15] In the same vein, Vives considers *laetitia* a different emotion from love and makes a distinction between cheerfulness (*levis laetitia*), gladness (*gaudium*), joy proper, and pleasure (*delectatio*), which is full joy.

Spinoza's classification of emotions represents a return to ancient Stoic sources. The taxonomy of the *Ethica* differs from that of the *Perí Pathōn* in only few details. The quartet of the Pseudo-Andronicus is scaled down to the tripartite division of Spinoza by the simple device of making fear a kind of sadness. Otherwise the important distinction between desire on one side and joy and sadness on the other remains intact. The only difference is that Spinoza's *laetitia* combines into one category the passions listed by Pseudo-Andronicus under the headings of *delectatio* and *eupathéiae* (rational appetites such as *gaudium*). The polarity separating joy and sadness and the basic drive of desire serve Spinoza well in studying the interaction between emotions, a subject dear to Vives which I shall consider in Chapter 19.

The differences in the classification of emotions written by the ancient Stoics, medieval scholastics, Renaissance writers and modern rationalists are only moderately enlightening regarding the philosophical direction of their authors. They are, however, significant in the history of ideas because they illustrate the relish that Western philosophers have evinced for centuries in attempting to arrange both their mental and their linguistic apparatus according to well-defined patterns. The subtle differences in these classifications reveal different stages of human consciousness, different levels of human discourse, and the different emotional traits of their authors. To a certain extent, these taxonomies of emotions are also a form of linguistic analysis. The appeal to ordinary usage as an authority is explicitly made by Saint Thomas, Descartes, and Vives. Saint Thomas writes that joy and pleasure cannot be identical for the simple reason that, while we say that animals experience pleasure, we do not say that animals experience joy (Iallae. 31, 3, and Iallae. 35, 2). In the introduction to the third book of *De Anima et Vita* (M 3.424), Vives makes an explicit appeal to context in order to determine the meaning of his words. Even Spinoza, who had some philosophical reservations about the accuracy of ordinary language and did not hesitate to depart from it on some occasions, made clear in the *Ethica* that, although his own definitions were not subject to the constraints of ordinary language, neither were they wholly stipulative. Spinoza, therefore, did not hesitate sometimes to use terms that "in their common usage mean something else," provided "their usual meaning was not entirely opposed to the meaning" that he wished to give them (III, 20, *explicatio*).

17
The Basic Emotions

THE PURPOSE OF THIS chapter is to compare Vives' analysis of the basic emotions mostly with those of Saint Thomas and Descartes, which writers are the outstanding representatives respectively of the Aristotelian tradition that preceded Vives and the rationalist schools of thought that followed him.

As I noted in the preceding chapter, traditional philosophers have always assumed that all the varieties of emotional reactions can be comprehended under a limited number of more generic, more primitive, and original emotions. In the *Summa Theologiae,* Saint Thomas organizes his study of *De Passionibus Animae* around the following emotions: love, hatred, desire, pleasure, pain, hope, despair, fear, daring, and anger. But this list can be further reduced by subsuming despair and daring under the analysis of fear and hope as effects are subsumed under their causes (IaIIae. 45, 2). In fact, Saint Thomas is inclined to agree with "the commonly held doctrine" (he quotes Boethius) that makes joy, sadness, fear, and hope the "principal emotions" (*principales passiones*). These four are called principal for different reasons. Joy and sadness because they are "the absolutely ultimate terms of the emotional process," hope and fear because they are at least "the culminating point of that part of the process that bears upon some objective lying in the future" (IaIIae. 25, 4). Saint Thomas, however, insists that in the etiology of emotions (*ordo consecutionis et generationis*) love is the principal emotion.[1] He nevertheless dismisses anger as one of the principal emotions because he considers anger to be an effect of courage, and courage itself to be "consequent upon hope" (IaIIae. 45, 2).

Descartes, as we saw in the previous chapter, is more incisive and explicit in this matter. All passions, he says, are composed of or are species of six "primitive" passions: wonder, love, hatred, desire, joy, and sadness (II, 59). Leaving aside for the moment the passion of "wonder" — a controversial and highly debatable addition to the traditional catalogues of emotions — the main difference between Descartes and the scholastics is the former's omission of hope and fear; Descartes considers these to be a "disposition of the soul" (*une disposition de l'âme*) caused respectively by joy and desire and by sadness and desire (III, 165).[2] Anger, to Descartes, is not a primitive emotion but a species of hatred (III, 199).

In *De Anima et Vita,* Vives refuses to speculate about which emotions are generic and primitive, a speculation uncongenial to his intellectual temper. But in fact, as a result of Vives' own analysis, most emotions emerge as constellations gravitating toward or centering upon some more generic and original emotions. If we ignore the initial attempt to classify emotions in the first chapter of the treatise and rely instead on the headings and content of the chapters that make up the book, we obtain the following catalogue of basic emotions: love (preceded by attraction, fondness, and respect; Chapters 2, 4, 5, 6), desire (Chapter 3), joy (Chapters 8 and 10), pleasure (Chapter 9), hatred (preceded by irritation and contempt and followed by envy, jealousy, indignation, and desire of revenge; Chapters 11, 12, 15, 16, 17, 18), sadness (Chapters 19 and 20), anger (Chapter 13), fear (Chapter 21), hope (Chapter 22), shame (Chapter 23), and pride (Chapter 24). Leaving aside the chapters that deal not with emotions but with the expression of some emotions (Chapter 10 on laughter and Chapter 20 on tears) and the chapter on pride (which Vives himself admits is not an emotion), our list shrinks to the following: love and hatred, desire, joy and sadness, hope and fear, anger, and shame.

Such a listing is very close to that of Saint Thomas, except for the importance Vives attaches to the analysis of anger as a complex but independent emotion and to the analysis of shame, which Saint Thomas reduces to a kind of fear (IaIIae. 41, 4). Descartes' "primitive emotions" differ from Vives' basic emotions in several respects. Unike Vives, Descartes emphasizes wonder as a prelude to our encounter with either good or evil, subsumes hope and fear under the heading of desire, and considers anger and shame as emotions derived from the primitive emotion of sadness.

In this chapter, I plan to deal with three pairs of contrary emotions: love-hatred, hope-fear, and joy-sadness, and with desire and anger as they relate respectively to love and to hatred. The study of these basic emotions includes, first, an understanding of their definition, and, second, an analysis of their distinctive nature. Definitions play a secondary but still significant role in Vives' treatise on emotions. The traditional philosophical impulse to arrange, structure, and classify the elements of reality goes hand in hand with the will to define the terms used to refer to them. If taxonomy is clearly connected with the Greek philosophy of nature and with Aristotelian biology in particular, the emphasis on definition is an inseparable part of Greek dialectic and of the Aristotelian logic of substantive and predicative terms. In this chapter I shall try to review Vives' definition of the basic emotions listed above and to analyze what Vives had to say about their specific nature while comparing his analysis to that of the scholastic tradition (Saint Thomas) and modern rationalism (Descartes). In spite of its emphasis on descriptive analysis, *De Anima et Vita* pays a considerable tribute to tradition. The definitions of each emotion follow traditional lines, with only a few original touches that I intend to bring out.

Love and Desire

Vives deals with love and desire in three lengthy, poorly organized, and occasionally repetitious chapters. Chapter 2 deals with love (*De amore*) Chapter 3 with desire (*Cupiditates*), and Chapter 4 discusses love and desire under the curious heading of "Two Kinds of Love Intermingled" (*De utroque amore mixtim*). Together with the chapters on fondness (*De favore*) and reverence (*Veneratio seu reverentia*), this entire section on love and desire makes up about one-third of the treatise *De Anima et Vita*, Book 3.

To some extent, Vives' lengthy analysis of love is explained by his own concept of love as an emotion, a concept that includes without distinction the motions of the soul toward sensible and intelligible good, motions such as the attraction of our senses toward a beautiful face and the attraction of our will toward the Infinite Goodness of God. This large scope allows Vives to mix without any particular order high metaphysical considerations about the role of love within the universe and psychological warnings about the way to cure the excesses of passionate attachment between human lovers.

Throughout the book Vives emphasizes the central, pivotal, and fundamental role of love in the dynamics of human emotions. "The will," Vives writes, "is the controlling ruler of the entire soul, but love is the ruler of the will. Love is by far the strongest and the most powerful of all emotions. All emotions proceed from love" (*Voluntas est animi universi dominatrix et rextrix, voluntatis amor. Affectionum omnium fortissima et potentissima amor. Ex amore affectus omnes profluere;* M 3.440). From this perspective, all emotions are effects and manifestations of love because our will is primarily moved toward the good and rejects evil only because it is the contrary of the good. "We are similar in this respect to our Creator who is the Supreme Good, since we avoid evil for the sake of the good and seek the good for its own sake" (M 3.421).

Obviously, these are not original ideas. They echo a tradition of Christian philosophers and moralists who, departing radically from Stoic thought, gave Plato's *Symposium* a transcendent religious significance. Vives' words on love can be found almost literally in both Saint Augustine and Saint Thomas. Saint Augustine wrote: "When love longs for the things loved, that is desire; when it possesses and enjoys them, that is joy."[3] And Saint Thomas states in the *Summa Theologiae* that love "is the first of the affective emotions" (IaIIae. 25, 2), because it is the cause of all emotions, even the cause of hatred (IaIIae. 29, 2); for "a thing can be hated only because it runs counter to some agreeable thing" (*contrariatur convenienti*) that is loved.

It is therefore very likely that Vives' musings on the primacy of love were perceived by Descartes as scholastic commonplaces without much analytic insight into a subject he was writing about as though he were "treating of a matter which no one had ever touched on before" (I, 1). Vives' devout and Platonizing emphasis on love fades away in the cool, rational analysis of the *Traité des passions*. Love is characterized there as just one of the six primitive passions and as the opposite of hatred (II, 56), while desire itself becomes " a passion apart" from love (II, 80: *une passion à part*). The fact that evil is nothing but the contrary of the good is used by Descartes not to emphasize the centrality of loving, but rather to dispense with the emotion of aversion as the opposite of desire. "It is always an identical movement which makes for the search after good and at the same time for the avoidance of evil," although in one case it is accompanied by love, hope, and joy, and in the other by hate, fear, and sadness (II, 87). This Cartesian principle seems, however, to undermine both the contrast between love and hatred, and also that between hope and fear as two distinct and contrary emotions. Descartes himself admits that fear is nothing but a lack of hope (III, 175). Is hatred nothing but a lack of love? Are love and hatred as intertwined as hope and fear? Love is not the strongest of all emotions for Descartes, but rather desire, particularly the desire born from the expectation of pleasure (II, 101), a desire that "usually receives the name of love . . . and provides the principal material for the writers of romances and for poets" (II, 90).

Love, for Vives, is "an inclination or forward motion of the will toward the good, an outgoing of the will to embrace the approaching good that results in the craving to be united with it" (*amorem licet intelligere voluntatis sive inclinationem sive progressum ad bonum, exit enim voluntas obviam bono venienti ut id complectatur, unde nascitur conjunctionis expetitio;* M 3.428). The emphasis on love as a merging of lover and beloved object is corroborated by the mandatory reference to the *Symposium* (M 3.439), although Vives seems to be less impressed than Descartes by the Aristophanic account of love as a mythical searching "for the other half." While Vives makes no reference to Aristophanes' speech, Descartes explains sexual desire between people "of a certain age" as though they were "but the half of a whole, of which an individual of the other sex should be the other half" (II, 90). Descartes' restriction to "people of a certain age" seems to reveal some apprehension about the weakening of the sexual drive in old age, even though he himself seems to have had no problems of the sort in his own life.

This traditional account of love as a merging is enriched by Vives with some reflections on the several degrees of contact that satisfy love's cravings. Wine and food must be eaten, perfume must be close enough to be enjoyed, clothes are put on, money is kept in safes to be always at our disposal, friends want to be in the same place, the dead are remembered by visiting the places where they used to live, the soul seeks to be transformed unto God (M 3.443). These observations seem to echo in Descartes' remarks on the different degrees of desire that spring from delight. "The beauty of flowers," Descartes writes, "incites us only to look at them and that of fruits to eat them" (II, 90).

Vives divides love into "desire" or "love of concupiscence" (*cupiditas seu concupiscentia*) and "true and authentic" love (*verus hic et germanus amor*). Desire, he writes, is only a false pretense of love (*falsus fictusque cupiditatis amor;* M 3.438). He characterizes the former as the love of what is "convenient" (*conducibile*) to us, either because it is useful (*utilia*) or pleasant (*iucunda*) to our body, our soul, or in general to our personal well-being. Authentic love, on the other hand, seeks no self-interest and has no considerations of utility. Such is the love among friends, the love of parents toward children, and the love of God toward us (M 3.428).

Vives' language and definitions signify a departure from Saint Thomas and those scholastics who considered desire as an emotion whose object is the pleasurable *qua* absent, specifically different from both love (which precedes desire) and from pleasure (which follows desire), and an effect of love (IaIIae. 30, 2).[4] Vives, on the other hand, identifies desire with selfish love and reserves the name of love (in most cases) to what scholastics called "love of friendship" (*amor amicitiae; Summa Theologiae*, IaIIae. 26, 4), a term Vives reserves to the cases where true and authentic love is mutual: "Friendship is born out of love when the person loved loves in return and there is reciprocal benevolence" (*ex amore amicitia nascitur quum id quod amatur redamat et reciprocatio est in benevolentia;* M 3.428). Vives repeats also the Aristotelian commonplace that the best kind of friendship is found only "among the best people" (M 3.451). Descartes makes desire an emotion different from love but improves Saint Thomas' definition by emphasizing that desire looks toward the future in the sense that it seeks not only the "presence of the absent good" but also the conservation of the present good and the absence of evil "which we already have" or "might experience in time to come" (II, 86).

Vives' novel manner of speaking creates some difficulties for the reader. Is desire incompatible with "true love"? Is it not true that even the purest love is permeated by the desire to be or to remain united with the beloved? Even if, as Vives teaches, true love seeks union with the beloved not "as reward" (*tamquam operae mercedem*) but "as its goal" (*sed est meta*) and the fulfillment of its natural inclination, and, even if, as Vives insists on saying, such union is desired not for the sake of the pleasure it might bring to the lover, how can we understand the inclination of the lover toward his object except by the desire for the object, a desire that either follows or is inextricably mixed with the emotion of love? In this respect, as in many others, Descartes' analysis sounds more convincing when he rejects the distinction between the love of concupiscence and the love of friendship (which he attributed to "the schools"), and claims that both benevolence and desire are inseparable from love and effects of love (II, 81). In fact, one could go even further and claim that love *is* a blending of benevolence and desire, and that the only difference between self-centered and self-giving love is the different proportion between the two. After all, Vives himself admits that even the love of parents toward their children—one of the paradigmatic cases of unselfish love—is born out of their love of themselves: "From this love of ourselves proceeds the love of our children as parts of ourselves" (*ex hoc amore nostri oritur amor erga filios nostros tamquam partem nostri;* M 3.429).

Vives' doctrine of desire is further weakened by the sharp contrast he draws between desire and unselfish love regarding their different objects and effects. To Vives, desire is not a separate emotion or a distinct stage in the emotional process from initial attraction to the consummate pleasure of possession, but rather a misguided form of love, a centripetal form of love, a love poisoned by excessive attention to the interest of the lover and by the wrong values it pursues. Although Vives recognizes that man was endowed with desire to make him seek what was needed for his conservation and welfare (M 3.436–37), and although he proclaims that human desire extends all the way from earthly things to the union with God, he still insists on contrasting "true and authentic Love" to the "false and pretended love of desire" (M 3.438) by relegating to desire the love of false goods. This is why in Chapter 3 he makes a distinction between the desire for what "is naturally necessary to us "(*necessitates naturales*) and the desire for those things we "ourselves have invented" (*nos alia confiximus*). The former, he says, is not desire but "appetite" (*appetitus potius dicuntur*). This is also why in Chapter

2 he describes at length the noble, admirable, and beautiful characteristics of what one should think "worthy of love" (M 3.429) as opposed to the characteristics of the objects of desire. In most cases, desire is to Vives the selfish love of what one should not love at all or one should not love in excess, such as the love of money (avarice), or the love of honor (ambition), or the intemperate love of food (gluttony) and sex (lust [M 3.438]).

The difference between unselfish love and selfish desire disguised as love is most striking when one considers their disparate effects. True love, to be considered later in more detail, brings out the joyful union of the lover and the beloved, such as in the union of the soul and God. Desire leads also to possession but makes possession "trivial and without joy" (M 3.444). The love that seeks pleasure is a torture, not because of love itself, "which is the sweetest of all things" (*quo nihil fieri potest suavius*), but because of desire "that distresses our soul if it is not satisfied" (M 3.444). Selfish love makes people "reluctant to love others" and eager "to relate everything to themselves" because by its very nature desire "looks inward toward itself" (M 3.444). The love of desire makes others into objects. Man loves the beauty of a woman as he loves the taste of a good wine or the strength of a horse (M 3.444). Unlike true love, desire is apprehensive and worrisome, "full of anxious dread" (*plena timoris amor*) and "the cause of trouble in human affairs" (ibid.). The desire for sexual pleasure in particular (*amor Cupidinis*) is irritable, impudent, arrogant, suspicious, "probably invented in a torture chamber" (M 3.447). The possessive love of concupiscence or desire is the cause of rivalries and envy while true love causes sincere communication and thrives with expansion and sharing (M 3.447). The love of concupiscence leads often to flattery and hypocrisy (M 3.447) while true love inspires great deeds, reinforces courage and trust, grows with compassion, and perfects knowledge (M 3.448).

Vives' negative attitude toward desire in general might betray some Stoic influence and a stern moralistic attitude, but Vives' rhetorical praise of true love is firmly rooted in "the deeper explanations of the Platonists" (*Platonici rei huius altius radices inquirunt;* M 3.433). Although it is difficult to pinpoint exactly the written sources of Vives' thought on love, one can think of several books by classical and Renaissance authors. Plato's *Symposium* and *Phaedrus* were obviously familiar to Vives, most likely in the fifteenth-century Latin translations of Leonardo Bruni. It is also probable that Vives was acquainted with Marsilio Ficino's commentaries on them.[5]

Vives' early studies of the church fathers, particularly Saint Augustine, was another important source of his familiarity with Platonic and Neoplatonic ideas on Love. It is less likely, however, that Vives was conversant with

troubadour poetry, medieval romances, or such medieval doctrinal formula-
tions as Andreas Capellanus' *Tractatus Amoris et de Amoris Remedio*.[6]
Vives' minitreatise on love in Book 3 of *De Anima et Vita* seems only
indirectly influenced by the tensions between the Christian principle of
charity and the demands of human love that emerge in the poems of Petrarch,
Cavalcanti, and Dante. The three chapters on love in Vives' treatise are
nevertheless significantly linked to the Italian Neoplatonic literature on love
that flourished under the influence of Marsilio Ficino's partially successful
attempt to harmonize human and religious concepts of love and to bring to a
synthesis the central claims of Platonism and Christianity. To Ficino, God's
love for man and man's love for God and other humans were an integral part
of the cosmic order. All love originates in God's love for creation. Human
love, when humans love the proper object in the proper way, is love of God.
Unlike the scholastics and even more radically than Saint Augustine, Ficino
borrowed from Plato and the Neoplatonists the central insight about the
identification of the Good and the Beautiful and the sacramental character of
all created Beauty. Vives' less than flattering remarks about the "philosophaster Ficino" seem to suggest, however, that Ficino's thought reached him
only indirectly through the works of Ficino's disciples, most of all Pico della
Mirandola, for whom Vives had a great admiration, and perhaps through
Leone Ebreo, another Iberian Jew in exile, and through Pietro Bembo, Mario
Equicola, and others.[7] From these writers, Vives learned first of all to speak
of Love in terms of a "most profound, recondite, and incomprehensible
mystery" (*maxima sunt amoris profundissima, reconditissima et incom-
prehensibilia mysteria;* M 3.453). "Love created us, perfected us and makes
us happy" (*amore sumus conditi, amore perficimur, amore beamur;* M 3. 453).
The first "mystery of Love" is the attraction the lover feels for the object
loved. To Saint Thomas, such attraction was simply based on the "sense of
affinity" between the two (IaIIae. 26, 2). To the Italian Neoplatonists and to
Vives, such attraction was cosmic and mysterious, a part of the "spiritual
sympathy" and "secret and natural interconnection of all things" that ties
together like to like throughout the universe and results in a joyous harmony.
Similarity between lover and loved is itself a cause of love, because in loving
the other the lover partially loves himself, "as children kiss mirrors where
they see their own image" (M 3.429). "The souls of lovers," Vives writes,
"become mirrors in which the form of the beloved is reflected" (*amantis
animus speculum quodam redditur in quo amati relucet forma;* M 3.433).

   Physical beauty is also a cause of love not only because we interpret "a
beautiful face as a silent credential" for a beautiful soul and are used to judge
inward goodness from outward deeds, but for other profoundly metaphysical

and theological reasons. Created beauty is only a ray of Divine Beauty and Divine Beauty is only the "blossom of Divine Goodness" (M 3.431). In a passage clearly inspired by Ficino's *Commentarium in Platonis Convivium,* Vives describes the hierarchically ordained "gleams of God's Infinite Light," (*divinae illius ac immensae lucis splendores;* M 3.431) as contemplative intelligence, sense cognition, the seeds of life, and material forms.[8] Human love, therefore, is nothing but the love of the image of beauty and thus an image of love: "As Divine Beauty is the cause of true Love, so too its image is the cause of the image of Love" (*quemadmodum divina species veros amores elicit, ita imago illius imaginem quoque amorum;* M 3.430). In comparison with the love of God, "the only authentic, permanent, and joyful" love, all other loves are "trivial and unrewarding" (*inanes sunt et absque fructu;* M 3.444). But, no matter how trivial and unrewarding, unselfish human love, as the image of true love, also has wonderful effects. Love "transforms the many into one," "ties together whatever it touches," "reinforces trust," "seeks no advantage," "binds and levels what it binds," "is never idle," "never refuses to suffer anything," "leads to the execution of great and admirable deeds," "brings the fulfillment of knowledge," "increases with compassion, and blossoms in mutual friendship."

Hatred and Anger

Hatred has always been considered the opposite of love. Saint Thomas gives clear expression to that tradition: "Just as anything agreeable (*conveniens*), precisely insofar as it is agreeable, is what we call good; so anything disagreeable (*repugnans*), precisely insofar as it is disagreeable, is what we call evil. Just then, as the object of love is that which is good, so the object of hatred is that which is evil. That is why hatred is the contrary of love" (IaIIae. 29, 1). Descartes repeats Saint Thomas' doctrine in the *Traité des passions* (LVI) and uses similar words (*convenable, mauvaise ou nuisible*). Vives, however, gives a definition of hatred that makes it the contrary of benevolence rather than the opposite of love, an emotion directed exclusively at persons: "Hatred is a deeply rooted aggravation in which we wish to hurt seriously those we think have offended us" (*odium est offensio radicata qua quis cupit graviter illum laedere in quem tendit offensae existimatio;* M 3.483). This is why Vives emphasizes the role of suspicion and fear in the generation of hatred and the intimate relation between hatred, anger, cruelty, and the desire for revenge. Distrustful and cowardly people are obviously more inclined to feel offended than the self-confident and the strong. Those who are at the same time powerful and fearful become cruel in excess (M 3.484).

In spite of his narrow definition of hatred, Vives remains faithful to the traditional concept of hatred as the opposite of love whenever he makes general comparisons about their contrary natures and effects. The first of such topical comparisons has to do with the relative intensity of love and hatred. Hatred, Vives teaches, "overcomes us faster and strikes deeper roots than love" because, while the good "is never pure and enduring," evil "finds in us a place to entrench itself" (M 3.485), a pessimistic observation that deviates significantly from Saint Thomas' better conceived analysis. Love, the *Summa Theologiae* teaches, is stronger than hatred because "no effect can be stronger than its cause" and because "a thing is moved more strongly toward its end than toward the means to that end; and movement away from evil is a means toward the attainment of some good" (IaIIae. 29, 3). Having upheld these principles, Saint Thomas proceeds nevertheless to explain psychological appearances by admitting that hatred can either "be more keenly (*magis sensibile*) felt" than love or seem stronger when compared to the love for a lesser thing (ibid.). Descartes, too, engages in these traditional contrasts, but he adds to them a very modern feeling for the value of positive emotions. Descartes compares joy and love to sadness and hatred and comes to the conclusion that love and joy are preferable to sadness and hatred even when both are "badly founded." "Even a false joy is often of more value than a sadness whose cause is true," although a just hatred is preferable to a false love because, while the former separates us from a true evil, the latter might bring us to it (II,142). The effects of hatred are also described by Vives as the opposite effects of love. While love is the source of unity, hatred "plants the seed of discord," a topic that permeates Vives' entire treatise *De Concordia*.[9]

Vives' definition of hatred as the emotional reaction to a personal offense makes it difficult to establish a clear distinction between hatred and anger. His hesitations begin with his choosing of a point of departure. In the first chapter of *De Anima et Vita,* Book 3, the definition of hatred precedes that of anger. In the treatise, the analysis of anger (Chapter 13) precedes the study of hatred (Chapter 14). Hatred and anger share some generic characteristics. Both are intense emotions or passions. Anger, Vives writes, is "a vehement perturbation of the soul" (*concitatio animi acerba;* M 3.475). Hatred is "a deeply rooted aggravation" (*offensio radicata;* M 3.483). Both of them are caused by the thought that we have been unduly hurt by another, and both of them lead to the desire for revenge. Having said that, Vives tries to find the differences between the two by specifying the distinct ways in which the angry and the hateful may think they have been hurt and the different ways they go about in seeking revenge.

The offense that causes anger is called by Vives *contemptus,* the word used by the Pseudo-Andronicus in the definition of anger and which, I think, should in this context be translated as "slight." The offense that provokes hatred is anything that "hurts" (*laedere*). But since being slighted hurts, anger would appear to be a kind of hatred, a conclusion obviously at odds with ordinary language usage. Parents get angry every day at their own children without hating them. If anger excluded love, lovers would have to resign themselves to the idea that their love could and would be interrupted by moments (or days or weeks) of hatred every time they got angry at each other.

To find a more distinctive contrast between hatred and anger, Vives tries to differentiate between the revenge angry people seek and the revenge hateful people strive after. Angry revenge, he says, consists "in repaying pain with pain" (*ultio irae est dolorem reponere;* M 3.478). Hateful revenge consists in "hurting and hurting badly" (*ultio odii est malefacere et valde nocere;* ibid.). The angry man seeks revenge to show off his power to hurt the person he thinks hurt him. The hateful man seeks revenge for the sole purpose of hurting the other. For that reason it is important to the angry man that his revenge be noticed by his victim and that the victim be clearly informed of the source of the punishment. To a man full of hatred, these considerations are irrelevant. Vives seems also to suggest that the revenge of the angry man tends to be proportionate to the received offense. The man full of hate sees no limits whatsoever.

Vives rejects the Aristotelian claim that anger "must be always felt towards some particular individual."[10] Dido, Vives writes, became angry at the entire nation of the Trojans. One can, may I add, certainly be angry with the Ku Klux Klan without having the doubtful privilege of being acquainted with any of its members. Nor is Vives much interested in asking whether it is in the nature of anger to be explosive, as Seneca claims, or capable of gradual growth, as Plutarch teaches. Vives, however, thinks that Plutarch is more accurate because anger, he says, is like fire: it always flares up even after a long time of brooding and increasing aggravation. Vives seems nevertheless congenial to the Aristotelian teaching that anger diminishes while hatred increases with the passing of time (M 3.478), although he often admits that hatred itself, like any other emotion, tends to abate when its object is remote in space or time, forgotten or otherwise inoperative.

Finally, Vives repeats the cryptic Aristotelian remark that while the angry man "suffers" (*dolet*), the man who hates does not (M 3.478).[11] Translation does not suffice here. A benevolent interpretation is in order. Vives' context provides only modest help in adding that anger makes the strong weak and the weak ridiculous. Does Vives mean to say that hatred is more destructive than anger because it disguises better its own malice, because it eats away at one in a more insidious way? Is Vives suggesting that of the two passions anger is the one that more clearly reveals to oneself and to others its capacity to weaken our power of dealing with reality in a reasonable manner? Is anger explosive and less durable than hatred because it brings with itself an uncomfortable and in the long run unbearable dislike of ourselves? Is it true that one can get used to living in peace with one's hatred, but one finds it distressing and exhausting to live in constant anger? Is the fact that anger inflicts more pain than hatred its only redeeming quality? And if this is a significant difference between hatred and anger, why does Vives quote with approbation the old saying that "hatred is nothing but inveterate anger" (*unde et odium dixerunt quidam iram esse inveteratam;* M 3.485).

The catalogue of the Pseudo-Andronicus, had it been known to Vives, would not have helped him invent clearly distinct definitions of hatred and anger for the simple reason that it does not even include a definition of hatred or love, a significant feature of Stoic thought. To Saint Thomas, the main difference between hatred and anger lay in the fact that while hatred is a concupiscent emotion directed at evil as such, anger is the irascible emotion par excellence, an emotion directed against an evil as an evil that cannot be avoided because it has already taken place. Anger, furthermore, is a complex emotion that includes pain and desire for revenge, not as a genus includes the species, but "as an effect embodies its cause" (IaIIae. 46, 1 ad 3). What Saint Thomas seems to forget in the midst of all these subtle distinctions is the obvious fact that it is difficult to hate another person without wanting to hurt that person. What, then, is the difference between the revenge that the angry man seeks and this desire to hurt the other that seems inseparable from hatred?

Neither Descartes nor Spinoza add much to Vives' understanding of the finer distinctions between hatred and anger. Descartes includes anger (*la colère*) in the third part of the *Traité* dedicated to what he calls "particular passions." He does not hesitate to describe anger as a species of hatred or aversion (the hatred of things ugly), a position that, as I said before, seems too hard on lovers of any kind. To Spinoza, anger is a desire to hurt those we hate and is different therefore from the sadness of hatred (III, 36.7). But once again, according to Spinoza, we can only be angry at those persons we hate.

Fear and Hope

Vives begins the chapter on fear (Chapter 21) with a partial quotation from Aristotle that emphasizes only the cognitive ingredient of fear rather than the effect of fear upon the soul: "Fear is the imagination of an approaching evil" (*mali appropinquantis phantasia;* M 3.502).[12] This short definition, which leaves out the element of pain involved in fear as registered by Aristotle himself, is nevertheless complemented by another, and, as Vives says, a "better definition" that applies to fear the Stoic metaphor "contraction of the soul": "Fear is a contraction of the soul caused by what seems to an individual bad and imminent" (*contractio animi de eo quod cuique malum videtur cum cogitatur adventare;* M 3.502).[13]

Vives' definition of fear is followed by a strikingly long description of its physiological concomitants and effects in terms of blood and bowel movements, the warming up of black and yellow bile, the role of the heart's size, voice changes, and so on. The reader has the impression that Vives considers fear to be one of the most "bodily" emotions and that descriptions of this sort, which can hardly be found in the writings of Saint Thomas, might have had some influence upon Descartes' thought. Vives, however, follows very closely Saint Thomas' steps in considering fear one of the basic human emotions. Saint Thomas emphasizes that fear is a specific emotion with a specific object: "an object which is future, disagreeable, difficult, and irresistible" (*malum futurum difficile cui resistit non potest*; IaIIae. 41, 2). Fear is not just the emotional avoidance of any evil, but the emotional reaction to a future, disagreeable, difficult, and irresistible object. Saint Thomas emphasizes that fear cannot be confused with sadness (as he claimed Aristotle had done) nor be considered as a variation of desire, as Saint John Damascene had taught (quoted by Saint Thomas in IaIIae. 41, 1). Fear, Saint Thomas says, cannot be a form of sadness because fear is a contending, not an impulse emotion (as sadness is) directed against what is disagreeable not as such but as it is difficult and irresistible. Fear, however, can be described as sadness only in the sense that the object of fear is saddening when it is present (ibid.). By the same token, fear is not desire but can be linked to desire in the sense that the avoidance of the disagreeable is a function of seeking the agreeable. In fact, Saint Thomas considers fear second only to sadness as a passion, since in the most precise sense of that word "those affects are called passions which touch their subject adversely" (IaIIae. 41, 2).[14] Furthermore, Saint Thomas considered fear one of the four principal passions (together with joy, sadness, and hope) because it represents the last stage of the orectic movement with respect to evil (aversion-hatred-fear).

Descartes abandons both Saint Thomas and Vives by refusing to recognize fear as one of the "primitive emotions." To him fear is "a disposition of the soul which persuades it that the thing hoped for will not come to pass" (III, 145), a disposition that could coexist with hope when "at the same time we represent to ourselves the reasons which cause us to judge that the accomplishment of desire is easy" (ibid.). Fear to Descartes is nothing but insecure hope, a hope aware of its own weakness.

Although Vives considers fear a separate emotion, his analysis of fear adds little to the Aristotelian remarks in the *Rhetoric*. Vives emphasizes the special effects of fear, particularly its disturbing effect upon our ability to think in a straightforward manner (M 3.504). Vives underlines also the "tyranny of the imagination" in causing fear (M 3.508) and the impact of personal dispositions and circumstances. Unlike Saint Thomas, however, Vives fails to ponder the different kinds of fear, except the fear of shame (Chapter 23). The reader also misses a few reflections on the feeling of anxiety, an emotion that looms so large in contemporary existential philosophy and psychopathology. Vives merely describes anxiety as a mixture of grief, fear, irritation, and repressed desire (M 3.504), and remarks in passing that one can be anxious without feeling any emotion whenever "a thick humor weighs upon the heart" (ibid.). Was Vives afraid of dealing with an emotion to which he was probably most vulnerable? Was he compelled to keep silent by what Saint Thomas had called "the fear of fear itself" (IaIIae. 42, 2)?

Vives' chapter on hope (Chapter 22) is dishearteningly short (half a page) and extremely thin in content. Vives considers hope a "form of desire, the confidence that what we want will take place" (*spes cupiditatis est forma, nempe fiducia eventurum quod cupimus;* M 3.508). In this respect, there are strong similarities between Vives' thought on the relation of hope to desire and Descartes' reflections on the nature of fear. To Vives, hope is confident desire. To Descartes, fear is insecure hope. In spite of its clear opposition to fear, hope, in Vives' analysis, emerges not as a basic emotion (such as fear) but as a form of confident desire. I have nevertheless decided to deal with it as a basic emotion to emphasize, as Vives seems to do himself, its opposition to the basic emotion of fear. The confidence of hope, Vives reminds the reader, need not have the evidence of scientific knowledge, but is content with mere probability. In fact, writes Vives in a somber tone, "there is nothing so light, so small, so distant, or so strange that the soul will not seize in its search for the support of hope" (*nihil denique est tam leve, tam minutum, tam procul dissitum, tam alienum, ad quod animus non adhaerescat facile dum spei adminicula conquirit;* M 3.508). Without hope, life would be intolerable.

Vives' hesitations regarding the basic character of the emotion of hope also represent a departure from scholastic thought. Saint Thomas had clearly made hope one of the basic human emotions, the object of which is a future good that is arduous but possible. As seeking the good, hope is opposed to fear; as directed toward the future, hope is different from joy; as caused by an arduous good as arduous, hope is a contending emotion different from the impulsive emotion of desire; as facing a good that is difficult but possible, hope is opposed to despair (IaIIae. 40, 1). Hope differs from expectation that is "of what one hopes for with outside help" (ibid., 2).

Descartes seems to follow Vives in describing hope as a derivative emotion, as desire "mingled with joy" (III, 165) and accompanied by the representation that there is much probability of obtaining the object of our desire (II, 58). But Descartes is more consistent than Vives in classifying fear as an emotion similarly derivative of desire, the desire accompanied by the representation that there is little probability of obtaining the object of our desire (ibid.).[15]

The relations of contrariety between fear and hope and other emotions are also understood by Vives, Saint Thomas, and Descartes in different ways. In the first chapter of *De Anima et Vita*, Book 3, Vives contrasts fear to sadness in the sense that the latter is about a present evil and the former about a future one. By the same token he contrasts anger, indignation, and envy with confidence and daring as being movements of the soul against either a present or a future evil. In the same chapter, Vives subsumes hope under desire but has nothing to say about despair. Saint Thomas considers despair the opposite of hope, much as withdrawal is the opposite of approach. Fear is the contrary of hope because the objects of fear and hope are themselves contrary to each other, the disagreeable and the agreeable. Despair, on the other hand is not concerned with the disagreeable as such. The object of despair is only disagreeable by an accidental consideration, because it is an unattainable good. The object of despair remains desirable while unattainable. Without such conflicting sentiments one could not begin to understand the painfulness of despair (IaIIae, 40, 4). To Descartes, despair is not the opposite of hope but a case of extreme fear (III, 146) in the same way that confidence is nothing but strong hope (ibid.).

Joy and Sadness

Vives' definitions of joy (*laetitia*) and sadness (*moeror*) and their relations to pleasure and pain represent an interesting departure from traditional manners of speaking. To make this point clearer I shall begin by considering the language of Saint Thomas' *Summa Theologiae*. It is important to remind ourselves that to Saint Thomas passions of the soul were in the strict sense movements of the soul in response to sense perception. For that reason, pleasure and pain were for him basic passions that we experience in common with all living things capable of perception, that is, with all animals. Pleasure is a movement of the soul caused by the perception that the soul has come to be established in a condition harmonious with its nature. Or, to put it slightly differently, pleasure is caused by the awareness that the soul is in the actual possession of some good for which it has a natural propensity (IaIIae. 31, 1). Joy is only one species of pleasure, the pleasure of the mind, the pleasure that follows from obtaining an object of rational desire, a desire that arises from the exercise of reason. Pleasures are common to humans and animals; joys are exclusively human. Therefore all joys are pleasures, but not all pleasures are joys, not only because the pleasures of animals are not joys but also because there are some physical pleasures that humans experience that are not the fulfillment of rational desires (IaIIae. 31, 3). There are, in fact, physical pleasures that impede the use of reason because they absorb the mind's energies, undermine judgments about action, and fetter the exercise of reason through the physiological disorders they entail (IaIIae. 33, 4). Joy, on the other hand, strengthens the exercise of reason for it complements the operation of reason with the pleasure it finds in the repose of rational desire (IaIIae. 33, 4).

To Saint Thomas, pain (*dolor*) is the union of the soul with some evil together with the awareness of that union. Sadness (*tristitia*) is applied only to such pain as results from interior perception. Sadness (or sorrow) is therefore one species of pain as joy is one species of pleasure. Sadness is the opposite of joy as pain is the opposite of pleasure. This clear distinction between generic pleasures and pain on the one hand, and specifically human joys and sorrows on the other, allows Saint Thomas to explore in interesting ways the complicated relations between the two orders. Sorrow over the absence of one thing can make us seek more eagerly the object of pleasure, as much as the desire for some pleasure may make a person endure sorrow so as to attain the pleasure. Even pain can indirectly cause some pleasure by the surprise that goes with it, as in the theatre, or by bringing back the memory of something we have loved in the past (IaIIae. 35, 4). Sorrow and pleasure with regard to different objects are not themselves opposite species. The sorrow over a friend's death is not opposite to the pleasure of contemplating a beautiful landscape (IaIIae. 35, 5).

In a section rather similar to Descartes' reflections on the relative value of false joys and true sadness (II, 142), Saint Thomas compares the power of emotions that have the good as an object and the emotions that have evil as an object. Saint Thomas reaches the conclusion that, since good is stronger than evil, the desire for pleasure is stronger than the aversion from sorrow.

Pleasure can sometimes be perfect, but sorrow is always partial, "because it is impossible to find anything totally evil with nothing good in it" (IaIIae. 35, 6). Movements, too, are stronger at the finish (the movement toward pleasure) than at the beginning. The soul is more powerfully moved when it approaches the pleasure that it seeks than when it leaves "a point unbefitted to its nature," the object of its aversion. For extrinsic reasons, however, a man may shun sorrow more eagerly than he seeks pleasure. The present sorrow might be a threat to a greater good than the one he is enjoying, and love might be felt more keenly when we are without the thing we love (ibid.).

In sharp contrast with Saint Thomas and the scholastic tradition, Vives considers joy (*laetitia*)[16] "a movement of the soul caused by the perception of a present or clearly approaching good" (*motus animi ex judicio praesentis jam boni vel pro certo appetentis;* M 3.463). Vives remarks that although the absence of evil is equivalent to the good, it is not always enough to cause "the strong excitement" (*laetitia enim concitationem habet vehementem*) that accompanies joy. Furthermore, joy always results from the possession of a good that we have desired very intently or have worked hard to obtain, or from the possession of something that happens suddenly and beyond our wildest expectations. The end of an evil merely causes in us a weaker feeling that Vives calls *hilaritas,* a term I translate as "cheerfulness." If something good happens to somebody whom we like but do not love, we experience *gaudium* (the term Saint Thomas uses for joy) or gladness, but not joy. Nor is joy a species of pleasure, but rather pleasure is a species of joy, the consummation of joy: "pleasure is a movement of the soul that follows joy, when the soul settles down to enjoy the congenial good" (*post laetitiam autem quum resedit animus at bono sibi congruenti fruitur et acquiescit, voluptas est seu delectatio;* M 3.464). Having defined pleasure as the last stage of the movement of the soul by which the soul rests in the possession of the good, Vives proceeds to establish a hierarchy of pleasures. Now, since emotion for Vives comprehends both the reactions of the soul's sensitive appetite to objects known through the senses and also those of the will to objects known by the understanding, this hierarchy extends all the way from the lowest physical pleasures to the highest pleasure of intellectual contemplation. The quality of pleasure is in direct proportion to the quality of the corresponding faculty. Vives draws a sharp contrast between the sense of touch and the sense of sight. Touch causes the lowest pleasure because it is "a sense of things earthly" (*sensus terrestris*); sight is the "noblest sense" (*ceteris praestat sensibus*) because it is "of fiery and almost ethereal nature" (*ad igneam naturam et aethereae proximam;* M 3.466). This distinction between sight and touch was clearly inspired by Renaissance Neoplatonism.

For Marsilio Ficino and his disciples, sight made possible the ascent from created to uncreated Beauty while the other senses merely served the ends of material survival.[17] As a good Aristotelian, Vives places contemplation at the very top of all human pleasures, for it is a pleasure incompatible with the low pleasures of the body. Vives completes his reflections on pleasure by contrasting the pleasures derived from artificial objects with those derived from the contemplation of natural beauty, once again an echo of fashionable Neoplatonism. The chapter ends with a pessimistic observation on the power of small physical pains to prevent the enjoyment of noble and spiritual pleasures.

While the contrast between joy and sadness (*moeror*) is clearly emphasized by Vives in Chapters 8 and 9, and while the chapter on laughter (10) and the chapter on tears (20) neatly preserve the symmetry of the entire plan, one is struck by the fact that the pair joy-pleasure finds no counterpart in the column of evil, where the consideration of sorrow seems to preempt the analysis of pain. This lack of symmetry is not clear to the reader. If pleasure is radical joy, what is the name of radical sorrow? If we call pleasure the total enjoyment of a possessed good, what do we call the total surrender to an overwhelming evil?

Descartes follows Saint Thomas in considering the passions of the soul as "the perceptions, feelings or emotions caused, maintained and fortified" by bodily changes. Joy is therefore "an agreeable emotion of the soul which consists in the enjoyment that the soul possesses in the good which the impressions of the brain represent to it as its own" (II, 91). Sadness is "a disagreeable languor which consists in the discomfort and unrest that the soul receives from evil or from the impressions of the brain set before it as pertaining to it" (II, 92). These passions of the soul have to be distinguished from those emotions that are caused by the judgments of the soul about good and evil (II, 89) and on which "our good and harm mainly depend" (II, 147). The passion of joy needs to be distinguished from "a purely intellectual joy" caused by the representation of some good to the soul by the understanding alone, although even in this case it is accompanied by the passion of joy caused simultaneously by the imagination of the same good (ibid.). By the same token, sadness has to be distinguished from intellectual sadness, although the latter "hardly fails to be accompanied by passionate sadness" (II, 92).

The distinction between passionate and intellectual joy and sadness is further complemented by the distinction between the sensation of either pleasure or pain and the passions that accompany those sensations. The passions of joy and sadness that accompany "the titillation of the senses" or physical pain must be distinguished from them, although they are so closely connected "that the greater part of mankind does not distinguish the two" (II, 94). According to Descartes, therefore, we have physical sensations of pleasure and pain, passions of joy and sadness, and intellectual emotions of joy and sadness connected to the passions by the mediation of the imagination. The intellectual or "interior emotions," as Descartes also calls them (II, 147), are sometimes united to the passions that are similar to them, but sometimes can find their origin in other passions and even in passions that are contrary to them. Such conceptual apparatus allows Descartes to make shrewd observations about their interrelationships, observations that are anticipated by Saint Thomas but cannot be found in Vives. It is, for instance, possible to suffer pain with joy and to be saddened by pleasurable sensations. It is also possible to find some "intellectual joy" in being moved by sadness and hatred when these passions "are only caused by the strange adventures which we see represented in a theatre" and which, not being able to harm us in any way, seem pleasurably to excite our soul in affecting it (II, 94 and 147). It is also possible for a husband to feel at the same time sadness, love, and pity for his dead wife while being unable to repress a "secret joy" caused by the knowledge that she will not be brought to life again (II, 147).

18
Derivative Emotions

IN ATTEMPTING TO DEFINE the emotions that in some sense are derived from those generally accepted as basic, differences emerge among philosophers that are at least as significant as the ones I have analyzed in the preceding chapter. In dealing with these derivative emotions, the analysis has been extended beyond Descartes and includes Spinoza because, perhaps more than any other thinker, Spinoza tried to provide a network of definitions aimed at showing the dependence of all emotions on the basic ones of desire, sadness, and joy. This chapter will try to preserve some symmetry with the preceding by grouping all derivative emotions around love, desire, hatred, fear, hope, joy, and sadness.

Emotions Related to Love and Desire

The first movement of the soul toward an apparent good is called by Vives *allubescentia,* a word used by Plautus and Apuleius, mostly, if not only, in an erotic context to signify sexual allurement and enticement.[1] Vives' choice of this word to describe what Saint Thomas had characterized in a less titillating manner as "the attachment, the sense of affinity with some good, the feeling of its attractiveness" (*Summa Theologiae,* IaIIae. 26, 2) remains startling in spite of its probable Neoplatonic ancestry. To translate *allubescentia* by the more mechanical metaphor of "attraction," as I have done, represents a small but, I think, practical concession to tradition.

Neither the term *allubescentia* nor the feeling designated by it have fared well in the philosophical tradition. Descartes, for instance, concurs with Vives in characterizing love, hatred, desire, joy, and sadness as "simple and primitive" emotions, but sees no need to give any particular name to the initial enticement of the good. He departs further from Vives and established tradition by selecting as the first of the primitive passions what he calls "wonder," a "sudden surprise" of the soul to whatever appears as "rare and extraordinary." The unique characteristic of this passion—which Descartes considers very relevant to the process of learning—is that its object is neither good nor evil (although, Descartes warns the reader, excessive wonder or astonishment "can never be otherwise than bad") but novel and rare (I, 70–78). Vives has no name for such a value-neutral and anomalous emotion, and with less subtlety than Descartes seems to assume that whatever strikes our initial attention is immediately assessed by us as potentially lovable or hateful. Surprise, however, plays an important role in the Vivesian analysis of emotion-reinforcers. Descartes, on the other hand, has no name for the initial attraction of the good—an attraction thriving on its novelty and even surprise—and uses the French term *agrément* (which has been translated as "attraction") to describe the love of things beautiful (II, 85). The Cartesian emphasis on surprise was probably inspired by the Aristotelian sense of wonder that is said to be the beginning of philosophical reflection.[2] Vives' more erotic sense of the good as "alluring" was a rare tribute by an otherwise extremely austere man to the Renaissance's philosophy of love.

Spinoza refuses to recognize admiration as an emotion and describes it as simply the imagination of a thing "in which the mind remains fixed because this singular imagination has no connection with the others" (III, 4). By the same token, he rejects the alleged feelings of disdain, veneration and contempt (III, 5). Spinoza's definition of *propensio,* the emotion closest to *allubescentia,* fails to convey the dynamic sense of attraction, of being pulled and allured by the good, a sense which Vives clearly expresses through his erotic metaphor. To Spinoza *propensio* is simply the joy that is accompanied by the idea of something that is accidentally its cause (III, 8).

Vives has some problems in making a clear distinction between attraction and what he calls *favor,* which together with reverence and compassion falls, he says, "under love" (*sub amore*). In classical Latin *favor* can mean goodwill, good disposition toward something or somebody, popularity, fanaticism, enthusiastic support, applause, and even fanatic admiration (as in the case of admiration for actors, athletes, etc.). The description of this emotion in Chapter 5 of *De Anima et Vita,* Book 3, makes it imperative, I think, to translate the Latin *favor* by the English "fondness," which Vives describes as "a form of benevolence very close to love" (*proximus amori est favor et est quaedam benevolentia*), "incipient love" (*amor inchoatus*) and, more poetically, "a shade of love" (*umbra amoris;* M 3.453). One can be fond of somebody without being in love with that person—Vives says—but one cannot love another without being fond of him or her. Although the text does not provide more clues, the differences between *allubescentia* and *favor* seem to correspond rather neatly to the difference between attraction and fondness. Attraction comes first; fondness follows sometimes upon better acquaintance. Attraction is an early and sometimes fleeting emotion. Fondness is normally a more stable and almost habitual attitude toward another. Vives fails to make explicit whether fondness is a feeling reserved to relations between persons, but he seems to suggest that much by the examples he constantly gives (neighbors, relatives, fellow citizens, companions, servants). If this is the correct interpretation, pet lovers have few reasons to be fond of Vives.

Descartes narrows the definition of favor to a form of love toward those "who do the things which we esteem to be good, even though no good comes to us from it" (III, 192). Spinoza defines favor as the love for some one "who has benefited another" (III, 19). Both definitions, however, would unnecessarily limit the meaning of fondness. One can, I think, be fond of somebody who is not the benefactor of a third party.

Fondness and *reverentia* (the Latin term includes feelings of awe, misgivings, and shyness) share the same generic characteristic of disposing somebody to have a favorable attitude toward another person. Reverence, however, is, as Vives writes, always mixed with some fear, shyness, and admiration (M 3.454–55) caused by the greatness of the other.

Vives' analysis of fondness and reverence enriched both the Stoic analysis of *eupathéiae* and the more abstract and metaphysical study of love conducted by Saint Thomas and the scholastics. Descartes' analysis of esteem (*vénération;* II, 55), favor (*la faveur;* II, 64), and simple affection (*la simple affection;* II, 83) differs also in significant respects from the Vivesian feeling of "fondness." Esteem, for Descartes, is nothing but admiration for the novel and the great, favor is love excited by the good action of another, and simple affection is the love of something we esteem less than ourselves (we esteem flowers or horses, but we do not esteem people equal to ourselves). In a similar fashion, Spinoza fails to convey the feeling of "being fond of another person." Benevolence for Spinoza is the desire to do good to the person we feel sorry for (III, 35), devotion is the love of a person we admire (III, 10), and favor the love of those who help others (III, 19). In this point, as in several other aspects of the philosophical analysis of emotions, the philosophers' definitions and observations seem, when taken separately, inadequate to the task of describing the rich variations and interactions of emotions. Each author appears able to see but a limited perspective of a highly varied landscape.

Vives' narrow conception of desire as the unwarranted love of false goods (greed, ambition, gluttony, lust) preempted the possibility of his considering the desire for worthy objects, such as the desire for knowledge (curiosity) that Descartes mentions in the *Traité* (II, 88). Nor did Vives see any need to recognize as an emotion our desire not to have any desire toward a particular object, our determination to show cold indifference (different from disdain) to another person, or in a more radical way, our callousness and hardness of heart with respect to the other. Neither Descartes nor Spinoza added anything to Vives on this particular point.

Emotions Related to Hatred

The initial reaction of the soul away from evil is called by Vives *offensio,* the opposite of *allubescentia*. It is no easy task to convey in one single English term all the possible meanings and connotations of the Latin *offensio*. Literally, the word means striking against an obstacle. Stumbling was for the Romans a case of *offensio*. To be offended could also have meant to be upset, to have a setback, to resent, to receive an affront. An *offensio* could also be a violation, a crime, a provocation, or an indignity. In Chapter I, Vives preserves the parallelism with *allubescentia* by teaching that hate is nothing but an *offensio* that has become deep-set and stable: "when *offensio* is confirmed, it becomes hatred" (*offensio quae confirmata, fit odium;* M 3.426). But, in Chapter 11, he provides a lengthy and probably biographi- cally revealing description of *offensio* that makes it difficult, if not impos- sible, to understand this feeling as merely the initial repulsion for something or somebody, even if the term *repulsion* would have tidily preserved the dynamic antithesis with attraction. In Chapter 11, Vives seems to oppose *offensio* not only to attraction but to fondness. Offensio, he says, can lead not only to hate but also to envy and anger. It applies to the irritation we feel toward unpleasant sounds, the annoyance caused by bad weather or insect pests, or what we experience with the unusual behavior of others. Exaspera- tion and even rage are more intense degrees of *offensio*. Forced to make a choice, I have translated *offensio* by either "annoyance"'or "irritation." I am nevertheless aware that extreme cases of *offensio,* such as exasperation and rage, are only improperly called cases of annoyance or irritation.

To complicate matters, Vives includes a short chapter (Chapter 12) on an emotion not even mentioned in Chapter 1, an emotion he calls *contemptus,* the act of despising or scorning somebody. Contempt, he says, is caused by annoyance toward an evil that is harmless but "vile and abject" (*vile atque abjectum;* M 3.475). The lack of parallelism between the basic emotions toward the good (attraction-fondness-reverence-love) and the emotions away from evil (annoyance-contempt-hatred) is probably the reason why Vives fails to provide us with a name for a feeling that mediates between annoyance and contempt, a feeling that would correspond to that of fondness between attraction and reverence. Are we doomed to despise everything that even so slightly irritates us? What is the name for the feeling opposite to fondness?

The failure of the Stoics to name even such passing and initial feelings as attraction and annoyance was no doubt owing to their emphasis on violent and extreme emotions. Vives was not only free from the Stoic fallacy of equating emotions with uncontrolled ones, but also much more sensitive to the subtle but psychologically powerful link between embryonic feelings, strong emotions, habits, and motives. In this respect, Vives' analysis of the dynamics of emotional life is occasionally more perceptive and richer than the methodical study of Descartes or the highly systematized tract of Spinoza. Descartes does not even name the feeling of annoyance, and Spinoza provides a definition of *aversio,* which as with the definition of its opposite, *propensio,* lacks any sense of motion and direction. Aversion, he says, is a sadness "accompanied by the idea of something that is its accidental cause" (III, 9). Once again, the traditional dynamic metaphors about emotions seem semantically richer than Spinoza's highly rationalistic idiom.

Annoyance and contempt are movements of the soul away from an evil (*a malo*) that is present or remembered in the present. But the soul, Vives says, is also capable of moving against (*in malum*) an actual evil. Its motions are anger, envy, jealousy, indignation, desire for revenge, and cruelty. Following a well-established scholastic tradition, Vives teaches that these emotions have no contraries as the emotions caused by the good do, because the good can attract as good or challenge as an arduous good, while an inevitable evil can move the soul in but one direction. The opposite of anger can only be "the cessation of anger," an obviously pleasant feeling for which neither Vives nor Aristotle seemed to find the proper term.[3] Saint Thomas admits that calmness is the opposite of anger by way of privation. But he insists on teaching that anger has no contrary emotion, because an angry man can have no attitude contrary to the same object and none based on having a contrary object. When we face a present evil, we either capitulate and feel sad or attack and feel angry. The contrary of a present evil, a good already possessed, can only elicit the emotion of joyful possession.

Vives' classification of emotions places an inordinate emphasis upon those that in his own words are caused by evil and "degrade and brutalize the human spirit in an amazing manner." Human reaction to the good seems to Vives much more simple and single-minded than our tortuous, complex, devious, and multifaceted response to the presence of evil in the world. Our minds, he says, apprehend much faster (*celerius apprehendunt*) what is vicious and evil in the world simply because imperfection is "familiar and similar to us" (*sibi cognata et similia;* M 3.457).

Vives' attempts to describe the fine distinctions between hatred and anger, envy and jealousy, indignation, revenge, and cruelty are not more than partially successful and are highly unsystematic. In the preceding chapter I have dealt with the relations between hatred and anger, because the former occupies a prominent place in the Vivesian analysis of emotions, and seems to emerge as a complex but basic emotion. Here I shall deal with indignation, envy, desire for revenge, and cruelty.

If the difference between anger and hatred remains hazy in *De Anima et Vita,* the difference between anger and the emotion Vives calls *indignatio* is outright obscure. In Latin the word *indignatio* means "anger aroused by a sense of wrong" or "an angry outburst" (the flaring up of anger and its bodily expression). Vives' account of indignation (Chapter 17) is not his most successful one. It begins with the Aristotelian definition of indignation: pain at the unmerited good fortune of another.[4] But Vives also says that indignation includes a movement of compassion for those who undeservedly suffer. At the end of the chapter, however, Vives returns to the Aristotelian teaching by remarking that indignation and compassion are contrary emotions because one is about an undeserved good and the other is about an undeserved evil. In fact, Vives uses another word for the mixture of the two, *zeal.* Zeal, Scripture says, is what the just feel when they witness the happiness of sinners, an emotion that hardly includes elements of compassion, except perhaps for oneself. After quoting Scripture, Vives remarks that we feel zealous when God or our own country is unfairly treated, two examples that in no way seem to include any element of compassion. In any case, if indignation is mixed with compassion, how, then, can indignation be "often caused by envy," as Vives hastens to add? Is it possible, as he claims it is, to be indignant at ourselves when we admit to ourselves that we do not deserve the happiness we are actually enjoying? How can joy and indignation coexist in the same person and about the same object? Vives tries to help us by remarking that this can happen "when happiness is mixed with some inconvenience," as when we get a job we had desired for a long time and later we find it to be more burdensome than expected (M 3.493). But is "indignation" the best word to describe the feelings one might experience in such a situation, feelings of disappointment, apprehensive joy, misgiving, mild regret, uneasiness, wariness, and frustration?

Aristotle emphasizes the fact that indignation is directly opposed to pity, that both indignation and pity are associated with moral character, since both have to do with the "undeservedness" of either the bad (pity) or the good fortune (indignation) of another moral agent. Aristotle also points out that indignation is different from envy in that the latter does not underline the prosperity of the underserving but the mere fact that something good that is not threatening to us (otherwise it would become fear) is happening to people who are like us or equal to us, that the converse of indignation is the feeling of satisfaction at seeing the merited distress of others, like the punishment of parricides and murderers.[5]

By mixing compassion with indignation, Vives abandoned the reliable guidance of Aristotle and neglected the important fact that our feelings of indignation, like our feelings of pity, are intimately related to our sense of justice. Whatever is undeserved by another, whether it is the prosperity of the sinner (as the Bible constantly teaches) or the suffering of the just (particularly when such suffering has been inflicted upon them by human agents), provokes our indignation. In the first case, indignation is easily mixed with envy; in the latter, it is often blended with anger and hatred toward the perpetrator of the injustice and with compassion toward its victim. Like anger itself, indignation is an emotion that belongs exclusively to moral beings.

The Aristotelian teaching on indignation—heavily oriented toward its use in forensic rhetoric—did not fare well in the Stoic tradition. The *Perí Pathōn* provides no definition of indignation in its otherwise lengthy and minute catalogue, although it lists three sorts of envy (*invidia, zelus,* and *zēlotypia*) and two kinds of compassion (*misericordia, oiktos*). Cicero makes not a single reference to indignation in the *Tusculanae Disputationes*. It also seems strange that even Christian philosophers such as Saint Augustine and Saint Thomas found little or nothing to say about an emotional response to the distribution of prosperity and evil among the just and the wicked that plays such an important role in Judaeo-Christian piety. Saint Thomas merely understands indignation (and jealousy) as a species of envy (IIaIIae. 36, 2). Descartes and Spinoza, for their part, make explicit if not entirely satisfactory references to indignation. The former departs radically from the Aristotelian tradition by narrowly defining indignation as the opposite of benevolence, as an emotion caused "by the evil done by others and not having any relation to us" (II, 65). Spinoza follows Descartes by defining indignation as hate toward "someone who has done evil to another" (III, 20). Descartes and Spinoza, therefore, limit indignation to an emotional reaction against an injustice committed against a third party, and leave out those cases of indignation that verge upon envy rather than upon anger and hatred.

Unlike Aristotle, Vives makes no explicit effort to differentiate indignation from envy, but goes a long way toward distinguishing several kinds of envy. In so doing, he enriches in some interesting ways the traditional Aristotelian teaching. Another person's good fortune can be perceived by us in four different manners, he says: as harmful to ourselves, as something not harmful to us but that we ourselves would like to possess, as something we do not want others to possess because we think it should be exclusively ours, and finally, as something that makes us feel bad without any consideration of our interest, simply because we think it is bad that others do well. According to Vives, the first three kinds of envy are so called only by analogy to the fourth, "the authentic and most characteristic form of envy." Vives calls the third kind *zelus* (M 3.486). A special kind of *zelus* is what he terms *zēlotypia*. This idiosyncratic use of untranslated Greek terms poses some thorny problems for the interpreter and translator into English. The word *zelus* was almost unknown in classical Latin. In the *Tusculanae Disputationes,* Cicero translated it into *aemulatio,* warning the reader that it could mean something good and something bad (*et in laude et in vitio hoc nomen sit*). In the first sense, it means "eager rivalry"; in the second, the sorrow (*aegritudo*) that we feel when we see others enjoy what we desire but do not possess.[6] I think it rather revealing of Vives' pessimistic outlook on life that, although familiar with Cicero's distinction, he never considers the positive aspects of emulation, not even as an educational tool. Vives' terminology becomes further confusing when, at the end of the chapter on indignation (Chapter 17), he adopts what he calls the biblical term *zelus* to mean what Saint Thomas describes as an effect of love, the antipathy to anything prejudicial to my friend's (or God's) interests (IaIIae. 28, 4). Unfortunately, the English word *zeal* has become almost synonymous with enthusiasm and devoted dedication, except in its derivative noun *zealot,* which, besides its historical reference to a Jewish sect existing before the Christian era, has come to mean a fanatic. That Vives is aware of the danger of excessive religious zeal is obvious from his comment on the Biblical sense of the term: "Under this pretext many people often become enslaved to their evil desires and cater to their bitter hatred" (M 3.495). The son of a victim of the Inquisition had some reason to fear the dangerous consequences of self-righteous zeal!

The use of the Greek term *zēlotypia,* which the Pseudo-Andronicus defines as "the sadness we experience when others have what we do not have" (*zēlotypia autem tristitia in aliis existere et nobis non existere;* 224) is equally whimsical. Vives wrongly believes that the Greek term meant "envy of beauty" (*zelus est de forma;* M 3.490), whereas in fact it means "smitten with envy."[7] His definition of *zēlotypia* as "envy of beauty" restricts it to cases of erotic jealousy. In fact, Vives explicitly admits that what he mostly has in mind is the jealousy men feel about their wives and lovers. As such, the discussion in Chapter 16 lacks the philosophical amplitude that one could expect from a less narrowly defined topic.

In Chapter 18 of this third book of *De Anima et Vita,* Vives deals with revenge and cruelty. The desire for revenge was, as we have seen, an element of the emotion of anger. "When the soul is afflicted with some pain, it wishes to inflict a similar pain on the person who caused it." This emotional reaction is only an example of a general rule that applies to all emotions: "Whatever strikes up our emotions, good or evil, tends to call forth an emotional response similar to itself" (*Quicquid affectus accipit, cupit in idipsum refundere unde accepit, sive bonum sit sive malum;* M 3. 495). The desire for revenge is the culmination of prolonged irritation, hatred, anger, or envy. Revenge born from anger and jealousy is open and public. Revenge caused by hatred or envy can be crafty and secretive while revenge caused by irritation is generally violent, explosive, and rabid (M 3.495–96). Cruelty is an intense act of punishment carried out without compassion and mercy. Any violent passion, such as extreme fear or ambition, predisposes us to cruelty.

Love begins with attraction, is helped by fondness and reverence, and culminates in joyful possession. Hatred begins with irritation, is reinforced by disdain, and leads to sadness. Anger, envy, indignation, and desire for revenge are emotions against evil and seem to have no direct opposites in our relations to the good.

Emotions Related to Fear

In the preceding chapter I pointed out that Vives' analysis of fear adds little to Aristotle's, and that, with the exception of the fear of shame, he fails to deal with other kinds of fear, particularly with the feeling of anxiety. The fear of shame, on the other hand, is the subject of a lengthy chapter (Chapter 23). Shame or *pudor* is the fear of "a disgrace from which harm does not follow" (*metus dedecoris ex quo non sequitur damnum;* M 3.508). Custom and received opinion play an important part in our decision to perceive something as "disgraceful." The fear of shame was given to us, Vives says, as a tutor; without it life in society would be practically impossible. The social value of such fear explains Vives' sustained interest in its analysis, an analysis which is deeply rooted in the classic tradition, the Greek sense of honor, and the Roman emphasis on decorous and proper behavior. To these, however, Vives adds a characteristic note of Catholic prudishness in his remarks on the Christian doctrine of modesty and decency related to sexual organs and acts, and the latter's relation to Adam's sin in paradise (M 3.509). We are ashamed of our "pudenda," Vives explains, the same way a master is ashamed of a rebellious servant or slave. Against the Cynics, Vives observes that the reason why we are not ashamed of talking about murder but are ashamed of talking about "procreating, having a bowel movement, blowing our noses, or urinating" is that, while being reminded of a crime "does not excite our fantasy" to do something similar, being reminded of the obscene (*aliquid turpe*) provokes us to do something obscene.

Vives' analysis of shame as a kind of fear continues a long Stoic tradition. The Pseudo-Andronicus lists *aischunē* (a Greek term for which Grosseteste found no proper Latin translation) as the second species of fear. Saint Thomas, on the authority of Saint John Damascene and Saint Gregory of Nyssa, accepts the division of fear into six different kinds: laziness, embarrassment, shame, amazement, stupor, and anxiety. Shame in particular is the fear of a future reproach because of a past action. Embarrassment is the fear of a future reproach because of an act one is performing at present (IaIIae. 41, 4).

Descartes and, under his influence, Spinoza, abandon the tradition and see the feeling of shame not as a species of fear but as a species of sadness and an effect of the fear of being blamed for something. Descartes considers shame a species of sadness and a species of modesty and mistrust of self (III, 205). Spinoza makes a further distinction between the *pudor* we experience when we fear being reproached for something we have done, and the *verecundia* we experience when the fear of being reproached prevents us from doing something dishonorable (*turpe;* III, 31, *explicatio*). Both writers totally abandon the more medieval and Manichaean sense of shame with regard to the body's erogenous parts. To Descartes and Spinoza, shamelessness is not an emotion but the inability to feel ashamed. Both of them call it *impudentia*. Descartes specifies that impudence is a vice opposed to shame as ingratitude is to gratitude and cruelty is to pity, and that it proceeds from having being often affronted and from coming to the cynical realization that our bodily well-being does not always depend on our being honored by others (II, 207).

The main objection to the traditional view of shame as a form of fear is the commonly accepted convention that fear's object always lies in the future. If shame is a form of fear, how could one be ashamed of something while one is being reproached for it—or after having been reproached for it? In that sense, the Cartesian analysis of shame as a form of sadness seems more correct, a sadness that might be caused by the fear of a future reproach or by the pain of a present one. That Vives was vaguely concerned with these fine distinctions can be seen from the odd way he begins the chapter on shame. First he says that shame is a form of fear. Then he quotes Aristotle to the effect that shame is a form of pain, and, like Aristotle himself, he insists on saying that "shame applies to all times, present, past, future, and possible" (*omnia respicit tempora, praesens, prateritum, futurum, possibile;* M 3.508).[8] In any case, it is also strange, to say the least, that Vives' analysis of shame did not include any reference to the sense of guilt, an obviously important ingredient of Christian piety and a necessary condition for repentance and conversion. Confidence (*fiducia*) and daring (*audacia*), which are listed in the catalogue of emotions in Chapter 1, are virtually left out of consideration in the chapter on fear (or in the short chapter on hope), where Vives is satisfied with giving a timeworn definition of each (M 3.506). Nor does Vives betray any concern about establishing clear relations of contrariety between fear and hope, hope and courage, courage and cowardice, hope and despair, probably because he thinks that such an enterprise was nothing but a futile scholastic exercise.

Emotions Related to Hope

Vives' extremely short analysis of hope never permits him to consider the possible relations among hope, fear, and despair. In fact, *De Anima et Vita* does not even mention the emotion of despair, in spite of the fact that, according to a long-established tradition of Christian theologians, despair was not only a sin but the one sin against the Holy Spirit, the sin that Christ said could not be forgiven.[9]

Emotions Related to Joy

Regarding joy, Vives makes a distinction among *hilaritas,* a mild joy that follows the departure of what made us sad; *gaudium,* a pleasant feeling akin to joy occasioned by the memory of a past good, by the expectation of a future good, by the memory of past evils *qua* past, or by the good of somebody we are fond of; and *laetitia,* a strong feeling that follows the fulfillment of an ardent desire. These words have been respectively translated by "cheerfulness," "gladness," and "elation."

Vives' different kinds of joy have no counterpart in the austere list of the Pseudo-Andronicus' *eupátheiae.* Saint Thomas seems exclusively intent upon making a clear distinction between the pleasure (*delectatio*) animals experience and the joy (*gaudium*) which is exclusive to rational beings (humans and angels) on one hand and between the swelling of the heart that is characteristic of joy and its external manifestations (*exultatio, jucunditas;* IaIIae. 31, 3) on the other.

Descartes elaborates on Vives' richer terminology but shows a much more refined psychological sense by clearly defining the feelings of satisfaction, self-satisfaction, gratitude, gaiety, and cheerfulness. Descartes was even capable of detecting an element of joy in the scorn we feel when we perceive a small evil in a person who deserves it, a joy that, linked with surprise, can sometimes provoke laughter (III, 178). Spinoza, in a most characteristic manner, defines the Cartesian sense of self-satisfaction or self-esteem as the pleasure we experience when we contemplate our own power (III, 26, *explicatio*) and gives a highly intellectual description of confidence by characterizing it as a joy born of the idea of a future or past thing, concerning which the cause of doubt has been removed (III, 14).

In the first chapter of *De Anima et Vita,* Part 3, Vives defines pride as "a monster composed of many emotions, joy, desire and confidence" (*superbia monstrum est ex multis mixtum, ex laetitia et cupiditate et fiducia;* M 3.426). But in the last chapter of the book, a lengthy and revealing one (Chapter 24), Vives fails to explain which kind of joy is part of pride or how joy adds to the complexity of pride. In fact, Vives says that "expansive joy" (*laetitia effusa*), like other emotions such as fear, is an emotion "which borders on being a humbling experience" (*affectus demissioni vicini;* M 3.519) to the proud. In another context, Vives characterizes pride as "a swelling of the soul" (*tumor animi*) caused by "a thoughtless love of oneself" (*inconsideratus cuique amor sui ipsius;* M 3.514, 515). This excessive love of oneself causes an excessive desire for honor and recognition, arrogance, ostentatiousness, irritability, anger, self-indulgence, envy, intellectual blindness and stubbornness, disdain for others, love of novelty, and more of this sort.

This emphatic and moralistic condemnation of the passion of pride is clearly derived from Christian rather than from pagan sources. Although the Pseudo-Andronicus included "the immoderate desire for honor" (*filotimía*) in his list of passions, and although Stoic philosophers recommended a prudent detachment from personal glory, a keen sense of personal humility as the source of all virtues and the condemnation of pride as a capital sin and the origin of all vices were (and still are) essential ingredients of evangelical piety as understood by the fathers of the church.

Vives' preachy condemnation of pride contrasts rather sharply with Descartes' analysis. Obviously, Descartes, too, condemns pride as "a very vicious, unreasonable, and absurd vice" (III, 157), but unlike Vives, he hastens to condemn also what he calls "vicious humility" (*l'humilité vicieuse;* III, 159), a humility caused by feebleness and lack of resolution (ibid., 159), and directly opposed to noble-mindedness and leading to either servility or insolence. Furthermore, Descartes' recognition of the positive value of internal self-satisfaction, "the sweetest of all joys" (*la plus douce de toutes les joies;* III, 190), represents a novel and important departure from all the exaggerated forms of self-depreciation and submissiveness that more often than not disguise themselves as manifestations of Christian humility. Descartes' analysis of pride and humility bespeak a more secularized version of humanistic values, an interesting retrenchment from Christian ideals of human perfection.

Spinoza's comparatively favorable treatment of humility in the small treatise *God, Man and his Well-Being* has been taken by some interpreters as evidence of Christian influence upon his youthful work. But the *Ethica* recognizes that self-esteem is reasonable (IV, P 52) and condemns humility as a form of sadness caused by a false reflection about our lack of power (IV, P 53). Although Spinoza denies that humility is a virtue, he still admits that it frequently offers more advantages than disadvantages, because weak-minded persons can be more easily guided by the reason of others. "The mob," writes Spinoza in a cryptic and almost Machiavellian manner, "is terrifying, if unafraid" (IV, P 54, S). Spinoza gives Cartesian secular humanism an almost Nietzschean twist.[10]

Emotions Related to Sadness

Although sorrow is the opposite of joy, Vives does not try to contrast the various shades of sorrow to those of joy. In Chapter 19, he uses four Latin words as synonyms, *moeror, moestitia, tristitia,* and *aegritudo.* For reasons not totally apparent to his reader, the author complains that Cicero's analysis of *aegritudo* (Cicero's favorite term for sadness) in the *Tusculanae Disputationes* was not carefully done. One might suspect that Vives found less than congenial the long catalogues of different kinds of *lupē* characteristic of the Stoic tradition, which Cicero translated in part. The Pseudo-Andronicus gives twenty-five definitions of different kinds of sorrow. Nemesius gives four. Neither listing, however, seems particularly enlightening on the nature of sorrow or the interaction of contending and related emotions. The only varieties of sorrow that Vives mentions are *desiderium, desperatio,* and *rabies. Desiderium* is the sorrow that follows the loss of something good, and in that sense it could be considered the opposite of cheerfulness, although Vives is not explicit here. I have translated this complex Latin term as "nostalgic yearning," or as "bereavement" in the case of sorrow for the loss of a beloved person. Vives' explicit comments on the sadness of yearning enriched the stereotypical scholastic division of sorrow into four kinds (torpor, anxiety, envy, and pity; *Summa Theologiae,* IaIIae. 3, 35, 8), although Saint Thomas had given us an interesting insight into the complexity of sorrow. He notices that the sorrow we feel when we actually remember a lost good is or can sometimes be mixed with some pleasure, the pleasure of thinking about a beloved person (IaIIae. 32, 5). In a more pessimistic vein, Descartes uses the term *regret* "to name that "kind of sadness which has a particular bitterness inasmuch as it is always united to a certain despair" (III, 209). *Desiderium* therefore names an acute sense of personal loss intermingled with delightful moments of sweet memories and with profoundly distressing moments of despair brought about by the thought of the irretrievable character of fateful separations, particularly the final separation of death.

As I have previously stressed, despair, a popular emotion in existential literature and an important one in Christian piety, is mentioned by Vives only in passing and not in contrast with hope, but rather as an extreme form of sorrow and self-hatred (M 3.498). Rage seems to belong to the expression of violent anger. Pity and the desire of revenge are two emotions for which Vives does not find a clear location. In the first chapter of *De Anima et Vita*, Part 3, Vives classifies pity as an emotion related to love (*sub amore*). Envy, anger, and indignation are grouped together as emotional reactions against evil (*in malum*). Having dealt with envy and desire for revenge in connection with anger, I shall discuss here Vives' chapter on pity (Chapter 7). Vives begins by defining pity as a form of sadness caused by the undeserved evil fortune of another (M 3.458). In agreement with Aristotle, Vives emphasizes that the emotion of pity is only possible under certain conditions.[11] First, it must be clear that the evil fortune of the other is fully undeserved. It is obvious, Vives says, that "we feel no compassion at all for criminals" (*quale est quod impiorum animis quotidie accidit, nec nos miseret;* M 3.459), a sober commentary that sounds more like a reflection on our natural inclinations than an ethical precept inspired by Christian morality. In fact, Vives' teaching represents a departure from medieval scholasticism and a significant espousal of naturalistic ethics. The Aristotelian proviso about the undeservedness of the evil suffered by another—an important consideration in forensic rhetoric—had not been included by Saint Thomas in the definition of pity, among other reasons because Christian piety rejects any human pretense to judge the just deserts of another (IaIIae. 35, 8). Vives' remark is especially surprising since in the preceding paragraph he himself has criticized Aristotle for having dealt with pity from an exclusively "political" standpoint (M 3.458).

Like Aristotle and Saint Thomas, Vives emphasizes that pity is mostly directed at people similar to ourselves and regarding evils likely to befall ourselves. In fact, Saint Thomas had forcefully argued that pity as a form of sorrow is possible only in as far as we regard another person's misfortune "as our own" (*misericordia est tristitia de alieno malo inquantum tamen aestimatur ut proprium;* IaIIae. 35, 8). Vives' thoughts on pity represent a strong repudiation of Stoic attitudes toward the emotions. The Pseudo-Andronicus' definition of compassion (*misericordia*) as the first kind of sadness was clearly dependent upon the Aristotelian tradition, but most Stoics, particularly the Roman, saw compassion and mercy as debilitating passions in direct conflict with virile virtue. Vives explicitly rejects Seneca's teaching that one could help the miserable without oneself being burdened with the negative and sad feeling of pity. With uncharacteristic eloquence, Vives insists on the natural link between emotions as motives and their corresponding forms of behavior. Without feeling pity for others, Vives writes, one would not help them under strenuous circumstances or for a long time. It is easier to help others when one feels moved to help them. Without such feeling, help would not be long lasting (M 3.460). Furthermore, Vives goes on, nothing is more consoling to those who suffer than the knowledge that others share their pain. Pity, Vives says, is a "most gentle emotion" (*affectus mansuetissimus*) given by God to man as a gift of mutual consolation and a substitute for love (M 3.461). Cruelty for Vives is "the complete lack of sympathy for others," especially in carrying out a revenge inspired by hatred, indignation, anger, or envy (M 3.496).

It can hardly be denied that Vives' chapter on pity represents a persuasive and deeply felt apology of some fundamental Christian values. But it was not persuasive enough to prevent the eventual resurgence of Stoic patterns of thinking. Both Descartes and Spinoza consider pity a form of sadness. Like Vives, Descartes emphasizes that pity is a species of sadness opposed to envy and "mingled with love or good-will" (III, 185). But unlike Vives, Descartes strikes a clearly Stoic note by teaching that pity is a passion to which the feeble and the self-centered are particularly disposed (III, 186). The noble minded (*les plus généreux*) feel pity without the bitter sadness of the weak, because the object of their pity is not the suffering of the weak but their weakness in suffering (III, 187). There is something, nevertheless, that is worse than the proclivity of the weak to feel sorry for others, and that is the incapacity of the cruel, the envious, the proud, and the callous to feel any compassion at all for anyone (III, 188).

Spinoza's attitude toward "effeminate compassion"[12] represents a merciless return to harsh Stoic values. Pity or *commiseratio* and *misericordia*, Spinoza says, is nothing but sadness accompanied by the idea of an evil that has happened to another whom we imagine to be like us (III, 18). Pity is sadness "and therefore, of itself, evil" (II, P 50). Furthermore, "in a man who lives according to reason," pity is "useless." Still, Spinoza tempers his doctrine with a remark of obvious Cartesian origin: "One who is moved to aid others neither by reason nor by pity is rightly called inhuman" (ibid.). Pity, for Spinoza, is only human nature's last resort to compensate for the lack of reason.

Vives' language in the definition of these derivative emotions betrays not only the complexity of his own emotional makeup but also subtle influences of Platonic, Aristotelian, Stoic, and Christian sources. What makes Vives original and interesting is precisely the complete lack of systemic constrictions that this language reveals. Like most philosophers today Vives was more than willing to sacrifice rigid unity in order to expose the tensions, endless combinations, and variations of the emotions that human beings experience in life.

19
The Dynamics of Emotion

VIVES' LUKEWARM EFFORT TO define and classify emotions according to more or less traditional parameters contrasts vividly with his eagerness to probe and describe the complex interaction and intermeshing of our emotional reactions, motivations, and attitudes. Although he makes no explicit statement to this effect, his entire work on the emotions seems to be guided by the firm persuasion that our emotional life is more than a molecular juxtaposition of discrete emotional units, units that obligingly correspond to our mental categories and to our limited vocabulary. In spite of the division of the tract into chapters dealing with particular emotions, what makes Vives' book novel and influential is the constant effort to unravel by means of concrete description the inner dynamics of emotional processes. Emotions fluctuate in intensity, interact with others, change into different emotions either gradually or explosively, and form constellations and mixtures that defy naming and definition. As is typical of Vives, this descriptive enterprise is carried through in the most unsystematic manner. Analytic details, insights, and resolutions are practically never synthesized into high-level generalizations or principles. Even the headings I have used to organize the material of this chapter are only suggested by the author of *De Anima et Vita,* sometimes in a very distant, indirect manner.

Vives compares the inner dynamics of emotions to waves and to the career of a fire. Like waves, emotions have a crest and a trough. They rise, reach a peak, and then die out. But not every emotion rises with the same intensity, at the same pace, or according to the same pattern. Some emotions seem to thrive with resistance, to grow when they are challenged and meet stiff opposition. Other emotions, on the other hand, recede and yield to the sway of stronger ones. Fires, too, burn in different ways. In some people, the desire for revenge heats up quickly and "burns out in a very short time, as burning flux does" (*tamquam in stupa brevissime restinguitur;* M 3.497). But among melancholics envy catches fire very slowly and in a most stubborn manner (ibid. 67–69). Love is sometimes invigorated by small altercations between lovers, as "the furnace burns more vigorously with the sprinkling of some drops of water" (M 3. 452). The love of the young resembles "a passing flame." The love of cooler, more sanguine temperaments is like "burning lumber," less ebullient but more stubborn and longer lasting (M 3.436).

Some circumstances in the emotion's object tend to add momentum to the rising motion, others seem to weaken it or to hold it at bay. The rhetorical procedure of going through the *loci* (commonplaces) that Vives had learned from old masters (Aristotle, Cicero, Quintilian) and modern (Rudolph Agricola) was ideally suited for a detailed, rich, and occasionally super-fluous analysis of circumstantial variables. The chapters on anger (Chapter 13), jealousy (Chapter 16), and fear (Chapter 21) provide typical examples. The intensity of anger depends on local circumstances (in front of one's disciples, in hot weather), time (before or after winning a political cam-paign), personal situation (in prosperity or in hard times), the rank of the person who has offended us (inferiors, superiors, friends, people who owe us a favor, relatives), the tools used by the offender (a fist, a cane), the manner of the offense (whether it was public or private, preventable or not), the aims of the offender (to ridicule us), and our own expectations (whether the offense could have been anticipated or not; M 3.479–81). Jealousy, too, varies in intensity according to persons (the person who is jealous, the person of whom one is jealous, and the person on account of whom one is jealous), places (open, secret, sacred, or secular), time (a religious holiday), and occupations (M 3.491–92). Fear varies with our appraisal of the danger involved, and such appraisal depends greatly on the circumstances of location, time, and the power of the people involved (M 3.506–7). It can generally be said that persons tend to provoke in others emotions that correspond to their own personal qualities: benevolent people tend to provoke the benevolence of others and cruel people provoke hatred and instill fear in others.

Novelty intensifies emotion; experience and repetition weaken it. Nothing makes us indignant more quickly than the sudden good fortune of someone we think unworthy of it (M 3.494). A novel joy and an unexpected pleasure provoke us to laughter while the old and the usual leave us indifferent and unmoved (M 3.469). Lack of experience is a constant source of irritation (M 3.473). In the case of fear, experience can work either way. Veteran soldiers who have repeatedly faced the same dangers and escaped without injury are more confident than those who go to war for the first time, but gladiators who have been badly wounded in an early encounter become more fearful and are more afraid of combat (M 3.505 and 507). Repeated experiences of some sort can even prevent the possibility of harboring certain emotions: prolonged suffering, for instance, can make us callous and impervious to sadness and compassion (M 3.500).

The process by which emotions rise in intensity is not the same in all of them. There are emotions that seem to feed on themselves, such as sorrow, which "invites more sorrow" (M 3.498) and escalates into self-hatred, despair, and rage (M 3.35–37); or love, since "nothing provokes love as much as love itself" (M 3.433). Jealousy, too, thrives among people given to suspicion and brooding self-absorption (M 3.492). Other emotions, on the other hand, seem to exhaust themselves once they have reached a maximum. Such is the case of anger and revenge. Some emotions increase gradually and slowly; others are by their very nature explosive and tumultuous. Hatred can be harbored for a long time with no overt expression. Anger, on the other hand, even when it has been slowly nurtured, often flares up in violent and dramatic fashion (M 3.478). Envy, too, like anger, can become uncontrollable and intemperate, sometimes for the most unexpected reasons (M 3.489).

Sharing emotions with other people weakens some emotions and reinforces others. Envy, for instance, is lessened when we share our feelings with others (M 3.490). Joy and sadness are increased when shared with people dear to us. When joy is shared with people indifferent to us, our joy remains unaffected but our sadness is alleviated (M 3.499).

Although emotions have some inertia of their own and occasionally remain vigorous even after their object has either vanished or radically changed, time and distance generally tend to weaken and even dispel some of them. Envy fades with respect to those who are far away in space or time. We can envy the dead only when we are at the present time disturbed by the memory of their wealth, their talents, or their good fortune (M 3.490). Anger toward the dead cools in time because the dead have suffered the ultimate evil and cannot any more be the victims of our revenge (M 3.497). Time sooner or later provides some relief to the angry soul, depending on one's bodily temperament, personal attitudes, and perceptions (M 3.497). On the other hand, the attempt to repress and delay the execution of an act of revenge can make our desire for revenge more virulent and intense (M 3.497). Objects that are unrelated to us for one reason or another behave like objects distant in space or time. Those who do not go to sea do not care about shipwrecks and monks are unmoved by the miseries of a soldier's life (M 3.459).

Whatever has been said about the dynamics of particular emotions needs to be qualified by Vives' constant warning that emotions are seldom experienced in isolation but merge and interact with other emotions. Blurred emotions, poorly defined and hard-to-identify feelings in transitional stages, dominate our emotional life. Emotions are not indifferent to each other. They are attracted or repelled, curbed or reinforced, caused or prevented by other emotions.

Some emotions are so neighborly to other emotions that they seldom arise without their company. These congenial emotions are normally experienced in constellations and mixtures often identified and named according to their dominant ingredient at any given time. The exasperation we feel when people repeatedly deny our requests is a baffling mixture of irritation, anger, envy, and hatred (M 3.480). Irritation is often blended with anxiety and fear (M 3.473) and often evolves into hatred, anger, envy, and the desire for revenge (M 3.495). Indignation is often caused by envy and includes the feeling of compassion toward the person who undeservedly suffers or a strong fear that we ourselves might suffer some inconvenience, a fear that easily leads to hatred (M 3.495). The sadness of fear can provoke feelings of self-hatred, despair, and rage (M 3.498–99). Envy and hatred are the companions of pride, which is itself followed by anger, desire of revenge, and constant irritation (M 3.515). The indignation of the proud is permeated with anger and envy (M 3.494).

There are idiosyncratic mixtures of emotions that appear to be rooted in the personality characteristics of the person who has the emotion. Reflective types of persons are more likely to experience a mixture of hatred and envy than those who are thoughtless and empty-headed. The latter usually feel a combination of hatred and fear (M 3.484). Hatred is mixed with joy when those whom we hate suffer, unless we normally have strong feelings of compassion (M 3.485). Fearful people experience fear with many other emotions: the fear involved in respect, the fear that accompanies jealousy, the fear that is inseparable from desire, the fear that trails hope, the fear implied by sadness.

Some emotions appear in bundles simply because they evidently thrive in the company of each other, even when they seem disparate and inconsistent. Love of concupiscence, for instance, surrounds itself with such odd fellows as envy, hatred, or anger when somebody hurts or threatens to harm the beloved (M 3.446). But love is also inseparable from desire and hope, and hope itself is inextricably linked to fear (M 3.441). If the hope of the lover is fulfilled, hope leads to joy. If the lover's fears materialize, sadness ensues (M 3.427). The fear of disgrace is proportionate to the desire for honor (M 3.509). It is impossible to be ashamed of having been denied the respect one feels entitled to without wallowing also in feelings of irritation and anger

(M 3.511). In love among unequals, the respect for the greatness of the beloved is frequently mixed with feelings of shame and embarrassment (M 3.428). Love and compassion seem to reinforce each other (M 3.462), as much as hatred and anger depend on each other (M 3.497).

There are, however, emotions that seem incompatible with each other, that exclude or weaken each other. In some cases, this incompatibility is unexceptionable and final: joy excludes sadness and compassion repels jealousy (M 3.427). Love makes jealousy impossible, unless the former is mixed with desire and concupiscence (M 3.491). In other cases the incompatibility is enough to change the intensity of other emotions: confidence decreases desire, while fear increases it (M 3.437). The feeling of contempt sometimes dulls the emotions of hatred and envy (M 3.475). Anger, envy, hatred, and even love cause debilitation in any feeling of respect and admiration (M 3.457). And, in general, strong emotions tend to dislodge weaker emotions whether of the same or of different kind. Thus sorrow is canceled by a more intense sorrow, hatred is weakened by an even stronger hatred, and sadness disappears in the presence of a violent fear (M 3.427). The desire for revenge against a given person vanishes when we get violently angry against another (M 3.497). The strong desire for something makes us invulnerable to embarrassment (M 3.513), as much as intense fear destroys any pride (M 3.519). Any violent passion makes compassion impossible (M 3.496), and envy yields to a stronger envy, compassion, or fear (M 3.491–92).

Sometimes emotions are connected to each other as causes and effects. Pride causes envy (M 3.486), fear makes us suspicious (M 3.505), desire causes jealousy (M 3.490), hatred causes cruelty and the desire for revenge (M 3.485), and anger can cause daring and confidence (M 3.506). In other cases, the emotions seem to evolve into other emotions, to lead into them, either gradually or suddenly. Reverence toward somebody can turn into love (M 3.455), compassion can lead to fondness (M 3.453), and irritation invites contempt (M 3.475) and anger (M 3.476). By the same token, sustained anger can evolve into hatred (M 3.476), and envy can resolve itself into indignation (M 3.493). Some emotions seek to disguise themselves as other emotions. Envy, for instance, refuses to be openly recognized and seeks to be identified as anger or hatred or fear (M 3.487). Pride attempts to pass as humility and courtesy (M 3.519). Under certain conditions, emotions of a certain kind abruptly switch into their opposites. Thus love turns into violent hatred when we discover that the beloved is not the person we thought him or her to be (M 3.484), and envy turns into compassion when the happiness of the other turns into misery (M 3.489). The intense and fleeting pleasure of a joyful holiday can degenerate into the morbid sadness of a daily routine (M 3.498). Indignation and compassion seem to be mysteriously linked by our sense of just desserts (M 3.494).

Vives' rich albeit unsystematic observations on the dynamics of emotions reveal perhaps better than any other feature of *De Anima et Vita* his strong penchant for observation and introspection in the service of moral perfection and emotional control and therapy. To this final therapy we now turn our attention.

20

The Control and Therapy of Emotion

VIVES BEGINS HIS STUDY of emotions by solemnly announcing that to know our emotional life is necessary "for remedying grave evils" and providing "medication for severe diseases" (M 3.421). Remedying those evils and curing those diseases was not only the purpose of Vives' reflections on the nature and working of our emotional reactions, but the purpose of the entire treatise *De Anima et Vita,* and, to some extent, the final purpose of all Vivesian thinking. It is therefore important to know what evils Vives had in mind and the nature of the diseases he tried to cure before we proceed to discuss some of the remedies he prescribed for them.

Emotions are movements of the orectic part of the soul toward the good and away from evil. Human beings, like all animals, are thus directed by the Creator to the pursuit of their goals — self-conservation and happiness. The difference between human beings and animals is that while the latter are exclusively guided by inborn natural instincts, human emotions are directed by cognitive assessments that are themselves influenced by a variety of internal and external factors. Wrong value assessments are the source of man's most destructive "fraud" (*fraus*). In spite of the fact that God has also endowed us with some generic and "seminal truths" about right and wrong, human beings are capable of deceiving themselves about the good they should seek and the evil they should avoid, capable of throwing themselves into "enormous precipices" (*grandia praecipitia;* M 3.422).

If erroneous judgment about value is the greatest human evil, the kind of emotion or the degree of emotion that is caused by such judgment is man's "most severe disease." This highly Augustinian manner of thinking does not amount to a flat condemnation of emotion. At any given moment there is an emotion of some kind and intensity that is life-enhancing, humanly fulfilling, and divinely ordained. The disease does not consist in having the emotion, but in having the wrong one or even the right emotion in either an excessive or deficient degree. Emotions need to be controlled because they can adversely affect the choices we make and distort our judgment about the true value of things. Violent emotions need to be tempered because under their influence we lose control of ourselves and are "carried away by a storm" (M 3.425) that can take us into unpredictable situations. Under the influence of uncontrolled emotion we become like beasts; we are guided by the blind forces of "nature" rather than by the free choices of our will (M 3.426). "Man is human when he lives by the mind, uses his mind, and acts in a way worth his humanity; but the man who lives according to his passions, does not use his reason, and does what is contrary to God, becomes a brute and degenerates into a vile and rotten nature."[1] Human moral perfection therefore requires that emotions be controlled, excited, soothed, or sometimes eradicated.

Well within the Stoic tradition that still echoes in the thought of Descartes and Spinoza, Vives profoundly believes that emotions could and should be controlled. Since emotions and the degree in which they are felt are mostly caused by thought, the control of emotions to Vives is mostly, but not exclusively, a matter of thought control and cognitive enlightenment. "A mind which has been properly educated and trained to face different situations, should be able to increase or to decrease, to eradicate or to change the direction and power of its emotions" (*mente ergo aliter atque aliter edocta atque instituta mutantur affectus augmento vel decremento vel tolluntur prorsus atque in aliorum vim et quasi jus concedunt;* M 3.422). The Stoic ideal of the sage, although significantly enriched and complemented by Vives' observations on the noncognitive ingredients of emotional life, was the central inspiration of *De Anima et Vita*, in spite of Vives' harsh words on the scholastic "fallacies" of Stoic masters. "The Sage," Vives writes, "never fails to choose the good, seeks always a well-defined goal and follows the few and well-explored paths toward it" (*sapiens in eligendo bono non fallitur et unum aliquod sibi proponit paucasque ad illud vias, easque exploratas et certas;* M 3.425). The sage does that "by the rational restraint of those emotions that naturally surge in us and by forcing them to yield to right judgment" (*ut surgentem vi naturae affectum statim rationis freno compescat cogatque recto judicio cedere;* M 3.425).

The first remedy that Vives prescribes for emotional control and therapy is the knowledge of ourselves. To know what emotions are and how they work is the first condition of emotional control. Self-knowledge is the first step toward emotional therapy. That is why philosophical reflection into the nature of emotion was to Vives the foundation of private and public morality. "The supreme form of liberal education is that philosophy which provides a remedy for the diseases of the soul."[2] The third book of *De Anima et Vita* was written with this high purpose in mind.

The second most effective medicine for emotional health is to Vives the most difficult to procure, the habit of judging well about the value of our choices. Like Socrates, Vives was convinced that most human evils were the result of "blind ignorance," "errors," and "deceptions." As a Christian, Vives is convinced that the enslavement of reason to "perverse emotions" (*pravus affectus*) was one of the most devastating consequences of Adam's sin.[3] In his more Erasmian years Vives had taught that the highest purpose of Christianity was precisely to silence the storm of passion and to bring to the individual soul "the joy that comes from the serenity of mind."[4] In *De Disciplinis* (I, 3), Vives diagnosed the corruption of culture as a massive case of "emotional disorder" (*affectus immoderatus*). In *De Concordia* he warned that unless passions were restrained (*ni passiones cohibeantur*) humanity would see no end to war and social conflict.

Vives' teaching that emotional disorder was caused by bad judgment was a commonplace of a long philosophical tradition that goes back to Socrates, Aristotle, and Zeno. But Vives, always sensitive to the complexities and twists of human existence, realized that correct and accurate judgment was not only the main cause of emotional equanimity but also, partially at least, its effect. Emotional disorder caused by bad judgment leads to further emotional disorder, a disorder which itself distorts judgment. Emotional therapy, therefore, requires not just a simple lesson on values but an elaborate, complicated, and *ad hoc* strategy that takes into account the many-faceted aspects of emotional response, its cognitive, physiological, and situational components. Vives, however, does not present this strategy in a systematic manner. *De Anima et Vita* includes no manual of set rules to deal with emotional disorder. But as its author is wont to do, he writes a book containing a rich variety of practical suggestions and procedures, most of them original and interesting. We shall begin with those techniques and reminders that in one way or another have something to do with our cognitive operations.

"The same factors," Vives writes, "that . . . are capable of affecting our judgment and shaping our opinions, are also capable of exciting and soothing the emotions of our soul" (M 3.422). Judgment is greatly affected by emotional states. Any emotional therapy that attempts to correct false assessments should therefore take into consideration the emotional condition of the person. Emotions that have made deep inroads into the psyche or have become habits have a much stronger hold on our patterns of thinking than emotions with a short history or emotions in their initial stage. It is the task of educators to foster those emotional habits that are in harmony with the proper judgments in life. Mothers ought to impress upon their children the love of that which alone is "beautiful, worthy of admiration, worth having, reliable and solid," such as the love of justice, piety, moral strength, continence, knowledge, compassion, and benevolence toward others.[5] The first obligation of public schools is to teach children "the right opinions about things" (*rectas opiniones de rebus*).[6] Furthermore, spiritual counselors should try to eradicate dangerous and emotional inclinations as soon as they begin to take hold of our soul. "At the beginning love can be restrained without much difficulty; therefore the master in the art of loving (Ovid) recommends to resist it in the early stage" (M 3.450).

Thought can either weaken or reinforce an emotion. Pride can be checked by the thought that "there is nothing for a mortal to be proud of." That is why truly wise and intelligent people are less likely to be proud than the partially educated and the ill-tempered (M 3.515). Anger ceases when we realize that the person we thought had offended us was unable to do so because he was stupid, unaware, or mentally sick; or because what he did was his normal behavior or was done out of necessity (M 3.482). Reflection helps to control the "tyranny of the imagination" and to subdue our exaggerated fears (M 3.508). The wise are not ashamed of their parents' faults because they know that the parents bear no responsibility for them (M 3.510–11). When we are struck by grief, it helps for us to remind ourselves that the cause of our grief is often not in proportion to our suffering, that we lose more by feeling sad than by losing the things whose loss we deplore (M 3.500). We become more courageous if we often think how beneficial it is to us to face and overcome the perils confronting us and how harmful it is to run away from them (M 3.504). Jealousy is undermined when we recognize that "one is tormented for nothing and that all one gains from it is irritation" (M 3.492). Emotions that thrive on surprise, such as fear, can be prevented or weakened by thinking frequently about all the eventualities that might cause them.[7] People who have been trained in despising things transient and terrestrial and are exclusively interested in their heavenly destination are immune to the emotion of hatred (M 3.486).

Thought can not only weaken and eradicate dangerous emotions, but also reinforce those emotions that enhance our moral worth. Joy can be increased by considering how scarce and remarkable is the good that we have acquired. It can also be weakened by thoughts contrary to these (M 3.464).

Since emotional response is, at least partially, caused and supported by thought, there will be cases when the best way to control a harmful emotion will be to distract the mind and draw its attention to a different object. Lovers who are being carried way by their passions should be "brought back home from their wanderings" through music, parties, meals, wine, games, dancing, fishing, hunting, sailing, and more (M 3.452). Hard work and strenuous exercise can sometimes be the best remedy for emotional upheaval (M 3.452). Anger abates when we are engaged in cheerful occupations, during holidays and celebrations (M 3.481). The blow of irritation can be cushioned with a good joke (ibid.). An entertaining story is sometimes enough to dismiss sadness (M 3.500).

Emotions can also be controlled with the help of other emotions, or as Vives would say in one of his favorite metaphors, it is possible "to drive out a nail with the help of another nail" (M 3.497 and 500). Lawyers, spiritual counselors, teachers, and parents should be perfectly aware of the complex interaction between emotions themselves and of those subtle processes by which emotions of one kind gradually evolve into emotions of a different kind. They should know that the fear of getting hurt if we do not control ourselves is as useful to blunt anger as the hope of deriving some benefit from forgiving our enemies (M 3.497); that the fear of a present evil might suffice to control our fears of possible threats (M 3.500); that irritation and sadness can be minimized by seeking the company of those who are joyful and have a good sense of humor (M 3. 474). Vives goes so far as to suggest that people who are victims of a strong passion should be exposed to the seduction of a passion that is incompatible with the former, in the hope, I presume, that both passions would end in neutralizing each other. Persons blinded by passionate love should be treated with a proportionate diet of greed, ambition, fear, indignation, or anger until emotional balance has been achieved (M 3.453).

Emotional therapy to be complete must also take into account the physiological side of emotional response. Bodily temperament, climate, season, time of day or night, diet, sickness, health, and age affect our emotional dispositions and reactions. Whatever affects them affects the quality and intensity of our emotional life. "The more our judgment is infected by its contact with the body and the deeper it is immersed in it, the more and more frequently do our emotions grow, upsetting and distorting not only the intellect but even the external senses of the soul" (M 3.435). Vives does not hesitate to recommend bleeding the victim of a violent passion in order to bring in a new stream of blood and a different emotional disposition (M 3.453). A realistic attempt to control our emotions should also be aware of the inner conflict between bodily and mental inclinations. The pleasures the body seeks are often incompatible with the pleasures of the soul (*voluptates corporis et animi extrudunt sese mutuo;* M 3.467). Peace of spirit, therefore, demands sometimes that the pleasures of the body be sacrificed to the pleasures of the spirit, that our entire hierarchy of desires, loves, pleasures, hopes, and fears be arranged in accordance with such priorities. Finally, emotional guidance and control should be aware of and use for their higher purposes the impact of situations, social ties, rank, occupation, ethnic background, and other environmental circumstances.

Vives' recommendations for emotional control and therapy thus betray the highly eclectic character of a mind seeking to cure humanity's "diseases" not with a single magic panacea but with a complex and diversified stock of drugs.

21
Retrospect

In SPITE OF ITS profound indebtedness to tradition, Vives' tract on the
emotions manages to convey a personal flavor that is unique in the literature
on the subject. It is almost impossible to read the third book of *De Anima et
Vita* without reflecting on the character of its author, the people, and the life
events that helped to shape and define it. The book contains not only
scattered references to individuals whom Vives admired much (Pico della
Mirandola, Erasmus, Sir Thomas More, Catherine of Aragon), but also
personal anecdotes (laughing after a long fast, being unable to eat food that
had upset his stomach as a child), and frequent references to the positive and
negative influence of his own physical and social environment. The Valencian
exile was positively impressed by the good manners, the controlled behavior,
the cooperative and sociable temperaments of the people in the Low
Countries and in England, while noticing at the same time that northerners
were more vulnerable to melancholy and sadness. One also has the impression that Vives grew increasingly disenchanted with the proclivity of
southerners to effusive demonstrativeness, excessive laughter, and melodramatic jealousy. He disliked their parochial lack of adaptability to new
situations and was uncomfortable with their demonstrative eroticism. On the
other hand it seems clear that Vives also grew progressively weary of
northern stodginess, intellectual snobbery, and the abnormally frequent
occurrence of lunatic infatuations in cold and wet climates.

On the basis of Book 3 of *De Anima et Vita* one can venture to draw a
profile of Vives' character and *ingenium*. It is clear that as a Jewish exile from
Valencia who had been educated in Paris and was forced for a long time to
commute between Oxford and Bruges or Louvain, Vives had a profound
feeling for the relativity of values, tastes, and opinions. Emotions, he
constantly repeats, do not give us a picture of reality but only of an
individual's perspective and interpretation of reality. The young, the old,

women, children, intellectuals, the sick, the rich, the poor, rulers, citizens, soldiers, merchants, and teachers all have their own emotional profiles, profiles also affected by the climate in which those persons live, by their bodily temperaments, by their food and their drink, by their social rank and profession, by their memories and their expectations.

The first ten chapters of Book 3 introduce us to an austere, serious, intense, and highly moralistic man. The excesses of passion are described in passionate metaphors. Mistakes in value are compared to "precipices," intense emotions to "murky agitations," trivial desires to "swarms of dangerous bees." Vives' musings on love, concupiscence, desire, fondness, reverence, compassion, joy, pleasure, and laughter echo his almost Manichaean thoughts on sex and marriage as expounded in the moral treatises. The Neoplatonist content of the chapters on love seems only an unusual concession to popular literature. The real Vives comes to the surface in the impassioned condemnation of Cupid's sway, the harsh caricature of lovers' behavior, the cold contempt for "enticing looks," the downplaying of bodily pleasure, the eloquent condemnation of all forms of hedonism, the emphasis on the "vexations and tortures" of all human love. Probably nothing characterizes Vives better than his enthusiastic support for Saint Augustine's stern warning that the pleasures of the spirit are totally incompatible with the pleasures of the flesh. Vives' spirited defense of compassion against Seneca and the Stoics has as much autobiographical flavor as his description of the qualities that make other people lovable to us. These are people who can be counted upon, fulfill their duties (and life, Vives emphasizes, is full of duties!), well-mannered, modest, frugal, fair, unassuming, serious, respectable, and loyal, the very qualities that he himself strove after. Vives' reflections on friendship cannot be read without thinking of Craneveld, the loyal and close confidant; of More, the rich and influential but complicated friend; of Erasmus, the revered master who was so difficult to please; of Catherine of Aragon, the dear patroness who, when under pressure, misunderstood Vives' personal intentions. His fear and apprehension regarding political activism—which More exemplified for a while—can be felt in Vives' pronouncements about the dangers of power, the irritations and intrigues of the ambitious, the cruelty of those in command.

The second portion of Book 3, all the lengthy and ponderous chapters on those passions that "transform man into a beast," bespeak in mournful tones the unmitigated pessimism of a man who constantly dreamed of death as the end of all pain. Even hope—which occupies the shortest chapter of the entire book—is offered to the reader in the company of such low-ranking emotions as irritation, contempt, anger, hatred, envy, jealousy, revenge, and pride.

The chapter on irritation—one of the longest of the book—is not only an indictment of human nature but also the confession of a perfectionist who has found most people hard to tolerate, the outburst of a man who writes a brilliant masterpiece on education but is exasperated by the dull and annoying students at Oxford University. The portrayal of anger is also the revealing confession of a man easily insulted, who hates all histrionic displays of temper and who is occasionally tempted to think of the human animal as nothing but a devious monster. Vives' reflections on objectless sadness and depression, his strange opinion that sadness is increased when shared with people we love, cast a dim light into the somber recesses of a man absorbed in himself, a lonely man in a cherished, self-imposed exile. Vives' repeated attempts to disguise his Jewish origin, his inclination to think that his father's brutal execution has reflected in some strange way on his own character, and his eloquent words on the tyranny of the imagination, provide the chapter on fear with a historical context that no reader should forget. Vives' strong dislike of intellectual snobbery—a fundamental trait of both his pedagogy and his character—shines through the colorful and derisive denunciation of pride in the last chapter of the book.

The third book of *De Anima et Vita* also represents a lucid statement of Vives' world view and the clearest expression of his intellectual vocation as a moral philosopher and a pioneer of modern education. Nonhuman reality, the domain of natural entities determined by physical laws or by instinct to bring about and preserve their own being, is to Vives nothing but the fascinating, useful, and indispensable stage upon which humans seek self-fulfillment and moral excellence through free choice. His relentless effort to understand the possibilities and dangers inextricably attached to the exclusively human privilege of choice betrays the profoundly humanistic character of his thought. It is by choice that we can sink below the level of the beast as it is by choice that we can ascend to that of the angel. Choices made in time decide our fate in eternity.

I think one can claim without exaggeration that Vives' entire philosophy turns upon the complex interaction between emotion and the value judgments that affect choice, obviously a major concern of traditional philosophical reflection. What makes Vives' thought particularly interesting is his constant inclination to link individual human choices to the quality of the culture that humans create through history. Vives' philosophy of choice becomes a philosophy of history and a philosophy of a culture as the results of human choices. Culture and history are to Vives realities mediated by time and conditioned by choice. The same emotions that affect choice determine also the shape of culture at any time in a given moment of history. Historical manifestations of culture are expressions of the emotional temper of the age in which they were produced. Culture, Vives could have said, has its own *ingenium.*

In *Adversus Pseudodialecticos,* Vives criticizes and rejects terminist logic not so much for its technical shortcomings (about which, I am afraid, he had no clear idea), but mostly because it represented a misdirected form of human energy, a useless, wasteful display of contentiousness, vanity, and lack of interest in the challenges faced by humans in their daily life both as individuals and citizens. In *Fabula de Homine* and *In Sapientem Praelectio* Vives explains his opposition to any form of narcissistic speculation by emphasizing the vital connection between thought and emotion, and between emotion and life. The *Aedes Legum* is not only a testimonial to Vives' lifelong concern with legal reform but also a profoundly humanistic restatement of the Aristotelian teaching that equity cannot be fully guaranteed by the rewording of the law, but requires the unprejudiced and emotionally untainted judgment of those called upon to interpret it. Vives' somber reflections on contemporary European events (*De Europae statu ac tumultibus, De Europae Dissidiis et Bello Turcico, De Conditione Vitae Christianorum sub Turca*) are thoroughly permeated by the conviction that war is always the painful symptom of emotional disease. *De Subventione Pauperum* combines in a most striking manner Vives' profound compassion for those who suffer poverty and are emotionally disfigured by it with Vives' apprehensions about the dangers of professionalizing social assistance. Would bureaucrats become greedy in the business of helping others? Would the recipients of assistance lose any incentive to work and perpetuate forever the ugly spectacle of their profitable begging?

Vives' views on the role of emotion in the domain of political, social, and cultural events found their most explicit and comprehensive expression in the books he wrote or planned to write during his English period. The *Introductio ad Sapientiam,* one of his most successful and influential works, characterizes virtue and wisdom as the supreme accomplishment of reason, the control of emotional upheaval. His *Satellitium Animi* reiterates the same message in a different literary form. His *De Concordia et Discordia* brings to a magnificent synthesis the demands of individual ethics and the lessons drawn from Vives' political writings. His history of nations is nothing but a grand-scale projection of the moral achievements and failures of both citizens and leaders. His concept of political justice is only a larger version of the justice that prevails among the individuals making up the republic. International peace is but an echo, on the political level, of the individuals' emotional control and harmony.

Vives' pedagogical and psychological works, the last and also the most important parts of his intellectual production, represent an attempt to meet head-on the key challenge of reforming the individual through education and self-knowledge. *De Disciplinis* brings to fruition all the previous efforts made by Vives in the field of education. The grand ideal of *De Disciplinis* is to review the entire history of culture and to offer an ambitious blueprint for the reform of education. Cultural failures, Vives claims, are only manifestations of emotional disorder. The reform of education presupposes once again the reform of the individual. Individual perfection consists in the control of passion by reason. *De Anima et Vita,* Vives' most mature work, was written with the noble intention of laying the foundation of all educational reform: a thorough knowledge of human nature in its rich, complex, unique—and to some extent mysterious—individual manifestations.

The book on the emotions is without any doubt a typically Renaissance recapitulation of traditional (classical, patristic, and medieval) commonplaces on the subject, perhaps the most comprehensive and influential of such recapitulations in the sixteenth century, a clear mirror of the Renaissance's heightened sense of human individuality and dignity. The book displays the early and tentative attempts to liberate psychology from the tyranny of systemic rigidity, although by doing so it sometimes deteriorated into a poorly organized discourse. Vives' *De Anima et Vita* took the first steps toward a description of emotional reactions, a description that remained close to real life and was guided by introspection and observation rather than steered by metaphysical concepts and principles as scholastic thought had tried to do with moderate success. In some ways, Vives' approach signifies a return to the more descriptive treatment of the emotions by Aristotle.

But Vives' treatise on emotion is more than just one more expression, no matter how authoritative, of Renaissance discourse on human nature. The book is also a compelling proof of Vives' creativity and originality. Vives' programmatic commitment to constructive syncretism shines through every page of *De Anima et Vita*. Vives' open-minded but critical direction manages to compose a harmonious pattern out of such diverse voices as those of Socrates, Plato, Aristotle, the Greek and Roman Stoics, Saint Augustine, Saint Thomas, and the Renaissance Neoplatonists. From classical philosophy all the way from Socrates to the Roman Stoics of the Imperial Age, Vives accepted the basic teaching that passion could and should be controlled by knowledge. But Vives' careful observations on the cognitive determinant of emotion and on the mutual and complex interaction between emotion and thought removed some of Plato's hesitations on the matter, enlarged the scope of Aristotle's rhetorical approach, and provided a much-needed corrective of

Stoic exaggerations. Emotions, Vives claims, are not judgments but imply judgments. But these judgments implied by emotions do not need to be—Vives hastens to remark—propositions about beliefs. A mere stirring of the imagination often suffices to provoke a matching emotion. And since the imagination is closely bound to memory and its idiosyncratic associations, to habits and personal traits, emotions are highly subjective. They are not objective pictures of reality but are pictures of the unique picture of reality that individuals harbor in their minds. Emotions are therefore as relative to individuals as their opinions, tastes, values, character structure, memories, expectations, and motives. Emotions are as much shaped and defined by the social and physical environment as the cognitive experiences and traits of the individual. Vives' reflections on the influence of diet, climate, age, health, education, culture, social position, and situation reveal an intense and original interest in the study of the sociocultural, biological, and psychological determinants of emotion.

Vives' analysis of the intentionality of emotion is not the only significant departure from early Stoic doctrine. His positive attitude toward the constructive purposiveness of emotional responses—an attitude that was suggested but not fully developed by the Roman Stoics of the Imperial Age—differs radically from the Stoic confusion between emotional expression and emotional excess. It brought Vives closer to a Christian interpretation of Peripatetic philosophy under the guidance of medieval scholasticism. Emotions, he said, have a definite role in the divine plan of creation. Human beings incapable of feeling and expressing them would fall victims to the threats of the environment and find impossible the realization of their social nature. Without fear, human beings would be helpless; without compassion and shame, society would be impossible. Hope is the indispensable companion of all striving and even pride is the necessary condition of self-respect. For all these reasons, Vives strongly rejects the inhuman ideal of apathy and refuses to subscribe *in toto* to the Stoic ideal of wisdom or to accept as meaningful and valid the Stoic fallacies and subtleties aimed at proving that apathetic people are not touched by the misfortunes of life or by the evil actions of wrongdoers.

Again, the strong emphasis on the physiology of emotion distinguishes Vives from both Aristotle and Saint Thomas. That his physiology is in fact couched in the then fashionable idiom of Galen's temperaments, humors, and animal spirits—an idiom adopted also by Descartes—is less significant than his firm persuasion that emotional responses are irrefutable proofs of the mysterious union of mind and body. In fact, he seems to think that this union, for which speculation fails to provide a satisfactory explanation, is directly perceived and felt in the actual experience of any emotion. Vives' emphasis on description at the expense of grand conceptual schemes is deeply rooted in his mildly skeptical belief that life-experiences transcend theoretical constructions. One can even surmise that Descartes' *Traité des passions,* which was inspired by the same attitude in spite of the early insistence on "clear and distinct" ideas, was at least partially influenced by Vives' *De Anima et Vita.*

Vives' attention to the physiology of emotion goes beyond the traditional interest in the description of expression (facial configurations, voice changes, and so on), a description he freely borrows from Aristotle's *Rhetoric* and from the Stoics, particularly from Seneca. More original are Vives' reflections on the impact of bodily temperament upon character structure and emotional make-up and the occasionally detailed descriptions of the internal bodily changes that precede, accompany, and result from emotion.

De Anima et Vita's taxonomy of emotions was indeed more principled and richer in philosophical interest than the merely rhetorical nomenclatures of the early Stoics, but much less rigid than the systematic scheme of Saint Thomas or the austere and occasionally contrived array of Spinoza. Vives' catalogue of basic and derivative emotions can itself be classified halfway between the incomplete and unpretentious list of emotions in the second book of Aristotle's *Rhetoric* and the explicit and more tightly organized scheme of Descartes' *Traité.* Vives greatly enlarged the Aristotelian list of emotions. The more significant differences between Vives and Aristotle can be traced back to some of Vives' patterns of thinking. The Christian and Neoplatonic aspect of Vives' philosophy is evidenced by the emphasis on the emotion of love and its derivatives (fondness, respect, joy). Aristotelian friendship and kindness are transformed into the central emotion of love, the cosmic law of attraction between equals, the reflection on the human level of the Love that created and beautified the Universe. More Christian than Neoplatonic are Vives' reflections on compassion and shame. The reader is nevertheless puzzled by Vives' inattention to such religiously important emotions as regret, guilt, or despair. Vives' highly moralistic and didactic temper is revealed by his severe analysis of desire, his admonitions on pleasure, his harsh condemnation of cruelty, and the full and haunting chapter on pride. The detailed, even piercing description is best displayed in his reflections on the initial attraction of the good (*allubescentia*) and the multifarious annoyances humans are constantly subjected to (*irritatio*).

The similarities and differences between Vives and Descartes are both significant and enlightening. Descartes' catalogue of the six basic emotions (wonder, love, hatred, desire, joy, and sadness) differs from that of Vives (attraction, love, hatred, desire, joy, sadness, hope, fear, anger, and shame) by subsuming hope and fear under the description of desire and the analysis of anger and shame under that of sadness. Descartes' effort to reduce the primary emotions to small number was clearly exaggerated by Spinoza, who in this respect returns to an early Stoic position. But the similarities and differences between Vives and Descartes go beyond the listing of emotions. The Cartesian physiology of emotion is indeed expressed in language similar to that of Vives, but is also dictated and guided by highly methodological assumptions and principles that Vives never professed. The Cartesian distinction between passion and intellectual emotion could not be justified in Vives' philosophy. Still, the *Traité* is richer than *De Anima et Vita* in fine psychological insights. Descartes' observations on the mixed emotions of a widower or the secret pleasures experienced by the theatergoer in sharing the sadness of a play belong to a more mature stage of human consciousness. The same can be said about the Cartesian views on the positive and constructive aspects of self-esteem, about the joy derived from the contemplation of justice, about the relative value of unfounded hopes and justified fears, about the dangers of tediousness or vicious humility, and about the intimate connection between the nobility of the soul and consciousness of freedom.

One of the greatest features of *De Anima et Vita* is Vives' constant attention to the study of the dynamics of emotions. His talent for description shines through in his observations on the different courses of particular emotional reactions, on the complex interrelations between thought and emotion and between emotions themselves, on the impact of circumstance on the intensity and direction of emotion, on the role of novelty and habit, on the part that sharing emotions with others plays on the emotions themselves, on the effects of distance and time, on the merging of emotions, on the incompatibility or congeniality between emotions, and on their etiology and effects. Unfortunately, Vives' own detachment from any attempt to synthesize or systematize his observations was reinforced in this case by a long and often tiresome discourse through all the rhetorical list of *loci* (where, who, when, with what instrument, why, etc.). The almost anarchic and frequently redundant character of Vives' therapeutic recommendations on the ways to control and heal emotional excess was partially reinforced by the ever-popular appeal to rhetorical amplification.

It is no easy matter to trace the influence of *De Anima et Vita* on the subsequent literature on the emotions. We know for certain that the treatise was repeatedly published in Basel, London, Lyons, Freiburg, and Zurich.

The fact that Descartes mentioned it in the *Traité* seems to suggest that in the middle of the seventeenth century Vives' tract was widely accepted as one of the leading documents of Renaissance literature on the subject of emotional responses. But a more accurate assessment of such influence would require a research effort that goes far beyond the self-imposed limitations of the present study.

Notes
Bibliography
Index

Notes

Chapter 1. The Exile from Valencia

1. The date of Vives' birth is still uncertain. The traditional date of 1492 seems too early to fit with the declarations made to the Inquisitors of Valencia by Vives' father the day before his execution (not a good day to remember anything with great accuracy!). See Angelina García's "Una familia de judío-conversos: Vives," *Erasmus in Hispania. Vives in Belgio. Colloquia Europalia 1*. Acta Colloquii Brugensis, 1985, ed. J. Ijsewijn and A. Losada, 293–309. (Henceforth *Vives Europalia*.)

2. Since the publication of my book *Juan Luis Vives* in 1970 and its Spanish translation by Antonio Pintor Ramos in 1978, no new complete biography of Vives has been written, but some important periods of his life, especially his Valencian background and early years in the Low Countries have been thoroughly investigated by, respectively, Spanish and Belgian scholars.

3. What we knew through Vergara's correspondence has now been confirmed by the letter sent by the University of Alcalá to Vives in May 1522. See J. Delgado, *Juan Luis Vives. Epistolario*, 140.

4. See, for instance, the letter of Vives to Juan de Vergara, August 1527, in "Clarorum Hispaniensium Epistolae Ineditae," *Revue hispanique* 8 (1901): 181–308.

5. Simon Markish, *Erasme et les Juifs*, trans. M. Fretz, has suggested that Erasmus' apparent anti-Semitism was really a rejection of Pharisaic piety. This seems to me a generous interpretation of Erasmus' frequent outbursts. In "The Elaboration of Vives' Treatises on the Arts," *Studies in the Renaissance* 10 (1963): 69, William Sinz says that "in a letter to More that the young man [Vives] was to have taken with him to England, [Erasmus] treats him [Vives] plainly as an ingenuous bore." The wording of this commentary appears a little unfair to both Vives and Erasmus, although it is likely that Erasmus' opinion of the Spaniards as excessively ceremonious and expansive might have rubbed off on Vives himself, at least for a while.

6. On Vives' and Erasmus' views on Spanish cultural life, see C. G. Noreña, *Juan Luis Vives*, 26–28, 139–43.

7. A thorough "Rezeptionsgeschichte" of Italian humanism in the Iberian peninsula is still lacking, but recent efforts to chart its spread through other European countries (France, the Low Countries, England, and Germany) have indirectly helped to a reassessment of the biased pronouncements made by Klemperer, Morf,

and Wantoch at the beginning of this century. See *Itinerarium Italicum: The Profile of the Italian Renaissance in the Mirror of its European Transformations*, ed. H. A. Oberman and Th. A. Brady (Henceforth *Itinerarium*); A. Chastel and R. Klein, *El Humanismo;* R. Trevor Davies, *El gran siglo de España, 1501–1621;* F. B. Pedraza and M. Rodriguez, *Manual de literatura española: El Renacimiento;* J. L. Abellán, *Historia crítica del pensamiento español,* 2. *Edad de oro (siglo XVI).*

8. References to the third book of *De Anima et Vita* include the volume and the page of the Gregorio Mayans' edition of *Opera Omnia,* both in Arabic numerals and preceded by the letter M.

9. See André Rochon, *Présence et influence de l'Espagne dans la culture italienne de la Renaissance.* Also, Myron P. Gilmore in "Italian Reactions to Erasmian Humanism," *Itinerarium,* 99–107, where the author discusses the impact of the Spanish Erasmists on Italian religious life. Gilmore emphasizes the influence of Juan de Valdés, who according to José Nieto, *Juan de Valdés y los orígenes de la Reforma en España e Italia,* 108, was more influenced by the Spanish "alumbrados" than by Erasmus. On Vives' influence in Italy, see Tullio Gariglio and Agostino Sottili, "Zum Nachleben von Juan Luis Vives in der italienischen Renaissance," *Juan Luis Vives,* Arbeitsgespräch in der Herzog August Bibliothek Wolfenbüttel, from 6 to 8 November 1980, in *Wolfenbütteler Abhandlungen zur Renaissanceforschung,* Band 3, 211–43. (Henceforth *Vives WA.*)

10. All of the Vives' references to the American Conquest and continent are presented by Angel Losada in his interesting "La huella de Vives en America," *Vives Europalia,* 147–81.

11. Americo Castro's classic work on the subject is *De la edad conflictiva: Crisis de la cultura española en el siglo XVII.* Castro himself has applied this principle to the study of *El Lazarillo de Tormes,* in *La realidad histórica de España,* 143–66. *La Celestina* has been studied by Stephen Gilman in his *La España de Fernando de Rojas: Panorama intellectual y social de "La Celestina";* Juan del Encina has been investigated by Francisco Ruiz Ramón in *Historia del teatro español.* On the situation of the Jewish conversos, see Antonio Dominguez Ortiz, *Los judeoconversos en España y América;* Joseph Silverman, "Some Aspects of Literature and Life in the Golden Age of Spain." In *Estudios de literatura española ofrecidos a M. M. Morinigo.*

12. All this information is contained in *Procesos Inquisitoriales contra la familia judía de Luis Vives,* M. de la Pinta y Llorente and J. M. de Palacio y Palacio, eds.

13. All of these expressions are literally taken from Vives' correspondence. See H. De Vocht, *Literae virorum eruditorum ad F. Craneveldium, 1522–1528,* 32, 45, 47, 48, 56, 128, 136, 163, 167, 251, 261. Also *Opus Epistularum Desiderii Erasmi Roterodami,* ed. P. S. and H. M. Allen, 12 vols., 1306, 2208, and 2932. (References to this work include the number of the letter, the volume, and [sometimes] the lines within the letter.) See also two letters from Vives to Vergara in Delgado, *Juan Luis Vives. Epistolario,* 129 and 164.

14. De Vocht, *Literae,* 32

15. We know, however, that in Bruges Vives lied about the name of the Valencian church where he had been baptized because it was located very close to the Jewish ghetto.

16. Delgado, *Juan Luis Vives. Epistolario,* 123.

Chapter 2. The Parisian Student

1. On Paris and the French monarchy in the first two decades of the sixteenth century, see J.-C. Margolin, *L' Avènement des temps modernes,* Chapter 4. The influence of Petrarch as a moralist in France, the retrieval of the Aristotelian works by Lefèvre d'Etaples, the attitudes of Budé toward Hellenic culture, the Neoplatonist impact on French literature and the Renaissance awareness of French humanists have been studied by N. Mann, E. F. Rice, Jr., R. R. Bolgar, A. H. T. Levi, and F. Simone in *Humanism in France at the End of the Middle Ages and in the Early Renaissance,* A. H. T. Levi, ed.; Margolin, *L' Avènement des temps modernes,* 229–33, emphasizes the growing nationalistic feeling of French humanism and rejects Renaudet's claim in *Préréforme et humanisme à Paris pendant les premières guerres d'Italie, 1494–1517,* passim, that French humanism represented a radical rupture with medieval culture and that it was torn between devotion and literary aestheticism. Margolin pays special attention to Gaguin, Lefèvre, Fichet and his circle (Clichtove and Charles de Bouvelles). J. Ijsewijn traces back Italian influence to the times of Avignon, particularly in French Neo-Latin literature, in his concise but extremely useful book *Companion to Neo-Latin Studies.*

2. On Montaigu College, see Renaudet, *Préréforme et Humanisme,* 175–77, 463–67, 655–58; and R. Garcia Villoslada, *La Universidad de Paris durante los estudios de Francisco de Vitoria, O.P. (1507–1522).* Erasmus wrote a bitter description of Montaigu in his dialogue *Icthiophagia;* and Rabelais called Montaigu the "Collège de pouillerie" in Chapter 37 of *Gargantua.*

3. The introductory arts course was being gradually changed in other European universities (especially in northern Italy) to suit their more secular aims. Terminist logic was only preserved in institutions where the arts course was envisioned as an ideal preparation for scholastic philosophy and theology. See Lisa Jardine, "Humanism and the Teaching of Logic," in *The Cambridge History of Later Medieval Philosophy,* 709–808.

4. Contemporary scholars admit that our present knowledge of late medieval logic is still precarious. See N. Kretzmann, "Syncategoremata, exponibilia, sophismata." In *The Cambridge History of Later Medieval Philosophy,* 211–46.

5. In 1979 there were two bilingual (Latin-English) editions of the book. The first was prepared by Rita Guerlac under the title *Juan Luis Vives. Against the Pseudodialecticians: A Humanist Attack on Medieval Logic.* This edition contains also three chapters of the third book of *De Disciplinis* and some related passages of Saint Thomas More. Guerlac adopts with minor corrections the Mayans edition of 1782. The second was prepared by Charles Fantazzi under the title *Juan Luis Vives. In Pseudodialecticos. A Critical Edition.* Fantazzi has chosen the Louvain edition of 1520 as the basic text and relegated to the apparatus the variants found in the Selestat edition of 1520 and those in the 1555 text of the Basel edition reproduced by Mayans. Both editions have been reviewed and harshly criticized by J. Ijsewijn in "Methodische Ueberlegungen zu zwei Ausgaben von J. L. Vives' *Adversus Pseudodialecticos,*" *Wolfenbütteler Renaissance Mitteilungen* 4 (1980), 131–35. Ijsewijn criticizes both authors for "working in America and ignoring Dutch" and "das Neederlandische Milieu." Ijsewijn—who has characterized Vives as Catalan (See note 45, Chapter 5)—blames Guerlac for such intellectually irrelevant faults as calling

Craneveld Flemish (he was born at Nijmegen but lived for seven years in Bruges) and Fantazzi for having preferred the Louvain to the Selestat edition.

6. At least this is the way Charles Fantazzi interprets More's remarks in his letter to Dorp in defense of Erasmus. See "Vives, More and Erasmus," *Vives WA,* 170.

7. The *Christi Jesu Triumphus,* published in 1514, demonstrates Vives' extraordinary acquaintance with classical Latin literature. Its second half, entitled *Virginis Dei Parentis Ovatio,* mentions Erasmus by name and calls him "my dearest friend," an obvious exaggeration since Vives and Erasmus did not meet until 1517. In 1514, Vives was also asked to write the introduction to the new edition of *Hyginii Poeticon Astronomicon* and the preface to Adrian Cornelissen van Baarland's book on Vergil. In spite of Delgado's misreading of the Latin text, Vives does not recommend to his friend Fort that he dwell on the "suicetical cavillations," but rather set them aside for a few days, forget Gaspar Lax (a professor of terminist logic at Montaigu), and dedicate three or four days to the reading of Hyginius. Riber's translation of the same text seems to make better sense in *Juan Luis Vives. Obras Completas,* Spanish trans. Lorenzo Riber, 2 vols., 1.536b. (The letters a or b in the references to Riber apply to the columns on each page.)

8. See Franco Simone, "Une entreprise oubliée des humanistes français: de la prise de conscience historique du renouveau culturel à la naissance de la première histoire littéraire," in *Humanism in France at the End of The Middle Ages and in the Early Renaissance,* ed. A. H. T. Levi, 106–32.

9. On the study of quantifiers, see E. J. Ashworth, "Multiple Quantification and the Use of Special Quantifiers in Early Sixteenth-Century Logic," *Notre Dame Journal of Formal Logic,* 19 (1978): 599–613.

10. In *De Causis Corruptarum Artium,* 1.7 (M 6.44–49), Vives condemns the scholastic practice of classroom debate as a corruption caused by passionate disorders and responsible for sectarian narrow-mindedness and intellectual stubbornness.

11. In *Studies in Spanish Renaissance Thought,* I myself was as excessive in my judgment about the Spanish logicians at Montaigu. Modern scholars have pointed to some of their achievements and placed in the proper perspective their overall significance in the history of late terminist logic. E. J. Ashworth has emphasized the contributions of Domingo Soto in kinematics and the developments in the semantics of terms and propositions brought about by Dolz, Enzinas, and Celaya. "The Eclipse of Medieval Logic." In *The Cambridge History of Later Medieval Philosophy,* 787–97.

12. Recent scholars have probed some of these implications, particularly in the works of Valla. See H.-B. Gerl, *Rhetorik als Philosophie;* R. Waswo, "The 'Ordinary Language Philosophy' of Lorenzo Valla," *Bibliothèque d'humanisme et renaissance* 41–42 (1979): 256–71; S. I. Camporeale, *Lorenzo Valla: umanesimo e teologia;* L. Jardine, "Lorenzo Valla and the Origins of Humanist Dialectic," *Journal of the History of Philosophy* 15 (1977): 143–64; C. Vasoli, *La dialettica e la retorica dell' Umanesimo: 'Invenzione' e 'Metodo' nella cultura del XV e XVI secolo.*

Chapter 3. The Northern Humanist

1. It was assumed for a long time that Vives had settled down in Bruges about 1512. But Enrique González y González has provided convincing evidence that Vives was still active in Paris in 1513 and even in 1514, where he published some devotional

works, *Praelectio in Convivia Philelphi*, *Praelectio on leges Ciceronis*, *Praelectio in quartum Rheotricorum ad Herennium*, and *Praelectio in suum sapientem*. See his *Joan Lluís Vives: de la escolástica al humanismo*, 127–32. González's research has clearly demonstrated the influence of Parisian humanism upon Vives.

2. For a characteristically accurate and cautious reconstruction of the 1512–17 period, see J. Ijsewijn, "J. L. Vives in 1512–17: A Reconsideration of Evidence," *Humanistica Lovaniensia* 26 (1977): 82–100. See, however, the previous note.

3. For more information on Croy, see A. Poschmann, "El Cardenal Guillermo de Croy y el arzobispado de Toledo," *Lusitania Sacra* 75 (1919): 201–82.

4. I think, however, that William Sinz has slightly exaggerated this point in his "The Elaboration of Vives' Treatises on the Arts," *Studies in the Renaissance* 10 (1963): 68–90. Sinz's obvious purpose in this article is to emphasize the central importance of *De Disciplinis*, a work that according to him emerged as Vives' masterpiece after many years of doubt, reflection, and forced delays.

5. There is no doubt that Vives sought and finally obtained the patronage of the English king. G. E. McCully has suggested that Vives tried also to become a papal advisor and that he asked Aleander to mediate with Pope Adrian on his behalf. See "A Letter of Juan Luis Vives to Jerome Aleander, December 17, 1522," *Renaissance Quarterly* 22 (1969): 121–28. McCully's interpretation of Vives' cryptic expressions is only moderately persuasive. It seems clear that Vives was trying to obtain some papal favor, and it is much less likely that his ambition was to join the papal court as an advisor.

6. Most of Vives' references to recent Italian writers can be found in *De Ratione Studii Puerilis* (M 1.257–81), *De Tradendis Disciplinis*, 3.8 and 9 (M 6.332–45), and *De Causis Corruptarum Artium*, 4.4 (M 6.171–81). See also Vives' correspondence in Allen, *Opus Epistularum Desiiderii Erasmi Roterodami*, 4.1108, lines 110–15.

7. On the cultural background of the Low Countries at the beginning of the sixteenth century and the impact of Italian humanism, see J. Ijsewijn, "The Coming of Humanism to the Low Countries," in *Itinerarium*, 193–305. See also, by the same author, *Companion to Neo-Latin Studies*, 3.2.6. Sister Alice Tobriner in *A Sixteenth-Century Urban Report*, 13–15, presents a good picture of Bruges at the beginning of the century.

8. The young man from Valencia always liked Bruges better than Louvain, a city he found "too far inland" and one where the fish was "rotten." Allen, *Opus Epistularum Desiderii Erasmi Roterodami*, 3.1271.

9. I think that August Monzón exaggerates a little Vives' allegiance to the monarchy, the nobility, and the high bourgeoisie of the Low Countries when he suggests that Vives was *un dels ideólogues mès destacats* (one of the most eminent ideologues) of the new political and cultural conceptions that would bring the demise of regional cultural life in Aragon and Cataluña and the growth of political centralization. See "Joan-Lluís Vives. Orientacions per a una visió renovada," *Afers* 1 (Catarroja, 1985): 307. There is not much doubt, however, that Vives' bourgeois spirit—already apparent in his *De Subventione Pauperum* (see note 30 to Chapter 4)—dictated his opposition to the popular revolt of the "Germanías" in Valencia, as Monzón himself suggests, 308. On Vives' reaction to the "Germanías," see Ricardo García Cárcel, *Orígenes de la Inquisición española: el tribunal de Valencia, 1478–1530*, 228; and *La revolta de les Germanies*, 30–39 and 77–78.

10. The relations between Erasmus and Vives have been studied by several authors. See A. Tobriner, "Juan Luis Vives and Erasmus," *Moreana* 24 (1969): 35–44; C. G. Noreña, "Was Juan Luis Vives a Disciple of Erasmus?" *Journal of the History of Philosophy* 7 (1969): 263–72; Yvonne Charlier, *Erasme et l'amitié d'après sa correspondence,* 224–28, 261–67; A. Etchegaray Cruz, "Juan Vives según Erasmo de Rotterdam," in *Homenaje a Luis Vives,* 113–21; R. García Villoslada "Luis Vives y Erasmo. Cotejo de dos almas gemelas," *Humanidades* 5 (1953).

11. This is also the general conclusion reached by Y. Charlier in *Erasme et l'amitié,* after a meticulous study of Erasmus' relations with such people as Aleander, Amerbach, Baarland, Beda, Briard, Budé, Colet, Dorp, Fisher, Froben, Gaguin, Goclenius, Hutten, Lefèvre, Linacre, Aldo Manuzio, Paludanus, Rhenanus, Roger Servais, Vitrier, and Zasius.

12. Charlier, *Erasme et l'amitié,* 224–25. Also, C. Fantazzi, "Vives, More and Erasmus," *Vives WA,* 172–74.

13. *Vives WA,* 261–62.

14. On Erasmus' literary taste, see Benoit Beaulieu, *Le Visage littéraire d'Erasme,* 11–55.

15. See, C. G. Noreña, "Juan Luis Vives and Henry VIII," *Renaissance and Reformation* 13 (1976): 85–87.

16. See the dedication to Croy, which, for reasons unknown to me, was printed by Mayans at the end of the fourth meditation (M 1.217).

17. Allen, *Opus Epistularum Desiderii Erasmi Roterodami,* 5.1106.

18. I owe some of these insights to Professor Edward George's "The Sullan Declamations: Vives' intentions," *Acta Conventus Neo-Latini Guelpherbytani,* 55–61. Antonio Fontán in "Juan Luis Vives, la antiguedad como sabiduria," in *Tres grandes humanistas,* 27–29 ("Las declamaciones Silanas, ensayo de filosofía política") emphasizes also the novelty of Vives' piece: rhetoric, history, and philology are combined not only to learn about the art of *recte dicendi,* but also to extract from ancient examples the art of government.

19. *The Renaissance Philosophy of Man,* E. Cassirer, P. O. Kristeller, J. H. Randall, eds., 387–97 (trans. N. Lenkeith).

20. M. Colish has written an intelligent commentary on the *Fabula* in "The Mime of God: Vives on the Nature of Man," *Journal of the History of Ideas* 23 (1962): 3–21. Colish emphasizes the differences between Vives and Pico and corrects some of the hasty comments made by Lenkeith and Cassirer on the similarities between Pico and Vives. For an interesting comparison between Vives' allegory and a classic Castilian dialogue on the same topic, see Fernán Pérez de Oliva, *Diálogo de la dignidad del hombre,* J. L. Abellán, ed.

21. The text proves great familiarity with the writings of Plato, Aristotle, Cicero, Pliny the Elder, Varro, Ovid, Vergil, Eusebius, Diogenes Laertius, Plutarch, Saint Isidore, Boethius, and so forth.

22. Adrianna Bongiovanni has recently (1984) examined very carefully the sources, purpose, and content of Vives' *De Initiis* in her excellent but still unpublished doctoral dissertation "Il *De Initiis Sectis et Laudibus Philosophiae* di Juan Luis Vives. Temi e problemi di storiografia filosofica nel primo Rinascimento" (University of Pavia). See also her article "Juan Luis Vives, filosofo converso: interpretazioni

storiografiche," *Il confronto letterario. Quaderni del Dipartimento di Lingue e Letterature Stranniere Moderne dell' Universita de Pavia*, Anno II, n. 3 (Maggio, 1985): 53–67.

23. I want to thank Professor Edward George of Texas Tech University for allowing me to use his still-unpublished English translation, critical edition of the Latin text, and magnificent commentary on this important work of Vives. In his "Imitatio in the *Somnium Scipionis,*" *Vives WA*, 81–85, Professor George has called our attention to the obvious influence of Seneca's *Ludus de morte Claudii* upon Vives' *Somnium*. See also D. Baker-Smith, "Juan Vives and the *Somnium Scipionis,*" in *Classical Influences in European Culture, A.D. 1500–1700*, R. R. Bolgar ed.; and W. H. Stahl, trans., Macrobius' *Commentary on the Dream of Scipio*.

24. See the introduction to the dialogue *In Sapientem Praelectio* (M 4.20).

25. J. Ijsewjin, "Vives and Poetry," *Roczniki Humanistycne* 26 (1978): 26.

26. Allen, *Opus Epistularum Desiderii Erasmi Roterodami*, 4.1108.

27. On Vives' significance in the history of humanist jurisprudence, see Guido Kisch, *Erasmus und die Jurisprudenz seiner Zeit*, 69–90. In a recent doctoral dissertation, "El derecho en Joan Lluís Vives" (1986), Professor August Monzón Arazo, University of Valencia, Law School, has analyzed in detail the sources, philosophical content, and influence of Vives' philosophy of law. Professor Monzón has rightly emphasized Vives' philosophical approach to the study of law, his opposition to an uncritical, literal, and dogmatic subservience to the Corpus Iuris Civilis (as exemplified by the tradition of the *glossatores*), Cicero's and Valla's influence upon Vives, the intimate connection between Vives' ideas on equity and Vives' Stoic doctrine on the rational control of emotions, the parallel between Vives' philosophy of law and his opposition to terminist logic, the linkage between Vives' political and legal thought, and the influence of the Low Countries' milieu upon Vives. Professor Monzón's doctoral dissertation is a magnificent exponent of contemporary Valencian research on Vives.

Chapter 4. The Amphibious Man

1. De Vocht, *Literae*, 175.

2. Ibid., 122 and 157. See the epitaph dedicated to Dorp in Delgado, *Juan Luis Vives. Epistolario*, 429.

3. De Vocht, *Literae*, 185.

4. Allen, *Opus Epistularum Desiderii Erasmi Roterodami*, 7.2040.

5. *Opus Epistularum Desiderii Roterodami*, 7.1830. R. Stupperich in "Das Problem der Armenfürsorge," interprets Erasmus' remark as a reference to Vives' Jewish ancestry and Christian education, but nothing in the letter's content supports this interpretation. It is true, however, that Vives himself was puzzled by the expression and confessed to Erasmus he could not make any sense of it. Allen, *Opus Epistularum Desiderii Erasmi Roterodami*, 7.1847.

6. De Vocht, *Literae*, 261.

7. Delgado, *Juan Luis Vives. Epistolario*, 142 (Vives to Vergara).

8. De Vocht, *Literae*, 90.

9. Delgado, *Juan Luis Vives. Epistolario*, 43.

238*Notes to Pages 34–40*

10. Nicholas Orme, *English Schools in the Middle Ages*, Chapters 5, 7, and 9; also in *Itinerarium* "England and the Humanities in the Fifteenth Century," by Denys Hay, 305–67, on fifteenth-century English patrons of the humanities.

11. On princely education in England see Orme, *English Schools*, Chapter 1; and *Itinerarium*, 358–59.

12. De Vocht, *Literae*, 80.

13. Ibid.

14. Orme, *English Schools*, Chapter 9.

15. J. McConica, *English Humanists and Reformation Politics under Henry VIII and Edward VI*, 80–83.

16. De Vocht, *Literae*, 90.

17. More's private correspondence was partially destroyed after his tragic end. Vives, however, refers to the letters he wrote to More, as given in Allen, *Opus Epistularum Desiderii Roterodami*, 4.1222. We also know that occasionally at least Craneveld send his letters to Vives to More's address, that in 1525 Vives stayed for a full month in More's household at Chelsea, and that More and Erasmus often exchanged comments on Vives.

18. See J. A. Guy, *The Public Career of Sir Thomas More*.

19. Allen, *Opus Epistularum Desiderii Roterodami*, 4.506.

20. Guy, *The Public Career*, 8.

21. The harshest critic of More is probably J. Ridley in his recent book *The Statesman and the Fanatic: Thomas Wolsey and Thomas More* .

22. C. G. Noreña, *Juan Luis Vives*, 88–89.

23. G. E. McCully has studied these documents in detail in his unpublished doctoral dissertation "Juan Luis Vives (1493–1540) and the Problem of Evil in His Time," (Columbia University, 1967).

24. Jean-Claude Margolin, "Conscience européene et réaction à la menace turque d'après le *De Dissidiis Europae et Bello Turcico* de Vivès (1526)," *Vives WA*, 107–41.

25. R. P. Adams, in his *The Better Part of Valor*, thinks, however, that even in this dialogue Vives maintained the principle of unexceptional pacifism.

26. In this respect see the thought-provoking "La política europea en la perspectiva de Vives," by Antonio Fontán, *Vives Europalia*, 27–73.

27. For the recent bibliography on the subject, see Robert Stupperich, "Das Problem der Armenfürsorge bei Juan Luis Vives," *Vives WA*, 49–63.

28. This is De Vocht's interpretation of Vives' cryptic remarks in *Literae*, 160.22, 167.45, 178.22, and 182.26. William Sinz, however, thinks that Vives was referring to *De Disciplinis*. See "The Elaboration of Vives' Treatises on the Arts," 69.

29. De Vocht, *Literae*, 157, 163, 167, and 171.

30. This is the feeling one derives from Geldenhouwer's letter to Craneveld, De Vocht, *Literae*, 198.4–10. Geldenhouwer, the author of Wessel's and Agricola's biographies, eventually became a reformer. See also Ibid., letter 246 (date: 8/16/1527).

31. Sister Alice Tobriner, *A Sixteenth-Century Urban Report*, 9–10. M. Bataillon has made an interesting study of Vives' proposals and their European background in "Luis Vivès, réformateur de la bienfaisance," *Bibliothèque d'humanisme et renaissance* 14 (1952): 141–58. Bataillon suggests that Vives' attitudes toward the poor and the unemployed was characteristically bourgeois. See also Constant Matheeussen, "Quelques remarques sur le *De Subventione Pauperum*," *Vives Europalia*, 87–97.

32. Matheeussen, "Quelques remarques," 95, emphasizes, however, that Vives suggested the possibility of using ecclesiastical riches to alleviate the needs of the poor. Vives, nevertheless, never bothered to explain how civil authorities would administer such ecclesiastical endowments.

33. Sister A. Tobriner, in *A Sixteenth-Century Urban Report*, 4–14, 22–29, traces Vives' influence through the Low Countries, England, and the American colonies.

34. Alistair Fox, *Thomas More, History and Providence*.

35. Ibid., 41.

36. Allen, *Opus Epistularum Desiderii Roterodami*, 4.1.

37. Ridley, *The Statesman and the Fanatic*, 30 .

38. De Vocht, *Literae*, 9.

39. Chapter 12 of *Institutio Feminae Christianae*. See also letter 74 in Delgado, *Juan Luis Vives. Epistolario*.

40. Delgado, *Juan Luis Vives. Epistolario*, 404 (date: 6/20/1525).

41. Vives' opinions on the education of women have recently been the target of intense and well-deserved feminist criticism, especially in the United States. See Gloria Kaufman, "Juan Luis Vives on the Education of Women," *Signs. Journal of Women in Culture and Society*, 3–4 (1978): 891–96; Deborah S. Greenhut, "Persuade Yourselves: Women, Speech, and Sexual Politics in Tudor Society," *Proteus: A Journal of Ideas*, 3–2 (1986): 42–48; Valerie Wayne, "Some Sad Sentence: Vives' "Instruction of Christian Woman," in *Silent but for the Word*, ed. Margaret Patterson Hanny, 15–29.

42. Allen, *Opus Epistularum Desiderii Roterodami*, 4.1455.

43. Delgado, *Juan Luis Vives. Epistolario*, 129 (Vives to Vergara).

44. Such is, for instance, the considered opinion of José María de Palacio y Palacio, the publisher of the Inquisitorial processes against the Vives family and a doctor of medicine, who in an oral presentation to the Erasmus-Vives Bruges Convention in 1985 claimed to have enough evidence for it.

Chapter 5. The Mature Thinker

1. These new friends include Galcerano Cepello, a distant relative and childhood friend; Antonio Barquero, a friend of the Valdaura family; Honorato Juan, his disciple in Louvain and later professor at the University of Valencia; Pedro Maluenda, also a Louvain disciple and later a theologian in Trent; Rodrigo Manrique, a Spanish humanist in Paris; Juan Maldonado, who has been characterized as "the first historian of the Erasmian revolution in Spain"(Bataillon, *Erasme et l'Espagne*). Vives' main patrons in this period and the people he dedicated his books to were Charles V; the king of Portugal; the duke of Gandía (Valencia); Princess Margaret of Austria; the archbishop of Sevilla; Prince Philip, the future Philip II; and Doña Mencía de Mendoza (M 4.302–4; 6.1–4; 7.41–42, 139–41, 221–22).

2. The most important testimony is that of Luis Polanco, Saint Ignatius' secretary. On this topic see Miquel Batllori, "Las obras de Vives en los colegios jesuiticos del siglo XVI." in *Erasmus in Hispania. Vives in Belgio*, 122, note 2. Batllori, a prestigious Jesuit historian, thinks that my reluctance to place great significance upon this alleged encounter is a sign of an "uncritical supercriticism." (*Un hipercriticismo muy poco crítico.*)

3. G. E. McCully in his unpublished doctoral dissertation "Juan Luis Vives and the Problem of Evil in His Time," has correctly emphasized the central importance of this book. Much of what follows has been inspired by his remarks on the subject.

4. Charles Trinkhaus in *In Our Image and Likeness: Humanity and Divinity in Italian Humanist Thought,* and, more recently, W. J. Bouwsma in "The Two Faces of Humanism," *Itinerarium,* 3–61, have discussed the similarities and differences between Stoic and Augustinian views as the "genuine alternatives" of humanist thought.

5. Allen, *Opus Epistularum Desiderii Roterodami,* 7.2061 and 8.2208. Vives' interest in Seneca might have been reawakened by Erasmus' intense work in preparing a new critical edition of the Roman Stoic. Vives' desire to revise the commentaries on Saint Augustine was reinforced by his unrealistic belief that the first edition had not been a financial failure to Froben.

6. On the transformation of the medieval "Seneca legend" into the new critical attitude of sixteenth-century humanism, see K. A. Blüher, *Seneca in Spanien.*

7. Vives was certainly familiar with Erasmus' first edition of Seneca's works, published in 1515. It is also very likely that he knew the Castilian translation of Alfonso de Cartagena, published in the first half of the fifteenth century. Erasmus' criticism of Seneca's contrived style (*declamatoria affectatio*) was initially rejected by Vives, but *De Anima et Vita* and *De Veritate Fidei* echo the same criticism and reject the hair-splitting and verbal games of the Roman sage.

8. L. Zanta's *La renaissance du stoicisme au XVIè siècle* remains one of the most illuminating studies on the subject.

9. On Petrarch's influence on European, particularly French, humanism, see N. Mann, "Petrarch's Role as a Moralist in Fifteenth-Century France," in *Humanism in France at the End of the Middle Ages and in the Early Renaissance,* ed. A. H. T. Levi.

10. G. E. McCully, "Juan Luis Vives and the Problem of Evil," was the first to correct the traditional mistake (that can be found in my own book *Juan Luis Vives,* 109, and Appendix II, 308) of assigning the date of publication to 1526. In the essay, Vives makes a clear reference to the sack of Rome in 1527. It is more likely that the pamphlet was written after Suleiman's moves in the Danube valley, moves that brought panic to Christian Europe.

11. In this sense, *De Concordia* belongs to those somber Renaissance writings that convey what Robert S. Krisnan has called *The Darker Vision of the Renaissance,* and reinforces the opinion of those who have emphasized the turbulent historical background of the Renaissance.

12. In the third chapter of the second book of *De Tradendis Disciplinis,* Vives quotes from *De Anima et Vita* (M 5.286).

13. This treatise is sometimes called *De Disciplinis,* but in most cases, as in the Leyden edition of 1612, this title is used to include also *De Causis.*

14. In the second chapter of the fourth book of *De Tradendis Disciplinis,* Vives asserts that he himself has written a book on metaphysics "so that we may not have to follow the heathen to so great an injury of our religion" (M 6.351).

15. Mayans' decision to print the books on the arts under the heading of "Philosophy" rather than "Education" tends to conceal the unity of purpose behind the 1531 Antwerp edition. *De Artibus* attempts to translate into the writing of textbooks on metaphysics and dialectic the prescriptions given in *De Tradendis Disciplinis.*

16. In her review of Vives' writings in the Herzog August Bibliothek (Brunswick-Lüneburg), "Vives' Schriften in der Herzog August Bibliothek und ihre Bedeutung für die Prinzenerziehung im 16. and 17. Jahrhundert," *Vives WA*, 193–210, Maria Von Katte reports that the *Exercitatio* (closely followed by another educational work, *De Conscribendis Epistolis*) leads all of Vives' works in the number of printed editions. D. Briesemeister, "Die gedruckten deutschen Uebersetzungen von Vives' Werken im 16. Jahrhundert," ibid., 177–79, has emphasized the great impact of Vives' dialogues in the German schools toward the end of the sixteenth and the first half of the seventeenth century. T. Gariglio and A. Sottili, "Zum Nachleben von Juan Luis Vives in der italienischen Renaissance," ibid., 211–60, have reached the same conclusions with respect to Italy.

17. See the Introduction by R. R. Bolgar in his *Classical Influences on European Culture, A.D. 1500–1700*, 1–33.

18. In this sense, I think that R. R. Bolgar, whose writings in general have been a great inspiration to me, is unduly harsh on Vives when he characterizes him as "bogged down in the humanist curriculum," and accuses him of being more concerned with style than content. See "Humanism as a Value System, with Reference to Budé and Vivès," *Humanism in France*, 199–216.

19. This latter point plays an extremely important part in Vives' pedagogy and finds its psychological explanation in the pioneering analysis of *ingenia* provided by *De Anima et Vita* (Book 2, Chapter 6; M 3.364–69) and in Vives' frequent references to the *ingenium*-conditioned character of emotional responses in the third book of the same treatise.

20. See E. Grassi, *Rhetoric as Philosophy*, 10–14. Also, *De Causis Corruptarum Artium*, 5.1 (M 6.181–85).

21. "Juan Vives and the *Somnium Scipionis*," by D. Baker-Smith, in *Classical Influences*, 242.

22. In Chapter 8, I will analyze Chapters 3–8 of the first book of *De Anima et Vita* where Vives discusses the senses and their input into man's cognitive life.

23. See "La première querelle des 'anciens' et des 'modernes' aux origines de la Renaissance," by C. Vasoli in *Classical Influences on European Culture*, 74–75.

24. *De Tradendis Disciplinis*, 1.6 (M 6.266–71): *In tam multa librorum copia, qui sint in scholis publice enarrandi.*

25. *De Vita et Moribus Eruditi*, Appendix to Book 5 of *De Tradendis Disciplinis*, Chapter 2 (M 6.426).

26. *De Causis Corruptarum Artium*, 1.1–5 (M 6.8–35).

27. In *De Causis Corruptarum Artium*, 1.4 (M 6.31), Vives claims that Aristotle was intentionally obscure and ambiguous whenever he thought that in time he might be compelled to change his opinion.

28. *De Causis Corruptarum Artium*, 6 (M 6.208–22).

29. *De Causis Corruptarum Artium*, 3.1–4 (M 6.110–24); 6.2 (M 6.351–56). J.-C. Margolin in "Vives, lecteur et critique de Platon et d'Aristote," in *Classical Influences*, 245–58, has carefully analyzed Vives' critical views on Plato and Aristotle. Margolin rejects also my opinion (*Juan Luis Vives*, 165) that Vives became increasingly critical toward Plato. Margolin's contention that Vives remained basically Platonic in his ideas on the relations between reason and morality was never questioned by me. I still think that pedagogical considerations became gradually

more important to Vives and led him to become less sympathetic toward Plato's poetical and loose style, a style he considered less suited to training in philosophy.

30. *De Causis Corruptarum Artium*, 4.4 (M 6.172). On Vives' part in the lingering Ciceronian controversy, see his letter to Cepello in September 1528. The Spanish translation of the letter is given by Delgado, *Juan Luis Vives. Epistolario*, 505–9. On Vives' Latin style, see Antonio Fontán, "El latín de Luis Vives," *Homenaje a Luis Vives*, 33–63.

31. Miquel Batllori has emphasized the importance of early Renaissance vernacular literature in the domains of the crown of Aragón in his "Joan-Lluís Vives en l'Europa d'Avui," *Miscellània Sanchis Guarnier, Quaderns de Filología* (Universitat de Valencia, 1984), 33–39.

32. Book 1, Chapter 2, and Book 2, Chapter 11 (M 4.70, 121, 258).

33. *De Tradendis Disciplinis*, 3.2 (M 6.306–7). C. Uhlig and C. K. Arnold in "Vives in England," *Vives WA*, 141–64, have argued that Vives' enthusiasm for Nebrija's Latin-Spanish dictionary had a lasting impact on the attitude toward the English language in such educators as Th. Elyot, Ascham, and Mulcaster.

34. On Erasmus, see M. M. Phillips, "Erasmus and the Classics," in *Erasmus*, ed. T. A. Dorey. On More, see C. Weinberg's "Thomas More and Use of English in Early Tudor Education," *Moreana* 59/60 (1978): 21–30.

35. *De Tradendis Disciplinis*, 3.1 (M 6.302): *In sermone qui ore totius populi teritur, nihil necessum est artem aut regulas formari; ex populo ipso promptius ac melius discetur. De Causis Corruptarum Artium*, 2.1 (M 6.78): *Mutatur subinde sermo, usque adeo ut centesimo quoque anno prope jam sit omnino alius.*

36. On dialectic as "the speech which is the basis of rational thought" and the art of "uncovering the first *arjai* of any knowledge," see E. Grassi, *Rhetoric as Philosophy: The Humanist Tradition*.

37. In *Classical Influences*, 81–91 and 91–123, professors D. McFarlane and W. J. Ong present two fascinating examples of that tradition in their articles "Reflections on Ravisius Textor's *Specimen Epithetorum*," and "Commonplace Rhapsody: Ravisius Textor, Zwinger, and Shakespeare."

38. As A. Buck implies in the "Einleitung" to the *Juan Luis Vives. Wolfenbütteler Arbeitsgespräch*, 9.

39. *De Tradendis Disciplinis*, Book 5, Appendix (M 6.431).

40. On the relations between Vives and Rudolph Agricola, see my "Vives and Agricola in the Low Countries," in *Vives Europalia*, 99–121.

41. In "Vives and Poetry," *Roczniki Humanistyczne* 26 (1978), 21–34, J. Ijsewijn claims that this "anti-humanistic pamphlet" was written by Vives as an attack on humanist literature to preempt the criticism of Johannes Briardus and other Louvain theologians.

42. Compare Ijsewijn's "Vives and Poetry" with K. Kohut's "Literaturtheorie und Literaturkritik bei Juan Luis Vives," *Vives WA*, 35–49.

43. In *De Causis Corruptarum Artium* (Book 2, Chapter 6; M 6.108), Vives praises Froissart, Monstrelet, Commines, and Valera.

44. The simile of the "dim light" of paganism and the "solar beam" of Christ was adopted by Comenius as the motto of his *Physicae Synopsis*.

45. Jan Dullaert (1480?–1513), one of Vives' teachers at Paris, published in 1512 a

commentary to Aristotle's *Meteorology,* as Vives himself mentions in his 1514 letter to Johannes Fortis. This letter and its historical context are analyzed by J. Ijsewijn in "J. L. Vives in 1512–1517: A Reconsideration of Evidence," *Humanistica Lovaniensia* 26 (1977): 82–100. In this article, Ijsewijn wrongly describes Vives as a "young Catalan." I do not think that Vives ever perceived himself or was known to others as a Catalan. This remains true no matter how one chooses to think about the historically complex and politically sensitive problem of the relations between Valencia and Cataluña.

46. On the influence of ancient literature in sixteenth- and seventeenth-century applied science, see G. Oestreich's "Die Antike Literatur als Vorbild der Praktischen Wissenschaften im 16. und 17. Jahrhundert," *Classical Influences,* ed. R. R. Bolgar, 315–25.

47. Professor Ijsewijn ("J. L. Vives in 1512–1517: A Reconsideration of Evidence") is wrong in accusing me of having misdated this lecture in my book *Juan Luis Vives,* 55–56, n. 20. If the reader deems this detail important enough, he or she is invited to consider the language of that note.

48. *De Tradendis Disciplinis,* 4.6 (M 6.371). Professor A. G. Debus takes these words of Vives out of context and misrepresents or at least oversimplifies his thought on the usefulness of the study of mathematics in *Man and Nature in the Renaissance,* 3. It is also worth warning the reader that this "Renaissance book" stretches all the way to Descartes and Kepler.

49. G. Oestreich, in the article mentioned above in note 46, claims that between 1490 and 1597 there were 660 different editions of Galen, 18 of them *Opera Omnia.* Dioscorides' *De Materia Medica* was published thirty-two times in the first half of the sixteenth century. Vives explicitly recommended the translation of Galen's *Methodus Medendi* published in 1519 by his friend Linacre, the founder and first president of the Royal College of Physicians. See *De Tradendis Disciplinis,* 3.9 (M 6.342).

50. In *De Tradendis Disciplinis,* Vives uses different Latin terms to refer to schools without making any effort to specify the level of education he has in mind. It can, however, be safely assumed that *pedagogium* refers to elementary schools and that *Academia* corresponds roughly to our undergraduate universities. *Schola* and *ludus litterarius* would cover the period between elementary school and university education (junior high school and high school).

Chapter 6. Nature

1. M. Sancipriano in "La pensée anthropologique de J. L. Vives: l'entelechie," *Vives WA,* 63–70, has carefully pondered the meaning of these words in their proper context, a context I intend to discuss later.

2. *Anima quid sit, nihil interest nostra scire, qualis autem et quae ejus opera, permultum; nec qui jussit ut ipsi nos nossemus, de essentia animae sensit, sed de actionibus ad compositionem morum; De Anima et Vita,* 1.12 (M 3.332).

3. *Hoc est vetita septa transcendere, et impudenter ingerere se in arcana divinitatis; De Prima Philosophia,* 1 (M 3.187, 191, and 198).

4. *Sed nos quemadmodum perficiatur opus artis, perspicimus, quoniam ars nostra; quemadmodum opus naturae non perspicimus, quoniam illa est Dei; De*

Prima Philosophia, 3 (M 3.273).

5. *Nos conjunctione et commistione et detractione utimur extrorsus, natura in intimis versatur; De Prima Philosophia,* 3 (M 3.273).

6. *Ornatus quoque stupendus et decor ineffabilis ex difformibus; De Prima Philosophia,* 3 (M 3.94).

7. *Nam materiam et formam, quia partes sunt, causas nominari inusitatum est;* (M 3.230).

Chapter 7. Life

1. Unless otherwise explicitly stated, all the quotations in this chapter are taken from the first book of *De Anima et Vita.*

2. Aristotle's *History of Animals* (Book 8, 588b4–18) proves that Aristotle was fascinated by the apparently unbroken ascending line between vegetal and animal life and that he felt at a loss to determine in certain cases whether a given species was a plant or an animal.

3. Vives' language in this context has created some problems for his translators. Riber—always polished but not always precise—leaves out the Latin word *animus* (designating what is usually understood as the seat of reason) and translates *vita cogitativa* as "*vida inteligente,*" and *cogitatio* as "*entendimiento*" (*Obras Completas,* 2.1149). M. Sancipriano in his critical edition and Italian translation of *De Anima et Vita* (p. 91) translates *vita cogitativa* as "*attivita psichica,*" and *cogitatio* as "*imaginazione.*" The first translation, however, neutralizes the Latin original: both for Aristotle and Vives all the manifestations of life are "psychical" in origin. The second translation amounts to a benevolent interpretation of Vives' language. Sancipriano also writes that the higher animals "*poseggono una certa vita mentale,*" but such expression is only a free translation of Vives' *vi quadam animi sunt praedita ad memoriam et cogitationem.*

4. *Metaphysics,* Book 1, 980a28–980b24. Also, *On Memory,* 1.450a15–23.

5. This Galenic principle meant a certain departure from Aristotle, who seemed to hesitate in this matter. See *On the Soul,* II. 4, 416a20–416b8.

6. *De Anima,* II. 4, 416a18–19.

7. See Aristotle's *Generation of Animals,* 4. 3.

8. For these and other details, see Pliny, *Naturalis Historia,* 14.45.

Chapter 8. Sensation

1. Notice the clever distinction between "thick air" or "smoke" (the object of smell) and air in motion (the object of hearing), which conveniently makes room for five senses. Vives' reasonable conjecture about the sufficiency and adequacy of the five senses contrasts sharply with the almost unintelligible deductive reasoning presented by Aristotle in the first chapter of the third book of *On the Soul* (III. 1, 424b24–425a13).

2. Although Vives was willing to make some exceptions, his theories about the propagation of sound through air led him to believe that most fish are naturally deaf.

3. In Chapter 10, Vives deals with "interior cognition" and makes explicitly clear that it is not an exclusively human faculty.

4. In the same passage, Vives describes this intellectual inference as "another sensation that belongs to the mind rather than to the senses" (*substantia sentitur aliena sensione, quae magis est mentis quam sensus;* M 3.322–23).

5. Aristotle mentions wool, sponges, and needles. *On the Soul,* II. 8, 419b7–14; and 420a24.

6. Vives' description of the internal "humor" of the ears is certainly closer to the contemporary anatomy of the ear, which includes the cochlea fluid whose waves activate the sensory cells in the organ of Corti (M 3.316).

7. This example is taken from Aristotle (*On the Soul,* III. 2, 426b9–10) and is mentioned here to suggest that this or a similar case was in Vives' mind when he provided the aforementioned definition of common sense.

8. In the case of sessile animals, such as shells and sponges, these motions are limited to expansions and contractions. The heartbeat of animals is not a motion caused by appetite, but by the heat involved in nutrition. From the context it seems obvious that Vives is using the term *iudicium* in a loose sense, not in the strict sense that applies exclusively to rational life. The same loose sense of *judicium* reappears in Book 3, Chapter 1, when Vives tries to explain the cognitive ingredient of all emotions (M 3.422–23).

Chapter 9. Intelligence

1. *On Memory,* 2.453a 5–15.

2. *On Memory,* 1. 451a15–19. Aristotle's conception is basically similar to William James' notion of "secondary memory," the knowledge of an event plus the consciousness that we have experienced it or thought about it before. The object of memory is therefore an object imagined in the past to which the "emotion of belief" adheres. This "emotion of belief" is similar to the Aristotelian notion of the "state and affection" that accompanies the presentation as a likeness of a past one. James rightly emphasizes that memory requires not only that the fact imagined be expressly referred to the past, but that it be referred to *my* past. See *Principles of Psychology,* Chapter 16, 425.

3. In the dedication of the treatise, Vives says that Book 2 deals with the rational soul. In the introduction to Book 2, he lists memory as one of the three faculties that, as Saint Augustine had taught, make man into an image of the Trinity (*imago divinae Trinitatis*). See Dedication (M 3.299) and Introduction to Book 2 (M 3.341–42).

4. *On Memory,* 2.451b7–10, 452a4–14, 452b7–453a4.

5. Lactantius was thought to be one of the first to have engraved characters in copper for the purpose of printing.

6. See Plutarch, *Moralia, De liberis educandis* (The Loeb Classical Library), 1.45.

7. *Institutiones Oratoriae,* 12.2.

8. Only within the context of language learning did Vives emphasize the importance of memory cultivation in an early age. See *De Tradendis Disciplinis,* 3.3 (M 6.310–11).

9. This care and concern explains why, as James said, "Most men have a good memory for facts connected with their own pursuits." *Principles of Psychology,* Chapter 16, "The Conditions of Goodness in Memory," 433.

10. Vives often gave detailed instructions on writing notes. See, for instance, *De Tradendis Disciplinis*, 3.2 (M 6.310), and *De Ratione Studii Puerilis* (M 6.268).

11. I think that Riber, the Spanish translator of Vives' *Opera Omnia*, perceived here some problems when he misleadingly translated the Latin term *contemplatio* into the Spanish *reflexión*. To Vives, contemplation was the pleasurable rest of the mind in possession of a congenial truth reached through reasoning.

12. Notice how in one and the same sentence Vives includes scientific and practical knowledge.

13. One of Vives' favorite strategies is to accumulate rich metaphors to state rather than to prove difficult speculative claims.

14. I am thinking in particular of the passage in *Posterior Analytics*, I. 9, 76a25–30, where Aristotle seems to imply that, even if the premises of an argument appear "true and primitive" our mind will not accept the conclusion unless it is "of the same genus as the primitives."

15. Although Vives declares that the knowledge of God requires "a supernatural light," he does not mean to deny the possibility of natural theology. See *De Prima Philosophia* (M 3.185–88).

16. These thoughts seem to reverberate in Descartes' *Meditations* and *The Discourse on Method*. In dedicating the *Meditations* to the theologians of Paris, Descartes asserts that the demonstrations used in the book are more certain and evident than those used in geometry, but "cannot be adequately understood by many" because they are lengthy and "dependent the one on the other" and also because they demand a mind totally free from prejudice.

Chapter 10. Ingenium

1. On Quintilian, see *Institutiones Oratoriae*, 1.3. On Galen, *On the Physical Powers* or, as the Loeb Classical Library translates the title (A. J. Brock trans.), *On the Natural Faculties*, Chapter 19.

2. I think it is slightly exaggerated to say that Vives "introduced the term ingenium to the modern age" (*ch' gli introduce nell' eta moderna*), as M. Sancipriano claims in his critical edition and Italian translation of *De Anima et Vita*, 287, note 1. The word was obviously well known to the Latinists of the age. What Vives did was to enrich the anthropological and psychological meaning of the word.

3. Descartes' *Traité des passions* represents also an attempt to understand the union of body and soul not through clear and evident ideas but through the experience of passion in real life. As in the case of Vives, Descartes' significant shift in method was also prompted by ethical and humanist considerations. The relations between Vives and Descartes will be discussed in Chapters 15 through 18.

4. This reference to Democritus is taken from Cicero's *De Divinatione*, 1.37. The quotation is almost literally taken from Seneca's *De Tranquillitate Animi*, 17.10. Vives compares the influence of black bile to that of wine, an idea taken from the treatise *Problemata*, 30.32, which was attributed in the sixteenth century to Aristotle.

5. *De Tradendis Disciplinis*, 2.3 (M 6.291).

6. On the relation of age to emotional control, see Chapter 15, second section ("Emotion and the Body").

7. *De Tradendis Disciplinis*, 2.2 (M 6.288).

Chapter 11. Language

1. *De Concordia et Discordia*, 1 (M 5.197).

2. *Introductio ad Sapientiam*, 15, "*De verbis*" (M 1.36); *De Concordia et Discordia*, 1 (M 5.197).

3. *De Ratione Dicendi, Praefatio* (M 5.89). Also in *De Causis Corruptarum Artium*, 4.1 (M 6.152).

4. *De Causis Corruptarum Artium*, 4.1 (M 6.152).

5. *De Ratione Dicendi, Praefatio* (M 5.89).

6. *De Ratione Dicendi*, 1, Introduction (M 2.93).

7. *De Tradendis Disciplinis*, 3.1 (M 6.298).

8. As a good Aristotelian, Vives constantly teaches that language separates human beings from the brutes. See, for instance, *In Quartum Rhetoricorum ad Herennium* (M 2.87).

9. *De Ratione Dicendi*, 1 (M 2.93). See also *De Anima et Vita*, 1.7 (M 3.369): "*Democritus sermonem apte nominavit rivum rationis.*"

10. *De Prima Philosophia*, 1 (M 3.190).

11. On the position of Vives within this humanist tradition, see C. Vasoli, *La dialettica e la retorica dell' Umanesimo: "Invenzione" e "Metodo" nella cultura del XV e XVI secolo;* also, by the same author, "Juan Luis Vives e un programa umanistica di reforma della logica," *Academica Toscana di Scienze e Lettere "La Colombaria." Atti e Memorie* 25 (1960): 219–63.

12. *De Inventione Dialectica, Proemium.*

13. According to C. Vasoli (*La dialettica*, 160), Agricola considered *ornamentum* an indispensable quality of all kinds of discourse, including the language of mathematics and the natural sciences.

14. See *De Ratione Dicendi, Epistula nuncupatoria* (M 2.91), where Vives warns against the practice of teaching rhetoric to children immediately after grammar. On the relation between rhetorical eloquence and political freedom—a recurrent topic of humanist literature—see *De Ratione Dicendi*, 1 (M 2.94) and *De Consultatione*, 1 (M 2.249).

15. Some scholars have attempted to portray Valla as a radical opponent to traditional views on language. R. Waswo, for instance, in his article "The 'Ordinary Language Philosophy' of Lorenzo Valla," *Bibliothèque d'humanisme et renaissance* 41–42 (1979): 255–73, has attempted to prove that Valla rejected the "ontologically bound grammar and semantics of his age" (256), "entirely denied both the correspondence theory of Truth and the referential theory of meaning" (268) and all "venerable dichotomies between word and thing." To Valla, so Waswo believes, language was not the sign but the measure and creation of all meaning and reality. Ordinary language—what Valla called *communis loquendi consuetudo*—was to him much more than "a canon of oratorical good taste." It was "the measure of sensible reality," the "creator of meaning," one and the same as knowledge itself. Hanna-Barbara Gerl maintains similar interpretations in her *Rhetorik als Philosophie, Lorenzo Valla.* According to Gerl, Valla considered language *die menschliche Shöpfung der Welt* (65) and taught that words are necessary to bring objects into consciousness (*Um das Nicht-Wort in das Bewusstsein heben zu können, muss man sich des Wortes bedienen;* 221). Waswo's article was harshly criticized by M. Szymanski in "Philosophy and

Language," *Bibliothèque d'humanisme et renaissance* 44 (1982): 150–52. A careful reading of the Valla's texts quoted by Waswo and Gerl in G. Zippel's new and magnificent critical edition of Valla's *Repastinatio dialectice et philosophie,* has convinced me that Waswo's and Gerl's interpretations are not sufficiently justified. But there is little doubt that some ambiguities in Valla's pronouncements and his constant and exclusive appeal to received linguistic usage in deciding philosophical questions could provide some excuse for the inevitable comparisons between his thought on language and that of post-Wittgensteinian analytic philosophers. That is certainly not the case in Vives, whose philosophical approach was decidedly more conservative. This radical difference between Vives and Valla might be an important reason for Vives' mixed feelings toward a man he both admired and often criticized severely. Vives' severity toward Valla has puzzled some scholars. See, for instance, Rita Guerlac, *Juan Luis Vives: Against the Pseudodialecticians,* passim.

16. *De Anima et Vita,* 2.7 (M 3.369).

17. *De Censura Veri,* 1 (M 3.145).

18. *De Censura Veri,* 1 (M 3.142).

19. On Ockham, see G. Leff, *William of Ockham: The Metamorphosis of Scholastic Discourse,* 125, where Leff explains the differences between Ockham and Scotus.

Chapter 12. The Will

1. *De Veritate Fidei,* 1.1 (M 8.5–9). See also *De Prima Philosophia,* 1 (M 3.188–89).

2. See, for instance, Marsilio Ficino, *Five Questions Concerning the Mind,* in *The Renaissance Philosophy of Man,* ed. E. Cassirer et al., 196–206.

3. On this topic, see Wilhem Dilthey's *The Individual and the Cosmos in the Renaissance,* trans. by M. Domandi, Chapter 3, "Freedom and Necessity in the Philosophy of the Renaissance," an interesting introduction to the study of this subject.

4. *De Anima et Vita,* 2.11 (M 3.382–83).

Chapter 13. Sleep and Dreams

1. In his dedication of *Somnium* to the archbishop-elect of Valencia, Vives facetiously declares that the writing of the book had kept him awake for a long time: *vigiliandum nobis fuit in enarrando illo somnio* (M 5.63). To Erasmus, however, he wrote that the book was "dreamed" in Paris and that, upon awakening, he returned to Louvain (M 7.151–57). Thomas More found the book "superior to the vigils of the most alert wise men," but difficult to understand. See Allen, *Opus Epistularum Desiderii Erasmi Roterodami,* 1106, 4, lines 266–90.

2. See *The Realism of Dream Visions: The Poetic Exploitation of the Dream-Experience in Chaucer and His Contemporaries,* by Constance B. Hieatt.

3. Although Vives' own dream does not clearly fit into any of the medieval classifications of dreams—such as those of Macrobius or John of Salisbury—the description of Sleep's watchmen is clearly inspired by that tradition. See C. B. Hieatt, *The Realism of Dream Visions,* 27–30. See also Edward V. George, "Imitatio in the *Somnium Scipionis,"* Vives WA, 81–85.

4. See, for instance, the 1531 letter to the duke of Béjar, where Vives narrates the story of the drunkard who was brought to a palace and was royally treated for a day, became drunk again, and was returned to the streets the following morning. "What is the difference," Vives writes, "between that drunkard's day and our own life? There is no difference at all, except that our own dream is a bit longer" (M 7.144). Although this is an interesting letter, to say as J. J. Delgado and Félix G. Olmedo insinuate, that Calderón's drama *La Vida es Sueño* might have been inspired by Vives' private correpondence, seems to me farfetched and unrealistic. See Félix G.Olmedo, *Las fuentes de "La vida es sueño,"* and Delgado, *Juan Luis Vives. Epistolario,* 570, footnote 1. The letter merely proves that Vives shared a typically Spanish attitude toward life as a dream, a recurrent theme of Spanish literature (Seneca, Calderón, Quevedo, Lope de Vega, etc.). See *El sueño y su representación en el barroco español,* ed. by D. Cvitanovic.

5. *De Anima et Vita,* 1.9 *"De sensibus in genere"* (M 3.322–23).

6. *De Anima et Vita,* 3.2, 13, 19, and 21 (M 3.435, 477, 499, and 503).

7. Vives' mother-in-law, to whom he seems to have been more attached than the average married man, suffered greatly from insomnia during the last months of her long illness. See De Vocht, *Literae,* 171.

8. *De Somnis,* 458b, 15.

9. For a careful discussion of this Aristotelian teaching and its implications in the Cartesian attitude toward dreams, see *Dreaming,* Norman Malcolm.

10. The last concrete example might be more autobiographical than generic. We know that Vives suffered greatly from insomnia when pressed by Erasmus to complete his commentaries on Saint Augustine's *The City of God.* See De Vocht, *Literae,* 6.

Chapter 14. Death and Immortality

1. See, for instance, *Preces et Meditationes Diurnae* (M 1.99); *In Orationem Dominicam Commentarius, ad "Adveniat regnum tuum"* (M 1.147); *Institutio Feminae Christianae* (M 4.284–85), and *De Veritate Fidei* (M 8.51).

2. *Preces et Meditationes Diurnae* (M 1.71: *nihil sepulturae similius quam lectus*).

3. Ibid., 101.

4. De Vocht, *Literae,* 251.

5. M 7.136, 139–41. See also Delgado, *Juan Luis Vives. Epistolario,* 576. In spite of these obviously sincere remarks, Vives was prudent enough to leave Bruges in a hurry at the time of the plague known as *sudor anglicus,* even if that meant a temporary separation from his wife who, according to his explicit testimony, was much less afraid of the disease. See letter to Antonio Barquero (M 7.220).

6. In *De Institutione Feminae Christianae,* Vives characterizes the old age of women as a time of liberation from the sexual drive, the time "to taste heavenly rather than earthly things" *(coelestia potius quam terrena sapiet;* M 4.278). The implication is, I guess, that women succeed better than men at doing that and, consequently, live longer.

7. *De Anima et Vita,* 2.17 (M 3.401–3).

8. In her magnificent book *Probability and Certainty in Seventeenth-Century*

England: A Study of the Relationships between Natural Science, Religion, History, Law and Literature, Barbara Shapiro studies what she calls "the erosion of the traditional dichotomy between 'science' and 'probability'" (267), and "the enormous expansion of the realm of the probable and the contraction of the certain" (4), as the "crucial development[s]" (267) of English intellectual life in the seventeenth century. Professor Shapiro recognizes Vives' "interest in natural observation, the practical arts and the utility of knowledge" (8), and timidly suggests that in his writings one can see "the beginnings of a breakdown, or, at least, an erosion of the boundary between demonstrative certainty and probability" (8). Nevertheless, when she describes the achievements of sixteenth-century humanists (she mentions Agricola, Melanchthon, and Ramus), she claims that "in their hands, dialectic would take much of what had previously belonged to rhetoric" (230). In Agricola's concrete case that meant, Professor Shapiro writes, that "the techniques of amplifying, embellishing or illustrating" were now included in "the new dialectic"(231). It seems obvious to me that Vives' chapter on the immortality of the soul cannot be described as a mere amplification, embellishment, or illustration of a philosophical *locus,* and that both Vives' theory and practice of "the new dialectic" represented much more than the beginning of an erosion of the boundary between moral certainty and high probability. In that sense, I think, Professor Shapiro has partially failed to recognize the explicit and distinctive features of Vives' contribution to the history of dialectic.

9. The notion that the soul belongs only to God is central to the understanding of Calderón de la Barca's concept of personal honor. In *El Alcalde de Zalamea,* Primera Jornada, lines 874–77, the main character recognizes that the king has some claims to the material possessions of his subjects, but not their honor, "porque el honor es patrimonio del alma, y el alma sólo es de Dios" (Because honor is the soul's patrimony, and the soul belongs only to God).

10. This argument is echoed by Descartes in his fourth *Meditation.*

11. Vives mentions Theophrastus whose lamentations are referred to by Cicero, *Tusculanae Disputationes,* 3.28, 69; Seneca, *De Brevitate Vitae,* 1.2; and Saint Jerome, *Ad Nepotianum,* 52.3.

12. Vives' disparate judgments on Aristotle, like those on Plato, do not seem to reveal a linear process of intellectual change, but betray, rather, the different moods of an eclectic and complex thinker who saw with varying clarity the shortcomings and achievements of two philosophers whose literal interpretation was at least partially inconsistent with his Christian vision of life and the universe.

Chapter 15. The Nature of Emotion

1. Declarations of this sort are not limited to this topic, but are particularly strong and emphatic when writers deal with it. In his *Traité des passions,* Descartes declares that he would write on the passions of the soul "as though I were treating of a matter which no one had ever touched on before" (I, 1). In the *Ethica,* Spinoza complains that, although some eminent philosophers had written magnificently on the right conduct of life, no one had ever explained "the nature and power of the emotions" (III, Introduction). Here and henceforth the references to the *Traité des passions* include the Part of the Treatise (Roman numerals) and the number of the Article (Arabic numerals). The references to Spinoza's *Ethica* follow the traditional

manner of quotation.

2. On Plutarch, see *Plutarque et le stoicisme*, by Daniel Babut, 318–34. On Seneca, see here Chapter 17, second section ("Hatred and Anger").

3. See xxi–xxiii of Eric D'Arcy's Introduction to the nineteenth volume of the *Summa Theologiae*, Blackfriars Edition.

4. Galen's and Plutarch's expositions of Chrysippus' doctrine seem to favor this interpretation. See Galen, *De Placitis Hippocratis et Platonis*, in *Stoicorum Veterum Fragmenta*, III, 461; and Plutarch, *De Virtute Morali*, ibid., 459. In his *The Philosophy of Chrysippus*, 181–86, Josiah B. Gould convincingly rejects Bréhier's interpretation of Chrysippus' teaching. According to Bréhier the judgment that Chrysippus identified with emotion was not a judgment about the value of the emotion's object, but rather about the appropriateness of our emotional response to it. See *Chrisippe et l'ancien stoicisme*, 250–52.

5. See Sartre, *The Emotions: Outline of a Theory*; and Robert Solomon, *The Passions*.

6. See nevertheless *De Anima et Vita*, 2.4 (M 3.355).

7. *De Anima et Vita*, 2, Chapters on memory (2), on judgment (5), and on *ingenium* (6)—M 3.345–53, 362–64, 364–69.

8. One cannot, however, expect to find in Vives any counterpart to the subtle and rich analysis of the rationality of emotions carried out by contemporary philosophers trained in the refined idiom of analytic philosophy. Nor is there but a rough Latin equivalent to such expressions as "magnetized dispositions," "habits of selective attention," "patterns of salience," "paradigmatic scenarios," and so forth. See Amelie Rorty and Ronald de Sousa in *Explaining Emotions*, Amelie O. Rorty, ed., 103–27 and 127–53.

9. The context makes clear that Vives means "dispositions toward certain emotions" rather than the emotions themselves.

10. This short passage is the one quoted by Descartes in his *Traité des passions*, II, 127. I have used the English translation of the *Traité des passions* by E. S. Haldane and G. R. T. Ross in *The Philosophical Works of Descartes*. The French text is quoted from the edition of the *Traité* by F. Mizrach. Roman numerals indicate the part of the treatise and arabic numerals the number of the article. Descartes, however, interprets Vives by saying that laughter in such a case was provoked not by the eating of food, but by the "mere imagination" of eating. Should Descartes be right, Vives would have laughed even more during the fast.

11. *De Tradendis Disciplinis*, 2.1 (M 6.272–73).

12. Vives nevertheless wrote that jealousy is also felt by such animals as swans, pigeons, hens, and bulls (M 3.491).

Chapter 16. The Classification of Emotions

1. These or similar expressions are used by Amelie Rorty in her introduction to her *Explaining Emotions*.

2. See the magnificent critical edition of the Greek text and the medieval Latin version prepared by A. Gilbert-Thierry.

3. *Perí Pathōn*, Gilbert-Thierry edition, 230.

4. Hope is characterized by Vives as a form of desire (M 3.508), but because of

its opposition to fear it could be considered one of the basic emotions.

5. See *De Civitate Dei*, XIV, 3. For Boethius, see *De Consolatione Philosophiae*, I, 7.

6. Saint Thomas attempts to justify his terminology by explaining that the two groups are named by those emotions within the group which are either most keenly felt *(concupiscentia)* or most readily perceived *(ira;* IaIIae. 25, 2 ad 1, and 3 ad 1). The Dominican translators of the *Summa Theologiae,* Blackfriars Edition, translated the terms in different ways. D'Arcy sought to avoid any problems by translating *appetitus concupiscibilis* into "affective orexis" and *appetitus irascibilis* into "spiritual orexis" (vol. 19). But Reid preferred to translate the same terms into "impulsive" and "contending" (vol. 21).

7. In my article "Vives and Agricola in the Low Countries," I have given other examples of Vives' topical method. See *Vives Europalia,* 99–121.

8. In II, 87, Descartes rejects the scholastic doctrine that aversion is the opposite of desire on the grounds that "it is always an identical movement which makes for the search of the good and at the same time for the avoidance of evil which is contrary to it" (II, 87). In Article 89, however, Descartes emphasizes the difference between desire born from delight and desire born from revulsion. The latter, Descartes says, is accompanied by hatred, fear, and sadness.

9. Saint Thomas teaches that although there are many species of sorrow (pity, envy, anxiety, and torpor) there are not many species of pleasure (IaIIae. 35, 8 ad 1). Vives teaches that the good makes only "a weak impression on us," while evil, deeply entrenched in ourselves, "leaves a more permanent mark and is therefore more lasting and burdensome" (M 3.485).

10. Notice that Descartes uses the term *aversion* to signify both the opposite of delight and one kind of desire.

11. Descartes describes favor as a species of love mixed with pity and as a species of desire (II, 92).

12. In spite of Descartes' claim to novelty, Vives describes gaiety and regret in Chapters 8 and 19 of *De Anima et Vita.*

13. In *De Anima et Vita* (M 3.469) Vives tells us that he could not keep from laughing after taking the first or second bite of food after a long fast. The explanation that Vives offers—food expands the contracted diaphragm—differs slightly from the Cartesian. Descartes teaches that laughter is caused by the inflation of the lung, which is itself caused by "the first juice which passed from his stomach to his heart" (II, 127).

14. H. A. Wolfson defends the rendering of *laetitia* by "pleasure" on the ground that some Latin translators of Aristotle had used that term for the Greek *ēdonē.* See H. A. Wolfson, *The Philosophy of Spinoza,* 2 vols., 2:206. But Edwin Curley, in his *The Collected Works of Spinoza,* 1:642, argues that "joy is more suggestive of the overall sense of well-being that Spinoza has in mind" and thinks it is preferable to reserve pleasure for the Latin term *titillatio* or *delectatio.* The same applies to "pain" and "sorrow" with respect to *tristitia.* Curley thinks that "pain" is the translation of *dolor,* something more tied to a specific sensory stimulation. *Collected Works,* 1:654.

15. Saint Thomas derives the word *laetitia* from the Latin adjective *latus,* which means broad and wide (IaIIae. 31, 3).

Chapter 17. The Basic Emotions

1. D'Arcy's translation of these words into "the order of actual occurrence" (Blackfriars Edition of the *Summa Theologiae*, vol. 19, 57) seems to me inappropriate because it makes no explicit reference to causal relationships.

2. Descartes speaks only about joy and desire as causes of hope, but the clear contrast with fear suggests that fear is caused by a mixture of desire and sadness.

3. *De Civitate Dei*, XIV, 7.

4. The relations between love and desire are discussed at length in the first dialogue of Leone Ebreo's *Dialoghi d'amore*, but it is difficult to know whether this book was available to Vives during the writing of *De Anima et Vita*. See *Amour et intellect chez Leon l'Hebreu* by Suzanne Damiens. Ebreo's book appeared in Rome in 1535, three years before the publication of *De Anima et Vita*. There is an English translation of the first dialogue in *The Italian Philosophers: Selected Readings from Petrarch to Bruno*, edited, translated, and introduced by Arturo B. Fallico and Herman Shapiro, 172–227.

5. Besides the influential commentary *In Convivium Platonis de Amore*, printed in 1484, Marsilio Ficino wrote extensively on the *Hymn of the Phaedran Charioteer* in his *Theologia Platonica*, *De Voluptate*, and *Commentarium in Philebum*. For further details, see *Marsilio Ficino and the Phaedran Charioteer*, introduction, texts, and translations by Michael J. B. Allen.

6. For a good summary of this tradition, see Volume 1, Chapter 1 of *The Nature of Love, Courtly and Romantic*, by Irving Singer.

7. For further details see *Renaissance Theories of Love*, by John Charles Nelson.

8. Ficino speaks of four "cycles" of irradiated Beauty: the Ideas, Reasons, Seeds, and Forms.

9. See Book 4, Chapter 11: *Ni passiones cohibeantur nec servare in agendo modum possumus nec ullus erit rixarum et discordiarum finis;* M 5.373–80.

10. *Rhetoric*, II. 2, 1378a33–34.

11. *Rhetoric*, II. 4, 1382a11–12.

12. *Rhetoric*, II. 5, 1382a21.

13. The metaphor of "contraction" was cherished by Saint John Damascene and passed on to the scholastic tradition through the work of Saint Thomas (IaIIae. 41, 1 and 2; see also IaIIae. 44). Saint John Damascene himself was evidently influenced by ancient Stoic sources, probably by the work of the Pseudo-Andronicus.

14. The word *passio* is derived from the verb *pati* which literally means "to suffer." Obviously sadness and fear are more "suffered" than desire or love.

15. Although Descartes failed to make it explicit, it seems obvious that fear must be intermingled with sadness as much as hope is intermingled with joy. Spinoza, probably inspired by Descartes, makes fear "an inconstant sadness" and hope "an inconstant joy" (II, definitions 12 and 13).

16. Saint Thomas uses the term *laetitia* to signify one of the effects of pleasure, the swelling (In Latin: *dilatatio*) of the heart.

17. It is obvious that this philosophical emphasis on the visual was of great consequence to the aesthetic ideals of the Renaissance. See Singer, *The Nature of Love*, 1:172–74. Saint Thomas, following a questionable interpretation of Aristotle's

words in the *Ethics* (3.10.1118a33), had previously taught that "taking the senses as useful, it is touch that affords the greatest pleasure; taking them as source of knowledge, it is sight"(IaIIae. 31, 6). On the other hand, Saint Thomas emphasized that, while the pleasure derived from usefulness is common to men and animals, the pleasure derived from knowledge is exclusively human (ibid.). Although Vives considered hearing second only to sight, his reflections on music in the educational treatise *De Disciplinis* and in *De Initiis Sectis et Laudibus Philosophiae* are strikingly short and perfunctory. See M 6.371 and 3.6–7. Vives' references to music in *De Initiis* are placed within their contemporary context by Adriana Bongiovanni in her excellent but as yet unpublished doctoral dissertation "Il *De Initiis Sectis et Laudibus Philosophiae* di Juan Luis Vives. Temi e problemi di storiografia filosofica nel primo Rinascimento."

Chapter 18. Derivative Emotions

1. This and other observations in this chapter on the usage of concrete Latin names of emotion are taken from the *Oxford Latin Dictionary*.

2. *Metaphysics,* I. 2, 982b12–13.

3. Aristotle says that the opposite of anger is "calmness," which consists, he says, in "the quieting of anger." *Rhetoric,* II. 3, 1380a5–9.

4. *Rhetoric,* II. 9, 1386b11.

5. *Rhetoric,* II. 9, 186b9–29.

6. IV. 17. Also, *Stoicorum Veterum Fragmenta,* 415.

7. Vives, who was familiar with Cicero's *Tusculanae Disputationes,* seems to forget Cicero's explicit distinction between *invidentia, aemulatio,* and *obtrectatio.* The first corresponds to the Greek *phthonos,* the second to *zelus,* and the third, to *zēlotypia.*

8. See the Aristotelian definition of shame in *Rhetoric,* II. 6, 1383b14–16.

9. Mark 3:28–29.

10. The affinity between Spinoza's and Nietzsche's ideas on pity, humility, and repentance has been discussed by C. Appuhn, *Oeuvres de Spinoza,* 4 vols., 3:371.

11. *Rhetoric,* II. 8, 1385b14.

12. *Muliebris misericordia,* II, P 49, *scholium.*

Chapter 20. The Control and Therapy of Emotion

1. *Preces et Meditationes Generales,* M 1.82–83.

2. *Introductio ad Sapientiam,* 204; M 1.17.

3. See *Preces et Meditations Generales* (M 1.82–83), prayer 12, *Adversus Pravos Affectus.*

4. *Introductio ad Sapientiam,* 209; M 1.17.

5. *De Institutione Feminae Christianae,* 2. 11; M 4.260.

6. *De Subventione Pauperum,* 2. 4; M 4.476.

7. The advice is almost literally repeated by Descartes in the *Traité des passions,* III, 176.

Bibliography

1. Primary Sources

Aquinas, Saint Thomas. *Summa Theologiae.* Blackfriars edition. London: McGraw-Hill, 1975.

Aristotle. *The Complete Works of Aristotle: The Revised Oxford Translation.* 2 vols. Ed. Jonathan Barnes. Princeton: Princeton University Press, 1984.

Arnim, Hans F. A. von. *Stoicorum Veterum Fragmenta.* Leipzig: Teubner, 1903–24.

Calderón de la Barca, Pedro. *El Alcalde de Zalamea.* Ed. José Díez-Borque. Madrid: Castalia, 1976.

Descartes, René. *Traité des passions.* Trans. E. S. Haldane and G. R. T. Ross. In *The Philosophical Works of Descartes.* Reprint, 2 vols. New York: Dover, 1973.

———. *Traité des passions de l'ame.* Ed. F. Mizrach. Paris: Union Générale d'Editions, 1965.

Ficino, Marsilio. *Five Questions Concerning the Mind.* In *The Renaissance Phisosophy of Man,* 196–206. *See* Cassirer, Kristeller, and Randall under 2.

———. *Marsilio Ficino and the Phaedran Charioteer.* Introduction, texts, and translations by Michael J. B. Allen. Berkeley: University of California Press, 1981.

James, William. *The Principles of Psychology. The Great Books.* Vol. 53. Chicago: Encyclopedia Britannica, 1952.

Macrobius. *Commentary on the Dream of Scipio.* Trans. W. H. Stahl. New York: Columbia University Press, 1952.

Pérez de Oliva, Fernán. *Diálogo de la dignidad del hombre.* Ed. José Luis Abellán. Barcelona: Cultura Popular, 1963.

Pseudo-Andronicus. *Perí pathōn.* Critical ed. and Latin trans., A. Gilbert-Thierry. Leiden: Brill, 1977.

Sartre, Jean Paul. *The Emotions: Outline of a Theory.* Trans. B. Frechtman. New York: Philosophical Library, 1948.

Spinoza, Baruch. *Oeuvres de Spinoza.* 4 vols. Ed. C. Appuhn. Paris: Garnier, 1964.

————. *The Collected Works of Spinoza.* 2 vols. Trans. and ed. Edwin Curley. Princeton: Princeton University Press, 1985.

Valla, Lorenzo. *Repastinatio dilalectice et philosophie.* Critical ed. Gianni Zippel. Padua: Antenore, 1982.

Vives, Juan Luis. *Against the Pseudodialecticians: A Humanist Attack on Medieval Logic. The Attack on the Pseudodialecticians and on Dialectic. Book III, v, i, viii from the Causes of the Corruption of the Arts with an Appendix of Related Passages by Thomas More.* Trans. and critical ed. Rita Guerlac. Dordrecht-London-Boston: Reidel, 1979.

————. "Clarorum Hispaniensium Epistulae Ineditae." *Revue hispanique* 8 (1901): 181–308.

————. *Concerning the Relief of the Poor.* Trans. Margaret M. Sherwood. New York: New York School of Philanthropy, 1917.

————. *De Anima et Vita.* Trans. and critical ed. Mario Sancipriano. Padua: Gregoriana, 1974.

————. *De Communione Rerum.* Trans. and critical ed. L. Gallinari. Florence: La Nuova Italia, 1973.

————. *De Subventione Pauperum.* Critical ed. A. Saitta. Florence: La Nuova Italia, 1973.

————. *De Tradendis Disciplinis.* Trans. Foster Watson. Totowa, N.J.: Rowman and Littlefield, 1971.

————. *Early Writings: De Initiis Sectis et Laudibus Philosophiae, Veritas Fucata, Anima Senis, Pompeius Fugiens.* English trans. and critical ed. C. Matheeussen, C. Fantazzi, and E. George. Leiden: Brill, 1987.

————. *Epistolario.* Ed. and trans. José Jimenez Delgado. Madrid: Editora Nacional, 1978.

————. *In Pseudodialecticos. A Critical Edition.* Ed. Charles Fantazzi. Leiden: Brill, 1979.

————. *Instruction of a Christian Woman.* Trans. R. Hyrde. London: Berthelet, 1540.

————. *J. L. Vives' Somnium et Vigilia in Somnium Scipionis.* Introd., critical ed. and trans. Edward V. George. (In preparation.)

————. *Joannis Ludovici Vives Valentini Opera Omnia.* 8 vols. Ed. Gregorio Mayans y Síscar. Valencia: Monfort, 1790. Reprint, 8 vols. London: Gregg Press, 1964.

————. *Obras Completas.* 2 vols. Trans. Lorenzo Riber. Madrid: Aguilar, 1947–48.

————. *On the Citie of God: With the Learned Comments of J. L. Vives.* Trans. J. Healey. London, 1620.

————. *Praefatio in Leges Ciceronis et Aedes Legum.* Critical ed. Constantius Matheeussen. Leipzig: Teubner, 1984.

————. *The Fable of Man.* In *The Renaissance Philosophy of Man.* 2nd ed. Ed. E. Cassirer, P. O. Kristeller, and J. H. Randall, Jr., et al. Chicago: University of Chicago Press, 1963.

2. Secondary Sources: Books

Abellán, José Luis. *Historia crítica del pensamiento español.* 4 vols. Madrid: Espasa-Calpe, 1979.

Adams, Robert Pardee. *The Better Part of Valor: Erasmus, Colet and Vives on Humanism, War and Peace, 1496–1535.* Seattle: University of Washington Press, 1962.

Allen, Percy Stafford, and H. M. Allen. *Opus Epistularum Desiderii Erasmi Roterodami.* 12 vols. Oxford: At the Clarendon Press, 1906–58.

Babut, Daniel. *Plutarque et le stoicisme.* Paris: Presses Universitaires de France, 1969.

Baron, Haron. *The Crisis of the Italian Renaissance: Civic Humanism and Republican Liberty in the Age of Classicism and Tyranny.* Princeton: Princeton University Press, 1955.

Bataillon, Marcel. *Erasme et l'Espagne.* Paris: Droz, 1937.

————. *Erasmo y el Erasmismo.* Trans. Carlos Pujol. Barcelona: Editorial Crítica, 1977.

Beaulieu, Benoit. *Le Visage littéraire d'Erasme.* Quebec: Presses de l'université Laval, 1973.

Blüher, Karl Alfred. *Seneca in Spanien.* Munich: Francke Verlag, 1969.

Bohatec, Josef. *Budé und Calvin. Studien zum Gedankenwelt des französischen Frühumanismus.* Graz: H. Bohlaus Nachf., 1950.

Böhmer, Edward. *Spanish Reformers.* 3 vols. Strassbourg-London: K. Trubner, 1970.

Bolgar, R. R., ed. *Classical Influences on European Culture, A.D. 1500–1700.* Cambridge: At the University Press, 1976.

Bonilla y San Martín, Adolfo. *Historia de la filosofía española.* Madrid: V. Suárez, 1908.

————. *Luis Vives y la filosofía del Renacimiento.* 3 vols., 2nd edition. Madrid: L. Rubio, 1929.

Brady, Th. A. *See* Oberman, under 2.

Bréhier, Emile. *Chrisippe et l'ancien stoicisme.* Paris: Presses Universitaires de France, 1951.

Buck, August, ed. *Juan Luis Vives. Wolfenbütteler Arbeitsgespräch.* Hamburg: Hauswedell, 1981.

Camporeale, Salvatore. *Lorenzo Valla: umanesimo e teologia.* Florence: Nella sede dell' Instituto, 1972.

Cassirer, Ernest, Paul O. Kristeller, and Herman Randall, Jr. *The Renaissance Philosophy of Man.* Chicago: University of Chicago Press, 1948.

Castro, Américo. *De la edad conflictiva: crisis de la cultura española en el siglo XVI*. 3rd edition. Madrid: Taurus, 1973.

———. *España en su historia: cristianos, moros y judíos*. 2nd edition. Barcelona: Editorial Crítica, 1983.

———. *La realidad histórica de España*. 6th edition. Mexico: Porrúa, 1975.

———. *The Structure of Spanish History*. Trans. E. L. King. Princeton: Princeton University Press, 1954.

Charlier, Yvonne. *Erasme et l'amitié d'après sa correspondance*. Paris: Les Belles Letres, 1977.

Chastel, A., and R. Klein. *El Humanismo*. Estella: Salvat, 1971.

Cvitanovic, Dinko. *El sueño y su representación en el barroco español*. Bahia Blanca, Argentina: Instituto de humanidades, Universidad Nacional del Sur, 1969.

Damiens, Suzanne. *Amour et intelect chez Leon l'Hebreu*. Toulouse: Privat, 1971.

Debus, A. G. *Man and Nature in the Renaissance*. 2nd edition. Cambridge: University Press, 1980.

De Vocht, Henry. *Literae virorum eruditorum ad F. Craneveldium, 1522–1528*. Louvain: Librairie Universitaire, 1929.

Dilthey, Wilhelm. *The Individual and the Cosmos in the Renaissance*. Trans M. Domandi. New York: Barnes and Noble, 1963.

Domínguez-Ortiz, Antonio. *Historia de la filosofía española*. Madrid: V. Suárez, 1908.

———. *La clase social de los conversos en Castilla en la edad moderna*. Madrid: Istmo, 1955.

———. *Los judeoconversos en España y América*. Madrid: Istmo, 1978.

Fallico, Arturo B., and Herman Shapiro, ed. and trans. *The Italian Philosophers: Selected Readings from Petrarch to Bruno*. New York: Random House, 1967.

Fox, Alistair. *Thomas More, History and Providence*. Oxford: Blackwell, 1982.

García Cárcel, Ricardo. *La revolta de les Germanies*. Valencia: Institució Alfons el Magnànim, 1981.

———. *Orígenes de la inquisición española: el tribunal de Valencia, 1478–1530*. Barcelona: Península, 1976.

García Villoslada, Ricardo. *La Universidad de Paris durante los estudios de Francisco de Vitoria, 1507–1522*. Rome: Gregorian University, 1938.

———. *Loyola y Erasmo. Dos almas, dos épocas*. Madrid: Taurus, 1965.

Garin, Eugenio. *Italian Humanism: Philosophy and Civic Life in the Renaissance*. Trans. Peter Munz. Westport, Conn.: Greenwood Press, 1975.

———. *La cultura filosofica del rinascimento italiano: ricerche e documenti*. 2nd edition. Florence: Sansoni, 1979.

Gerl, Hanna-Barbara. *Rhetorik als Philosophie. Lorenzo Valla.* Munich: Fink, 1974.

Gilbert, Neil Ward. *Renaissance Concepts of Method.* 2nd edition. New York: Columbia University Press, 1963.

Gilman, Stephen. *La España de Fernando de Rojas: panorama intellectulal y social de "La Celestina."* Madrid: Taurus, 1978.

González y González, Enrique. *Joan Lluís Vives: de la escolástica al humanismo.* Valencia: Soler, 1987.

Gould, Josiah B. *The Philosophy of Chrysippus.* Albany: State University of New York Press, 1970.

Grassi, Ernesto. *Rhetoric as Philosophy: The Humanist Tradition.* University Park: Pennsylvania State University Press, 1980.

Guy, Alain. *Vives, ou l'humanisme engagé.* Paris: Seghers, 1972.

Guy, J. A. *The Public Career of Sir Thomas More.* Brighton, Sussex: The Harvester Press, 1980.

Hieatt, Constance B. *The Realism of Dream Visions: The Poetic Exploitation of the Dream-Experience in Chaucer and His Contemporaries.* The Hague-Paris: Mouton, 1967.

Ijsewijn, Jozef. *Companion to Neo-Latin Studies.* Amsterdam-New York-Oxford: North Holland, 1977.

———. *Erasmus in Hispania. Vives in Belgio, Colloquia Europalia* I. Acta Colloquii Brugensis, 1985. Ed. J. Ijsewijn and A. Losada. Louvain: Peeters, 1986.

Kelso, Ruth. *Doctrine for the Lady of the Renaissance.* Urbana: University of Illinois Press, 1956.

Kisch, Guido. *Claudius Cantiuncula: ein Basler Jurist und Humanist des 16. Jahrhunderts.* Basel: Helbing und Lichtenhahn, 1980.

———. *Erasmus und die Jurisprudenz seiner Zeit: Beiträge zu einer Geschichte.* 2nd edition. Sigmaringen: Thorbecke, 1978.

———. *Gestalten und Probleme aus Humanismus und Jurisprudenz: neue Studien und Texte.* 2nd edition. Berlin: D. Gruyter, 1969.

Krisnan, R. S. *The Darker Vision of the Renaissance: Beyond the Fields of Reason.* Berkeley: University of California Press, 1974.

Kristeller, Paul Oskar. *Eight Philosophers of the Italian Renaissance.* Stanford: Stanford University Press, 1966.

———. *Renaissance Concepts of Man and other Essays.* New York: Harper, 1972.

———. *Renaissance Thought and its Sources.* New York: Columbia University Press, 1979.

Leff, Gordon. *William of Ockham: The Metamorphosis of Scholastic Discourse.* 2nd edition. Manchester: Manchester University Press, 1977.

Levi, A. H. T., ed. *Humanism in France at the End of the Middle Ages and in the Early Renaissance.* New York: Manchester University Press, 1970.

McConica, James. *English Humanists and Reformation under Henry VIII and Edward VI.* Oxford: Clarendon Press, 1968.

Malcolm, Norman. *Dreaming.* London: Routledge and Paul, 1959.

Margolin, Jean-Claude. *L'avènement des temps modernes.* Paris: Presses Universitaires de France, 1937.

———. *L'humanisme en Europe au temps de la Réformation.* Paris: Presses Universitaires de France, 1981.

Markish, Simon. *Erasme et les Juifs.* Trans. M. Fretz. Lausanne: L'Age de l'homme, 1979.

Menéndez y Pelayo, Marcelino. *Ensayos de Critica Filosófica.* In *Obras Completas.* 65 vols. Vol. 49, 164–74. Madrid: Consejo Superior de Investigaciones Científicas, 1954.

———. *La Ciencia Española.* In *Obras Completas.* Vol. 58, 110–12, 184–88, 218–24, 309–25; and vol. 59, 57–67, et passim.

Monsegú, Bernardo Gómez. *Filosofía del humanismo de Juan Luis Vives.* Madrid: Consejo Superior de Investigaciones Científicas, 1961.

Nelson, John Charles. *Renaissance Theories of Love.* 2nd edition. New York: Columbia University Press, 1963.

Nieto, José. *Juan de Valdés y los orígenes de la Reforma en España e Italia.* Mexico: Fondo de Cultura Económica, 1979.

Noreña, Carlos G. *Juan Luis Vives.* The Hague: Nijhoff, 1970.

———. *Juan Luis Vives.* Revised edition by author, translated into Spanish by Antonio Pintor Ramos. Madrid: Ediciones Paulinas, 1978.

———. *Studies in Spanish Renaissance Thought.* The Hague: Nijhoff, 1975.

Oberman Heiko A., and Th. A. Brady. *Itinerarium Italicum: The Profile of the Italian Renaissance in the Mirror of its European Transformations.* Leiden: Brill, 1975.

Olmedo, Félix G. *Las fuentes de "La vida es sueño."* Madrid: Voluntad, 1928.

Orme, Rodolfo. *English Schools in the Middle Ages.* London: Methuen, 1973.

Palacio y Palacio, José María de. *See* under Pinta Llorente.

Pedraza, F. B., and M. Rodriguez. *Manual de Literatura Española: El Renacimiento.* Tafalla: Cenlit, 1980.

Pinta Llorente, Miguel de la, and José María de Palacio y Palacio. *Procesos Inquisitoriales contra la familia judía de Juan Luis Vives.* Vol. I (only one published). *Procesos contra Blanquina March, madre del humanista.* Madrid: Instituto Arias Montano, 1964.

Rashdall, Hastings. *The Universities of Europe in the Middle Ages.* New York: Oxford University Press, 1970.

Renaudet, Augustin. *Préréforme et humanisme à Paris pendant les premières guerres d'Italie, 1494–1517.* 2nd edition. Geneva: Slaktine Reprints, 1981.

Ridley, Jasper. *The Statesman and the Fanatic: Thomas Wolsey and Thomas More*. London: Constable, 1982.

Rochon, André. *Présence et influence de l'Espagne dans la culture italienne de la Renaissance*. Paris: Université de la Sorbonne Nouvelle, 1978.

Rorty, Amelie O., ed. *Explaining Emotions*. Berkeley: University of California Press, 1980.

Ruiz Ramón, Francisco. *Historia del Teatro Español*. 2nd edition. Vol. 1. Madrid: Alianza, 1967–71.

Shapiro, Barbara. *Probability and Certainty in Seventeenth-Century England: A Study of the Relationships between Natural Science, Religion, History, Law and Literature*. Princeton: Princeton University Press, 1983.

Shapiro, Herman, *See* Fallico, Arturo B. under 2.

Singer, Irving. *The Nature of Love, Courtly and Romantic*. 2 vols. Chicago: University of Chicago Press, 1984.

Solomon, Robert. *The Passions*. New York: Doubleday, 1976.

Tobriner, Sister Alice. *A Sixteenth-Century Urban Report*. Chicago: University of Chicago Press, 1971.

Trevor Davies, R. *El gran siglo de España 1501–1621*. Madrid: Akal, 1973.

Trinkhaus, Charles. *In Our Image and Likeness: Humanity and Divinity in Italian Humanist Thought*. Chicago: University of Chicago Press, 1970.

Vasoli, Cesare. *La dialettica e la retorica dell'Umanesimo: "Invenzione" e "Metodo" nella cultura del XV e XVI secolo*. Milano: Feltrinelli, 1968.

———. *Umanesimo e i Rinascimento*. Palermo: Palumbo, 1969.

Watson, Foster. *Les relacions de Joan Lluís Vives amb els anglesos i amb l'Anglaterra*. Barcelona: Institut d'Estudis Catalans, 1918.

———. *The Spanish Element in Luis Vives*. Barcelona: Institut de Estudis Catalans, 1917.

Wolfson, Harry A. *The Philosphy of Spinoza*. 2 vols. Cambridge: Harvard University Press, 1934.

Zanta, L. *La Renaissance du stoicisme au XVe Siècle*. Paris: Champion, 1914.

3. Secondary Sources: Articles and Dissertations

Ashworth, E. J. "The Eclipse of Medieval Logic." In *The Cambridge History of Later Medieval Philosophy*, 787–97. New York: Cambridge University Press, 1982.

———. "Multiple Quantification and the Use of Quantifiers in Early Sixteenth-Century Logic." *Notre Dame Journal of Formal Logic* 19 (1978): 599–613.

Baker-Smith, D. "Juan Vives and the *Somnium Scipionis*." In *Classical Influences*, 239–44. *See* Bolgar, under 2.

Bataillon, Marcel. "Autour de Luis Vivès et d'Iñigo de Loyola." *Bulletin hispanique* 30 (1928): 184–86.

————. "Luis Vivès, réformateur de la bienfaisance." *Bibliothèque d'humanisme et renaissance* 14 (1952): 141–58.

Batllori, Miquel. "Joan-Lluís Vives en l'Europa d'avui." In *Miscel·lània Sanchis Guarner. Quaderns de Filologia*. Universitat de Valencia, 1984, 33–39.

Bolgar, R. R. "Humanism as a Value System, with Reference to Budé and Vivès." In *Humanism in France*, 199–216. See A. H. T. Levi, under 2.

Bonenfant, P. "Les origines et le caractère de la réforme de la bienfaisance publique au Payx-Bas sous le règne de Charles-Quint." *Revue Belge de philologie et d'histoire* 5: 4 (Oct.–Dec. 1926): 887–904.

Bongiovanni, Adriana. "Il *De Initiis Sectis et Laudibus Philosophiae* di Juan Luis Vives. Temi e problemi di storiografia filosofica nel primo Rinascimento." Ph.D. dissertation, University of Pavia, 1984.

————. "Juan Luis Vives, filosofo converso: interpretazioni storiografiche. *Il confronto letterario* 23 (1985): 53–67.

Bouwsma, W. J. "The Two Faces of Humanism." In *Itinerarium*, 3–61. *See* Oberman, under 2.

Briesemeister, D. "Die gedruckten deutschen Uebersetzungen von Vives' Werken im 16. Jahrhundert." In *Juan Luis Vives. Wolfenbütteler Arbeitsgespräch*, 177–91. *See* Buck, under 2.

Buck, August. "Juan Luis Vives' Konzeption des humanistischen Gelehrten." In *Juan Luis Vives. Wolfenbütteler Arbeitsgespräch*, 11–23. *See* Buck, under 2.

Colish, Marcia, "The Mime of God: Vives on the Nature of Man." *Journal of the History of Ideas* 23 (1962): 3–21.

Dudon, Paul. "La rencontre d'Ignace de Loyola avec Luis Vives à Bruges, 1528–1530." *Homenaje a Bonilla y San Martín* 2 (1930): 153–62.

Etchegarary Cruz, Adolfo. "Juan Vives según Erasmo de Rotterdam." In *Homenaje a Luis Vives. VI congreso de estudios clásicos*, 113–21. Madrid: Fundación Universitaria Española, 1977.

Fantazzi, Charles. "Vives, More and Erasmus." In *Juan Luis Vives. Wolfenbütteler Arbeitsgespräch*, 172–74. *See* Buck, under 2.

Fontán, Antonio. "El latín de Luis Vives." In *Homenaje a Luis Vives. VI congreso de estudios clásicos*, 33–63. Madrid: Fundación Universitaria Española, 1977.

————. "Juan Luis Vives, La antiguedad como sabiduría." In *Tres grandes humanistas*, 7–37. Madrid: Fundación Universitaria Española, 1975.

————. "Juan Luis Vives, un español fuera de España." *Revista de Occidente* 145 (1975): 37–52.

————. "La política europea en la perspectiva de Vives." In *Erasmus in Hispania. Vives in Belgio*, 27–73. *See* Ijsewijn, under 2.

García, Angelina. "Els Vives, una familia jueva." *Debats* 2 (1982): 25–31.

———. "Una familia de judeo-conversos: Vives." In *Erasmus in Hispania. Vives in Belgio*, 293–309. *See* Ijsewijn, under 2.

García Cárcel, Ricardo. "Notas en torno al contexto familiar de Luis Vives." *Cuadernos de historia de la medicina* 13 (1974): 337–45.

Gariglio, Tullio, and Agostino Sottili. "Zum nachleben von Juan Luis Vives in der Italienischen Renaissance." *Juan Luis Vives. Wolfenbütteler Arbeitsgespräch*, 211–61. *See* Buck, under 2.

George, Edward V. "Imitatio in the *Somnium Scipionis*." In *Juan Luis Vives. Wolfenbütteler Arbeitsgespräch*, 81–85. *See* Buck, under 2.

———. "The Sullan Declamations: Vives' Intentions." *Acta Conventus Neo-Latini Guelpherbytani, Wolfenbüttel 12 August to 16 August 1985*. Ed. Stella P. Revard et al. 55–61.

Gilmore, Myron P. "Italian reactions to Erasmian Humanism." In *Itinerarium*, 99–107. *See* Oberman, under 2.

Greenhut, Deborah S. "Persuade Yourselves: Women, Speech, and Sexual Politics in Tudor Society." *Proteus: A Journal of Ideas* 3-2 (1986): 42–48.

Guerlac, Rita. "Vives and the education of Gargantua." *Etudes rabelaisiennes* 11 (1974): 63–72.

Hay, Denys. "England and the Humanities in the Fifteenth Century." In *Itinerarium Italicum*, 305–67. *See* Oberman, under 2.

Ijsewijn, Josef. "Het humanism, de Nederlanden en Spanje." In *Luister van Spanje en de Belgische Steden, 1500–1700*. Bruxelles, 1985.

———. "J. L. Vives in 1512–1517. A Reconsideration of Evidence." *Humanistica Lovaniensia* 26 (1977): 82–100.

———. Methodischen Ueberlegungen zu zwei Ausgaben von J. L. Vives *Adversus Pseudodialecticos*." *Wolfenbütteler Renaissance Mitteilungen* 4 (1980): 131–35.

———. "The Coming of Humanism to the Low Countries." In *Itinerarium*, 193–301. *See* Oberman, under 2.

———. "Vives and Poetry." *Roczniki Humanistyczne* 26 (1978): 21–34.

———. "Vives' Jugendwerke neu datiert." *Wolfenbütteler Renaissance Mitteilungen* 2 (August 1987): 58–59.

———. "Zu einer kritischen Edition der Werke des J. L. Vives." In *Juan Luis Vives. Wolfenbütteler Arbeitsgespräch*, 23–35. *See* Buck, under 2.

Jardine, Lisa. "Humanism and the Teaching of Logic." In *The Cambridge History of Later Medieval Philosophy*, 797–808. New York: Cambridge University Press, 1982.

———. "Lorenzo Valla and the Origins of Humanist Dialectic." *Journal of the History of Philosophy* 15 (1977): 143–64.

Katte, Maria von. "Vives' Schriften in der Herzog August Bibliothek und ihre Bedeutung für die Prinzenerziehung im 16. und 17. Jahrhundert." In *Juan Luis Vives. Wolfenbütteler Arbeitsgespräch*, 193–210. *See* Buck, under 2.

Kaufman, Gloria. "Juan Luis Vives on the Education of Women." *Signs.*
   Journal of Women in Culture and Society 3–4 (1978): 891–96.
Kohut, K. "Literaturtheorie und Literaturkritik bei Juan Luis Vives." In
   Juan Luis Vives. Wolfenbütteler Arbeitsgespräch, 35–49. See Buck, under 2.
Kretzmann, Norman. "Syncategoremata, exponibilia, sophismata." In *The
   Cambridge History of Later Medieval Philosophy,* 211–46.
Lewis, G. "Une source inexplorée du *Traité des Passions.*" *Revue philoso-
   phique de la France et de l'étranger* 138 (1948): 341–81.
Losada, Angel. "La huella de Vives en América." In *Erasmus in Hispania.
   Vives in Belgio,* 147–81. See Ijsewijn, under 2.
McConica, James. "Northern humanists before the reform." In *The Study of
   Spirituality,* ed. C. Jones et al., 338–41. New York: Oxford University
   Press, 1986.
McCully, George Elliot. "A Letter of Juan Luis Vives to Jerome Aleander,
   December 17, 1522." *Renaissance Quarterly* 22 (1969): 121–28.
———. "Juan Luis Vives (1493–1540) and the Problem of Evil in His
   Time." Ph.D. dissertation, Columbia University, 1967.
McFarlane, D. "Reflections on Ravisius Textor's *Specimen Epithetorum.*" In
   Classical Influences, 81–91. See Bolgar, under 2.
Mann, Nicholas. "Petrarch's Role as a Moralist in Fifteenth-Century
   France." In *Humanism in France,* 6–29. See A. H. T. Levi, under 2.
Margolin, Jean-Claude. "Conscience européene et réaction à la menace
   turque d'après le *De Dissidiis Europae et Bello Turcico* de Vivès (1526)."
   In *Juan Luis Vives. Wolfenbütteler Arbeitsgespräch,* 107–41. See Buck,
   under 2.
———. "Vivès, lecteur et critique de Platon et d'Aristote." In *Classical
   Influences on European Culture,* 245–58. See Bolgar, under 2.
Matheeussen, Constant. "Das rechtsphilosophische Früwerk des Vives." In
   Juan Luis Vives. Wolfenbütteler Arbeitsgespräch, 93–107. See Buck, under 2.
———. "Quelques remarques sur le *De Subventione Pauperum.*" In
   Erasmus in Hispania. Vives in Belgio, 87–99. See Ijsewijn, under 2.
Millás-Vallicrosa, José María. "La ascendencia judaica de Luis Vives y la
   ortodoxia de su obra apologética." *Sefarad* 25 (1965): 59–66.
Monzón Arazo, August. "El Derecho en Joan Lluís Vives." Ph.D. disserta-
   tion, Universitat de Valencia, 1986.
———. "Joan Lluís Vives i la pau." *Sab* 62 (September 1984): 14–15.
———. "Joan Lluís Vives. Orientacions per una visió renovada." *Afers,
   Fulls de recerca i pensament* (Catarroja, Valencia) 1 (1985): 293–309.
———. "Juan Luis Vives y la enseñanza del Derecho." *Revista de la
   facultad de derecho en la Universidad Complutense de Madrid* 5 (1982):
   241–47.
Noreña, Carlos G. "Juan Luis Vives and Henry VIII." *Renaissance and
   Reformation* 13 (1976): 85–87.

————. "Vives and Agricola in the Low Countries." In *Erasmus in Hispania. Vives in Belgio,* 99–121. *See* Ijsewijn, under 2.

————. "Was Juan Luis Vives a Disciple of Erasmus?" *Journal of the History of Ideas* 7 (1969): 263–72.

Oestreich, G. "Die Antike Literatur als Vorbild der Praktischen Wissenschaften im 16. und 17. Jahrhundert." In *Classical Influences,* 315–25. *See* Bolgar, under 2.

Ong, Walter J. "Commonplace Rhapsody: Ravisius Textor, Zwinger, and Shakespeare." In *Classical Influences,* 91–123. *See* Bolgar, under 2.

Phillips, M. M. "Erasmus and the Classics." In *Erasmus,* ed. T. A. Dorey. London: Routledge and Kegan Paul, 1970.

Poschmann, A. "El Cardenal Guillermno de Croy y el arzobispado de Toledo." *Lusitania Sacra* 75 (1919): 201–82.

Sancipriano, Mario. "Il sentimento dell' Europa in Juan Luis Vives." *Humanitas* 12 (1957): 629–35.

————. "La pensée anthropologique de J. L. Vives: l'entelechie." In *Juan Luis Vives. Wolfenbütteler Arbeitsgespräch,* 63–70. *See* Buck, under 2.

Silverman, Joseph. "Some Aspects of Literature and Life in the Golden Age of Spain." In *Estudios de literatura española ofrecidos a M. M. Morinigo.* Madrid: Insula, 1971.

Simone, Franco. "Une enterprise oubliée des humanistes français: de la prise de la conscience historique du renouveau culturel à la naissance de la première histoire littéraire." In *Humanism in France,* 106–32. *See* A. H. T. Levi, under 2.

Sims, Edra. "The Antifeminist Element in the Works of Alfonso Martínez and Juan Luis Vives." *College Language Association Journal* 18 (1974–75): 52–68.

Sinz, William. "The Elaboration of Vives' Treatises on the Arts." *Studies in the Renaissance* 10 (1963): 68–90.

Steppe, J. K. "Mencía de Mendoza et ses relations avec Erasme, Giles de Busleyden et Jean-Louis Vivès." *Scrinium Erasmianum* 2 (1969), 449–506.

Stupperich, Robert. "Das Problem der Armenfürsorge bei Juan Luis Vives." In *Juan Luis Vives. Wolfenbütteler Arbeitsgespräch,* 49–63. *See* Buck, under 2.

Swift, L. J. "Somnium Vivis y el *El Sueño de Escipión.*" In *Homenaje a Luis Vives. VI congreso de estudios clásicos,* 33–62. Madrid: Fundación Universitaria Española, 1977.

Szymanski, M. "Philosophy and Language." *Bibliothèque d'humanisme et renaissance* 44 (1982): 150–52.

Tobriner, Sister Alice. "Juan Luis Vives and Erasmus." *Moreana* 24 (1969): 35–44.

Uhlig C., and C. K. Arnold. "Vives in England." In *Juan Luis Vives. Wolfenbütteler Arbeitsgespräch,* 141–64. *See* Buck, under 2.

Urmeneta, Fermin. "Senequismo y Vivismo." *Augustinus* 10 (1965): 373–83.

Urriza, Juan. "Universidades Españolas: Alcalá or Complutense." In *Diccionario de historia eclesiástica española,* 4.2612–16. Madrid: Centro Superior de Investigaciones Científicas, 1975.

Vasoli, Cesare. "G. L. Vives e la polemica antiscolastica nello *In Pseudodialecticos.*" *Miscelanea de estudios a Joaquín Carvalho* 7 (1961): 679–86.

———. "Juan Luis Vives e un programma umanistica di riforma della logica." *Academia Toscana di Scienze e Lettere "La Colombaria," Atti e Memorie* 25 (1960): 219–63.

———. "La première querelle des 'anciens' et des 'modernes' aux origins de la Renaissance." In *Classical Influences on European Culture,* 74–75. *See* Bolgar, under 2.

Waswo, R. "The 'Ordinary Language Philosophy' of Lorenzo Valla." *Bibliotèque d'humanisme et renaissance* 41–42 (1979): 255–73.

———. "The reaction of J. L. Vives to Valla's Philosophy of Language." *Bibliothèque d'humanisme et renaissance* 42 (1980): 595–609.

Wayne, Valerie. "Some Sad Sentence: Vives' 'Instruction of a Christian Woman.'" In *Silent but for the Word: Tudor Women as Patrons, Translators, and Writers,* ed. Margaret Patterson Hannay, 15–29. Kent, Ohio: Kent State University Press, 1985.

Watson, Foster. "The Influence of Valencia on Vives." *Aberystwyth Studies* 1 (1927): 47–103.

Weinberg, C. "Thomas More and the Use of English in Early Tudor Education." *Moreana* 59/60 (1978): 21–30.

Index

Acoustics. *See* Music

Adagia (Erasmus, 1508), 21, 30, 31

Adrian (pope), 18

Adversus Pseudodialecticos (Vives, 1519), 11–15, 27, 28, 51, 57, 115, 118, 222

Aedes Lequm (Vives, 1520), 30, 51, 222

Afterlife, existence of, 133

Age, and emotions, 8–9, 111, 152, 217. *See also* Old age

Agricola, Rudolph, 12, 16, 18, 19–20, 42, 52, 55, 56, 115–16, 167

Ailly, Pierre d', 14

Albert of Saxony, 14

Aleander, Hieronymous (Girolamo Aleandro), 22

Anger (*ira*), 142, 148, 149, 161, 180, 181–83, 196

Annotationes in Novum Testamentum (Valla), 21

Annoyance (*offensio*), 4, 161, 194–95. *See also* Irritation

Appetites: and emotions, 145–46; and knowledge, 119, 134

Argument, Vives' types of, 102

Aristotle: comments on dreams, 127; comments on emotions, 142, 159–60, 183–84, 185, 195, 196–97, 204, 224, 225; comments on life, 82, 84; comments on memory, 96–97, 98, 99; comments on the soul, 71–72, 75, 135; and study of deductive logic, 14; theory of four qualities, 110; Vives' admiration for and familiarity with, 16, 28, 51, 55, 63, 103; Vives' independence from, 141. *See also De Anima; Organon; Rhetoric*

Artes sermocinales, Vives' guidelines for the

study of, 56–57, 64, 115

Arthur (prince of Wales), 34

Ascham, Roger, 34

Astronomy, Vives' interest in, 63–64

Attraction (*allubescentia*), 161, 191–92

Augustine (saint): comments on emotions, 164, 175, 197; Vives' acceptance of ideas of, 48, 55, 178; Vives' commentary on, 22, 23, 33, 36, 47

Averroës (Ibn Rushd), 62

Barbaro, Ermolao, 12, 18

Barquero, Antonio, 239n.1

Beda, Noel, 9, 10, 11

Bembo, Pietro, 179

Bereavement (*desiderium*), 161, 203

Boccaccio, Giovanni, 18

Borgia, Alexander (pope), 3

Brethren of the Common Life, 10, 21

Bricot, Thomas, 11

Bruni (d'Arezzo), Leonardo, 51, 178

Bucolics (Vergil), Vives' interpretation of (1537), 46, 59

Budé, Guillaume, 12, 18, 22, 55

Bureau, Nicolas de, 40

Buridan, Johan, 14

Calvin, John, 10

Campeggio, Lorenzo (cardinal), 33

Capellanus, Andreas, 179

Castro, Américo, 5, 6

Catherine of Aragon (queen of England), 32–33, 219, 220

Catholicism: conversion of Vives' parents to, 3; criticism of, 24; insecurity among converts to, 5

Censura de Aristotelis Operibus (Vives, 1538), 51, 63
Cepello, Galcerano, 239n.1
Charles V (Holy Roman emperor), 49, 239n.1
Cheerfulness (*hilaritas*), 201–2
Cheke, Sir John, 34
Children, Vives' opinion of, 44
Christi Jesu Triumphus (Vives, 1514), 25
Chrysippus, 143, 147, 163
Cicero, 55, 105, 130, 164, 197, 198, 203
Ciceronianus (Erasmus, 1528), 23
Cleanthes, 143, 147
Clement VII (pope), 49
Climate: role in emotions, 153, 217; role in temperament, 111
Clypei Christi Descriptio (Vives, 1518), 25
Colet, John, 18, 21, 22, 34, 56
Common sense, Vives' opinion on, 92–93
Compassion (*misericordia*), 142, 157, 161, 196–97
Confidence (*fiducia*), 161
Contemplation, Vives' opinion on, 103, 107
Contempt (*contemptus*), 194–95
Craneveld, Francis: as friend of Vives, 7, 20, 30, 32, 33, 35, 39, 40, 42, 43, 44, 46, 66–67, 220
Croy, William de, 17, 26
Cruelty, 180, 196, 199, 205
Curiosity, 194

Daring (*audacia*), 161
De Anima (*On the Soul*, Aristotle), 71, 83, 86, 89, 91, 95, 159
De Anima et Vita (Vives, 1538): compared to Aristotle's *De Anima*, 71, 83, 86, 89, 91; dedication of, 81; English translation of, xv; influence of, 226–27; writing of, 6, 50, 223
—Book 1: comments on growth, 83–84; comments on reproduction, 83, 84–85; comments on sensations, 86–94; life defined in, 81–83
—Book 2: comments on contemplation, 103, 107; comments on human memory, 93, 95, 96–100; comments on *ingenium*, 108–12; comments on intelligence, 95–96, 101, 112; comments on judgment, 105–7; comments on language, 113–18; comments on old age and death, 27–28, 130–32; comments on opinion, 106, 108; comments on reasoning, 101–5; comments

on sleeping and dreams, 124–29; comments on the will, 119–23
—Book 3: autobiographical content of, xvi–xvii, 6–7, 162, 219–21; comments on death of Pico della Mirandola, 18; comments on knowledge of nature, 71–80 passim; comments on memory, 53; comments on sexual love and pleasure, 45; comparison of northern and southern Europeans in, 19; Vives' opinion of, 61. *See also* Emotions
De Anima Senis (Vives, 1518), 27–28, 130
Death, Vives' comments on, 130–32
De Causis Corruptarum Artium (Vives, M 3.143), 10, 50, 53, 54, 59, 60, 65, 117
De Censura Veri (Vives, 1531), 58, 116, 118
De Civitate Dei (Saint Augustine), 22–23, 33, 36, 47, 163
Declamationes Syllanae (Vives, 1520), 11, 26, 29, 60
De Concordia et Discordia in Humano Genere (Vives, 1529), 39, 47–49, 222
De Conditione Vitae Christianorum sub Turca (Vives, 1529?), 50, 222
De Conscribendis Epistolis (Vives, 1534), 51, 241n.16
De Disciplinis (Vives, 1531), 11, 15–16, 18, 50–51, 53, 54, 55, 57–58, 61, 66, 99, 118, 223
De Disputatione (Vives, 1531), 58
De Europae Dissidiis et Bello Turcico (Vives, 1526), 38, 222
De Europa statu ac tumultibus (Vives), 222
De Explanatione Cujusque Essentiae (Vives), 118
De Ingenuis Moribus (Vergerius), 51
De Initiis, Sectis et Laudibus Philosophiae (Vives, 1518), 28
De Institutione Feminae Christianae (Vives, 1523), 33, 42, 43, 44, 45, 51, 56, 59
De Instrumento Probabilitatis (Vives, 1531), 58
De Inventione Dialectica (Agricola, 1515), 16
De Legibus (Cicero), Vives' introduction to, 30
De Liberorum Educatione (Pius II), 51
Democritus, 114, 149
De Officio Mariti (Vives, 1528), 42, 43, 45, 51
De Ordine Docendi et Studendi (Guarino), 51

De Pacificatione (Vives, 1529), 49–50
De Prima Philosophia, sive de Intimo Naturae Opificio (Vives, 1531), 61–62, 71–72, 74–80 passim, 104, 135
De Ratione Dicendi (Vives, 1532), 51, 59, 60, 114
De Ratione Studii Puerilis (Vives, 1523), 33, 51
Descartes, René: classification of emotions, 151, 154, 161, 167–69, 171, 172–73, 175–76, 180, 181, 183, 184–85, 186, 189, 190, 191–206 passim, 224–27
De Senectute (Cicero): Vives' introduction to, 26, 27; Vives' writing based on, 130
Desire (*cupiditas*), 87, 142, 161, 174, 177–78, 193; for truth, 135
Despair (*desperatio*), 38, 201, 203, 204
De Studiis et Literis (Bruni d'Arezzo), 51
De Subventione Pauperum (Vives, 1526), 39, 51, 222
De Tempore quo, id est, de Pace in qua Natus est Christus (Vives), 60
De Tradendis Disciplinis (Vives, 1531), 59, 60, 62, 112, 114
De Veritate Fidei Christianae (Vives, 1543), 66–68, 73, 119, 132
Devotional works, by Vives, 26
Dialogues of the Dead (Lucian), 124
Diet: role in emotions, 152, 217; role in temperament, 111
Diet of Worms, 17
Discourse. *See* Reasoning
Disdain, 199
Dormitatio (state between sleeping and being awake), 128
Dorp, Martin, 32
Dreams, Vives' comments on, 124–29; memory of, 128
Dullaert, Jan, 64

Ebreo, Leone, 179
Education: humanist writings on, 51–52; Vives' reform of, 10, 11, 15, 35, 50, 51, 52–66 passim, 223
Elation (*laetitia*), 201–2
Elements, four, 79–80
Elizabeth I (queen of England), 34
Emotions: and action, 156–58; and age, 8–9, 111, 152; bodily responses to, 151–54; classification of, 159–71; control of, 213–18; divine origin of, 142; and the environment, 66, 154–56; and habits, 123,

215–16; interactions of, 207–12; and knowledge, 146–51, 214–15; and memory, 148, 149; nature of, 141–46; remedy through control of, 213–18
—basic, 172–90; anger (*ira*), 142, 148, 149, 161, 180, 181–83, 196; desire (*cupiditas*), 87, 142, 161, 174, 177–78, 193; fear (*metus*), 5, 142, 148, 161, 183–85, 186; hatred (*odium*), 158, 161, 180–81, 182, 183, 196; hope (*spes*), 161, 185–86; joy (*laetitia*), 161, 186–90; laughter, 142, 154, 189; love (*amor*), 142, 157–58, 161, 174–80; pain, 151, 186–87; pleasure (*delectatio*), 151, 161, 186–88; sadness (*moeror*), 6, 7, 161, 186–90; tears, 142, 154, 189
—derivative, 191–206; annoyance (*offensio*), 4, 5, 142, 161, 194–95; attraction (*allubescentia*), 161, 191–92; bereavement (*desiderium*), 161, 203; cheerfulness (*hilaritas*), 201–2; compassion (*misericordia*), 142, 157, 161, 196–97; confidence (*fiducia*), 161; contempt (*contemptus*), 194–95; cruelty, 180, 196, 199, 205; curiosity, 194; daring (*audacia*), 161; despair (*desperatio*), 38, 201, 203, 204; disdain, 199; elation (*laetitia*), 201–2; envy (*invidia*), 148, 161, 162–63, 198–99; fondness (*favor*), 4, 21, 161, 174, 192–93; gladness (*gaudium*), 201–2; humility, 202–3; indignation (*indignatio*), 142, 149, 161, 196–97; pity (*commiseratio*), 196–97, 204–6; pride, 142, 148, 162, 202–3; regret, 204; revenge (desire for), 180, 182, 196, 199, 204; reverence (*reverentia*), 142, 161, 174, 193; shame (*pudor*), 163, 199–201; zeal (*zelus*), 196, 198
Enchiridion Militis Christiani (Erasmus, 1504), 21, 25
Envy (*invidia*), 148, 161, 162–63, 198–99
Equicola, Mario, 179
Erasmists, Spanish: persecution of, 4; praise for Vives, 11; Vives' admiration for, 5; Vives' letters to Erasmus concerning, 23
Erasmus, Desiderius, 18; anti-Semitism of, 7; Colet's influence on, 34; edition of Seneca's works by, 47; offered Oxford appointment, 32; opinion of begging, 39; opinion of Montaigu College, 9; opinion of public service, 36; opinion of Spanish culture, 3–4; opinion of vernacular language, 56; opinion of Vives' treatment

of women, 5; praise for Vives, 21, 22; reputation of, 21; Vives' influence on, 99; Vives' intellectual debt to, 12, 23–25, 55; Vives' introduction to, 17, 21; Vives' praise for, 18, 21, 22. *See also* Vives, Juan Luis: friendship with Erasmus

Estimative sense, Vives' opinion on, 93

Ethica (Spinoza), 159, 170–71, 203

Eton Latin grammar, 34

Exercitatio Linguae Latinae (Vives, 1538), 10, 51, 57

Fabula de Homine (Vives, 1518), 27, 53, 222

Fall of man: and knowledge of nature, 73; and language, 114–15

Fantasy, and intelligence, 101. *See also* Imagination

Fear (*metus*), 5, 142, 148, 161, 183–85, 186

Ferdinand I (Holy Roman emperor), 26

Fevyn, John, 20

Ficino, Marsilio, 18, 178, 179, 189

Filelfo, Francesco, 18

Fisher, John (bishop of Rochester), 332

Fondness (*favor*), 4, 21, 161, 174, 192–93

Force of habit, Vives' comments on, 123

Forgetting. *See* Memory

Free will. *See* Will

Friendhsip: Erasmus' views on, 22; Vives' views on, 22, 176

Frivolity, of youth, 10

Froben, Johann, 23

Gaguin, Robert, 21

Galen, 65, 83, 89, 108, 110, 125, 126, 147, 151

Gaza, Teodoro, 18

Geneathliacon Jesuchristi (Vives, 1514), 25

Georgics (Vergil), Vives' writings on (1518), 59

Gladness (*gaudium*), 201–2

Goclenius, Conrad, 23, 32

God, Man and his Well-Being (Spinoza), 203

Greek language: revised use of, 52; use discouraged, 11; Vives' use of, 7, 25, 53–54

Grey, William, 34

Grocyn, William, 56

Grosseteste, Robert, 160, 163, 164

Guarino Veronese (Guarino da Verona), 51, 53, 115

Habits, and emotions, 123, 215–16

Hatred (*odium*), 158, 161, 180–81, 182, 183, 196

Hearing. *See* Sensations

Henry VII, 34

Henry VIII: education of, 34; patronage of Vives by, 7, 18, 33, 46; Vives' letters to (1526), 37, 38; Vives' letter to Luther on behalf of, 25

Heracleitus, 149

Hippocrates, 131

History, Vives' writings on, 37–39, 47, 60–61

Homer, 59

Hope (*spes*), 161, 185–86

Human nature, Vives' view of, 45. *See also* Nature

Humility, 202–3

Hyginus, Gaius Julius, 63, 64

Ignatius of Loyola, 10, 46

Imagination, Vives' opinion on, 92, 93, 94, 101–2

Immortality of the soul, 132–37

Indignation (*indignatio*), 142, 149, 161, 196–97

Individuality. *See* Ingenium

Ingenium, Vives' comments on, 108–12, 117, 148, 151

In Leges Ciceronis Praefatio (Vives), 51

Inquisition, Spanish: and Vives' father, 6, 17–18, 32; Vives' fear of, 5–7

In Sapientem Praelectio (Vives, 1522), 29, 222

Institutio Principis Christiani (Erasmus, 1516), 21

Intelligence, Vives' comments on, 95–96, 101, 112

Introductio ad Sapientiam (Vives, 1524), 45, 47, 222

In Vita C. Julii Caesaris, De Gente Julia, Caesarum Familia (Vives), 60

Irritation, 5, 142, 194. *See also* Annoyance

Isocrates, Vives' translations of (1526), 33, 37

Isocrates Oratio Areopagitica (Vives), 60

Italy, northern humanists' interest in, 18

James, William, 96

Jealousy, 148

Jerome (saint), 55

John XXI (pope), 13

Joy (*laetitia*), 161, 186–90
Juan, Honorato, 239n.1
Judaism: conversion of Vives' parents from, 3; insecurity among converts from, 5
Judgment, Vives' opinion on, 105–7, 148–49, 151, 215, 221, 224
Justice, and language, 113

Kant, Immanuel, 105
Knowledge: and emotions, 146–51; of self, 214–15

Langius, Rudolph, 19–20
Language: vernacular, 55–56; Vives' comments on, 113–18. *See also* Greek language; Latin language
Latin language: revived use of, 52; Vives' use of, 25, 53–54, 55
Laughter, 142, 154, 189
Laurin, Mark, 20
La Vita Civile (Palmieri), 51
Lefèvre d'Etaples, Jacques, 12, 18, 22
Legal reform, Vives' writings on, 30–31, 51, 64
Leto, Pomponio, 18
Life, Vives' opinions on, 81–85
Lily, William, 34, 56
Linacre, Thomas, 32, 56
Love (*amor*), 142, 157–58, 161, 174–80
Lucan (Marcus Annaeus Lucanus), 55
Lucian, 124
Ludes de Morte Claudii (Seneca), 124
Luther, Martin, 24, 25, 41–42

Macrobius, Ambrosius Theodosius, 29, 53, 124
Major, John, 10, 11, 39
Maldonado, Juan, 239n.1
Maluenda, Pedro, 239n.1
Manrique, Alfonso, 49
Manrique, Rodrigo, 239n.1
Manuzio, Aldo, 21
Margaret (princess of Austria), 239n.1
Marriage, Vives' opinions on, 42–45
Martens, D., 20
Mary Tudor, Vives as preceptor to, 32, 33, 37
Mathematics, Vives' opinions on, 63, 64
Medicine, Vives' writings on reform of, 64–66
Melanchthon, Philipp, 55
Memory: of dreams, 128; Vives' comments on, 53, 93, 95, 96–100, 148, 149
Mendoza, Doña Mencía de, 46, 90, 239n.1
Metamorphoses (Ovid), 124
Montaigu College. *See* University of Paris, Montaigu College
Moral conscience, Vives' notion of, 103
Morality, and immortality, 136
More, Thomas, 18; attitude toward women and sex, 40–42; Colet's influence on, 34; criticism of enclosure, 39; influence on Vives, 40–41; objection to passages in *Declamationes Syllanae*, 26; opinion of vernacular language, 56; patronage of Vives by, 7, 32; praise for Vives, 11; relationship with Erasmus, 22; relationship with Vives, 35–36, 219, 220
Mortality. *See* Immortality of the soul
Music, Vives' view of, 64

Nature, Vives' view of knowledge of, 62–63, 71–80. *See also* Human nature
Nature-nurture dichotomy, 109
Nebrija, Antonio de: Vives' admiration for, 5, 55, 57

Ockham, William of, 13–14
Old age, Vives' comments on, 27–28, 130–32
Ong, W. J., 58
On Memory and Reminiscence (Aristotle), 96–97, 98
Opinion, Vives' notion of, 106, 108
Organon (Aristotle), 14, 15, 55
Ortus Caesaris et Educatio (Vives, M 6.438–40), 60
Ovid, 124
Oxford University: Vives' readership at, 32, 34–35

Pacifism, of Vives, 38
Pain, 151, 186–87
Palmieri, Matteo, 51
Panaetius, 143, 147
Pardo, Jeronimo, 11
Patrizi, Francesco, 18
Paul III (pope), 66
Paul of Venice, 11, 14
Percy, Sir Thomas (earl of Worcester), 34
Perí Pathōn (Pseudo-Andronicus), 144, 159, 160–61, 163, 164, 197
Peripatos, Vives' relationship to, 141
Peter of Mantua, 11

Peter of Spain (later Pope John XXI), 11, 13
Petrarch (Francesco Petrarca), 12, 18, 19, 47, 51, 115
Philip II (king of Spain), 239n.1
Physics, Vives' understanding of, 62–64, 75
Pico della Mirandola, Giovanni, 18, 27, 123, 179, 219
Pity (*commiseratio/misericordia*), 196–97, 204–6
Pius II (pope), 51, 53, 63
Plato, 55, 63, 143, 178
Pleasure (*delectatio*), 151, 161, 186–88; and the soul, 135, 217
Pliny (Gaius Plinius Secundus), 131
Plutarch, 52, 53, 55, 60, 99, 103, 147
Poeticon Astronomicon (Hyginus), Vives' edition of (1514), 63–64
Poetry: reading forbidden, 11, 30; by Vives, 59; Vives' opinion of, 59–60
Poggio, Giovanni Francesco, 18
Politian (Angelo Ambrogini), 12
Politics, Vives' views on, 36–37
Posidonius, 143–44, 147
Praefatio et Vigilia in Somnium Scipionis Ciceroniani (Vives, 1521), 27, 29–30, 53, 124
Praet, Louis de, 39
Praise of Folly, The (Erasmus, 1511), 21
Pride, 142, 148, 162, 202–3
Psalms, penitential: Vives' writings on (1518), 25–26
Pseudo-Andronicus: classification of emotions, 144, 159, 160–61, 163–64, 182, 183, 198, 200, 201, 202
Ptojologia (Erasmus), 39
Public welfare, Vives' plan for, 39–40

Qualities, four, 79, 110
Quinam Fuerint Gothi, et Quomodo Romam Ceperint (Vives, M 6.440–49), 60
Quintilian, 16, 52, 55, 58, 99, 100, 105, 108

Rabelais, François, 9
Reason, Vives' opinion on, 82, 92
Reasoning (discourse), Vives' opinion on, 101–5
Regret, 204
Renaissance, in Spain, 4
Revenge, desire for, 180, 182, 196, 199, 204
Reverence (*reverentia*), 142, 161, 174, 193
Rhetoric (Aristotle), 159–60, 185, 225

Sadness (*moeror*), 6, 7, 161, 186–90
Salutati, Lino Coluccio di Piero, 12, 19
Sapientis Inquisitio (Vives, 1520), 59
Satellitium Animi (Vives, 1524), 33, 36, 222
Schools, location of, 66, 154
Scipio Africanus, 53
Seneca: comments on emotions, 144, 157; Erasmus' edition of works by, 47; Vives' admiration for, 55, 124
Sensata (perception of sensible objects), 75
Sensations: external, 86–92; fallibility of, 110; internal, 87, 92–94
Sensilia communia, 92. *See also* Common sense
Shame (*pudor*), 163, 199–201
Sight. *See* Sensations
Signification, and language, 117–18
Sleep: allegorical portrayal of, 124–25; and emotions, 126; Vives' comments on, 125–26
Smell. *See* Sensations
Socrates, 28, 147
Somnium Scipionis (Cicero), Vives' commentary on, 27, 29–30, 53, 124
Soul: immortality of, 132–37; and pleasure, 135, 217; Vives' view of, 45, 72, 73, 78, 110
Spinoza, Baruch: classification of emotions, 159, 161, 169–71, 183, 191–206 passim, 225, 226
Standonck, Jan van, 9, 10, 19
Stoic teachings: and emotions, 143–44; rejected by humanists, 47–48; summarized in *Perí Pathōn*, 160–61; Vives' admiration for, 48, 143, 147; Vives' independence from, 141, 144, 157, 224
Suetonius (Gaius Suetonius Tranqillus), 60
Suiseth, Richard, 62
Suleiman I, the Magnificent (sultan of the Ottoman Empire), 37, 38
Summa Theologiae (Saint Thomas), 145–46, 159, 161, 164–67, 172, 181, 186–88
Summulae Logicales (Peter of Spain), 11, 13
Symbolism, and language, 117

Tartaret, Pierre, 11, 14
Taste. *See* Sensations
Tears, 142, 154, 189
Theocritus, 59
Thomas (saint): classification of emotions, 145–46, 159, 161, 164–67, 171, 172, 173, 175, 176, 180, 181, 183, 184, 186–88,

195, 197, 200, 201, 203, 204, 224
Thomism, reaction against, 13
Touch. *See* Sensations
Tractatus Amoris et de Amoris Remedio
(Capellanus), 179
Traité des passions de l'âme (Descartes),
151, 159, 167–69, 175–76, 180, 225
Trilingue College (Louvain), 17
Truth, desire for, 135
Tusculanae Disputationes (Cicero), 164,
197, 198, 203

University of Alcalá: Vives offered chair in
rhetoric at, 3, 4, 18
University of Paris, Montaigu College:
reputation of, 9, 10–11; Vives as student
at, 8, 9, 11–12
Utopia (More), 36, 39, 41

Valla, Lorenzo: Erasmus' publication of
Annotationes in Novum Testamentum, 21,
25; influence on Vives, 12, 18, 20, 25,
52, 55, 56, 57, 103, 115–16
Vergara, Juan de: friendship with Vives, 3,
7, 46; persecution of, 4
Vergerius, Pietro, 51, 53
Vergil, 46, 55, 59
Veritas Fucata I (Vives, 1520), 59
Veritas Fucata II (Vives), 59, 60
Vitrier, Francisco de, 21
Vittorino da Feltre (Vittorini Ramboldini),
51, 63
Vives, Juan Luis: accused of heresy, 40;
attitude toward women and sex, 5, 10,
42–45; birth of (1493), 3, 231n.1; concern
for sisters, 6; death of (1540), 47;
education of, 3, 8, 9, 11–12, 18;
friendship with Erasmus, 3–4, 17, 21–25,
32, 46, 219, 220; health of, 6, 32, 46–47;
marriage of, 32, 42–45; opinion of Italian
culture and people, 18–19; opinion of
Spanish culture, 3–4, 13, 15; opinion of
Spanish people, 4–5; as pacifist, 38;
parents of, 3, 6, 7, 32; personality of, 5,
7, 8, 9–10, 24, 42, 198, 219–21;
reluctance to return to Spain, 3, 5;
secrecy of, 7
—in Bruges (1514–17): affection for as
"second home," 20; marriage in (1524),
32; as preceptor in residence, 17; return to
(1528–40), 33, 45; writings from this
period, 46, 47–68 passim

—in Brussels: trips to, 46; visit in 1516, 17
—in England: and execution of his father, 6,
32; at Oxford (1523–24), 18, 32, 34–35;
as preceptor to Princes Mary (1527), 32;
trips back and forth to (1523–28), 32–33,
37; writings from this period, 37–38,
39–40, 42–45
—in Louvain: move to (1517–23), 17–18;
trips to, 46; visit in 1516, 17; writings
from this period, 25–31
—in Paris: as a student (1509–12), 8, 9–10,
11–12; as a writer (1512–14), 8,
234–35n.1; move to (1509), 3; trips to, 46
Vives, Margaret Valdaura, 32, 42, 44–45,
47

Will, Vives' comments on, 119–23, 147
Wolsey, Cardinal Thomas: appointment of
More as Chancellor of the Duchy of
Lancaster by, 36; endowment of
Cardinal's College by, 35; patronage of
Vives by, 7, 32, 33; taxations opposed, 39
Women: as "incomplete males," 84;
emotions of, 42–43. *See also* Vives, Juan
Luis: attitude toward women and sex

Zeal (*zelus*), 196, 198
Zeno of Citium, 143, 147
Zuñiga, Francisco de (duke of Béjar), 81

CARLOS G. NOREÑA is Professor of Philosophy, Adlai E. Stevenson College, University of California, Santa Cruz. He is the author of numerous articles appearing in such journals as *International Philosophical Quarterly, Journal of the History of Philosophy, The New Scholasticism, Renaissance and Reformation,* and *Revista de Estudios Hispánicos,* as well as the author of *Juan Luis Vives* (also published in Spanish translation), *The Passions of the Soul* (English translation of Book 3 of Vives' *De Anima et Vita*), and *Studies in Spanish Renaissance Thought.*